The Sequential Intercept
Model and Criminal Justice

The Sequential Intercept Model and Criminal Justice

Promoting Community Alternatives for Individuals with Serious Mental Illness

EDITED BY PATRICIA A. GRIFFIN

KIRK HEILBRUN

EDWARD P. MULVEY

DAVID DeMATTEO

AND

CAROL A. SCHUBERT

OXFORD
UNIVERSITY PRESS

OXFORD
UNIVERSITY PRESS

Oxford University Press is a department of the University of
Oxford. It furthers the University's objective of excellence in research,
scholarship, and education by publishing worldwide.

Oxford   New York
Auckland   Cape Town   Dar es Salaam   Hong Kong   Karachi
Kuala Lumpur   Madrid   Melbourne   Mexico City   Nairobi
New Delhi   Shanghai   Taipei   Toronto

With offices in
Argentina   Austria   Brazil   Chile   Czech Republic   France   Greece
Guatemala   Hungary   Italy   Japan   Poland   Portugal   Singapore
South Korea   Switzerland   Thailand   Turkey   Ukraine   Vietnam

Oxford is a registered trademark of Oxford University Press
in the UK and certain other countries.

Published in the United States of America by
Oxford University Press
198 Madison Avenue, New York, NY 10016

Library of Congress Cataloging-in-Publication Data
The sequential intercept model and criminal justice : promoting community alternatives for
individuals with serious mental illness / edited by Patricia Griffin, Kirk Heilbrun, Edward Mulvey,
David DeMatteo, Carol Schubert.
pages cm
Includes bibliographical references and index.
ISBN 978–0–19–982675–9 (hardback)
1. Mentally ill offenders—United States.   2. People with mental disabilities and crime—
United States.   3. Criminal justice, Administration of—United States.   4. Alternatives to
imprisonment—United States.   5. Criminals—Mental health—United States.
I. Griffin, Patricia A.
HV6133.S39 2015
364.3'80973—dc23
2014027252

CONTENTS

Patricia A. Griffin, PhD, is an independent consultant who is also associated with the Pennsylvania Mental Health and Justice Center of Excellence and with Policy Research Associates. Her scholarly and practice interests include diversion, specialized training of first responders, and provision of services to justice-involved individuals with behavioral health disorders. She is a co-developer of the Sequential Intercept Model.

Kirk Heilbrun, PhD, is a Professor in the Department of Psychology at Drexel University and Co-Director of the Pennsylvania Mental Health and Justice Center of Excellence. His research and professional interests include risk assessment and management, forensic assessment, and diversion.

Edward P. Mulvey, PhD, is a Professor in the Department of Psychiatry at Western Psychiatric Institute and Clinic, University of Pittsburgh School of Medicine, and Co-Director of the Pennsylvania Mental Health and Justice Center of Excellence. His research interests include violence and mental illness, prediction of violence and crime, juvenile offenders and the juvenile justice system, and criminal justice policy. He is also interested in public agencies serving justice-involved individuals with mental health problems.

David DeMatteo, JD, PhD, is an Associate Professor of Psychology and Law at Drexel University, where he is also Director of the JD/PhD Program in Law and Psychology, and a consultant with the Pennsylvania Mental Health and Justice Center of Excellence. His research interests include psychopathy, forensic mental health assessment, drug policy, and diversion.

Carol A. Schubert, MPH, is a researcher with the Law and Psychiatry Program at the Western Psychiatric Institute and Clinic of the University of Pittsburgh School of Medicine, and a consultant to the Pennsylvania Mental Health and Justice Center of Excellence. Her research interests include violence risk and service provision; she has coordinated numerous large research projects focusing on these areas with justice-involved adults and adolescents.

CONTRIBUTORS

Dan Abreu is a Senior Project Associate at Policy Research Associates in Delmar, New York.

Natalie Bonfine, PhD, is Assistant Professor of Psychiatry and Instructor of Family and Community Medicine at Northeast Ohio Medical University.

Stephanie Brooks-Holliday, PhD, is a postdoctoral fellow in clinical and research neuropsychology at the DC WRIISC in Washington, D.C.

Samantha Califano was previously with Policy Research Associates, Delmar, New York.

Brian Case is a project associate with Policy Research Associates, Delmar, New York.

Tim Coffey is Coordinator of the Criminal Mental Health Project of the 11th Judicial Circuit, Miami, Florida.

Amanda Brown Cross, PhD, is a Research Specialist for the Pennsylvania Mental Health and Justice Center of Excellence in Pittsburgh, Pennsylvania.

David DeMatteo, JD, PhD (see "About the Editors")

Sarah Dorrell, MSW, is Case Manager for Student Life at Baylor University, Waco, Texas.

Jennifer Eno Louden, PhD, is Assistant Professor, Department of Psychology at the University of Texas at El Paso.

Hallie Fader-Towe, JD, is Program Director, Courts at the Justice Center, Council of State Governments.

Sarah Filone, MS, is an advanced student in the doctoral clinical psychology training program (forensic concentration) at Drexel University.

Christina Finello, JD, PhD, is Criminal Justice Policy, Grant, and Planning Coordinator at PMHCC, Philadelphia, Pennsylvania.

William Fisher, PhD, is Professor, Department of Psychiatry, University of Massachusetts Medical School.

Meghann Galloway, MS, is an advanced student in the JD-PhD training program at Drexel University.

Patricia A. Griffin, PhD (see "About the Editors")

Albert Grudzinskas, Jr., JD, is Clinical Associate Professor, Department of Psychiatry, University of Massachusetts Medical School.

Kirk Heilbrun, PhD (see "About the Editors")

Allison B. Hill, JD, PhD, is with Peachtree Psychological Associates in Atlanta, Georgia, and also supervises psychiatry residents and psychology interns through Emory University School of Medicine.

Kathleen Kemp, PhD, is Assistant Professor at Brown University School of Medicine.

Christopher King, MS, is an advanced student in the JD-PhD training program at Drexel University.

Casey LaDuke, MS, is an advanced student in the doctoral clinical psychology training program (forensic concentration) at Drexel University.

Steve Leifman, JD, is Associate Administrative Judge, Miami-Dade County Court Criminal Division of the 11th Judicial Circuit, Miami, Florida.

Siyu Liu, PhD, is Assistant Professor, Department of Criminal Justice at New Jersey City University.

Sarah Manchak, PhD, is Assistant Professor, School of Criminal Justice, University of Cincinnati.

Edward P. Mulvey, PhD (see "About the Editors")

Mark Munetz, MD, is Professor, Department of Psychiatry, Northeast Ohio Medical University.

Chanson Noether, MA, is Director of the Criminal Justice Division, Policy Research Associates, Delmar, New York.

Megan O'Connor, MA, is a graduate student in the Department of Psychology at the University of Texas at El Paso.

Fred Osher, MD, is Director, Health Services and Systems Policy, with the Council of State Governments Justice Center.

John Petrila, JD, LLM, is Chair and Professor, Department of Health Policy and Management, College of Public Health, University of South Florida.

Allison D. Redlich, PhD, is Associate Professor, School of Criminal Justice, University of Albany (State University of New York).

Melissa Reuland is Senior Research Consultant with the Council of State Governments Justice Center.

Michelle R. Rock, JD, is Director of the Illinois Center of Excellence for Behavioral Health and Justice.

Susan Salasin is the former director of the Trauma and Trauma-Informed Care Program at the Substance Abuse and Mental Health Services Administration (SAMHSA).

Carol A. Schubert, MPH (see "About the Editors")

Jennifer L. Skeem, PhD, is Professor, School of Social Welfare, Goldman School of Public Policy, University of California, Berkeley.

Henry J. Steadman, PhD, is President of Policy Research Associates, Delmar, New York.

Heidi Strohmaier is completing her final year in the doctoral clinical psychology training program (forensic concentration) at Drexel University.

Katy Winckworth-Prejsnar is Coordinator of the Pennsylvania Mental Health and Justice Center of Excellence.

Kento Yasuhara, PhD, is Assistant Professor, Department of Criminal Justice, College of Criminal Justice and Forensic Sciences, University of New Haven.

The Sequential Intercept Model and Criminal Justice

The Movement Toward Community-Based Alternatives to Criminal Justice Involvement and Incarceration for People with Severe Mental Illness

KIRK HEILBRUN, DAVID DeMATTEO, HEIDI STROHMAIER, AND MEGHANN GALLOWAY ■

Recent decades have seen growing interest in the use of community-based alternatives to the conviction and incarceration of certain individuals involved in criminal offending. This should not be viewed as an attempt to undermine our society's legitimate interests in prosecuting and convicting criminal offenders, particularly retributive and public safety priorities. However, there has been an increasing recognition that subgroups of offenders are involved in crime largely as a function of substance use or symptoms of severe mental illness (SMI).[1]

Much of the growth in this area has resulted from evidence demonstrating the high rates of individuals with SMI in the criminal justice system. Evidence has shown that many of these individuals can be rehabilitated in the community at less cost, without increased risk to public safety, and in ways that directly address their risk-relevant needs and improve their opportunities for recovery (Boccaccini, Christy, Poythress, & Kershaw, 2005; Case, Steadman, Dupuis, & Morris, 2009; Hiday & Ray, 2010; see Heilbrun et al., 2012, for a summary). Initiatives such as Crisis Intervention Team training for police, problem-solving courts, structured reentry, and empirically informed probation and parole case management are among the approaches focusing on enhancing effective practice with offenders with SMI in the community.

The Sequential Intercept Model (SIM; Munetz & Griffin, 2006) is a conceptual tool that identifies five points at which standard criminal processing can be interrupted to offer community alternatives. These "intercepts" are (1) law enforcement/emergency services, (2) booking/initial court hearings, (3) jails/courts, (4) reentry, and (5) community corrections/community support. Each intercept describes a stage at which a jurisdiction might divert a target population from further penetration into the criminal justice system. Although this book will focus on offenders with SMI, its description of the SIM and application strategies may generalize to other populations with specific rehabilitation needs.

This book has five major purposes. First, we review the changes in correctional policy and practice during the past decade, which reflect an increased focus on community-based alternatives for offenders. Second, we describe the SIM and review the relevant empirical evidence for interventions at each of its five points of interception. Third, we provide information about national and state-level initiatives that provide training, consultation, and research in this area. Fourth, we address specific challenges in using the SIM to promote community alternatives to incarceration (legislative, data gathering, information sharing, and systems mapping). Finally, we integrate these chapters and suggest how the process described in this book might be applied to other populations (e.g., veterans, juveniles, those with substance use only disorders or developmental disabilities).

The book involves collaboration between academic, policy, and practice experts in this area. There will be an emphasis on empirical evidence and its application toward best practice. There will also be a substantial amount of useful information provided for policymakers who are considering community-based alternatives to incarceration for offenders with SMI, for practitioners who carry out these changes, and for program evaluators who seek to document the impact of such changes. Finally, this volume will offer a coherent description of the relevant research, policy, and practice in this area for those who provide training or are in training themselves.

JUSTIFICATION FOR COMMUNITY-BASED ALTERNATIVES

The rationale and justification for providing community-based alternatives to standard prosecution and incarceration can be summarized in three domains: treatment appropriateness, cost savings, and humanitarian grounds (Heilbrun et al., 2012). Each will be summarized in this section. The first justification for community-based alternative alternatives involves the nature of the treatment that can be provided in communities. This stands in contrast with what is available in correctional settings, which must deal with security and cost priorities involving individuals with a range of healthcare needs. It is difficult to prioritize the needs of offenders with SMI (e.g., medication, co-occurring disorder treatment, psychosocial skills, and recovery) with the same precision in a correctional setting as can be done with a more homogeneous group in the community. Again, it is important to know about the range of interventions available and delivered in the community in order to demonstrate this "appropriateness of treatment" justification, as well as outcome data on diverted versus nondiverted individuals (or other comparison groups).

Second, the cost of providing of appropriate treatment to those with SMI (and sometimes co-occurring substance use disorders) is very high when compared with the cost of community-based treatment. The annual healthcare costs for California prison inmates now approaches $2 billion—about $11,600 for each inmate (Kiai & Stobo, 2010), with much of this cost from mental healthcare. Texas spends between $30,000 and $50,000 annually for a single inmate with mental illness, compared to $22,000 a year for other inmates (Torrey, Kennard, Eslinger, Lamb, & Pavle, 2010). By contrast, jail diversion programs targeting offenders with mental health or substance abuse issues can substantially lower state costs. The Bexar County Jail Diversion Program in San Antonio, Texas, is estimated to have saved the state's criminal justice system between $3.8 million and $5 million over the course of 2.5 years (Center for Healthcare Services, 2006). Not all jail diversion programs are as economical, however. Other investigators (Cowell, Broner, & Dupont, 2004) reported that only one of four jail diversion programs examined generated cost savings, while another actually produced a net financial loss. In addition, it appears that certain factors (e.g., inclusion of low-level felons, transfer of the cost burden to community-based treatment systems) play a crucial role in enhancing the cost benefits of jail diversion programs (Hughes, Steadman, Case, Griffin, & Leff, 2012). Drug courts and other substance abuse treatment alternatives to incarceration are also economically advantageous. For instance, Kings County, New York, was able to save $38,000 per year for each offender diverted to a mandatory drug treatment program rather than prison (Cummings, 2010). When community-based alternatives for treating and supporting justice-involved individuals with mental illness can be provided, and the criminal recidivism rates do not increase as a result, then state and local jurisdictions can save substantially. To determine whether this has occurred, of course, it is important to obtain outcome information in both financial and criminal justice domains.

Third, community-based alternative alternatives have been justified on humanitarian grounds. The majority of offenders with SMI appear to have risk-relevant needs that are similar to those of a general offender population (Skeem & Eno Louden, 2006). A subgroup, however, apparently become involved with the criminal justice system through atypical behavior that is influenced by a mental health condition. Such individuals would be classified as low or moderate risk in "risk–need–responsivity" terms (Andrews & Bonta, 2006) but high need (in clinical terms), and it is for these individuals that alternative justice sanctions are easiest to justify on humanitarian grounds, with strong potential for recovery.

THE STRUCTURE OF CHAPTERS

Each of the chapters in this book is structured to include several sections. Authors begin their topic by providing an introduction, which broadly defines and clarifies that topic in the context of diversion and community-based alternatives and examines how the SIM has been used with those with SMI and possibly co-occurring substance use. The introduction will also address why the SIM can provide an important contribution in this context.

The next section will summarize how the topic developed and will describe its current status. In addition, authors will discuss the current usage and impact of the SIM when it is applied in this area. In the section that follows, the authors will describe the empirical evidence as well as theoretical or practical support for using the SIM in this area. In a number of areas, relatively little research has been conducted, so the discussion is often limited to a description of how theory or practice guides the use of the SIM.

In light of the material discussed in their chapters thus far, the authors are finally asked to summarize the implications in three areas: research, policy, and practice. We hope that this summary will help to guide the empirical literature, the developing policy, and the application of the SIM over the next decade.

THE SIM: RELEVANT HISTORY

The movement toward diverting offenders with mental illness away from the criminal justice system began in the early nineteenth century, when it was observed that many individuals with mental illness were incarcerated in jails and prisons throughout the United States. Reformers such as Louis Dwight and Dorothea Dix described this practice as inhumane and successfully campaigned to have specialized treatment facilities built for those with mental illness and to have offenders with mental illness transferred to these facilities, beginning around 1830 (Torrey et al., 2010). The movement greatly reduced the number of those with mental illness in prisons and jails: They constituted less than 1% of the incarcerated population by 1880 (Torrey et al., 2010). Although this reformation was well intentioned, the lack of effective treatment in asylums meant that their primary function was confinement (Wright, 1997).

The National Mental Health Act of 1946, which created the National Institute of Mental Health, and the Community Mental Health Centers Act of 1963, which established community mental health centers and promoted deinstitutionalization, represented early efforts at utilizing community-based alternatives for individuals with mental illness (Rochefort, 1984). A handful of court-based initiatives aimed at providing therapy for defendants with mental illness surfaced in New York and Chicago in the 1960s, serving as a precursor to modern mental health courts (Goldkamp & Irons-Guynn, 2000). Unfortunately, these community programs and court initiatives could not handle the large number of individuals with mental illness released from state hospitals during deinstitutionalization. The limited planning associated with deinstitutionalization has been linked to homelessness among many of those released from state hospitals (Lamb, 1984). Combined with other influences, such as the enforcement of "quality of life" offenses, the "war on drugs," and the movement toward enhanced sentencing in the 1980s, deinstitutionalization resulted, according to some, in the criminalization of people with mental illness (Goldkamp & Irons-Guynn, 2000).

As the number of people incarcerated in the United States continued to grow, the percentage of offenders with mental illness increased substantially. In 1996, an estimated 283,800 offenders with mental illness were incarcerated in jails and prisons across America, making up 16% of the prison population (Ditton, 1999). By 2005, according to one estimate, the number of incarcerated offenders with mental illness had increased to 1.25 million (Glaze & James, 2006).

Community-based alternatives to prosecuting defendants with mental illness have expanded substantially in the past two decades. A landmark study by Steadman and colleagues (1994) found that in 1992, only 52 out of more than 1,200 jails surveyed across the United States utilized diversion programs for defendants with mental illness. The two primary types of diversion efforts they identified were prebooking initiatives, which occurred during the police contact stage, and postbooking initiatives, which occurred either before or after arraignment. By 2006, estimates of the number of jails operating diversion programs had increased to 610 (B. Case, personal communication, May 11, 2012).

In recent decades, specialized courts have emerged as a promising alternative to prosecuting defendants with mental health or substance use disorders. Drug courts, which have been established for more than two decades, represent the most established type of specialized court (McGaha, Boothroyd, Poythress, Petrila, & Ort, 2002). The first official mental health court followed the establishment of the drug court. These specialized courts aim to alleviate the overrepresentation of offenders with mental illness and substance use problems in the criminal justice system by diverting them to community-based treatment programs tailored to their needs. The early success and popularity of these courts and other emerging diversion models inspired other jurisdictions to adopt similar approaches. A revised mental health court model, known as the "second generation" of mental health courts, has emerged over the past several years. This type is distinguished from earlier versions in its acceptance of felony offenders, permissibility of jail sanctions, mode of mandated supervision, and adjudicative model (Redlich et al., 2005). As new diversion efforts continue to emerge and develop, the SIM may help researchers investigate the most effective strategies for the diversion of offenders with mental health and substance abuse problems.

The SIM (Munetz & Griffin, 2006) was conceived as a conceptual approach to the justice system involvement of those with SMI. It began with the observation that the criminal justice system has distinct "points of interception" at which an individual with SMI could be diverted into a path emphasizing appropriate treatment and alternative sanctions. The underlying philosophy of applying this model was described as follows:

Although the nature of mental illness makes it likely that people with symptomatic illness will have contact with law enforcement and the courts, the presence of mental illness should not result in unnecessary arrest or incarceration. People with mental illness who commit crimes with criminal intent that are unrelated to symptomatic mental illness should be held accountable for their actions, as anyone else would be. However, people with mental illness should not be arrested or incarcerated simply because of their mental disorder or lack of access to appropriate treatment—nor should such people be detained in jails or prisons longer than others simply because of their illness.

—MUNETZ & GRIFFIN, *2006, p. 544*

It is important to recognize that the SIM is basically descriptive, a view of the criminal justice system encompassing both the needs of people with SMI (e.g., treatment/rehabilitation, liberty interests) and the interests of the broader society (e.g., public safety, efficient and effective use of public funding). It is the *application* of the SIM, however, that generates questions that are relevant to research, policy, and practice. Moreover, the SIM does not dictate which interventions should be attempted at different intercepts; rather, it identifies the relevant intercepts at which various interventions might be attempted. The foundational assumption in applying the model is that people with mental disorders should not "penetrate" the criminal justice system at a greater frequency than people in the same community without mental disorders (Munetz & Griffin, 2006). Accordingly, the application of the model should yield higher rates of diversion from standard prosecution (for Intercepts 1, 2, and 3) or lower rates of offenders with mental illness in jail or returning to the criminal justice system from probation (for Intercepts 3, 4, and 5). Process and outcome questions, such as whether such interventions are effective, whether they result in appropriate treatment being delivered more frequently, how they are perceived by various constituencies, and what they cost, can be addressed through the use of the SIM at a single intercept, or at multiple intercepts.

In the time since the publication of the Munetz and Griffin (2006) article, it appears that the use of the SIM has grown quickly. It is used as an important educational tool in "cross-systems mapping" (also called Sequential Intercept Mapping; see http://www.prainc.com/expertise-services/services/training/) provided by the National GAINS Center (see Chapter 8) and other such trainings provided by state centers of excellence (see Chapter 10) and as requested by local jurisdictions (see Chapter 13). But this impression is anecdotal; we do not have sufficient data about the application of the SIM in training and consultation delivered in different jurisdictions. We do not know how it might have affected the development of law and policy in this area (see Chapter 11). It was this limited information, among other things, that prompted us to develop this book and try to fill some of these information gaps whenever possible—and identify the need for further study when it is not.

Fortunately, there are some empirical data regarding the application of the SIM and various outcomes. These studies have been reviewed in detail elsewhere (Heilbrun et al., 2012) and will be summarized in the next section. Studies have focused on the empirical support for the interventions described at each intercept. To date, there have been no studies describing the global effectiveness of interventions that are consistent with the SIM ("SIM-compliant").

RELEVANT LITERATURE

Theoretical and Practical Support

The SIM was developed to provide a theoretical framework to guide the provision of community-based alternatives to incarceration for individuals with mental illness. At each of its five intercept points (detailed in the first section of this chapter), it provides choices to decision makers that may offer a treatment-oriented disposition in the community as an alternative to standard criminal justice processing. The first theoretical and practical question, however, is whether there is sufficient need for such alternative dispositions at each of the intercepts.

The mere presence of mental illness among those who may interact with law enforcement and first responders (Intercept 1) appears to make such interaction significantly more likely. Having SMI increased an individual's risk of police contact by 250%, according to one estimate (Crocker, Hartford, & Heslop, 2009). A total of 28% of individuals who used mental health services reported being arrested at least once during a ten-year period (Fisher et al., 2006). Police officers who have not received specialized training in this area are more likely to arrest individuals with mental illness than to help them seek treatment (Levin, Hennessy, & Petrila, 2010). There may be a number of reasons for this, including the failure to recognize the symptoms of mental illness and the absence of treatment alternatives for individuals whose behavior might otherwise justify arrest.

Once the decision to arrest rather than treat has been made, people with mental illness tend to cycle between the criminal justice system and community services (Munetz & Griffin, 2006). This is due to a number of factors, including the complexity of their release back into the community. Approximately 75% of inmates with active mental illness also have substance abuse problems (Vogel, Noether, & Steadman, 2007). This creates particularly complex needs for treatment and rehabilitation, which offenders frequently do not receive. One approach to addressing this complexity of needs involves problem-solving courts, which are alternative courts that address the underlying reasons for offending (Berman & Feinblatt, 2005). Such courts target the needs of specific cohorts such as those with substance abuse, mental illness, domestic violence, and problems stemming from military service. Further into the justice system, those who receive the most intensive mental healthcare while incarcerated are also those who tend to leave prison with limited support or supervision (Metraux, 2008). Offenders with mental illness typically serve longer prison sentences and are less likely to be released on parole; without services to facilitate their reentry into the community, they are at risk for reincarceration (Osher & Steadman, 2007).

The fourth and fifth intercepts identify the specialized needs for offenders with mental illness during reentry from incarceration and while on probation or parole. If specialty parole is utilized, these offenders may be more likely to adhere to the conditions of their parole—and hence less likely to be reincarcerated—because they are receiving services targeted to their needs. As a conceptual tool, the SIM provides a useful framework for identifying the needs and corresponding interventions that can promote community-based resolutions of the justice system involvement of particular groups. But does it work? The following section discusses the scientific support for using specific interventions at different SIM intercepts.

Scientific Support

Law Enforcement and Emergency Services (Intercept 1). The recent review (Heilbrun et al., 2012) located 11 original studies on specialized police responding (SPR), most of them focusing on the Crisis Intervention Team (CIT) approach. Of these, 7 included a control or comparison group and 4 had samples of substantial size ($N > 200$). The research focused on three areas: characteristics and knowledge of specially trained officers, characteristics of individuals diverted through SPR, and the impact of SPR (using outcomes such as the number diverted, time incarcerated, services delivered, case dispositions, and subsequent arrests).

CIT-trained police reported feeling most prepared to handle encounters with individuals with mental illness (Borum, Williams, Deans, Steadman, & Morrissey, 1998), although their knowledge diminished in the period following training (Compton & Chien, 2008). CIT-trained officers were more likely to refer those they encountered to mental health treatment (Compton, Bahora, et al., 2008) and less likely to use physical force with them (Compton, Demir, et al., 2009; Skeem & Bibeau, 2008), even when they appeared at higher risk for violence. Individuals who were diverted did not differ in rearrest rates from those who were not (Steadman & Naples, 2005; Teller et al., 2006; Watson et al., 2010) but did differ in other respects (less time in jail, less costly in terms of criminal justice funding but more costly in terms of treatment funding). While this evidence suggests that SPR does increase the rate of diversion and referral to treatment, it does not yet solidly support the conclusion that such diversion reduces the rearrest rate. It should be noted that SPR is only one possible intervention on SIM Intercept 1. Other interventions (e.g., joint responder models) are also possible, but the research to date has apparently focused on the SPR model.

Post-Arrest: Initial Detention/Initial Hearing (Intercept 2). The review by Heilbrun and colleagues (2012) identified ten studies (nine original studies and one review) in the post-arrest diversion context described by Intercept 2, and all but one found differences between diverted and nondiverted individuals.

Bertman-Pate and colleagues (2004) cited no differences in revocation outcomes. Other studies, however, observed differences that included greater time in the community (Broner et al., 2005; Hoff et al., 1999; Lamberti et al., 2001; Steadman & Naples, 2005) and treatment participation for diverted participants (Steadman & Naples, 2005), as well as fewer hospital days in the community (Lamberti et al., 2001). Participation in a diversion program was also associated with fewer arrests and less homelessness (National GAINS Center, 2002), as well as more emergency room contacts but fewer subsequent arrests (Shafer et al., 2004). It should be noted that some studies include diversion at different intercepts (e.g., National Gains Center, 2002, included some diversion efforts from CIT programs at Intercept 1, making it difficult to judge the impact of intercept-specific diversion).

Diverted individuals at this intercept appear likely to spend more time in the community and to participate in various kinds of treatment activity, and they may possibly be rearrested less frequently than nondiverted individuals. This must be considered cautiously, however. There have been relatively few studies, and many of the studies have small sample sizes and do not employ a control or comparison group. These constraints may hide or distort patterns in the data. Also, investigators have considered different types of "diversion" at this intercept (e.g., diversion from jail, diversion from hospitalization following acquittal as not guilty by reason of insanity). The particular challenges in researching this area, therefore, include developing reliable and valid measures of the efficacy of different interventions and factoring in different programmatic goals in determining how well particular outcomes have been achieved.

Post-Initial Hearings: Jail/Prison, Courts, Forensic Evaluations, and Commitments (Intercept 3). Intercept 3, which includes specialty courts such as drug courts, mental health courts, and community courts, is where the majority of the research has been conducted. Not only have there been more studies to date, but the research designs for problem-solving courts, especially for drug courts, are consistently stronger than in the investigations described at the previous intercepts. Such strengths include the consistent use of experimental or quasi-experimental designs, as well as large ($N > 200$) samples. Outcomes are described separately for drug courts, community courts, and mental health courts. (Other problem-solving courts, such as those devoted to populations such as veterans or prostitutes, are too recent to have generated outcome research.)

In early reviews of nearly 100 drug court evaluations, Belenko (1998, 1999, 2001) found that participation in drug courts reduced jail and other justice-related costs and led to lower offending rates while under court jurisdiction. It also resulted in reduced recidivism following drug court completion for graduates and even some who did not graduate. These findings have been replicated (Belenko, Patapis, & French, 2005; Bhati, Roman, & Chalfin, 2008; Gottfredson & Exum, 2002; Gottfredson et al., 2003, but cf. Government Accountability Office, 2005), and one meta-analysis found significant reductions in criminal recidivism among drug court clients (Wilson, Mitchell, & Mackenzie, 2006). Criminal recidivism appears to be reduced more when drug courts focus on higher-risk and younger offenders, according to one meta-analysis (Lowenkamp et al., 2005). Although drug courts appear effective at reducing recidivism, it is less clear whether they also reduce drug relapse rates. A recent review of drug court research found that five of eight studies revealed statistically significant reductions in drug relapse rates (Government Accountability Office, 2005). Additionally, Belenko's (1998, 1999) meta-analyses revealed that although drug court graduates exhibited lower levels of relapse, the mean graduation rate was only 47%, and drug use during the program ranged from 0.8% to 71% (Belenko, 2001).

A high proportion of community court[2] participants were favorably disposed toward the goals of community court: working productively, assigning useful community service, and treating participants equally (Justice Education Center, 2002). Community courts have been perceived by participants as fairer than traditional courts, using criteria such as perceptions of the judge and quality of the courtroom communication (Frazer, 2006). Such courts were more inclined to use alternative sanctions and less likely to employ conventional incarceration (Hakuta et al., 2008). Compliance with sanctions was higher, targeted outcomes (e.g., prostitution, illegal vending arrests) occurred less often, and cost per case increased slightly (Kralstein, 2005).

A variety of studies have investigated the outcome of criminal recidivism after participation in mental health court. Investigators have observed such outcomes as fewer arrests and jail days (Case et al., 2009), lower recidivism rates (McNiel & Binder, 2007; Moore & Hiday, 2006; Steadman et al., 2010), reduced recidivism rates for both graduates and participants who did not graduate (Hiday & Ray, 2010), and possibly lower costs over time relative to traditional courts (Ridgely et al., 2007). When mental health courts use the pre-adjudication model, any record of arrest is expunged when the individual completes the requirements of mental health court. This model is most typical with minor offenses, however. Mental health courts have expanded to include felony charges; with such expansion has come the use of post-adjudication models that reduce the length of imposed sentences upon completion of mental health court (Redlich et al., 2005).

Intercept 3 of the SIM offers the most extensive and longstanding research of any of the interventions at any of the intercepts (Heilbrun et al., 2012). This is largely due to the presence of problem-solving courts and the extensive research available on drug courts, mental health courts, and community courts in particular. Studies have focused on the characteristics of participants, their ratings of favorability, and outcomes, including cost, services delivered, rearrest rates, and subsequent incarceration. Although there is mixed evidence on whether drug courts consistently reduce the drug-use relapse rate (Belenko, 1998, 1999, 2001; Government Accountability Office, 2005), the evidence is consistently favorable regarding the impact of problem-solving courts on favorable perception by participants, delivery of appropriate services, and reduction in the rates of rearrest and reincarceration for those who have completed the process associated with such problem-solving courts.

Reentry from Jails, State Prisons, and Forensic Hospitalization (Intercept 4). Three domains of research are apparent at Intercept 4 (Heilbrun et al., 2012): Assertive

Community Treatment (ACT)-based programs for justice-involved populations, Forensic Intensive Case Management (ICM)-based programs, and correctional reentry programs. Frequently studied outcomes include criminal justice involvement, such as arrest or conviction following return to the community, and quality of life indicators (e.g., employment, living situation, substance use, global functioning). Comparisons have been made within individuals (by looking at performance and functioning before and after participation in a specialized reentry program) and between individuals (by comparing one group participating in a specialized reentry program with another receiving standard intervention ["treatment as usual," such as standard parole services]).

Studies focusing on ACT for justice-involved populations yielded several findings. Enhanced treatment within the ACT model was associated with less substance use, greater economic independence, better criminal justice outcomes, and more improvement in global functioning relative to treatment as usual (California Board of Corrections, 2005). Evidence-based studies focusing on Forensic Assertive Community Treatment (FACT) demonstrated significant reductions in jail days, arrests, hospitalizations, and days spent in the hospital as well as lower average yearly service costs per client (Lamberti, Weisman, & Faden, 2004). Other studies showed similar results, including fewer hospital days, arrests, and incarceration days, when compared with their pre-ACT program functioning (McCoy et al., 2004; Thresholds, State, County Collaborative Jail Linkage Project, Chicago, 2001; Weisman, Lamberti, & Price, 2004). Additional benefits included improvements in psychological functioning and engagement in substance abuse treatment (McCoy et al., 2004). There has been substantial variability in the implementation of ACT-derived programs, however (Lamberti et al., 2004; Lamberti, Deem, Weisman, & LaDuke, 2011; Morrissey et al., 2007), with some models more closely approximating community support interventions as opposed to reentry initiatives. As such, efforts to standardize these reentry models are needed.

Some promise has also been demonstrated by ICM models of intervention designed for justice-involved populations. As with ACT programs, the implementation of ICM models varies significantly and may encompass both reentry initiatives and community-based support programs. Participants in one program showed significant decreases in legal problems and improvements in life situation and symptoms, although they did not show comparable improvement in income or residential circumstances (Goodley, Finch, Dougan, McDonnell, & McDermeit, 2000). Participants spent more time in the community (relative to treatment as usual), although they were also more likely to have emergency room visits or hospitalizations (Steadman & Naples, 2005). Another study reflected a high proportion (72%) of incarcerated individuals being rearrested during follow-up but indicated that those receiving even a small amount of case management in jail (1–59 minutes per month) had lower odds of rearrest—particularly for violent offenses (Ventura et al., 1998). Fewer subsequent jail incarcerations at 6, 12, and 18 months following release were observed for the group receiving assertive case management services (Wilson et al., 1995). Hartwell (2010) conducted a 3-month follow-up study of individuals provided with transition team services and found that 47% were engaged in community service, 21% were hospitalized, and 18% were reinvolved with the criminal justice system.

The available evidence for interventions at Intercept 4 supports better criminal justice outcomes (whether in terms of rearrest or reincarceration) for participants in programs that are based on ACT or ICM. The impact of these programs on mental health outcomes is less clear. Some evidence suggests consistently favorable mental health and community adjustment outcomes, while other studies show that certain health outcomes (such as hospital days) may actually be higher for those in specialized programs. Despite the generally promising nature of the evidence, there is a need for more well-designed studies (using large samples and comparison groups) in this area.

Community Corrections and Community Support (Intercept 5). The research on interventions at this intercept can once again be categorized in three domains: specialty mental health programs, either parole or probation; specialty probation; and specialty parole (Heilbrun et al., 2012). Outcome measures were similar. Studies tended to use criminal justice outcomes (rearrests, reconvictions, reincarceration) and mental health outcomes (receipt of appropriate services, responses to such services).

One detailed review suggests that specialty probation/parole services can have a substantial impact on improving clinical and criminal outcomes for probationers and parolees with mental illness (Skeem & Eno Louden, 2006). Psychotropic medication and treatment motivation played an important part in the risk of reincarceration; participants perceiving medication to be less helpful or having poorer treatment motivation were much more likely to be reincarcerated for a new charge or a technical violation. Participants were are also monitored more intensively using approaches which may combine the just-noted motivational finding to explain the results of one additional study: An ACT team's clients were *more* likely to be returned to jail (Solomon & Draine, 1995a, 1995b). Intensive monitoring has also been associated with higher failure rates among drug court clients. More recent research has yielded positive results for the impact of specialty probation/parole services on clinical outcomes. Specifically, FACT programs surveyed by Lamberti and colleagues (2011) found that 47% reported a positive impact and 40% reported a very positive impact of probation involvement in reducing criminal recidivism.

Both traditional and specialty parole/probation officers used graduated sanctions, according to one study, but traditional officers generally responded to noncompliance with more punitive strategies than did specialty officers (Eno Louden et al., 2008). This is consistent with the findings of another investigator (Perez, 2009): The treatment group was more likely to be charged with a probation violation, while comparison-group participants were more likely to be arrested for a new criminal offense. Specialty agencies were more likely to focus on monitoring medication and treatment attendance or to use problem-solving strategies and less likely to use threats of (or actual) incarceration (Skeem et al., 2006). This approach was described as particularly well suited for individuals on probation with co-occurring mental illness and substance use: Such individuals were more likely to have poor relationships with professionals and to feel coerced into treatment and were less likely to attend treatment (Skeem et al., 2009). Compared to traditional officers, specialty officers are more involved in supervising probationers with mental illness, meet with them more frequently, are more likely to function as a treatment team, and use problem-solving strategies more regularly (Eno Louden et al., 2008).

The research on interventions at this intercept has demonstrated the importance of the relationship between the case manager or specialty parole/probation officer and the individual under supervision. Individuals with mental illness appear to respond favorably to specialized interventions emphasizing treatment and rehabilitation, but there are several caveats. First, large caseloads are problematic, as the use of reincarceration (or its threat) seems to supplant a more rehabilitative emphasis when probation officers have less time to spend with each individual. Second, the individual's perception that medication and other aspects of treatment are helpful is strongly related to whether he or she will remain in the community without incurring criminal justice sanctions. Third, the subgroup of individuals with co-occurring disorders of mental illness and substance use has poorer relationships with treatment providers, engages in riskier behavior, and is more likely to feel coerced into treatment.

IMPLICATIONS

The chapters in this book will describe topics that include the development of the SIM, interventions at each of the five intercepts, national and state-level promotion and dissemination projects, developing a legislative framework, obtaining and analyzing data, sharing information across systems, applying the SIM to cross-systems mapping exercises, and transforming extramural support into sustainable funding. The detailed description of each of these topics will offer the opportunity for the chapter authors to draw conclusions regarding implications in the areas of research, policy, and practice. These implications will be discussed briefly.

Implications for Research

Each chapter will identify two domains of support for the SIM: theoretical and practical, and empirical. Often the available empirical research will be limited. One of the goals of this book, however, is to offer approaches to translating existing support in the area of theory or practice into testable models that can ultimately offer empirical support. Accordingly, the authors will comment on opportunities for operationalizing present support that is nonempirical into designs that investigators can use to conduct relevant research. Chapter 12 is devoted to strategies to identify, obtain, and analyze research data on these topics.

The brief review of research on interventions at each intercept provided in this chapter demonstrates the need for additional empirical research at each step. The respective chapters addressing each intercept will describe the existing evidence in more detail and expand on the needs for further research. One of the clear needs for all intercepts (particularly Intercepts 1, 2, and 5) is for additional studies that have a large number of participants (more than 200), employ multiple sites, and incorporate control or comparison groups.

Several national and state-level projects have used the SIM to provide information and initiatives relevant to community-based alternatives to prosecution. The National GAINS Center (discussed in Chapter 8) and the Council for State Governments are two of the most prominent examples. In addition, several states (Florida, Illinois, Massachusetts, Ohio, and Pennsylvania) have developed centers that have done similar work within their own states (discussed in Chapter 10). When such projects provide information, technical assistance, and education using the SIM, the impact of such interventions has typically not been gauged through evaluation or formal research. Yet there may be opportunities to do so. The chapters describing these projects (Chapters 8 and 10) will suggest ways in which the impact of their interventions might be measured empirically.

Implications for Policy

The implications of the SIM for helping to shape legal policy will be addressed at two levels. In Chapter 11, Leifman and Coffey describe a legislative framework into which community-based alternatives to standard prosecution, and the SIM, might be incorporated. This discussion will focus primarily on federal and state legislation. It will also touch upon the second level of policy consideration, which relates to the policy applicable in local jurisdictions such as communities and counties. The discussion of local policy implications will encompass the informality and local variability that are part of the change process as influenced by the SIM.

Implications for Practice

Several important practice questions regarding the SIM will be discussed in this book. The first of these is educational. The SIM has often been used in jurisdiction-specific cross-system mapping exercises conducted in the past decade. How can this be done most effectively? This is the topic of Chapter 13, in which several highly experienced trainers describe strategies for the effective use of this model in this context.

The second practice question is financial. Jurisdictions may begin the process of changing their policy and practice on community-based alternatives to prosecution through the application of funding provided by a grant or contract.

Unless this funding can be transformed from extramural to internal, however, there will be no stable basis on which to sustain the efforts that were initiated. This transformation is particularly challenging in the current political and economic climate in the United States. Moving from extramural to sustained, internal funding is the topic of Chapter 9.

The third practice question involves generalizability. The chapters in this book will review what we know and do not know about the application of the SIM to community-based alternatives to prosecution for individuals with SMI and often co-occurring substance use. Would such an approach be feasible with other populations? Such groups include veterans, individuals with substance use (but without mental disorders), juveniles, and those with developmental disabilities. The final chapter will address the feasibility and logistics of applying the SIM to other groups with the comparable goal of providing effective interventions that promote public safety.

NOTES

1. For the purposes of this chapter and this book, we consider SMI using the National Institute of Mental Health (1987) definition: a diagnosis of nonorganic psychosis or personality disorder, with a duration involving a two-year or longer history of mental illness or treatment, and functional disability. Our focus will also encompass co-occurring disorders of drug or alcohol use but will not consider such substance use when it does not co-occur with a mental illness.
2. Community courts are neighborhood-focused courts designed to address local problems. They use problem solving and strive to create relationships with outside stakeholders such as residents, merchants, churches, and schools (Center for Court Innovation, 2012).

REFERENCES

Andrews, D., & Bonta. J. (2006), *The psychology of criminal conduct* (4th ed.). Newark, NJ: Lexis Nexis/Mathew Bender.

Belenko, S. (1998). Research on drug courts: A critical review. *National Drug Court Institute Review, 1*, 1–42.

Belenko, S. (2001). *Research on drug courts: A critical review: 2001 update.* New York: National Center on Addiction and Substance Abuse at Columbia University.

Belenko, S., Patapis, N., & French, M. (2005). *Economic benefits of drug treatment: A critical review of the evidence for policy makers.* Philadelphia, PA: Treatment Research Institute.

Berman, G., & Feinblatt, J. (2005). *Good courts: The case for problem-solving justice.* New York: New Press.

Bertman-Pate, L., Burnett, D., Thompson, J., Calhoun, C., Deland, S., & Fryou, R. (2004). The New Orleans Forensic Aftercare Clinic: A seven-year review of hospital-discharged and jail-diverted clients. *Behavioral Sciences and the Law, 22*, 159–169.

Bhati, A., Roman, J., & Chalfin, A. (2008). *To treat or not to treat: Evidence on the prospects of expanding treatment to drug-involved offenders*. Washington, D.C.: Urban Institute.

Borum, R., Williams, M., Deans, M., Steadman, H., & Morrissey, J. (1998). Police perspectives on responding to mentally ill people in crisis: Perceptions of program effectiveness. *Behavioral Sciences & the Law, 16*, 393–405.

Boccaccini, M., Christy, A., Poythress, N., & Kershaw, D. (2005). Rediversion in two postbooking jail diversion programs in Florida. *Psychiatric Services, 56*, 835–839.

Broner, N., Mayrl, D., & Landsberg, G. (2005). Outcomes of mandated and nonmandated New York City diversion for offenders with alcohol, drug, and mental disorders. *The Prison Journal, 85*, 18–49.

California Board of Corrections (2005). Mentally ill offender crime reduction grant program: Overview of statewide evaluation findings. Retrieved January 8, 2011, from California Department of Corrections and Rehabilitation web site: http://cdcr.ca.gov/CSA/CPP/Grants/MIOCR/Docs/miocrg_report_presentation.pdf

Case, B., Steadman, H., Dupuis, S., & Morris, L. (2009). Who succeeds in jail diversion programs for persons with mental illness? A multi-site study. *Behavioral Sciences and the Law, 27*, 661–674.

Center for Court Innovation (2012). Community court. Retrieved April 25, 2012, from <http://www.courtinnovation.org/topic/community-court>.

Center for Health Care Services (2006). Providing jail diversion for people with mental illness. *Psychiatric Services, 57*, 1521–1523.

Compton, M., Bahora, M., Watson, A., & Oliva, J. (2008). A comprehensive review of extant research on crisis intervention team (CIT) programs. *Journal of the American Academy of Psychiatry and the Law, 36*, 47–55.

Compton, M., & Chien, V. (2008). Factors related to knowledge retention after crisis intervention team training for police officers. *Psychiatric Services, 59*, 1049–1051.

Compton, M., Demir Neubert, B., Broussard, B., McGriff, J., Morgan, R., & Oliva, J. (2009). Use of force preferences and perceived effectiveness of actions among crisis intervention team police officers and non-CIT officers in an escalating psychiatric crisis involving a subject with schizophrenia. *Schizophrenia Bulletin*, Advance online publication, doi:10.1093/schbul/sbp146.

Cowell, A., Broner, N., & Dupont, R. (2004). The cost effectiveness of criminal justice diversion programs for people with serious mental illness co-occurring with substance abuse. *Journal of Contemporary Criminal Justice, 20*, 292–315.

Crocker, A., Hartford, K. & Heslop, L. (2009). Gender differences in police encounters among persons with and without serious mental illness. *Psychiatric Services, 60*, 86–93.

Cummings, J. (2010). The cost of crazy: How therapeutic jurisprudence and mental health courts lower incarceration costs, reduce recidivism, and improve public safety. *Loyola Law Review, 56*, 279–310.

Ditton, P. (1999). Mental health and treatment of inmates and probationers. Retrieved August 7, 2011, from the U.S. Department of Justice, Bureau of Justice Statistics website: http://bjs.ojp.usdoj.gov/index.cfm?ty=pbdetail&iid=787

Eno Louden, J., Skeem, J., Camp, J., & Christensen, E. (2008). Supervising probationers with mental disorder: How do agencies respond to violations? *Criminal Justice and Behavior, 35*, 832–847.

Fisher, H., Roy-Bujnowski, K., Grudzinskas, A. J., Clayfield, J., & Wolff, N. (2006). Patterns and prevalence of arrest in a statewide cohort of mental health care consumers. *Psychiatric Services, 57*, 1623–1628.

Frazer, M. (2006). *The impact of the community court model on defendant perceptions of fairness: A case study at the Red Hook Community Justice Center.* New York: Center for Court Innovation.

Government Accountability Office (2005). *Adult drug courts: Evidence indicates recidivism reductions and mixed results for other outcomes.* Washington, D.C.: Author.

Glaze, L., & James, D. (2006). Mental health problems of prison and jail inmates. Retrieved August 7, 2011, from the U.S. Department of Justice, Bureau of Justice Statistics website: http://bjs.ojp.usdoj.gov/index.cfm?ty=pbdetail&iid=789

Goldkamp, J., & Irons-Guynn, C. (2000). Emerging judicial strategies for the mentally ill in the criminal caseload: Mental health courts in Fort Lauderdale, Seattle, San Bernardino, and Anchorage. Retrieved August 6, 2011, from U.S. Department of Justice, Office of Justice Programs website: https://www.ncjrs.gov/html/bja/mental-health/contents.html

Gottfredson, D., & Exum, M. (2002). The Baltimore City Drug Court: One-year results from a randomized study. *Journal of Research on Crime and Delinquency, 39*, 337–356.

Gottfredson, D., Najaka, S., & Kearley. (2003). Effectiveness of drug treatment courts: Evidence from a randomized trial. *Criminology & Public Policy, 2*, 171–196.

Goodley, S., Finch, M., Dougan, L., McDonnell, M., & McDermeit, M. (2000). Case management for dually diagnosed individuals involved in the criminal justice system. *Journal of Substance Abuse Treatment, 18*, 137–148.

Hakuta, J., Soroushian, V., & Kralstein, D. (2008). *Do community courts transform the justice response to misdemeanor crime? Testing the impact of the Midtown Community Court.* New York: Center for Court Innovation.

Hartwell, S. (2010). Ex-inmates with psychiatric disabilities returning to the community from correctional custody: The forensic transition team approach after a decade. In M. Peyrot & S. Burns (Eds.), *Research in social problems and public policy: Vol. 17. New approaches to social problems treatment* (pp. 263–283). Bingley, United Kingdom: Emerald Group.

Heilbrun, K., DeMatteo, D., Yasuhara, K., Brooks-Holliday, S., Shah, S., King, C., Bingham, A., Hamilton, D., & LaDuke, C. (2012). Community-based alternatives for justice-involved individuals with severe mental illness: Review of the relevant research. *Criminal Justice and Behavior, 39*, 351–419.

Hiday, V., & Ray, B. (2010). Arrests two years after exiting a well-established mental health court. *Psychiatric Services, 61*, 463–468.

Hoff, R., Baranosky, M., Buchanan, J., Zonana, H., & Rosenheck, R. (1999). The effects of a jail diversion program on incarceration: A retrospective cohort study. *Journal of the American Academy of Psychiatry and the Law, 27*, 377–386.

Hughes, D., Steadman, H. J., Case, B., Griffin, P. A., & Leff, H. S. (2012). A simulation modeling approach for planning and costing jail diversion programs for persons with mental illness. *Criminal Justice and Behavior, 39*, 434–446.

Justice Education Center, Inc. (2002). *Evaluation of the Hartford Community Court*. West Hartford, CT: The Justice Education Center, Inc.

Kiai, J., & Stobo, J. (2010). Prison healthcare in California. *UC Health*, 1-22-10. Available online at http://universityofcalifornia.edu/sites/uchealth/2010/01/22/prison-health-care-in-california/

Kralstein, D. (2005). *Community court research: A literature review*. New York: Center for Court Innovation.

Lamb, H. R. (1984). Deinstitutionalization and the homeless mentally ill. *Hospital and Community Psychiatry, 35*, 899–907.

Lamberti, J., Deem, A., Weisman, R., & LaDuke, C. (2011). The role of probation in forensic assertive community treatment. *Psychiatric Services, 62*, 418–421.

Lamberti, J., Weisman, R., & Faden, D. (2004). Forensic assertive community treatment: Preventing incarceration of adults with severe mental illness. *Psychiatric Services, 55*, 1285–1293.

Lamberti, J., Weisman, R., Schwarzkopf, S., Price, N., Ashton, R., & Trompeter, J. (2001). The mentally ill in jails and prisons: Towards an integrated model of prevention. *Psychiatric Quarterly, 72*, 63–77.

Levin, B., Hennessy, K., & Petrila, J. (Eds.). (2010). *Mental health services: A public health perspective*. New York: Oxford.

Lowenkamp, C., Holsinger, A., & Latessa, E. (2005). Are drug courts effective? A meta-analytic review. *Journal of Community Corrections*, Fall, 5–10, 28.

McCoy, M., Roberts, D., Hanrahan, P., Clay, R., & Luchins, D. (2004). Jail linkage assertive community treatment services for individuals with mental illnesses. *Psychiatric Rehabilitation Journal, 27*, 243–250.

McGaha, A., Boothroyd, R., Poythress, N., Petrila, J., & Ort, R. (2002). Lessons from the Broward County mental health court evaluation. *Evaluation and Program Planning, 25*, 125–135.

McNiel, D., & Binder, R. (2007). Effectiveness of a mental health court in reducing criminal recidivism and violence. *American Journal of Psychiatry, 164*, 1395–1404.

Metraux, S. (2008). Examining relationships between receiving mental health services in Pennsylvania prison system and time served. *Psychiatric Services, 59*, 800–802.

Moore, M., & Hiday, V. (2006). Mental health outcomes: A comparison of re-arrest and re-arrest severity between mental health court and traditional court participants. *Law and Human Behavior, 30*, 659–674.

Morrissey, J., Meyer, P., & Cuddeback, G. (2007). Extending assertive community treatment to criminal justice settings: Origins, current evidence, and future directions. *Community Mental Health Journal, 43*, 527–544.

Munetz, M., & Griffin, P. (2006). Use of the Sequential Intercept Model as an approach to decriminalization of people with serious mental illness. *Psychiatric Services, 57*, 544–549.

National GAINS Center for People with Co-Occurring Disorders in the Justice System (2002). *The Nathaniel Project: An alternative to incarceration program for people with serious mental illness who have committed felony offenses*. Program Brief Series. Delmar, NY: Author.

National Institute of Mental Health (1987). *Towards a model for a comprehensive community-based mental health system*. Washington, D.C.: NIMH.

Osher, F. C., & Steadman, H.J. (2007). Adapting evidence-based practices for persons with mental illness involved with the criminal justice system. *Psychiatric Services, 58*, 1472–1478.

Perez, D. (2009). Applying evidence-based practices to community corrections supervision: An evaluation of residential substance abuse treatment for high-risk probationers. *Journal of Contemporary Criminal Justice, 25*, 442–458.

Redlich, A., Steadman, H., Monahan, J., Petrila, J., & Griffin, P. (2005). The second generation of mental health courts. *Psychology, Public Policy, and Law, 11*, 527–538.

Ridgely, S., Engberg, J., Greenberg, M., Turner, S., DeMartini, C., & Dembosky, J. (2007). Justice, treatment, and cost: An evaluation of the fiscal impact of the Allegheny County Mental Health Court. Retrieved May 5, 2011, from Rand Infrastructure, Safety, and Environment website: http://www.rand.org/content/dam/rand/pubs/technical_reports/2007/RAND_TR439.pdf.

Rochefort, D. A. (1984). Origins of the "third psychiatric revolution": The Community Mental Health Centers Act of 1963. *Journal of Health Politics, Policy and Law, 9*, 1–30.

Shafer, M., Arthur, B., & Franczak, M. (2004). An analysis of post-booking jail diversion programming for persons with co-occurring disorders. *Behavioral Sciences and the Law, 22*, 771–785.

Skeem, J., & Bibeau, L. (2008). How does violence potential relate to Crisis Intervention Team responses to emergencies? *Psychiatric Services, 59*, 201–204.

Skeem, J., & Eno Louden, J. (2006). Toward evidence-based practice for probationers and parolees mandated to mental health treatment. *Psychiatric Services, 57*, 333–342.

Skeem, J., Eno Louden, J., Manchak, S., Vidal, S., & Haddad, E. (2009). Social networks and social control of probationers with co-occurring mental and substance abuse problems. *Law and Human Behavior, 33*, 122–135.

Solomon, P., & Draine, J. (1995a). Jail recidivism in a forensic case management program. *Health & Social Work, 20*, 167–173.

Solomon, P., & Draine, J. (1995b). One-year outcomes of a randomized trial of case management with seriously mentally ill clients leaving jail. *Evaluation Review, 19*, 256–273.

Steadman, H., Barbera, S., & Dennis, D. (1994). A national survey of jail diversion programs for mentally ill detainees. *Hospital and Community Psychiatry, 45*, 1109–1113.

Steadman, H., & Naples, M. (2005). Assessing the effectiveness of jail diversion programs for persons with serious mental illness and co-occurring substance use disorders. *Behavioral Sciences & the Law, 23*, 163–170.

Teller, J., Munetz, M., Gil, K., & Ritter, C. (2006). Crisis Intervention Team training for police officers responding to mental disturbance calls. *Psychiatric Services, 57*, 232–237.

Thresholds, State, County Collaborative Jail Linkage Project, Chicago (2001). *Psychiatric Services, 52*, 1380–1382.

Torrey, E., Kennard, A., Eslinger, D., Lamb, R., & Pavle, J. (2010). More mentally ill people are in jails and prisons than hospitals: A survey of states. Retrieved August 7, 2011, from: http://treatmentadvocacycenter.org/storage/documents/final_jails_v_hospitals_study.pdf

Ventura, L., Cassel, C., Jacoby, J., & Huang, B. (1998). Case management and recidivism of mentally ill persons released from jail. *Psychiatric Services, 49,* 1330–1337.

Vogel, W., Noether, C., & Steadman, H. (2007). Preparing communities for re-entry of offenders with mental illness: The ACTION approach. *Mental Health Issues in the Criminal Justice System, 45,* 167–188.

Watson, A., Ottati, V., Morabito, M., Draine, J., Kerr, A., & Angell, B. (2010). Outcomes of police contacts with persons with mental illness: The impact of CIT. *Administration and Policy in Mental Health and Mental Health Services Research, 37,* 302–317.

Weisman, R. L., Lamberti, J. S., & Price, N. (2004). Integrating criminal justice, community healthcare, and support services for adults with severe mental disorders. *Psychiatric Quarterly, 75,* 71–85.

Wilson, D., Mitchell, O., & MacKenzie, D. (2006). A systematic review of drug court effects on recidivism. *Journal of Experimental Criminology, 2,* 459–487.

Wilson, D., Tien, G., & Eaves, D. (1995). Increasing the community tenure of mentally disordered offenders: An assertive case management program. *International Journal of Law and Psychiatry, 18,* 61–69.

Wright, D. (1997). Getting out of the asylum: Understanding the confinement of the insane in the nineteenth century. *Social History of Medicine, 10,* 137–155.

2

Development of the Sequential Intercept Model

The Search for a Conceptual Model

PATRICIA A. GRIFFIN, MARK MUNETZ,
NATALIE BONFINE, AND KATHLEEN KEMP ■

This chapter addresses the development of the Sequential Intercept Model. It traces this development from its roots, through the collaboration of Mark Munetz, Patricia Griffin, and Henry Steadman, to its local, regional, and national implementation.

INITIAL DEVELOPMENT OF THE SIM

Summit County, Ohio

In the early 1990s, stakeholders in Summit County recognized that individuals with mental illness were overly represented in the local criminal justice system. In addition, the limited resources available to serve this growing population were straining the mental health system, jail, courts, and community corrections. They noticed similar patterns throughout the United States: frequent encounters of individuals with SMI with law enforcement, increased arrest and incarceration rates of individuals with SMI, an increased demand for mental health services at the local jail, and a reduction of psychiatric beds in general, accompanied by an increase in the proportion of remaining beds being used for forensic patients (Council of State Governments, 2002; Lamb & Weinberger, 1998; Munetz, Grande, & Chambers, 2001). Service administrators, including Mark R. Munetz, the Clinical Director for the County of Summit Alcohol, Drug Addiction and Mental Health Services (ADM) Board, were concerned about the overrepresentation of individuals with mental illness in the county jail and the lack of a coordinated, systematic approach to address this issue. By 1999, these problems led Summit County to seek assistance. The federally funded National GAINS Center for People with Co-Occurring Disorders in the Justice System (see Chapter 8) was offering technical assistance to communities to recognize and address such issues, and Summit County requested such assistance. The GAINS Center sent Patricia Griffin to Summit County as a consultant. Eventually, this consultation led to the collaborative development of the SIM by Munetz, Griffin, and GAINS Center Director Hank Steadman. The model would prove to be an effective approach to addressing the needs of individuals at the interface of the criminal justice and mental health systems (see Chapters 8, 10, and 13).

The technical assistance provided by the GAINS Center served as a catalyst for collaborative program development in Summit County. Griffin made a number of recommendations, including "As part of the planning process of the criminal justice—treatment forum, map out the process by which individuals go from initial law enforcement contact to jail through the court system and back into the community. . . . The flowcharts and resource directory should be used as a basis for future information sharing and collaboration between mental health, substance abuse, and criminal justice staff in Summit County." The recommendation went on to note: "This mapping helps everyone understand how the local criminal justice and treatment systems work, describes local resources, and identifies how each participant fits in the larger picture. In addition, mapping of criminal justice-treatment interactions can be used to identify the gaps between the current resources and the unmet needs of the criminal justice–involved population" (Griffin, January 2000). In April 2000, in consideration of the recommendations of the GAINS Center, the Summit County Mental Health/Criminal Justice Forum was convened, with major stakeholders from mental health, addictions, and criminal justice represented (American Psychiatric Association, 2003). The forum initially used the recommendations of the GAINS Center to proceed with two programs that had already been in the planning phase prior to Griffin's visit to Summit County: a CIT program and a mental health court. In 1999 the Summit County ADM Board sent a team, including then-Lt. Michael Woody of the Akron Police Department, to Memphis, Tennessee, to receive formal training in the CIT model. By late 1999, Summit County was planning an initial training for volunteer first responders in the Akron Police Department. The first CIT training, held in May 2000, provided police officers with training on recognizing mental illness and developing deescalation skills. The CIT program also established partnerships between law enforcement and mental health agencies so police officers and other first responders became aware of community treatment options when encountering individuals with mental illness. In 2001, another local champion (Judge Elinore Marsh Stormer) established the Akron Municipal Mental Health Court in collaboration with the Summit County mental health system. This Akron problem-solving court was the first mental health court in Ohio (indeed, among the first in the country) and was later selected as a learning site by the

Bureau of Justice Assistance to act as a model and source of reference for similar programs in development (Council of State Governments, 2006).

The Ohio Criminal Justice Coordinating Center of Excellence

Given the success of Summit County in implementing CIT and mental health court programs, local stakeholders became interested in jail diversion efforts at the state level, believing that the lessons learned in Summit County could inform others how to effectively address the criminalization of individuals with mental illness. At the same time, Director Mike Hogan of the Ohio Department of Mental Health (now the Ohio Department of Mental Health and Addiction Services) was facing a fragmented and decentralized mental health system. Hogan recognized the need to use existing expertise in best practices to address a number of areas related to mental illness. In 2000, the Ohio Department of Mental Health was developing a plan to support coordinating centers of excellence (CCoEs) to promote evidence-based practices throughout the state. The goals of such centers involved capitalizing on statewide expertise in effectively addressing the specific needs of individuals with mental illness. CCoEs developed and supported by the Ohio Department of Mental Health promoted evidence-based practices that emerged from successful collaboration between the mental health and addictions systems. Examples include the Integrated Dual Disorder Treatment CCoE and the Supported Employment CCoE. Other CCoEs focused on issues such as (a) wellness management and recovery and (b) mental illness and developmental disabilities.

CCoEs were typically located within a university or research setting, thus connecting an expert knowledge base with community mental health agencies, mental health boards, consumer advocates, and state administrators. The role of CCoEs generally was to (a) assist local mental health systems in identifying and implementing evidence-based practices, and in promoting the use of procedures required to implement such practices and (b) develop and disseminate educational and training materials. The CCoEs were also created to utilize and share fidelity scales to measure and evaluate program implementation and to promote cross-systems sharing of information and effective practices.

Following the successful jail diversion activities in Summit County, Munetz and the Ohio Department of Mental Health discussed creating a center of excellence focused on justice-involved individuals with SMI. Hogan and Steadman discussed the concept and shared a vision for a "mini-GAINS Center"—a technical assistance center focused on jail diversion that would serve Ohio as the GAINS Center served the country. In May 2001, the Ohio Department of Mental Health funded Summit County's Alcohol, Drug Addictions, and Mental Health Services Board to create the Criminal Justice Coordinating Center of Excellence (CJ CCoE) to help in the statewide elaboration of jail diversion programs (see Chapter 10). The Board collaborated with Northeast Ohio Medical University's Department of Psychiatry in operating the CJ CCoE.

The decision by the state to fund the CJ CCoE was not straightforward. At the time, jail diversion was an emerging and promising area but lacked a clear evidence base. However, the enthusiasm over CIT and mental health courts, and the possibility of replicating the work of the GAINS Center throughout Ohio, overcame the state's reluctance. The decision to fund the CJ CCoE was conditional. Hogan directed the CJ CCoE to develop a conceptual model for jail diversion in its first year of operation. This requirement, coupled with the work that had begun in Summit County, the work that Griffin was doing in Pennsylvania, and the ongoing consultation between Griffin and Steadman at the GAINS Center and Munetz and his collaborators with the CJ CCoE, led to the development of what would eventually become the SIM.

The Pennsylvania Southeast Region Forensic Task Force—"Road Testing" The Model

In 2001, the five southeastern counties in Pennsylvania (Bucks, Chester, Delaware, Montgomery, and Philadelphia) began using the developing SIM as an organizing tool to plan coordinated regional behavioral health and criminal justice initiatives. This was the second time the five counties had worked together in such an effort. The first meeting was an exercise in futility: contentious and wide-ranging discussion, but little consensus and few useful outcomes. This time, the organizers wanted to address the issues in a more coherent and productive fashion that would both utilize the wide range of participants' expertise (mainly in criminal justice and behavioral health) *and* generate positive results. A subcommittee, composed of representatives from the advocacy community, county and state behavioral health systems, forensic state hospital, and state prison[1] and Griffin, was formed to explore promising practices locally and nationally.

As part of their initial work, they searched for a larger conceptual model to guide the discussion. They found little that was helpful. Much of the literature at that time reflected traditional "forensic" approaches to the justice involvement of individuals with mental health issues by focusing on the evaluation of legal questions such as competence to stand trial and mental state at the time of the offense. Far less attention was devoted to treatment, continuity of care between jail or prison and the community, and helping people with behavioral health disorders to avoid the arrest/conviction/incarceration process that was standard for justice-involved individuals.

There were a few promising possibilities. For example, in describing the connections between the criminal justice and substance abuse systems, the Center for Substance Abuse Treatment (1995) identified nine potential linkage points: arrest, pretrial hearing, presentence (plea) hearing, jail, diversion program, trial/sentencing, probation, jail/prison, and parole. These offered important opportunities for intervention with justice-involved individuals with substance abuse problems. Landsberg and Shannon (2002) described a roadmap with six critical intervention points: preventive, pre-booking, post-booking, incarceration, probation, and post-incarceration. But it was Munetz's presentation on the use of the SIM in Ohio, which he gave at the 2001 Annual Forensic Division Conference of the National Association of State Mental Health Program Directors, that seemed most applicable to Griffin as she listened to the talk. Munetz was using the SIM as a conceptual tool to structure the work of the proposed Ohio Coordinating Center of Excellence on criminal justice and mental health. He described the evolving model as a systematic approach to the problem of criminalization of those with mental disorder that could not be solved with a single solution but must instead be addressed on multiple levels by the community as a whole (Munetz, 2001). At this time, the model was called the "Sequential Filters" Model and had four filters: best clinical practices, pre-arrest diversion, post-arrest diversion, and treatment in the criminal justice system and linkage. Griffin took this model back to the Promising Practices Subcommittee and proposed it as a possible approach for the work of the task force. The subcommittee saw the potential in the model but suggested modifications to more closely follow the flow of the criminal justice system process. Five intercepts were identified: Intercept 1—law enforcement and emergency services; Intercept 2—initial detention and hearings; Intercept 3—post-booking diversion, jails, courts, forensic evaluation, and forensic hospitalization; Intercept 4—reentry; and Intercept 5—community corrections and support services. The subcommittee proposed the revised SIM to the larger task force to help organize the discussion in important areas relevant to the movement of people with mental illness through the criminal justice system. The task force agreed and began to use the SIM in its regional planning (Promising Practices Subcommittee Report, 2002).

The task force met monthly and focused on one intercept per meeting. Between monthly meetings, the Promising Practices Subcommittee began a three-phase approach to working with the larger group. First, they surveyed each county on the status of current work on the specific intercept to be discussed at the upcoming meeting. Second, they developed a list of promising practices/models for each intercept. Finally, they described issues, barriers, strategies, and possible next steps for each intercept. Their larger goal was to move past the dissatisfactions typically expressed when criminal justice and behavioral health staff met. Instead, they wanted to (a) develop a common language of criminal justice–behavioral health and treatment linkages, (b) enhance the expertise of the task force in addressing these issues, and (c) produce a final report with meaningful recommendations based on increased knowledge of criminal justice–behavioral health intersections in each county and thoughtful consideration of the implications of this knowledge.

Using the version of the SIM available at that time, the task force was decidedly more successful in its second attempt. Such successes are apparent in considering some of the steps taken by participants after the second set of meetings:

- Bucks County organized a countywide planning effort based on the SIM to improve the local continuum of mental health–criminal justice interactions and services.

- The state's Department of Community and Economic Development helped fund a forensic position for the southeast regional behavioral health office to focus on forensic issues in the five counties in the future.
- The Pennsylvania Forensic Interagency Task Force sponsored by Pennsylvania's National Alliance on Mental Illness reviewed the work of the task force and recommended that the SIM be used as a planning and organizing tool at the state and local levels.
- The Office of Mental Health and Substance Abuse Services of the Pennsylvania Department of Public Welfare began to use the SIM as the organizing tool for its annual forensic plan and required each of Pennsylvania's sixty-seven counties to do so as well (Munetz & Griffin, 2006).

The GAINS Center

The contributions of the GAINS Center, particularly those of Steadman, were instrumental in the development and maturation of the SIM. Steadman advocated a public health approach to the problem of over-representation of people with mental illness in the criminal justice system, emphasizing alternatives to standard prosecution *and* to traditional forensic approaches that prioritized assessment over intervention. The work of the GAINS Center is national, so the development of a model that could illustrate steps in the penetration into the justice system would be useful for technical assistance, training, and consultation across the country.

Munetz visited the GAINS Center in 2001 for consultation on the development of the Ohio Criminal Justice Coordinating Center of Excellence. Upon Steadman's advice, the developing SIM began to incorporate the term "intercept" and dropped the use of "filter." More broadly, the application of the SIM using multiple levels, considering the larger community, was clarified. Arguing that justice involvement should not result solely because of symptoms of mental illness, Steadman advised Munetz to add "treatment in the criminal justice system" and "linkages upon reentry" as intercepts in the model.

The collaboration between Munetz, Griffin, and Steadman in developing the SIM is illustrated well in this 2001 meeting. While Munetz used the developing model to good advantage in Ohio and Griffin employed it in Pennsylvania, the GAINS Center applied the SIM nationally in the technical assistance, consultation, and education that it conducted across the country. (Since both Griffin and Munetz also used the SIM in presentations delivered in other states, each also contributed to the national application of the SIM.) In 2004–2005, the GAINS Center developed a brochure entitled *The Sequential Intercepts for Change: Developing a Comprehensive State Plan for Mental Health and Criminal Justice Collaboration*, which was widely disseminated across the country. The brochure used the SIM to highlight specific actions that could be taken to support criminal justice–mental health collaboration at both the state level and at the service level for each intercept. Communities now had a single, easy-to-read planning document that provided an overview of where criminal justice–mental health partnerships should go in the future and specific steps to reach that partnership. The brochure was revised in 2009 (CMHS National GAINS Center, 2009) to further refine the model/action steps for partnership, make it more broadly relevant to state and local planning, and to reflect the collaborative nature of the Munetz/Griffin/Steadman work on the model. By 2009, the brochure noted:

> The Sequential Intercept Model has been used by numerous communities to help organize mental health service system transformation to meet the needs of people with mental illness involved with the criminal justice system. The model helps to assess where diversion activities may be developed, how institutions can better meet treatment needs, and when to begin activities to facilitate re-entry (2009, p.4).

THE MODEL

The Sequential Intercept Model (SIM) is based on the goal that, in an ideal world, the prevalence of mental disorders among individuals in the criminal justice system would be, at minimum, no greater than the prevalence of mental disorders among all individuals living in the corresponding community. In other words, individuals with mental disorders would not be over-represented in the criminal justice system. Currently, some people with mental illness end up in the criminal justice system because of behavior resulting from untreated, symptomatic mental illness. This is known as the criminalization of mental illness and reflects a system failure. The problem of the overrepresentation of people with mental illness in the criminal justice system is complex. It has no single cause, and there is no single solution. Implementing a new program or change in policy is not sufficient; the problem must be approached systematically, at many levels, and as early as possible in the process. Further, the needs of people with mental illness are complex, going beyond what can be provided by the mental health and addictions systems. Individuals with serious mental illness (SMI) who enter the criminal justice system penetrate deeper into the system and often stay involved longer than people without serious mental illness (Ditton, 1999). Thus, the criminal justice system shares responsibility for this problem with the mental health and addiction systems. The SIM provides a framework for stakeholders to examine this failure from a multisystem perspective.

Collaboration across these systems is key to effective solutions and the collaboration is necessarily interdisciplinary. It has long been recognized that jail diversion requires "boundary spanners" (Steadman, 1992): individuals who are familiar with both the mental health and criminal justice systems. While roughly half of people with SMI in the community have a comorbid substance use disorder, 72% to 80% of justice-involved individuals with SMI have a co-occurring diagnosis (Abram & Teplin, 1991; Abram, Teplin, & McClelland, 2003). Thus, the key systems—addictions, mental health, and criminal justice— must coordinate their efforts to address the needs of overlapping populations. This challenge is exacerbated by limited funding for mental health and addictions treatment, overburdened correctional systems, and limited probation resources. The SIM offers a framework to help communities by encouraging the systematic development of initiatives to reduce the criminalization of people with mental illness. It also creates a lens that illustrates the "big picture" of justice-involved individuals with behavioral health disorders, which is more likely to resolve overarching problems (Steadman, 2011; see also Chapter 11).

The SIM is conceptually simple (Munetz & Griffin, 2006). It uses the flow of the criminal justice system to frame the issues. People move from the community through the criminal justice system in a reasonably predictable, linear fashion, from arrest, to an initial hearing, to jail awaiting trial or adjudication of competence to stand trial, to release or reentry, and finally to community supervision or support. Each of these points in the justice system provides opportunities to intervene and "intercept" the person, divert him or her from the justice system to the community treatment system when possible, and facilitate timely movement through the criminal justice system.

The Sequential Intercept Model originally assumed that the over-representation of people with serious mental illness in the criminal justice system was largely the result of symptomatic mental illness that directly resulted in behavior leading to criminal justice involvement. Thus if more people with mental illness received effective treatment in the community, the problem would be diminished. Accordingly, Munetz and Griffin called an accessible mental health system the *ultimate intercept*: "An accessible, comprehensive, effective mental health system focused on the needs of individuals with serious and persistent mental disorders is undoubtedly the most effective means of preventing the criminalization of people with mental illness" (Munetz & Griffin, 2006, p. 545).

Recent studies suggest that we have over-estimated the proportion of people with SMI who end up in the justice system because of untreated psychosis and under-estimated the proportion who end up in the justice system because of additional risk factors including criminogenic influences (e.g., substance abuse, unemployment, criminal thinking, family dysfunction, antisocial peers), trauma, situation stress, and environmental factors. For instance, Peterson and colleagues (2010) found that only 7% of offenders with a mental illness committed crimes that were a direct result of psychosis (5%) or minor "survival" crimes related to poverty. Recent research advances reveal that treating mental illness alone may not be sufficient (Epperson et al, 2011; Fisher, Silver, & Wolff, 2006; Peterson et al., 2010; Skeem et al., 2011). An adequate mental health system is clearly necessary, though not sufficient, to effectively keep people with SMI out of the criminal justice system. New evidence suggests that the mental health system as a whole needs to reconsider the goals of treatment to go beyond mental illness and substance use needs and incorporate criminogenic needs that also contribute to justice involvement. As the problem of over-representation of people with serious mental illness in the criminal justice system is better understood, it becomes increasingly clear that these criminogenic risk factors, in addition to the results of untreated, symptomatic mental illness, may increase the risk of people with SMI ending up in the justice system. So an accessible, effective mental health system, the "ultimate intercept," is still not the complete answer to the criminalization problem, unless that system includes expertise on the interventions addressing criminality.

Skeem and colleagues (2011) have suggested that we need to consider a paradigm shift. In a 2011 *Psychiatric News* article exploring the relationship between arrests and mental illness, Appelbaum was quoted noting "The new paradigm suggests that merely treating mental disorders may be insufficient to reduce criminality, including violence, unless specific criminogenic factors are addressed as well—for example, anger management and cognitive therapy for criminal cognitions. That is not a reason to reduce efforts to treat major mental disorders in the

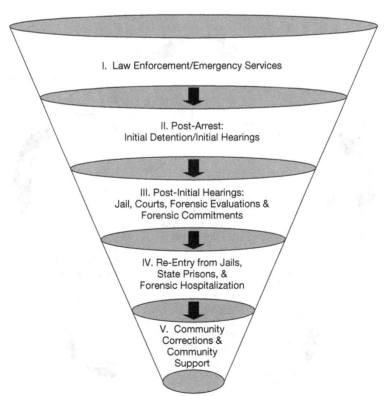

Figure 2.1 Sequential Intercepts as a Series of Filters.

offender population, but it is recognition that ordinary clinical treatments may not be enough" (Daly, p. 10). Epperson and colleagues (2011) suggest that mental health and criminal justice interventions must address a variety of factors that influence criminal behavior in an integrated and centralized format.

As a result of this evolving research and discussion, Munetz, Griffin, and Kemp (2013) have recently suggested that "the real ultimate intercept is a comprehensive, accessible, effective mental health and addiction system that is criminologically informed and working closely with criminal justice partners who understand the behavioral health needs of offenders" (p. 461).

The model has three graphic representations: a funnel, a circle, and a horizontal line. The funnel graphic illustrates that the earlier an intervention occurs, the larger the number of individuals potentially affected (Fig. 2.1). Accordingly, Intercept 1 interventions (law enforcement/crisis services such as a crisis intervention team [CIT]) may divert more individuals than Intercept 3 interventions (e.g., a specialty mental health docket). The circular graphic makes the point that people can get caught in a revolving door and that intervention at any of the intercepts can stop or at least slow the door (Fig. 2.2). From this perspective, an intervention at any of the intercepts is likely to be helpful to some people. The horizontal graphic in

Figure 2.2 The SIM: The Revolving Door Perspective.

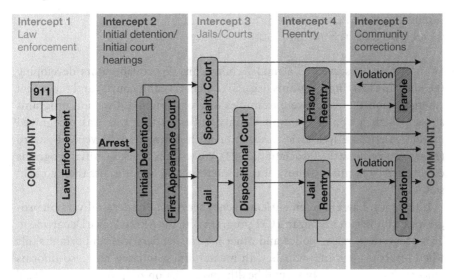

Figure 2.3 The National GAINS Center's Linear Version of the SIM.

Figure 2.3 illustrates that movement through the system is linear and predictable.

ADOPTION BY THE FIELD

In this section, we move from early development to some later indicators about the ways in which the SIM has influenced policy and practice. Although the SIM was developed for use in public mental health systems that typically prioritize SMI, it is no longer limited to people with SMI as a target population. It can be used to illuminate the flow of other target populations through the criminal justice system, including those with less severe mental illness, those with only substance use disorders, women with a history of trauma, and other particular groups. It has become an organizing and planning tool with a wide possible application.

Clearly the SIM was employed by the GAINS Center from very early in its development, with Steadman an active collaborator in the model's development. Four other examples, described in this section, will illustrate how the SIM has been influential during the past decade. We will describe Summit County Ohio in detail, as an example of a county in which there is important work being done at each of the five SIM intercepts. Two examples involve state-level centers of excellence in Ohio and Pennsylvania, which on a regional level do some of the work done by GAINS nationally (e.g., consultation, technical assistance, and continuing education in the areas of diversion and community-based alternatives to standard prosecution for people with behavioral health disorders). The last example involves the U.S. Department of Veterans Affairs and its Veterans Justice Outreach policy.

Illustrating the Impact at the Local Level: The SIM in Summit County

Summit County served as a model community for collaborators developing the SIM. The existing programs (e.g., CIT, mental health courts) and those that emerged soon thereafter were examples of promising jail diversion programs at each intercept point. Summit County's work in this area was recognized by the American Psychiatric Association with a Bronze Achievement Award (American Psychiatric Association, 2003). We will describe the initial programs established by Summit County at each intercept and then discuss their current status.

Intercept 1: Law enforcement/emergency services: Pre-arrest diversion programs. Summit County began a CIT program with the Akron Police Department. This program provides police and other first responders with important skills when responding to individuals with mental illness in crisis and also informs officers about community mental health and addiction resources. The first CIT training in Summit County occurred in 2000.

Summit County currently has a successful countywide CIT program that includes twenty-seven law enforcement agencies, including the county sheriff's office and the University of Akron Police Department. Corrections/court personnel, dispatchers, hospital police and security, mental health crisis workers, and park rangers have also participated in CIT training. One municipal court judge also went through a weeklong CIT training, subsequently became an instructor in the class, and also started a mental health court program in her jurisdiction! Summit County expanded CIT efforts with an innovative CIT outreach program involving follow-up with individuals who had a CIT encounter that did not result in emergency transport to treatment. The outreach team pairs a senior social worker with a CIT officer for home and community visits in the attempt to engage nonparticipating individuals in treatment. Using a "good-cop/bad-cop" approach (the officer may play either role), the pair is often successful in convincing reluctant individuals to engage in treatment. The Summit County CIT program has served as a model for other communities throughout Ohio and the nation.

Because of concerns expressed by former Sheriff Drew Alexander, a protocol was developed to identify individuals who may need psychiatric treatment beyond the capacity of the jail to deliver *before* such individuals are actually incarcerated. A similar protocol was developed to transfer current jail inmates needing more intensive treatment to a state psychiatric hospital, bypassing the usual prescreening process for state hospital admissions.

Intercept 2: Initial hearings/initial detention: Post-arrest diversion programs. As part of the Summit Link program created in Summit County, a mental health worker from Community Support Services, Inc., the county's primary agency for services for people with serious and persistent mental illness, visits the county jail every weekday morning to identify individuals with mental illness who had been booked the previous day. He or she has access to both the jail roster and the list of active and inactive clients of the mental health agency. Prior to an arraignment hearing, the linkage worker gathers information, performs psychosocial assessments when indicated, and makes suggestions to the municipal court judge regarding treatment options and alternatives. Such suggestions might include an order for a competency to stand trial assessment, release on conditions of bail or bond, dismissal of charges and recommend treatment, or order treatment as a condition of probation if the defendant was adjudicated guilty.

The Summit Link program has expanded to include a second large mental health agency serving a broader patient population. It also now includes linkage with addiction services. Further, the county ADM Board now tracks individuals with mental illness who are arraigned in the Akron Municipal Court so that mental health and probation personnel can intervene early in the process.

Intercept 3: Jails, courts, and forensic evaluation and hospitalization. Initially, staff from Community Support Services provided psychiatric and other mental health services, including psychotropic medications, to county jail inmates. While this was an expensive service, it had the advantage of enhancing continuity of care during and after incarceration. Also, as discussed previously, stakeholders created the Akron Municipal Mental Health Court in January 2001. The Akron mental health court intervenes post-conviction and offers treatment in lieu of incarceration (Munetz & Teller, 2004).

At present, Summit County has misdemeanor mental health courts in three jurisdictions, effectively serving the entire county. While mental services are still provided to county jail inmates, changes at the provider level have created some obstacles to continuity of care. Despite these challenges, the amount of psychiatric care provided at the county jail has been increased to seventeen service hours per week, with better integration of medical and psychiatric services so inmates are more likely to accept and take prescribed medication. Summit County stakeholders have also started a peer support in-reach program at the Summit County Jail. Most recently, the ADM Board received funding to begin offering long-acting injectable antipsychotic and anticraving medications for inmates with psychotic and addictive disorders, respectively, to increase the likelihood they will maintain stability prior to subsequent outpatient care.

Intercept 4: Reentry from local jails, state prisons, and state hospitals. In collaboration with the respective state agencies for corrections, criminal justice, mental health, and drug and alcohol, NAMI Ohio created a program, the Bridging the Gap Reentry Project, to facilitate transition from state correctional facilities to the community.

At present, Summit County participates in the Ohio Department of Mental Health and Addiction Services state linkage program. As part of this program, the ADM Board is notified of pending releases from the prison system and efforts are made to link with community-based services to reestablish individuals' benefits (e.g., Medicaid, SSI) as soon as possible following release. To bridge the time between release and subsequent involvement in community-based services, inmates are provided with long-acting injectable medications for psychosis and/or opiate addiction as needed. A full-time behavioral health linkage coordinator assists with this effort. Forensic peer support workers also continue to work with the individuals as they move from an in-reach model to an outreach model to further strengthen continuity of care.

Intercept 5: Community corrections and community support services. Summit County's Mental Health/Criminal Justice Forum developed a cross-systems training curriculum for mental health, addictions, and criminal justice personnel. This curriculum emphasizes enhancing the partnership between the mental health and addiction systems and probation/parole. Soon after the county CIT program was developed, probation officers also participated in CIT classes, strengthening the relationship between law enforcement, mental health, and probation.

The Summit County collaboration to develop various jail diversion programs provided valuable lessons. The process of forming community collaborations dealing with jail diversion was not a linear one. Many efforts occurred simultaneously, some coordinated and some not. Stakeholders began to align similar activities through the initial technical assistance provided by the GAINS Center. Eventually this process and the emergent programs in Summit County led to the development of the current iteration of the SIM. However, it was not until Summit County received additional technical assistance from Policy Research Associates that the community collaborative group adopted the SIM as an operating framework for jail diversion efforts. In 2009, Summit County (supported by the County Executive's Office and the ADM Board) completed a Sequential Intercept Mapping exercise with Griffin and staff from Policy Research Associates. The mapping exercise convened a large group of administrators and personnel from Summit County's mental health services board, mental health and addictions treatment provider agencies, the county sheriff's office, and other law enforcement, jail, courts, and probation/parole services. Other key stakeholders included consumer advocates, county public safety officials, and local researchers. The mapping exercise led to ongoing work to further improve the local system of care at the interface of the behavioral health and criminal justice systems.

Cross-systems training continues in Summit County. Such training, involving mental health, addictions, and criminal justice personnel, includes promoting a better understanding of criminogenic risk and needs. A Forensic Assertive Community Treatment team has been established to serve individuals with psychotic disorders who were frequently incarcerated. An adaptation of the Thinking for a Change curriculum is provided to patients on this team as part of a research project attempting to modify the evidence-based intervention for an SMI population.

Illustrating Impact at the State Level: The Ohio Criminal Justice Coordinating Center of Excellence

Today, the CJ CCoE uses the SIM with Ohio communities to guide the development of jail diversion programs (see also Chapter 10). The focus of the CJ CCoE is the promotion of systems-level partnerships and collaboration among stakeholders in criminal justice, mental health, and advocacy, with the awareness that such collaboration is necessary to form sustainable, coordinated efforts to divert individuals with SMI from the criminal justice system. At the local level, the CJ CCoE provides technical assistance to communities to identify and work with local resources. One strategy is to "go where the energy is"—communities are encouraged to take advantage of community leaders or emerging champions of a certain program to foster enthusiasm and build support for the program. The CJ CCoE's technical assistance is designed to support such local grassroots efforts in a coordinated and informed way.

Working with local communities, the CJ CCoE provides technical assistance in a number of areas. These include assistance in identifying and convening key stakeholders to begin a successful collaboration; planning and implementing jail diversion programs along the SIM (e.g., CIT with local law enforcement departments); informing communities about available training and cross-training programs for law enforcement, court, jail, and mental health professionals; and providing individualized community consultation and technical assistance.

Most recently, the CJ CCoE has expanded its technical assistance to Ohio communities by offering Sequential Intercept Mapping (see also Chapter 13). Derived from the cross-systems mapping project of Policy Research Associates, this activity brings together local stakeholders from mental health, criminal justice, and consumer advocacy. With a team of trained facilitators, the CJ CCoE uses the SIM with stakeholders to discuss available resources and challenges facing each system at each intercept. The mapping process highlights areas where change may be needed to implement jail diversion or improve existing efforts. Priority areas are identified and an initial action plan is developed. A detailed final report is created, providing community stakeholders with the foundation for sustained collaboration on jail diversion.

In addition to the technical assistance provided at the local level, the CJ CCoE engages in statewide efforts to address the needs of justice-involved individuals with mental illness. One key state partner has been the Supreme Court of Ohio. Former Justice Evelyn Lundberg Stratton developed the Advisory Committee for Mental Illness and the Courts, which consisted of representatives from state agencies and departments, mental health practitioners and administrators, court personnel, researchers, and consumers who met regularly to address important issues. This advisory committee encouraged the development of local task forces and/or advisory committees to bring stakeholders together to collaborate on the needs of justice-involved individuals with mental illness (Stratton, Blough, & Hawk, 2004). Further, the Supreme Court of Ohio's Specialty Docket section supported the use of the SIM in its promotion of mental health courts and other specialty dockets. After Stratton left the Supreme Court of Ohio, the Ohio Attorney General's Office convened a Task Force on Criminal Justice and Mental Illness. The task force builds upon the work that Stratton's group started, focusing on issues such as diversion and reentry, housing, juvenile justice, law enforcement, mental health and the courts, psychiatry and treatment, and research and best practices.

The Ohio chapter of the National Alliance on Mental Illness (NAMI) is another statewide partner that has been integral to the development and sustained success of the CJ CCoE. NAMI Ohio and the CJ CCoE work collaboratively with local community stakeholders to discuss the needs of each community and identify opportunities for jail diversion. This partnership ensures that the voices and concerns of consumers, family members, and advocates are included in local planning efforts for jail diversion. The CJ CCoE and NAMI Ohio also cosponsor statewide technical assistance efforts for CIT, including hosting an annual advanced CIT conference.

The success of the CJ CCoE has included building and sustaining partnerships with local and state mental health, criminal justice, and consumer advocacy stakeholders. The use of the SIM as a conceptual framework has proven quite effective, making Ohio a national leader in the promotion of jail diversion efforts.

The Pennsylvania Mental Health and Justice Center of Excellence

The use of the SIM in Pennsylvania, which began with the Southeast Region Forensic Task Force, served as a framework for the work solicited in a request for proposals issued in 2009 by the Pennsylvania Commission on Crime and Delinquency (with funding also contributed by the Pennsylvania Department of Public Welfare/Office of Mental Health and Substance Abuse Services). The request for proposals envisioned a state-level center, comparable to a "mini-GAINS Center," that would prioritize the diversion of individuals with serious mental illness (possibly with co-occurring substance use disorders) from standard prosecution. When the proposal submitted jointly by Drexel University and the University of Pittsburgh Medical Center was approved, the new Pennsylvania Mental Health and Justice Center of Excellence began operation in 2010 and has provided services continuously since that time.

A detailed account of this group's priorities and operation is available (see Chapter 10). Our purpose here is to emphasize the SIM's influence on its development, operation, and oversight. As noted earlier in this chapter, the SIM in Pennsylvania has become part of the standard conceptualization of the criminal justice process relevant to diversion; it is accepted at local, regional, and state levels. The request for proposals clearly indicated that the work of the new CoE should be guided by the SIM. Cross-systems mappings (see Chapter 13) conducted in Pennsylvania use the SIM as an organizing tool. The CoE's work with its immediate oversight committee and the larger Mental Health and Justice Advisory Committee uses the SIM for conceptualization, discussion, and clarification. Technical assistance and specialized projects routinely (and early in the process) seek focus from identifying the intercepts being prioritized. It is, quite simply, a fundamental tool on which the CoE relies heavily in providing consultation, technical assistance, system mappings, and continuing education.

Illustrating the Impact at the Federal Level: Veterans Justice Program

The U.S. Department of Veterans Affairs incorporates the SIM in its policies outlining outreach, diversion, and services provided by the Veterans Health Administration facilities to veterans involved in the criminal justice system (see http://www.va.gov/vhapublications/ViewPublication.asp?pub_ID=2019). The goal of the Veterans Justice Outreach initiative is to "avoid unnecessary criminalization of mental illness and extended incarceration among veterans" (Department of Veterans Affairs, 2009, p. 57).

Staff at the U.S. Department of Veterans Affairs again used the SIM in a review of case examples in the national dissemination of interventions for justice-involved veterans (Blue-Howells, et al, 2013). The authors noted:

> The utility of the SIM lies in its reduction of the complex and locally variable criminal justice process to five simple, universal components: it has provided a common point of reference for local planning efforts, and a common system for categorizing interventions according to target population.
> —BLUE-HOWELLS, *Clark, van den Berk-Clark, & McGuire, 2013, p. 50*

IMPORTANT CHALLENGES FOR THE FUTURE

As a descriptive schematic of the criminal justice system, the SIM is often used by local agencies, communities, and systems to share information, identify gaps and opportunities, and promote planning. Further development to facilitate the measurement of functioning at each intercept would require research and development going well beyond what has been accomplished to date with the SIM. This should be seriously considered, however. One of the strengths of the SIM is its application to questions of accountability and progress in planning diversion and community-based treatment alternatives. If quantifying the appraisal of these questions using the SIM would help to answer them better, this would be a welcome development.

Another important implication to be drawn from the development of the SIM is the importance of accessible, effective treatment services for individuals with mental disorders who might become involved with the criminal justice system. This is not in itself a preventive panacea, as there appear to be a number of differences between individuals with mental disorders who become justice involved and those who do not (see Chapter 7). But criminogenic risk factors often overlap with clinical needs, so the provision of services that directly address criminogenic factors along with those that help with family, work, housing, co-occurring substance use disorders, and social support, for example, will likely constitute an important strategic application of behavioral health and rehabilitative services provided for individuals under SIM-based planning for community services in the future.

NOTE

1. Roberta Altenor, MSN, Pennsylvania Department of Public Welfare's Office of Mental Health and Forensic Services; Edwin Camiel, MD, Norristown State Hospital; Lance Couturier, PhD, Pennsylvania Department of Corrections; Jeffrey Hunsicker, CCJs, Pennsylvania Protection & Advocacy; Lisa Keller, JD, Philadelphia Department of Behavioral Health; Marcella McGuire, PhD, Philadelphia Department of Behavioral Health; Rocio Nell, MD, Montgomery County Emergency Services; Nancy Wieman, Montgomery County Mental Health Services).

REFERENCES

Abram, K. M., & Teplin, L. A. (1991). Co-occurring disorders among mentally ill jail detainees: Implications for public policy. *American Psychologist, 46*, 1036–1045.

Abram, K. M., Teplin, L. A., & McClelland, G. M. (2003). Comorbidity of severe psychiatric disorders and substance use disorders among women in jail. *American Journal of Psychiatry, 160*, 1007–1010.

American Psychiatric Association (2003). Bronze Award to Summit County (Ohio) Alcohol, Drug Addiction and Mental Health Services Board: A systematic approach to criminalization of persons with mental illness. *Psychiatric Services, 54*, 1537–1538.

Blue-Howells, J. H, Clark, S. C., van den Berk-Clark, C., & McGuire, J. F. (2013). The U.S. Department of Veterans Affairs Veterans Justice Programs and the Sequential Intercept Model: Case examples in national dissemination of intervention for justice-involved veterans. *Psychological Services, 10*, 48–53.

Center for Substance Abuse Treatment (1995). *Planning for alcohol and other drug abuse treatment for adults in the criminal justice system.* Rockville MD: Substance Abuse and Mental Health Services Administration.

CMHS National GAINS Center (2009). *Developing a comprehensive plan for mental health and criminal justice collaboration: The Sequential Intercept Model.* Delmar, NY: Author.

Council of State Governments (2002). *Criminal Justice/Mental Health Consensus Project report.* Delmar, NY: National GAINS Center.

Council of State Governments (2006). *Mental health court learning sites.* Washington, D.C.: Bureau of Justice Assistance, Office of Justice Programs, U.S. Department of Justice.

Department of Veterans Affairs (April 30, 2009). Under Secretary for Health's Information Letter: Information and recommendations for services provided by VHA facilities to veterans in the criminal justice system. Washington, D.C.: Veterans Health Administration.

Ditton, P. M. (1999). *Mental health and treatment of inmates and probationers.* Washington, D.C.: Bureau of Justice Statistics, Department of Justice.

Drake, R. E., Essock, S. M., Shaner, A., Carey, K. B., Minkoff, K., Kola, L., Lynde, D., Osher, F. C., Clark, R. E., & Rickards, L. (2001). Implementing dual diagnosis services for clients with severe mental illness. *Psychiatric Services, 52*, 469–476.

Lamb, H. R., & Weinberger, L. E. (1998). Persons with severe mental illness in jails and prisons: A review. *Psychiatric Services, 49*, 483–492.

Landsberg, G., & Shannon, H. (2002). A roadmap of interventions for adults with mental illness in—or at risk of involvement with—the criminal justice system. *Community Mental Health Report, 2*, 33–34, 46–47.

Munetz, M. R., Grande, T. P., & Chambers, M. R. (2001). The incarceration of individuals with severe mental disorders. *Community Mental Health Journal, 37*, 361–372.

Munetz, M. R., & Griffin, P. A. (2006). Use of the Sequential Intercept Model as an approach to decriminalization of people with serious mental illness. *Psychiatric Services, 57*, 544–549.

Munetz, M., & Teller, J. L. S. (2004). The challenges of cross-disciplinary collaborations: Bridging the mental health and criminal justice systems. *Capital University Law Review, 32*, 935–950.

National GAINS Center (2005). *Developing a comprehensive state plan for mental health and criminal justice collaboration*. Delmar, NY: Author.

Promising Practices Subcommittee Report (2002). In *Pennsylvania's Southeast Region Inter-Agency Forensic Task Final Report*. Harrisburg, PA: Office of Mental Health and Substance Abuse.

Steadman, H. J. (1992). Boundary spanners: A key component for the effective interactions of the justice and mental health systems. *Law & Human Behavior, 16*, 75–87.

Steadman, H. J. (2011). Prison overcrowding in the context of the ACA. *Psychiatric Services, 62*, 1117.

Stratton, E. L., Blough, S., & Hawk, K. (2004). Solutions for the mentally ill in the criminal justice system. *American Jails, 16*, January/February, 14–17.

3

Law Enforcement and
Emergency Services

MELISSA REULAND AND KENTO YASUHARA ∎

For many citizens, police officers represent the "face of government." Police officers visibly patrol our communities and respond to our calls for assistance. They are charged with maintaining order and keeping community members safe from harm. They also act as the "gatekeeper" to the rest of the criminal justice system when they make the determination that a person must be deprived of his or her freedom and taken into custody. In this way, they clearly represent the "first intercept" at which all people—not just those with mental illness who are in crisis—encounter the criminal justice system.

In the decades following the widespread release of people with mental illnesses from institutions as part of deinstitutionalization, these roles have positioned police officers as the primary first responders to scenes involving someone experiencing a mental health crisis. These situations represent approximately 6% to 8% of the total volume of calls for service (Engel & Silver, 2006; Novak & Engel, 2005) and range in severity from relatively mild encounters, involving minor nuisance crimes, to more serious ones in which people with mental illness pose a danger to themselves or others.

Several characteristics of these encounters make them particularly challenging for law enforcement. For example, lack of experience deescalating crisis behavior and a paucity of community-based mental health resources can leave officers with few tools to effectively address mental health crises. Officers are often left either to put a short-term solution in place or to respond repeatedly to a small number of people for whom readily accessible mental health resources are insufficient.

Research has demonstrated that people with mental illness are no more likely than members of the general public to become violent unless they also experience co-occurring substance abuse (Steadman et al., 1998). However, when they do become violent, law enforcement officers are often called in to make the situation safe. These rare cases—often involving someone with a serious and persistent mental illness who may not be taking medication or who may have a co-occurring substance use disorder—have the potential for significant injury or even death. When tragedies do occur, they compel communities to change fundamental practices in a range of areas.

Several consequences have resulted from these circumstances. People with mental illness who neither meet the criteria for involuntary evaluation for civil commitment nor have committed a serious crime are either brought to jail because of a complaining victim or are left in the community with only a short-term solution in place. In addition, officers can spend substantial time transporting people with mental illnesses to emergency departments only to find them released back into the community before the officers have returned to patrol. This is an extremely poor use of limited law enforcement resources, is demeaning and ineffective for consumers, and has been frustrating for police officers for many years.

In response to these complex, potentially volatile encounters, law enforcement agencies across the United States—and the world—have created specialized policing responses (SPRs) to address issues related to safety and poor mental health service linkage. These programs are characterized by strong partnerships among law enforcement agencies, behavioral health service providers, family members, and consumers. They prioritize referral and transport to behavioral health resources over incarceration whenever appropriate. In this way, SPR programs divert people to therapeutic environments who might otherwise have been arrested and brought into the criminal justice system.

This chapter reviews the history of these programs and the circumstances that led to their creation. It details ten essential elements of these programs that the Council of State Governments (CSG) Justice Center and the Police Executive Research Forum (PERF) developed to guide programming. The chapter concludes with program examples from around the world that establish the critical need for SPRs to be tailored to specific communities to ensure success.

HISTORY OF SPR PROGRAM DEVELOPMENT

For several decades, law enforcement agencies have worked to address the problem of large numbers of people with mental illness coming into contact with police. The issue of police management of the mentally ill is complex, and solutions are constrained by tight and shrinking budgets for mental health services. However, several pioneering communities have developed innovative and promising approaches for addressing this problem by building collaborations between local law enforcement and mental health stakeholders.

Efforts to improve the police response began in the early 1980s when the Memphis, Tennessee, Police Department confronted a terrible tragedy—a person with mental illness had been killed by police. Through partnership with the National Alliance on Mental Illness, the police department developed an SPR designed to improve safety during police encounters with people with mental illness through enhanced, immediate crisis deescalation. For this agency and the many others who have adapted their model, one important part of this approach is the immediacy of the deescalation response—an immediacy that law enforcement can provide.

At the same time, law enforcement and mental health communities in Los Angeles, San Diego City, and San Diego County were confronting another dimension of this problem. These communities were concerned that people who were frequently in crisis and had repeated police contacts were not engaged in behavioral health treatments and services. Because police are limited by time and resource access and may have limited knowledge about behavioral health crisis, they often must conclude encounters with only a short-term resolution in place. For these agencies, the critical part of their approach is the linkage to behavioral health services—a linkage provided by behavioral health practitioners.

Two models—the crisis intervention team and the co-responder model—have gained popularity around the country and beyond as other communities struggled to address similar challenges. CSG and PERF researched these models and identified elements common to both models that communities achieve in different ways, depending on the problem they are trying to fix.

CURRENT PRACTICES

PERF and CSG focus broadly on programs that are police-based. "Police-based" programs are those that require substantial changes to law enforcement agency's policies and practices. CSG and PERF use the umbrella term of SPRs to refer to all three primary program variations:

- **Crisis intervention teams (CITs)**—A cadre of self-selected officers is deployed to calls involving probable mental health issues. These officers receive extensive training so they can identify signs and symptoms of mental illness, deescalate the situation, and bring the person in crisis to an efficient, round-the-clock treatment center if needed.
- **Co-responder teams**—A small group of officers pairs with a mental health professional to respond to the scene of a crisis involving mental illness. These teams handle calls that typically take longer to resolve or involve transportation to crisis centers. These teams also provide follow-up to address ongoing service needs.
- **Follow-up teams**—Specially trained officers work closely with mental health partners to identify people who repeatedly come to the attention of police to develop customized solutions.

TEN ESSENTIAL ELEMENTS OF SPR

The ten essential elements of these three approaches were derived from recommendations made by a broad range of practitioners and other subject-matter experts to provide a common framework for program design and implementation to promote positive outcomes (Schwarzfeld, Reuland, & Plotkin, 2008). The elements are sensitive to the distinctive needs and resources of each jurisdiction. As such, they reflect a process-oriented approach rather than a model replication approach. Table 3.1 lists the ten elements and how they are integrated into the crisis intervention team and co-responder program models.

The first element outlines key steps for developing effective collaborative structures that undergird all SPR approaches. This element discusses two types of groups, a planning group and a coordination group, each of which is multidisciplinary and whose members have operational decision-making authority. These two groups have distinct functions: The first group concentrates on planning the approach and the second group coordinates the work of the SPR that results from planning. Depending on the community's size, these two functions may be carried out by a single group.

The program design element (element two) describes a process that the planning committee goes through to determine the nature of the problem and its causes, and to use that information to design program approaches. This element is discussed in more detail below in the section "Tailoring SPRs."

The third element concentrates on features of the specialized training that is fundamental to these approaches. The element addresses the topics required in the specialized training. It also describes who should teach which modules and the variety of most effective teaching techniques that communities should use to convey the information so that the training not only informs its participants but transforms them as well. It is important both to have good information and to act on it.

The fourth element provides personnel field practice guidelines. It details procedures for call-takers and dispatchers so they can gather relevant information and relay that information appropriately to trained staff. The information obtained by call-takers is then used to prepare officers to respond effectively and safely. For many SPR agencies, call-takers are trained to ask about the person's history with mental illness, what strategies to employ or avoid when approaching the person in crisis, and the presence of weapons.

The fifth element is the core of the actual on-scene response. Officers must stabilize the scene using safety-focused deescalation techniques, observe for signs of mental illness, and use what they know about community behavioral health resources to determine the appropriate disposition. Deescalation techniques used by specially trained officers in SPR programs are fundamentally different from the techniques taught to officers for use in responding to citizens in general. Typically, officers are trained to gain control over situations using their authority as police officers. This authority is demonstrated by the officer's uniform, tone of voice, and implied threat of force. In situations involving a person with mental illness who is in crisis, however, these techniques can not only fail to control but can even make matters worse (Watson, Ottati, Morabito, Draine, Kerr, & Angell, 2010). SPR deescalation techniques depend instead on strategies to calm the crisis and communicate the desire to help. Depending on the program design, this element may be accomplished with or without on-scene mental health practitioners.

Element	Crisis Intervention Teams	Co-Responder
1. Collaborative Planning and Implementation	Organizations and individuals affected by police encounters with people with mental illnesses work together in one or more multidisciplinary groups; the purpose of these groups is to determine the response program's characteristics and guide implementation efforts.	Same
2. Program Design	The planning committee designs a specialized police-based program to address the causes of the problems that are impeding improved responses to people with mental illnesses and makes the most of available resources.	Same
3. Specialized Training	All law enforcement personnel who respond to incidents in which an individual's mental illness appears to be a factor receive training to prepare for these encounters; those in specialized assignments receive more comprehensive training. Dispatchers, call-takers, and other individuals in a support role receive training tailored to their needs.	All officers receive some training on crisis deescalation and a small group receives intense training on these skills.
4. Call-Taker and Dispatcher Protocols	Call-takers and dispatchers identify critical information to direct calls to the appropriate responders, inform the law enforcement response, and record this information for analysis and as a reference for future calls for service.	Same
5. Stabilization, Observation, and Disposition	Specialized police responders deescalate and observe the nature of incidents in which mental illness may be a factor using tactics focused on safety. Drawing on their understanding and knowledge of relevant laws and available resources, officers then determine the appropriate disposition.	Trained officers working in teams with mental health professionals make this assessment and select the appropriate disposition together.

(*continued*)

Table 3.1 (CONTINUED)

Element	Crisis Intervention Teams	Co-Responder
6. Transportation and Custodial Transfer	Police responders transport and transfer custody of the person with a mental illness in a safe and sensitive manner that supports the individual's efficient access to mental health services and the officers' timely return to duty.	Mental health professionals can assist in transporting those who are not a danger.
7. Information Exchange and Confidentiality	Law enforcement and mental health personnel have a well-designed procedure governing the release and exchange of information to facilitate necessary and appropriate communication while protecting the confidentiality of community members.	Same
8. Treatment, Supports, and Services	Specialized police-based response programs connect individuals with mental illnesses to comprehensive and effective community-based treatment supports and services.	Same
9. Organizational Support	The law enforcement agency's policies, practices, and culture support the specialized response program and the personnel who further its goals.	Same
10. Program Evaluation and Sustainability	Data are collected and analyzed to help demonstrate the program's impact and to inform modifications to the program. Support for the program is continuously cultivated in the community and police department.	Same

The transportation and custodial transfer element describes how SPR officers can ensure safety while minimizing the stress and indignity experienced by people with mental illness when police use restraints while transporting someone to a hospital. Emergency medical services may be dispatched in addition to police or alone to situations involving someone with a mental illness. When someone does not appear to present an immediate threat, ambulances are used to transport people in crisis to emergency departments a significant portion of the time. When the person is not willing to go to the hospital or presents a danger, police are required to conduct the transport. Officers can spend several hours waiting in hospital emergency departments with people who need an assessment or an inpatient admission. Best practices identified in this element include streamlining medical clearance practices and transferring custody of the person in crisis to the hospital staff so that patrol officers can resume their duties.

The seventh element addresses the need for developing procedures to guide the release and exchange of information while protecting the consumer's privacy and the confidentiality of medical records. For many communities, Health Insurance Portability and Accountability Act (HIPAA) laws have created needless complexity during program development (see Chapter 14). This law does not preclude law enforcement agencies from gathering and sharing information about people they encounter with mental health professionals. As such, law enforcement agencies are not "covered entities" under HIPAA. Behavioral health professionals and hospital employees, however, are covered by HIPAA laws; this prohibits them from releasing information to police. However, law enforcement agencies often insist they do not need private information about a person's health history to determine the most effective solution to a situation; their close partnership and their communication with mental health professionals make the critical difference in their response.

The eighth element details comprehensive and effective community-based treatment supports and services required for a law enforcement–based response program to succeed. If the community does not make its behavioral health resources more efficient, and often more numerous, training law enforcement officers in deescalation will have only limited success in addressing the critical issues communities face.

The ninth element describes how behavioral health and police organizations can support these initiatives through changes in officer evaluation procedures and enhanced opportunities for commendations. For example, in many police departments, officers are evaluated based on the number of arrests they make. For officers to be successful in a program designed to reduce arrests, police leaders may need to change those performance metrics.

The last element suggests how data should be collected and analyzed to demonstrate program impacts and enhance program sustainability. Although this is the last of the elements, it could just as easily have been the first. Communities must engage in data collection at the very beginning, ideally even before program implementation, so they are prepared to justify the program's existence by demonstrating its success.

SPR PROGRAM OUTCOMES

Most of the available literature on outcomes of SPR programs comes from data (collected in individual communities) that compare problems before and after program implementation. The most common outcome measures are arrests of people with mental illnesses, officer injuries, Special Weapons and Tactics (SWAT) deployment, and connections to mental health resources.

The limited empirical evidence on CIT and subsequent arrest does not support the conclusion that CIT training reduces the likelihood that officers will arrest an individual as part of an interaction. A study that compared the outcomes of calls handled by CIT-trained officers to those handled by non-CIT officers in Akron, Ohio, showed no difference between the two groups in numbers of arrests (Teller et al., 2006). A second study of CIT encounter outcomes in Chicago showed no significant difference in arrest rates between CIT-trained officers and officers with no CIT training (Watson et al., 2010). Of course, this is a very limited basis for judging whether CIT has an impact on subsequent arrest frequency, so clearly more empirical research is needed before any conclusion can be drawn with confidence. Indeed, there is some indirect evidence that CIT training may affect arrest rates. In a study examining two SPR programs (a CIT and co-response program) in police departments in Memphis and Birmingham, Alabama, arrest rates were 2% and 13%, respectively (Steadman, Deane, Borum, & Morrissey, 2000). These rates are lower than those observed in an earlier study that noted a 16% arrest rate in a different community without an SPR (Teplin, 1984). An analysis of the 1,439 CIT calls in Houston revealed that only seventeen people with mental illnesses had been arrested (Reuland, 2004). By contrast, a study that compared the outcomes of calls handled by CIT-trained officers to those handled by non-CIT officers in Akron, Ohio, showed no difference between the two groups in numbers of arrests (Teller et al., 2006). A study of CIT encounter outcomes in Chicago showed no significant difference in arrest rates between CIT-trained officers and officers with no training (Watson et al., 2010). So we need further research to determine whether the limited empirical research to date, reflecting no impact of CIT on subsequent arrest, is accurate— or whether any "arrest reduction" effect has not yet been detected.

There is some evidence that departments employing SPRs to people with mental illnesses also experience decreased injuries to officers. In San Jose, California, the CIT program reported a 32% decrease in officer injuries over a one-year period following program implementation (Reuland, 2004). In Memphis, the police department reported that the rate of injuries to officers responding to "mental disturbance calls" decreased from one in every 28,571 events in the three years prior to implementing a CIT program to one in every 142,857 events in the three-year period following its implementation. Other types of disturbance calls, including domestic violence calls, did not show a similar trend during this period (Dupont & Cochran, 2000). While it is useful to know that a jurisdiction experiences a drop in officer injuries following the implementation of CIT, it is also important to note that other influences could also account for such a decrease. From a research perspective, what is needed has apparently not yet been done: several studies, across multiple jurisdictions, comparing any change in officer injuries following the implementation of CIT with that change in a similar jurisdiction that has not implemented CIT. This is obviously an important area for applied research, given the high priority placed on the safety of both police officers and others involved in police–citizen encounters.

SPRs have the potential to reduce high-cost SWAT callouts, but this issue has received little research attention. The single study on this question did not show a relationship between CIT training and the use of SWAT callouts (Compton, Demir, Oliva, & Boyce, 2009). Other evidence suggests a possible relationship, however. The number of Tactical Apprehension Containment Team (TACT, similar to SWAT) calls in the Memphis Police Department decreased by nearly 50% after the implementation of its CIT program (Dupont & Cochran, 2000). Since the implementation of CIT in the Albuquerque Police Department, the use of SWAT teams involving a mental health crisis intervention has decreased by 58% (Bower & Petit, 2001). Not all departments experience an association between CIT and reduced use of tactical teams, however. Data comparing SWAT callouts in a large city did not show any correlation between the use of SWAT and the number of CIT-trained officers (Compton, Demir, Oliva, & Boyce, 2009). This is another question for which more evidence is needed—particularly from empirical research—in order to draw a well-informed conclusion.

Many promising research findings support the value of diversion (including CIT training) in linking individuals in crisis to behavioral health services. In one study of outcomes of pre- and post-arrest diversion programs (although not CIT), diverted individuals with mental illnesses incurred lower criminal justice costs and experienced greater access to behavioral health treatment than those who were not diverted (Steadman & Naples, 2005). People diverted from jail had significantly greater access to crisis services (emergency room and hospitalization) and noncrisis services (medication and counseling) than people who were not diverted from jail (Steadman & Naples, 2005). CIT-trained officers in Akron transported people with mental illnesses to psychiatric emergency services significantly more often than their counterparts without CIT training (Teller et al., 2006). In Memphis's CIT program, the referral rate from law enforcement to the emergency service increased by 42% in its first four years (Dupont & Cochran, 2000). CIT in two other sites has been associated with an increase in mental health services and a decrease in mental health symptoms (Cowell, Broner, & Dupont, 2004; Lattimore, Broner, Sherman, Frisman, & Sharer, 2003). Finally, data from ongoing work on the CIT program in Chicago revealed that CIT-trained officers transported significantly more people to mental health services than did their counterparts without CIT training (Watson et al., 2009).

TAILORING SPRS

The data on outcomes from SPR programs, although limited in scope, provide a good foundation for many communities to explore implementing these programs. The impetus for programs designed to improve the response to people with mental illness is typically a problem that community stakeholders can agree must—and likely can—be changed. These stakeholders are not, however, free to construct any response they wish; they are often limited by several important jurisdictional characteristics that represent a relatively rigid framework within which communities must operate to achieve their goals. Consequently, effective program design should consider both the problem and these characteristics.

This section describes a detailed program design process, the second of the ten essential elements. This process was derived from research that CSG Justice Center staff conducted in four communities in the United States (for more information on these communities and this project, see *Improving Responses to People with Mental Illnesses: Tailoring Law Enforcement Initiatives to Individual Jurisdictions*, available at http://consensusproject.org/issue_areas/law-enforcement). This research determined first and foremost that SPR program design depends on effective collaboration. A collaborative planning committee must identify community problems and problem causes, recognize the full range of community characteristics, and select program activities tailored to address the causes of the identified problems. The program design process has seven steps:

Step 1: Understand the impetus for change.
Step 2: Articulate program goals.
Step 3: Identify data collection procedures necessary to evaluate the program.
Step 4: Detail jurisdictional characteristics and their influence on program responses.
Step 5: Establish response protocols.
Step 6: Determine training requirements.
Step 7: Prepare for other evaluation tasks.

Tailoring to Problems

This research identified four common problems communities experience and the causes of those problems: lack of safety, strains on law enforcement resources, frequent arrests of people with mental illnesses, and repeated contacts with emergency services. "Problems" are defined as issues communities agree can be changed through program activities. The following discusses possible causes and characteristics of such problems and strategies used by SPR programs to address them.

Tailoring to safety concerns. About half of the communities surveyed began programs after someone—either a person with mental illness or a police officer—was killed during an encounter. In these cases, program planners often determined that the cause of this tragedy was a lack of information about mental illness and inadequate tools to deescalate crises. Program activities are aimed primarily at quick, on-scene deescalation of crisis behavior. They typically include (a) training call-takers and dispatchers to collect more information about the potential for violence and (b) providing officers with tools to identify signs and symptoms of mental illnesses so they can better (c) deescalate crises. Mental health professionals can also provide secondary response. Program responses resulting from concerns about safety are closely modeled after the elements of the original CIT pioneered by Memphis.

Tailoring to strains on law enforcement resources. Encounters between police and people with mental illnesses can be time-consuming and pose a drain on police resources because law enforcement officers may spend long periods of time waiting at hospital emergency rooms for a bed to become available. The cause of this problem is often inefficient access to a limited pool of mental health resources. Program responses include making the transfer of custody from the officer to the emergency room physicians more efficient. In addition, some law enforcement officers pair up with mental health practitioners to co-respond to incidents. In these cases, agencies must train all officers to understand which incidents require involvement of a co-responder team. If co-responder teams are used, they can also help transport and link people in crisis to a wide range of services because of mental health access to patient-specific information.

Tailoring to frequent arrests of people with mental illness. Many law enforcement agencies have experienced problems with arresting people with mental illness, when an officer either was not aware of the hallmarks of mental illness or had no other options for managing a person in the "gray area"—someone who did not meet the criteria for emergency evaluation but whose behavior was too disruptive to leave at the scene. Responses have focused on educating police about mental illness and available resources and training them to deescalate crises. Cross-training opportunities allow mental health professionals and consumers and family members to learn about the responsibilities of and constraints on police officers.

Tailoring to repeat contacts. Several of the communities studied have a small group of consumers who are not easily connected with services or maintained in treatment. In some cases, they are dually diagnosed (most often with severe mental illness and substance abuse), homeless, or both. Typically, these individuals stay in treatment for only a short period of time, and many do not follow through with treatment recommendations. This situation can result in law enforcement calls to the same locations, often involving the same people, without any indication of improvement in the person's well-being—and sometimes with clear signs of deterioration. To address these concerns, program activities include identifying individuals who repeatedly come into contact with emergency services and working closely with behavioral health professionals to develop customized, in-depth responses that include mental health treatment, services and supports, and rigorous follow-up.

Tailoring to Characteristics

The research for this project also identified several jurisdictional characteristics that shaped the nature of the SPR. These included aspects of the mental health system, the police department's leadership style, and the area's demographics and geography. These "characteristics" differ from problems in that they are relatively inflexible, so program activities must accommodate to them rather than aim to change them.

Tailoring to inadequate mental health system resources. It is almost universal for communities to experience significant problems related to a lack of behavioral health resources. Declines in inpatient hospital beds and inadequate outpatient community mental health services continue to plague many communities. When mental health practitioners have difficulty locating an inpatient bed for those who need one, people in crisis may be turned away from emergency medical facilities or released quickly, producing an apparent "revolving door." In the communities studied for this project, program planners had addressed this issue by helping officers identify who should be evaluated at the emergency room and who could be referred elsewhere. In one community, where the psychiatric emergency department was connected to an inpatient unit, the program planners addressed the problem of increased inpatient admissions following SPR implementation by contracting with a service that would assist clients to become enrolled in benefits programs.

Tailoring to law enforcement agency leadership style. The predominant law enforcement agency characteristic that affected program development was leadership style. Some law enforcement leaders believe a subset of officers must become "specialists" dedicated to particular areas of expertise (such as domestic violence). Others believe that all officers should be "generalists" prepared to respond to the wide variety of situations they will encounter. Underlying these preferences are opinions about the necessity of particular personality traits for particular tasks. In this context, many leaders believe that officers trained for SPR should be volunteers, specially selected to have compassion for people with mental illnesses. If law enforcement leadership style is an issue, program planners may need to be flexible about how many officers are trained and whether these officers volunteer for the training.

Tailoring to demographics and geography. A jurisdiction's population, population density, land area, and crime problems present important constraints on SPRs. Both very large and very small jurisdictions struggle with adequacy of resources, particularly those that must be deployed over large areas. Even in communities where the program impetus was concern over safety during police encounters, the size of the jurisdiction may limit effective deployment of CIT officers. As a consequence, in some sites CIT is localized to areas with the greatest number of people with mental illness. To manage large geographic areas with low population density, some jurisdictions use "force multipliers," such as ambulance services, and create agreements that allow jurisdictions to respond across a region, beyond their jurisdictional boundaries.

INTERNATIONAL SPR EXPERIENCE

Responding to large numbers of people with mental illness in the community is not an issue only for police agencies in the United States. Canada has been working on solving many of the same problems experienced in the United States over a similar period of time. The following section provides an overview of Canada's experience, along with that of other nations more recently implementing some aspects of SPR programs, including agencies in Australia, China, and Europe.

Canada

Due to the variety of police organizations, mental health systems, and geographic and demographic considerations in Canada, several different strategies have been deployed in various locations. A common feature is the existence of community-based liaisons for various members of the criminal justice and mental health systems, such as consumer groups, firefighters, police, and housing agencies. Many police departments have taken the approach of having a designated mental health officer, an individual tasked with being the contact between the mental health and criminal justice systems. These individuals may also function as the first responders to provide support and information as well as case management services for mentally ill individuals with frequent police contact. Another prominent model is the mobile crisis team model, which involves a nurse or mental health professional who travels with a designated police officer. The mental health worker can provide immediate assessment and can facilitate a seamless entry into the mental health system.

Most of the urban areas in Canada have adapted this model to their particular jurisdictions, although there are adaptations in rural areas that might involve telephone consultations by mental health workers (Coleman & Cotton, 2010). Although less common, the CIT model is also used in many jurisdictions, with specialized training for officers to respond to problematic situations involving behavioral health crisis. An enhanced model was developed in British Columbia; it offers CIT training to a core group of first responders with appointment of CIT liaisons in each of these agencies. This model is used in many smaller jurisdictions that may not have the volume of police involvement with the mentally ill or where an immediate response by a mental health professional is impractical due to geographic difficulties. Toronto has developed a comprehensive police response in which all police officers receive advanced mental illness education and training. There are also two models—the sequential response model and community development model—that involve police departments working with mental health service providers. The sequential response model involves an agreement with mental health agencies; once a situation has stabilized, the mental health agency is tasked to take over and assume immediate responsibility (Cotton & Coleman, 2013). The community development model requires a more active liaison between first responder officers and interagency committees.

Australia

The large number of individuals being diagnosed in Australia with mental illness and the increased interactions police have with these individuals have led to some fatal consequences. Although few individuals are fatally shot by Australian police (only 41 between 1990 and 1997), at least one third of those were identified as suffering from a diagnosed mental illness that required psychiatric treatment. Due to these incidents, Australian police departments have undertaken several strategies to improve the police response. These approaches have included introducing specialist mental health training for police officers and implementing a variation of the Memphis CIT model called the Mental Health Intervention Team (Chappell, 2013). In the state of Victoria, the police, in partnership with Monash University, are investigating police practices, policies, and procedures for dealing with individuals with mental disorders (Chappell, 2013).

China

A recent article by Lo and Wang (2010) speaks to the challenges faced by police in China. In Beijing, for example, when a police officer determines that an individual may have a serious mental illness, he or she must also determine its severity. If the police officer decides that the individual is too severely ill, he or she may call a "special squad" (similar to the mobile crisis team concept) in which a mental health professional responds with the public security officers. Although China's police have attempted to standardize the procedures for responding to people with mental illness by adopting the Mental Health Act, this effort has been largely ineffective (Lo & Wang, 2010).

China, much like the rest of the world, also faces the problem of the lack of training of their officers. As Lo and Wang conclude, although it is important for police to be trained, it is not enough. The most important first step, though, is to increase police officers' awareness of the factors that contribute to their specific jurisdictional challenges and to develop effective strategies for that jurisdiction.

Europe

The European Commission has stated that the "handling of mentally ill offenders by a criminal justice system is an indicator of the ability of a society to balance public safety interests with the achievements of modern psychiatry and of its ability to incorporate basic human rights principles into penal and mental health practice" (2005, p. 6). One interesting diversion effort in the United Kingdom involves a forensic community psychiatric nurse who is attached to the local community mental health and social services team (James, 2000). These individuals are placed in the police stations so that seriously ill people can be identified early in the process. These processes have apparently been successful in less populous areas and in many local police stations, but there is little or no published information on outcomes of these efforts. The most firmly established services are in London and Birmingham, two of England's largest cities. Their model involves a community psychiatric nurse service in the courts and police stations with the backup of a consultant psychiatrist (James, 1999). In Belfast, a program was designed that involves rapid screening and assessment at the time of first contact with the criminal justice system, as well as a structure to appropriately refer such individuals to behavioral health services (Moore, 2010). Using this program in Belfast, mental health nurses, forensic medical officers, police officers, court officials, and probation officers can interact with health and social service professionals who provide services. A unique addition to this is that the nurses can coordinate follow-up care and ongoing support to the offenders, police officers, and health care professionals.

IMPLICATIONS FOR FUTURE RESEARCH

Several authors have summarized the literature on the police response to people with mental illness (Compton, Bahora, Watson, & Oliva, 2008; Heilbrun et al., 2012). They have concluded that there is a paucity of prospective, rigorous research on the nature and extent of the problems faced by police and the effectiveness of various model approaches to solving these problems. Until more reliable data become available, policymakers and community members must develop programs that make the most sense in light of local information, reflecting local needs and resources. Future researchers and policymakers should consider a number of critical areas for exploration. Most important would be projects that assess the relative impact of a program's elements on its effectiveness. Additional research questions include:

- What aspects of community collaboration are most effective in developing and sustaining SPRs? Examples might include the number and type of partners, meeting structures, participant activities, accountability measures, group processes, and so forth.
- What type of training and what amount of training are most effective in changing officers' attitudes and behavior on scene?
- What tactics are most effective in safely deescalating situations involving people with mental illness?
- What training protocol is most effective in ensuring that an officer trained in deescalation is on the scene quickly—training all patrol officers extensively, training only a subset of officers extensively, or training all officers with deescalation techniques while a subset receives more intensive training?

- What situational factors affect the disposition police officers choose?
- What police referrals and treatment protocols are associated with long-term wellness and reduced encounters with police?

Although the available empirical research at this time is minimal, a strong argument can be made for the "face validity" of the programs described in this chapter, especially when communities do not have the luxury of time to wait before planning and acting to address some of the important problems discussed in this chapter.

REFERENCES

Bower, D. L., & Petit, G. (2001). The Albuquerque police department's crisis intervention team: A report card. *FBI Law Enforcement Bulletin, 70*, 1–6.

Chappell, D. (Ed.) (2013). *Policing and the mentally ill: International perspectives.* New York: CRC Press.

Coleman, T. G., & Cotton, D. (2010). *Police interactions with persons with a mental illness: Police learning in the environment of contemporary policing.* Ottawa: Mental Health Commission of Canada.

Compton, M. T., Demir, B., Oliva, J. R., & Boyce, T. (2009). Crisis intervention team training and special weapons and tactics callouts in an urban police department. *Psychiatric Services, 60*(6), 831–833.

Compton, M. T., Esterberg, M. L., McGee, R., Kotwicki, R. J., & Oliva, J. R. (2006). Crisis intervention team training: Changes in knowledge, attitudes, and stigma related to schizophrenia. *Psychiatric Services, 57*, 1199–1202.

Compton, M., Bahora, M., Watson, A., & Oliva, J. (2008). A comprehensive review of extant research on Crisis Intervention Team (CIT) programs. *Journal of the American Academy of Psychiatry and the Law, 36*, 47–55.

Cotton, D., & Coleman, T. G. (2013). Improving Relationships Between Police and People with Mental Illnesses Canadian Developments. In: Chappell, D. (Ed.). *Policing and the mentally ill: International perspectives.* New York: CRC Press.

Cowell, A. J., Broner, N., & Dupont, R. (2004). The cost-effectiveness of criminal justice diversion programs for people with serious mental illness co-occurring with substance abuse. *Journal of Contemporary Criminal Justice, 20*, 292–315.

Dupont, R., & Cochran, S. (2000). Police response to mental health emergencies: Barriers to change. *Journal of the American Academy of Psychiatry and Law, 28*, 228–244.

Engel, R. S., & Silver, E. (2006). Policing mentally disordered suspects: A reexamination of the criminalization hypothesis. *Criminology, 39*, 225–252. doi:10.1111/j.1745-9125.2001.tb00922.x

European Commission (2005). *Placement and treatment of mentally ill offenders: Legislation and practice in EU member states (Final Report).* Mannheim, Germany: Central Institute of Mental Health.

Heilbrun, K., DeMatteo, D., Yasuhara, K., Brooks Holliday, S., Shah, S., King, C., Bingham DiCarlo, A., Hamilton, D., & LaDuke, C. (2012). Community-based alternatives for justice-involved individuals with severe mental illness: Review of the relevant research. *Criminal Justice and Behavior, 39*, 351–419. doi:10.1177/0093854811432421

James, D. (1999). Court diversion at 10 years: can it work, does it work and has it a future? *The Journal of Forensic Psychiatry, 10*(3), 507–524.

James, D. (2000). Police station diversion schemes: role and efficacy in central London. *The Journal of Forensic Psychiatry, 11*(3), 532–555.

Lattimore, P. K., Broner, N., Sherman, R., Frisman, L., & Sharer, M. S. (2003). A comparison of prebooking and post-booking diversion programs for mentally ill substance using individuals with justice involvement. *Journal of Contemporary Criminal Justice, 19*, 30–64.

Lo, T. W., & Wang, X. (2010). Policing and the Mentally Ill in China: Challenges and Prospects. *Police Practice and Research, 11*, 342–354.

Moore, R. (2010). Current trends in policing and the mentally ill in Europe: a review of the literature. *Police Practice and Research: An International Journal, 11*(4), 330–341.

Novak, K. S., & Engel, R. S. (2005). Disentangling the influence of suspects' demeanor and mental disorder on arrest. *Policing: An International Journal of Police Strategies & Management, 28*, 493–512.

Reuland, M. (2004). *A guide to implementing police-based diversion programs for people with mental illness.* Delmar, NY: Technical Assistance and Policy Analysis Center for Jail Diversion.

Schwarzfeld, M., Reuland, M., & Plotkin, M. (2008). *Improving responses to people with mental illnesses: The essential elements of a specialized law enforcement-based program.* New York: Council of State Governments Justice Center.

Steadman, H. J., Deane, M. W., Borum, R., & Morrissey, J. P. (2000). Comparing outcomes of major models of police responses to mental health emergencies. *Psychiatric Services, 51*, 645–649.

Steadman, H. J., Mulvey, E. P., Monahan, J., Robbins, P. C., Appelbaum, P. S., Grisso, T., Roth, L. H., & Silver, E. (1998). Violence by people discharged from acute psychiatric inpatient facilities and by others in the same neighborhoods. *Archives of General Psychiatry, 55*, 393–401.

Steadman, H. J., & Naples, M. (2005). Assessing the effectiveness of jail diversion programs for persons with serious mental illness and co-occurring substance use disorders. *Behavioral Sciences and the Law, 23*, 163–170.

Teller, J. L. S., Munetz, M. R., Gil, K. M., & Ritter, C. (2006). Crisis intervention team training for police officers responding to mental disturbance calls. *Psychiatric Services, 57*(2).

Teplin, L. A. (1984). Criminalizing mental disorder: The comparative arrest rate of the mentally ill. *American Psychologist, 39*(7), 794–803.

Watson, A., Ottati, V., Morabito, M., Draine, J., Kerr, A., & Angell, B. (2010). Outcomes of police contacts with persons with mental illness: The impact of CIT. *Administration and Policy in Mental Health and Mental Health Services Research, 37*, 302–317.

4

Initial Detention and Initial Hearings

Intercept 2

KIRK HEILBRUN, DAVID DEMATTEO,
STEPHANIE BROOKS-HOLLIDAY,
AND PATRICIA A. GRIFFIN ■

Diversion at the postbooking stage is important for several reasons. An individual with a mental illness may be overwhelmed by the pretrial jail setting, particularly if the jail is loud or crowded or induces safety concerns. According to the Center for Mental Health Services' National GAINS Center (2007), "inmates with mental illness become vulnerable to assault and are at risk of harming themselves or others" (p. 7). In addition, for offenders with mental illness who are receiving treatment in the community, post-arrest detention interrupts the provision of services (Clark, 2004; National GAINS Center, 2007). Diversion can help reduce the backlogging that courts often experience by offering deferred or waived prosecution and can reduce pretrial jail crowding via conditional release (Clark, 2004). Research also suggests that diversion may help to reduce costs to the criminal justice system, due to reduced time spent in jail and reduced need for special resources for individuals with mental illness (National GAINS Center, 2007). Therefore, diversion at Intercept 2 has important implications.

The Sequential Intercept Model (SIM) has focused attention on the importance of diversion at Intercept 2. By identifying alternatives to standard processing at each of the five intercepts, the SIM has further delineated the distinction between interventions at initial detention and hearings from those following initial hearings that use a special docket or judge (e.g., problem-solving courts). The application of the SIM is facilitated by creating a cross-systems map that depicts how people with mental illness flow through the criminal justice system. In conducting this mapping exercise, jurisdictions become more aware of the gaps in their diversion services and develop plans to address these gaps. Such mapping has helped jurisdictions become more deliberate in service planning, identifying opportunities for the criminal justice and community mental health systems to collaborate. Because Intercept 2 interventions have received relatively less attention, particularly when compared to pre-arrest or specialty court diversion, cross-systems mapping has been useful in clarifying needs for services at this point of contact.

Research regarding the characteristics of those served by Intercept 2 programming supports the important role these programs play. Broner and colleagues (2002–2003) examined the postbooking, pre-arraignment population in Brooklyn, excluding those identified by the police as "emotionally disturbed." Participants were administered a diagnostic interview, self-report scales of alcohol and drug abuse, and a symptom inventory. A total of 18.5% of participants met diagnostic criteria for major depressive disorder, bipolar disorder, or schizophrenia, and 7% presented with another mental health disorder (this 7% was not exclusive with those diagnosed with severe mental illness). Overall, 22.1% endorsed symptoms of a mental health disorder, 13% endorsed severe symptoms, and the lifetime prevalence rate of any mental disorder was 31%. Nearly half of the participants endorsed behaviors consistent with alcohol or drug abuse or dependence. The researchers found that those with both lifetime and current mental illness were more likely to be incarcerated for the current offense. Although only 19% of the sample was admitted to the Department of Corrections, half of those individuals had a lifetime diagnosis and 39% had a current diagnosis. Comparing individuals with (1) severe mental illness only, (2) co-occurring disorders, (3) substance use only, and (4) no diagnosis, those with co-occurring disorders endorsed the highest severity of psychiatric distress, followed by those with severe mental illness. Individuals with substance use and co-occurring disorders were more likely to have an arrest or incarceration history than those without a diagnosis, and those with substance use had a higher rate of arrest history than those with severe mental illness. In the year following arrest, those with co-occurring disorders spent more time in jail than those with no diagnosis, and individuals in all three diagnostic groups were more likely than those with no diagnosis to be jailed at least once. Although many clients acknowledged a need for employment and housing assistance, smaller proportions endorsed a need for mental health or substance abuse treatment.

RELEVANT HISTORY

Development of Intercept 2 Diversion

In 1994, Steadman and colleagues first described the status and effectiveness of jail diversion programs. Although jail diversion appeared potentially useful to facilitate the provision of treatment and support services to those with mental illness, the investigators noted that support for these programs at that time was largely anecdotal and observational. Whereas previous descriptions of jail diversion programs had encompassed a wide range of program types and models, Steadman and colleagues (1994) focused on creating a working definition of post-arrest jail diversion. They identified three hallmarks of a program at this stage: (1) screening offenders for mental illness, (2) evaluations by mental health clinicians for those who appeared eligible, and (3) negotiation among legal and mental health stakeholders to generate a community-based disposition to provide mental health services. Diversion outcomes including plea bargaining, reduced charges, and reduced pretrial jail time were included in this working definition.

Of the 115 interviews conducted with survey respondents who identified themselves as having a jail diversion program, only 18% (twenty-one programs) met this definition.

Jail diversion has expanded considerably since 1994, when Steadman and colleagues (1994) estimated that only 52 of the 1,106 identified eligible jails (capacity of at least 50 inmates) had a formal mental health diversion program. This expansion was facilitated in part by federal funding. For instance, nine jail diversion programs participated in a Jail Diversion Knowledge Development and Application project funded by the Substance Abuse and Mental Health Services Administration (SAMHSA) beginning in 1997 (National Association of Mental Health Planning and Advisory Councils [NAMHPAC], 2006; National GAINS Center, 2004), and four of these programs would now be classified as Intercept 2 programs. SAMHSA's Center for Mental Health Services funded ten diversion programs under Targeted Capacity Expansion grants in 2001, and 17 more programs were awarded Targeted Capacity Expansion grants in collaboration with the Department of Justice in 2003 and 2004 (National GAINS Center, 2004; NAMHPAC, 2006).

Challenges to Implementing Intercept 2 Diversion

Some research has identified reluctance to offer pretrial release and deferred prosecution to those with serious mental illness (SMI). Clark (2004) surveyed jurisdictions with formal pretrial release and deferred prosecution programs to determine whether these programs were available to individuals with mental illness and whether they met certain criteria, including screening for mental illness, formal evaluation by a mental health professional, and offering pretrial release or deferred prosecution near the time of the initial court appearance. Of the 203 programs, only 12 met these "model" criteria for pretrial release decision making, two of which also offered deferred prosecution (Clark, 2004).

Although jurisdictions may develop plans to improve services at Intercept 2, limited resources may impede their implementation. A review of the Sequential Intercept Maps and action plans of some jurisdictions (see Chapter 13, this volume) shows that although Intercept 2 services may be in place, several areas have been identified for improvement. For instance, an Intercept 2-related gap identified by Franklin County, Washington, was the lack of pretrial service staff to review cases and identify potential diversion clients (Policy Research Associates, 2007). A review of the Denver metropolitan region identified various gaps across six counties, including absence of (a) pretrial diversion, (b) validated screening measures to identify potential clients, and (c) an individual to serve as a liaison among stakeholders (Policy Research Associates, 2008).

In addition, specialty courts have garnered a significant amount of the research attention provided to postbooking diversion programs in recent years, including meta-analyses and more methodologically rigorous investigations (Heilbrun et al., 2012). Nonspecialty court diversion and jail diversion have also received attention in the empirical literature, but not this same degree of scrutiny. Therefore, we have limited empirical knowledge about the features of Intercept 2 interventions that maximize their effectiveness.

RELEVANT LITERATURE

Scientific Support

Baseline characteristics of diverted clients. Postbooking diversion programs are receiving increased empirical attention. Some studies have described populations served by postbooking diversion programs, particularly in contrast to pre-booking diversion programs that fall under Intercept 1. Naples and Steadman (2003) examined three prebooking and four postbooking programs, including one specialty court, and found wider variability among the postbooking sites (3% to 30%) compared to the prebooking sites (13% to 20%) associated with violent offending charges. Another study (Lattimore, Broner, Sherman, Frisman, & Shafer, 2003) described differences between clients of prebooking and postbooking programs on demographic variables, service utilization, mental health and substance use, and criminal activity. Three prebooking sites and five postbooking sites (including one specialty court model) were included. The postbooking sites served a significantly higher proportion of Hispanic and white clients and fewer black clients, who tended to be younger. They also had more baseline deficits with respect to employment and education and had fewer days in the community in the three months before the study. They were significantly more likely to have been arrested in the previous month and year and had higher incidences of certain types of crimes (e.g., drug, property, and person crimes). Their instant offenses were generally more serious than those in prebooking programs. Postbooking clients had lower overall quality of life, higher drug and alcohol use, and a higher level of mental health and substance abuse treatment.

Other research found that clients of diversion programs differ from other offenders who receive mental health services while incarcerated. Draine and colleagues (2005) examined a diversion program serving both prebooking and postbooking clients, comparing 68 clients of the jail diversion program located in an outpatient county behavioral health emergency services center to 70 individuals who received in-jail behavioral health services. Those served by the diversion program were more likely to have acute psychotic symptoms but less likely to have a history of parole or probation or to have been treated for substance abuse.

Other studies have been more specific in describing those served by the different models of postbooking diversion programs. Court-based programs are "decentralized, with diversion staff working in multiple courts with multiple judges (and prosecutors and public defenders) at any stage in the criminal justice process and in the community, providing a case management and monitoring liaison role between community service providers and the court" (Lattimore et al., 2003, p. 33). Jail-based models "identify, screen, assess, and divert the defendant from the jail . . . These programs are typically operated by pretrial service personnel or by specialized jail personnel for those defendants who have not been identified earlier in the process, may have more serious charges, or whose mental status may result in diversion occurring later in the criminal justice process" (Lattimore et al., 2003, p. 33). Evidence regarding both types of programs is described in the following sections.

Court-Based Programs

One study examined a court-based diversion program that provided mental health consultation to the court by a clinical psychologist and diverted eligible clients to community treatment programs (Lamb et al., 1996). Of the 96 participants, many had a history of inpatient treatment and presented with symptoms of severe mental illness. About half (48%) were charged with a violent crime, with an average time from arrest to disposition of 2.7 months. A total of 58% were mandated to mental health treatment with monitoring, 13% had their cases dismissed, 14% received a criminal sentence, and 16% received treatment referrals without stipulated monitoring. One-year follow-up determined whether participants' outcome was poor (experienced at least one of the following: psychiatric hospitalization, arrest, significant physical violence against persons, or homelessness) or good (none of these events). Those in court-monitored treatment had a higher frequency of good outcomes (59%) than those who were not (28%). Among the treated participants, a higher proportion of monitored participants had "good outcomes" than those in the unmonitored treatment group. This suggests the value of diverting clients to court-mandated, monitored treatment.

Steadman and colleagues (1999) considered the effectiveness of a pre-arraignment diversion program. Diversion participants were compared to individuals who were referred to and agreed to participate in the diversion program but were not ultimately diverted. The majority of participants had a history of mental health and substance abuse treatment. At two-month follow-up, all diverted participants had been released, compared to 64.4% of the nondiverted participants. Diverted participants experienced a higher rate of subsequent hospitalization, although this difference was not statistically significant. There was no significant difference with respect to rearrest. At follow-up, nondiverted participants showed greater improvement in some aspects of mental health functioning (Somatization, Interpersonal Sensitivity, Anxiety) and quality of life (Friends and Health). Both groups experienced improvements in symptomology and quality of life, however. This study suggests some benefit for clients in diversion programs in improving mental health and quality of life, but there was no clear effect for rearrest.

Another study focused on eight criminal justice diversion programs, including prebooking programs and jail- and court-based postbooking programs (Broner, Lattimore, Cowell, & Schlenger, 2004). Each program included a comparison group. One of the sites (in Connecticut) followed an arraignment court model (Frisman et al., 2006). Diversion program participants were 3.4 times more likely to be hospitalized at three-month follow-up and reported increased general life satisfaction at 12 months (Broner et al., 2004). However, diverted clients also reported a higher likelihood of alcohol use at 12 months. Participation in the diversion program was not significantly related to criminal recidivism. Therefore, despite more service utilization by diverted clients, there was no clear support for the effectiveness of the program in improving other outcomes.

Because the study by Broner and colleagues (2004) "reported that the [Connecticut] site showed worse outcomes with respect to alcohol use and mental health symptoms for diversion clients" (Frisman et al., 2006, p. 8), these investigators took a different approach to examining the data. The diverted participants were significantly different from the comparison group on ten baseline variables, including history of substance abuse treatment, history of depression without psychosis, psychosis, receipt of federal disability, and score on the Michigan Alcohol Screening Test. Those in the diverted group had more days at risk in the community; this was controlled when examining substance use, homelessness, and criminality. Diversion status was not significantly related to differences over time on substance use, arrests, or violent crime. Diverted clients spent an average of 71 fewer days incarcerated than nondiverted clients. The diverted group spent more days in the community before reincarceration (162 versus 150 days) and had a higher likelihood of avoiding incarceration during the six months following diversion or release (83% versus 70%). There was no significant relationship between diversion and rearrest. Providing a more detailed description of the relationship between diversion and outcomes such as symptoms, criminal justice involvement, and general quality of life, this study did not offer evidence of consistent and clear advantages for diversion compared to traditional criminal court.

The Treatment Alternatives to Dually Diagnosed (TADD) program is a postbooking diversion intervention in Brooklyn that adapted an existing program for drug offenders for use with offenders with co-occurring disorders (Broner, Nguyen, Swern, & Goldfinger, 2003). TADD primarily used a deferred sentencing model and had both general court diversion and a mental health court track. In addition to providing case management services, the case management agency provided monitoring and other services, and training for community and criminal justice stakeholders. Broner and colleagues (2003) examined TADD clients during a three-month period. Accepted clients had a lower proportion of violent offenses and a higher proportion of drug-related offenses. Psychotic and major affective disorders were most common in both groups. The diverted group reported significantly more polysubstance use. At the end of six months, 80% were still engaged in community services, with the majority of dismissals occurring during the first three months. This study did not describe this diversion program with respect to criminal justice, mental health, or substance use outcomes, but it described characteristics of clients "appropriate" for diversion and the connecting of participants to community-based treatment. Results suggest that participants received intended services during their first six months, and the rate of program dismissal or absconding was low.

One study compared diversion versus diversion with an adjunctive citizenship component (Rowe et al., 2007). Individuals randomly assigned to the experimental treatment participated in therapeutic and case management services but were also involved in a citizenship intervention. Rowe and colleagues (2007) described citizenship as "a measure of the strength of people's connections to the rights, responsibilities, roles, and resources available to people through public and social institutions and through the informal, 'associational' life of neighborhoods and local communities" (p. 956). After controlling for baseline differences, the effects on alcohol use, drug use, and criminal behavior were examined. Significantly lower alcohol use was seen among individuals in the citizenship intervention at six- and twelve-month follow-up, although the groups did not differ on criminal justice involvement at these two time points. The investigators concluded that participation in the diversion program was associated with reduced alcohol and drug use and criminal activity in general, while the citizenship components appeared only to significantly affect alcohol use.

Jail-Based Programs

Project Link, in upstate New York, is a jail diversion program that serves clients at "multiple points within the criminal justice, health care and community support systems" (Weisman, Lamberti, & Price, 2004, p. 74). Participants ($N = 41$) experienced significant decreases in average annual jail days, hospital days, arrests per patient, and number of incarcerations and hospitalizations, and community functioning improved compared to the year prior to program participation. A second evaluation examined the first 44 participants to complete one year in the program. This group had significant reductions in service utilization and increases in community functioning outcomes. In addition, enrollment in substance abuse programming increased during the first year of program participation. A cost analysis revealed average savings of nearly $40,000 when comparing service costs in the year prior to program participation to the first year of program participation.

Another study described a program that served clients with SMI (Hoff, Baranosky, Buchanan, Zonana, & Rosenheck, 1999) charged with misdemeanors or less serious felonies, and a comparison group of nondiverted individuals with a history of mental illness was used. To identify potential diversion clients, a psychiatric nurse from a community mental health center screened potential clients and negotiated for a mental health disposition to the charges. At baseline, the diverted (N = 314) and nondiverted (N = 124) groups differed with respect to dual diagnosis (more common among diverted clients) and severity of crime (higher severity for the diverted group). Diverted clients spent significantly less time incarcerated than their nondiverted counterparts (40.5 versus 172.8 jail days, respectively). Accounting for baseline differences, females had significantly more jail days, and an interaction between diversion and charge was identified; specifically, the benefit of diversion was more pronounced for those with more serious charges. The investigators offered several potential explanations for this interaction, including a potential floor effect for lesser crimes, acuity of mental health symptoms, and placement in mandated versus nonmandated treatment.

As described earlier, Broner and colleagues (2004) examined the effectiveness of eight prebooking and postbooking programs. Three programs followed a jail-based, postbooking model. At the first site (New York City[1]), participants were less likely to report mental health-related hospitalization at three months, were less likely to be receiving medication for mental health purposes at twelve months, and reported reduced satisfaction with their living situation. Diverted participants were also less likely to be the victim of recent nonviolent crimes at three months. Participants at the second site (Hawaii) experienced significant reductions in self-reported physical health at three months and increases in self-reported psychiatric symptoms at twelve months. At the final site (Arizona), diverted participants reported less alcohol use at twelve months. Across sites, there was no significant effect of diversion on recidivism (arrests in the 30 days prior to the interview), but diversion was associated with fewer institutionalized days in the previous 90 days at three and twelve months, and fewer jail days during the previous 90 days at the three-month follow-up. But these results were not described separately for prebooking and postbooking programs. The results suggest that diversion programs are not necessarily associated with consistent improvements. Although some benefits were described (e.g., reduced victimization, reduced alcohol use), other results were mixed (e.g., reduced satisfaction with living situation). In addition, the inconsistencies in results across the study sites suggest that there may be substantial site-specific factors in effect.

Shafer, Arthur, and Franczak (2004) further examined the postbooking diversion program in Tucson and Phoenix, Arizona (included in the previously described study). Program participants were eligible for one of three reduced sanction options: release on conditions, summary probation, and deferred prosecution. Participants were interviewed upon entry to the program and at three and twelve months after baseline. Charges included misdemeanors and lesser felonies, and eligible diagnoses included schizophrenia and mood disorders. There were few baseline differences between diverted and nondiverted participants, although diverted individuals reported higher rates of polysubstance use and emergency department service utilization. Individuals in the diversion group were more likely to report a history of arrests for violent crimes and fewer procedural violations. At twelve months, diverted clients had significantly lower anxiety/depression scores, higher rates of emergency department service use since the baseline interview and during the six- to nine-month period before the follow-up interview, less use of physical health services in the past three months, and fewer arrests for minor crimes in the past month. Both diverted and non-diverted participants had reductions in mental health symptoms and substance use. There were no significant reductions in antisocial behavior and no significant effect of diversion participation on these behaviors. This study indicates that diversion programs may have a positive impact on mental health symptoms and criminal justice outcomes, although these differences were seen in specific domains (e.g., anxiety/depression).

The Chesterfield County (Virginia) Dual Treatment Track Program is a diversion program for individuals with dual diagnoses of mental health and substance use disorders (Gordon & Barnes, 2006). Diversion program participants were identified through (1) an initial screen by a Community Corrections pretrial services officer, (2) a subsequent assessment by a program pretrial services officer, (3) a third evaluation by a program clinician, and (4) approval of the court. Although the program screened many offenders, a small number were accepted (during a two-year period, for instance, fewer than 2% of screened clients were found to be eligible). Study participants were recruited over a 22-month period, and progress was measured by comparing participant outcomes during the year prior to enrollment to the year following enrollment. During the program, drug screens were conducted, with clients testing positive on an average of 2.5/76 screens. As a consequence of positive drug screens, clients averaged 2.3 violations and 11 days in jail. Of the 68 participants, nearly 70% were terminated without completing the program, 4% were successfully released without completing the program, and 11% completed the program. The incidence of alcohol and drug use decreased when comparing the 30 days prior to the baseline interview versus the 30 days prior to the six-month follow-up. The arrest rate did not substantially change in the year before enrollment and the year following enrollment, but the incidence of felony offenses decreased while misdemeanors increased. The number of jail days increased from 65 to 72; however, when comparing clients who completed the program with those who were terminated, the completers had fewer jail days in the year following enrollment than in the year before enrollment (decreasing from 93 to 23 days). The researchers suggested that the program was more effective for higher-risk offenders, particularly in reducing substance use and jail days for those who completed the program. It also suggests the importance of monitoring compliance, as those who did not complete the program and were terminated did not obtain the same benefits as those who graduated from the program.

The St. Louis Jail Diversion Program provides "intensive, short-term case management (30-90 days) with the goal of optimizing the use of mental health services and to reduce re-arrest rates over time" (Tyuse, 2005, p. 86). The program considered mental status and incarceration history when determining eligibility. Clients could be referred to the program by criminal justice stakeholders, family members, self-referrals, probation office staff, mental health service providers, Crisis Intervention Team (CIT) police officers, or nurses at correctional facilities.

Diverted clients attended 30 to 90 days of mental health treatment to complete the program. This study examined the effectiveness of the program in connecting the 50 participants with housing and federal entitlements. Results revealed a significant increase in the proportion of participants receiving Social Security and Medicaid benefits from program entry to completion. Upon completion, the number of clients receiving Social Security benefits increased by 27.9%, and the number of clients connected to Medicaid benefits increased by 54.4%. There were no significant improvements with respect to housing.

Broner and colleagues (2005) examined the effect of mandated versus non-mandated programming on diversion program outcomes in the New York City NYC-LINK program, which had "two tracks or conditions: those diverted and case managed from jail without specific court involvement or any mandated sanctions (non-mandated diversion) and those diverted through the court with diversion conditioned on treatment involvement, mandatory case management reporting, and with court sanctions for noncompliance (mandated diversion)" (p. 21). A comparison group was composed of dually diagnosed offenders in the general jail population. To be eligible for diversion, clients must have had psychiatric treatment and a mental illness; felony and misdemeanor index offenses were considered. Program participants received case management through a community-based program. The Brooklyn-based program included sanctions for noncompliance, whereas the other programs had no legal consequences for noncompletion. Diverted clients received a variety of reduced sanction benefits, including charge reduction, conditional discharge, and deferred sentencing (for those in the mandated program). Those in the mandated group spent significantly less time in prison and significantly more time in the community than the comparison group; for both variables, there was a nonsignificant advantage for mandated clients compared to nonmandated clients. There were no significant relationships between diversion and residential treatment days, hospital days, number of emergency department visits, or outpatient counseling participation. Mandated clients had a significantly higher rate of residential or outpatient treatment participation—with 95% receiving treatment—than the nonmandated group and comparison group. This study indicates that clients of mandated diversion programs may have some advantages with respect to participation in treatment compared to those in programs without a monitoring component and suggests a trend in favor of mandated diversion for prison and community time.

Boccaccini and colleagues (2005) examined the incidence of rediversion—"a former or current diversion program participant being booked into jail on a new charge and being diverted once again through the same diversion program"—among participants of two postbooking diversion programs: one jail-based program and one mental health court. The jail diversion program (Hillsborough County, FL) identified clients through a screening procedure at the county jails. Those with misdemeanor-level charges were eligible for the program. Charges were typically dropped for program participants. Data were obtained for program participants over an 18-month period, and 22% had two or more diversions during this period. The researchers found that 6% of Hillsborough County jail diversion program participants with three or more diversions accounted for 17% of all diversions. Of clients who were rediverted, 20% reentered the program within 30 days, 49% within 90 days, and 82% within 180 days. The average time to rediversion was 115 days. The researchers found that clients who were rediverted at least twice had a shorter time to rediversion than those with a single rediversion (83 versus 127 days, respectively). Rediverted clients were more likely to be male, Caucasian, and older. Although this measure of recidivism is somewhat unconventional, it provides a new perspective on the diversion process—especially as diversion programs often intend to serve clients who may otherwise cycle in and out of the criminal justice or mental health system.

Model Not Specified

The Nathaniel Project, a two-year postbooking program in New York City, served individuals charged with a felony (National GAINS Center, 2002). Screenings were conducted at the jail or courthouse and included a semistructured interview and education about the diversion program. Program staff identified eligible clients and worked with legal stakeholders to enroll these individuals. Clients pled guilty, with the understanding that a failure to comply with the program would result in incarceration, and an enforcement component enabled the judge to issue a bench warrant for clients who abscond. Treatment plans were developed and often included housing or residential treatment components, intensive case management, medication, and counseling. Among the program participants included in this study, severe mental illnesses were the most common diagnoses; 85% of clients also had a substance use disorder. Over 90% were homeless when they began the program, and 50% had serious health issues. This study compared the participants in the year prior to program enrollment to the year following enrollment and found a substantial drop in arrests (from 101 to seven total arrests). Four fifths of clients remained enrolled for the full two years, and 79% achieved stable housing during the first year. All clients were participating in mental health treatment services.

Case, Steadman, Dupuis, and Morris (2009) examined clients of postbooking programs funded by the Targeted Capacity Expansion for Jail Diversion Programs grants. There were 546 participants from 14 sites included in the analyses. Study participants were interviewed at baseline, six months, and twelve months, and the criminal justice outcomes were arrests and jail days in the twelve months after diversion. The role of a number of baseline variables was examined, including gender, age, race, charge, drug use, symptomology, lifetime abuse victimization, and number of arrests and jail days in the twelve months before diversion. Approximately 48% of participants had no postdiversion arrests, and 75% had fewer arrests in the year after diversion than they did in the year prior to diversion. Stable housing was significantly associated with arrests after diversion, with nearly 75% of the individuals who were not arrested after enrollment in the program reporting stable housing. With respect to jail days after enrollment, half of participants did not spend any time in jail in the year following diversion, and approximately 75% of participants had fewer jail days after diversion than before diversion. As with postdiversion arrests, prior arrest and jail days were significant predictors of incarceration after enrollment: Those who did not spend any time in jail following diversion had fewer prior arrests (1.9 versus 2.8 arrests) and fewer prior jail days (42.6 versus 60.8 days). In addition, those who experienced decreases in jail days following diversion were compared to those who experienced no change or increased jail days. Individuals who had fewer jail days after diversion had significantly more arrests in the year before diversion (2.5 versus 1.7 arrests) and significantly more jail days in the year before diversion (55.6 versus 39.8 days). This study provides important data about the characteristics of individuals who are successful in diversion programs and demonstrates the relationship between prior and future criminal justice involvement.

Mitton, Simpson, Gardner, Barnes, and Mcdougall (2007) evaluated the effectiveness of the Calgary Diversion Program in Canada, a postbooking diversion program for offenders with less severe crimes. Following an assessment, clients had the opportunity to participate in a day program, were connected to community-based mental health and support services, and received monitoring and progress check-ins. For those who completed the program, staff recommended withdrawal of charges. To study whether this program reduced criminal justice outcomes and improved mental health, the researchers examined client changes from the 18 months prior to program enrollment to the 18 months following program enrollment. Those who had their charges withdrawn experienced large reductions in the number of complaints and charges when comparing the 18 months before and after the program, while those whose charges were not withdrawn also experienced reductions, but of a smaller magnitude. For instance, the number of charges for clients with withdrawn charges dropped from 250 to 32, versus a reduction from 139 to 122 for those whose charges were not withdrawn (i.e., those who were less successful in completing the program). Clients with and without withdrawn charges experienced substantial reductions in hospital admissions, inpatient hospital days, and emergency department visits during the 18 months before and after the program, although the magnitude was larger for those with withdrawn charges.

Looking at the full sample, participants experienced a significant improvement in psychiatric symptom severity from program entry to the end of the program. For a subset of participants who completed quality of life questionnaires, improvements were seen in six areas, including occupational activities, physical health, and social relations. A cost analysis suggested that participation in the program helped reduce costs associated with criminal justice and health system contact. The researchers noted that a substantial proportion of participants did not complete follow-up assessments, so the favorable outcomes of this study may be slightly inflated. However, this study does provide support for the role of diversion in improving mental health symptoms and quality of life and reducing contact with the criminal justice system.

Prebooking and Postbooking Combined

In their review of three prebooking and three postbooking diversion programs (including one specialty court model), Steadman and Naples (2005) focused on the effectiveness of jail diversion for individuals with co-occurring disorders. Some baseline differences were identified when comparing diverted and non-diverted clients, including a higher proportion of females, disorders with psychotic features, substance use, and past jail time among diverted clients, but these differences were not broken down by prebooking and postbooking sites. Follow-up data were drawn from interviews conducted twelve months after diversion (or twelve months after recruitment for the comparison group participants). Among the postbooking clients, diverted clients spent more days in the community than nondiverted clients (288.5 versus 222.1 days, respectively) and had higher rates of emergency department service utilization (30.9% versus 20.5%), hospitalization (27.1% versus 15.1%), prescription medication use (81.8% versus 75.5%), and mental health counseling (68.4% versus 59.7%). Differences in the number of arrests, rate of residential treatment, and psychiatric symptoms were less pronounced, but significance testing was conducted only on the overall differences between diverted and nondiverted participants (combining prebooking and postbooking clients). An additional cost analysis was conducted for four diversion programs. In two of the postbooking programs, no significant cost differences were observed; in the third, the average net savings per diverted participant was estimated at $6,260.

The Arapahoe County Diverts the Mentally Ill for Treatment (ADMIT) program in Colorado is a partnership among the county sheriff's office, a local mental health center, and a local research institute (Swanson, Ghokar, & Tolle, 2011). Eligible offenders included adults with SMI or co-occurring disorders with nonviolent offenses. Approximately 75% of the 117 participants in this sample had misdemeanor offenses, and 22% had felony charges. A comparison group was recruited from those considered for participation in ADMIT but not enrolled. A somewhat larger proportion of comparison group members had felony charges. To examine outcomes, this program evaluation focused on 81 individuals who completed the ADMIT program (i.e., completed the program without major incident). The diverted group had a significantly lower rate of new charges (12.3%) compared to nondiverted individuals (25.9%). The diverted group had a mean of 94 more days in the community before reoffending than the comparison group, and the average sentence diverted individuals received for their new charges was 36 days shorter than that of the comparison group (36 versus 72 days, respectively). Due to the small sample sizes, statistical significance could not be determined for these comparisons. Also, diversion program completers—who had at least one moderate incident during the program—had a 24.1% recidivism rate, compared to a 5.8% recidivism rate for program graduates (who had no major incidents). Finally, changes in clinical symptom measures were examined for diverted participants, who experienced significant improvements in depression and psychotic symptoms. Participants reported significant improvements in quality of life. Finally, the researchers calculated the total cost savings by the ADMIT program during 2008, 2009, and 2010. During this period, the program resulted in an estimated savings of $57,789 when comparing program costs to the costs of serving time at the local detention center.

Theoretical and Practical Support

Among the programs described in the previous section, there is considerable variability with respect to screening procedures, relationships among the associated agencies, and program models—including length of stay, eligibility criteria, and the effect that program participation has on legal outcomes. This probably reflects the variability across diversion programs nationally. As noted in a National GAINS Center (2007) publication on jail diversion: "While all diversion programs engage in some form of identification and linkage, *there is no definitive model for organizing a jail diversion program.* Jail diversion programs will be unique to the community and the services they provide will be tailored to the consumer" (p. 13). However, certain components have been recognized as important across program models.

The first essential step in the diversion process is *identification* and *screening/ assessment* of potential clients (Lattimore et al., 2003; National GAINS Center, 2007). To identify potential clients, jurisdictions such as Maricopa County, Arizona, have developed a "data link," allowing diversion program staff to identify existing clients when they have made contact with the criminal justice system and to screen for new potential clients (National GAINS Center, 1999). Similarly, in Virginia Beach, one method of identifying clients involves cross-referencing the arrest rosters with the Department of Human Services database (Morris, 2007). Other clients are identified via referral to the diversion program. These referrals may come from a variety of sources, including family members; law enforcement; probation and/or parole; community-based and advocacy organizations; court, pretrial, and jail staff; mental health providers; nurses; judges; and attorneys. Other programs place diversion program staff in the jail or court setting to identify potential clients after arrest (e.g., Allegheny County, 2010). To identify individuals who may be appropriate for diversion services, these referring sources may consider a history of mental health diagnoses or treatment, or raise the question due to current symptomology. In addition, many programs serve clients with co-occurring mental health and substance use disorders (e.g., Broner et al., 2003; Gordon & Barnes, 2006; National GAINS Center, 1999, 2002). After referral to a program, a follow-up evaluation may be conducted. Generally, it is recommended that this identification process take place within the first 24 to 72 hours (GAINS TAPA Center, 2006; National GAINS Center, 2007).

In addition to receiving referrals, the *screening and evaluation* process is an important step in the identification of appropriate diversion clients. Some programs conduct record reviews to assess for a history of mental illness or mental health treatment, and interviews with the client are often used (National GAINS Center, 2002; Steadman et al., 1999). Many jurisdictions use an initial brief mental health screen (Broner et al., 2003), while other programs use specific screening tools. For instance, the Sparrow Court Diversion Program in Vermont (Tolmie, Meyers, & Glesner, 2010) uses the Risk and Needs Triage (RANT), a screening tool designed to briefly assess risk and mental health needs. Screenings may be conducted by a variety of parties, such as specific jail diversion specialists (De Piano & Rodriguez, 2010).

Other programs utilize a series of assessments, first identifying potential clients and then using successively more specific and comprehensive evaluations to identify clients who are most appropriate for the program (e.g., Gordon & Barnes, 2006; Tyuse, 2005). These assessments are often conducted by psychologists, psychiatrists, and psychiatric nurses (e.g., Broner et al., 2005; Frisman et al., 2006; Gordon & Barnes, 2006), although correctional or court staff may also have a role (Gordon & Barnes, 2006). Some programs may look generally for individuals with SMI, whereas others may have more specific criteria with respect to diagnosis or severity. Part of the screening process is determining whether program clients are *eligible* with respect to both mental health needs and charges. Some programs serve clients with misdemeanor charges and/or low-level felonies, while other programs allow offenders with higher-level felonies or violent charges to participate.

Another important element of these programs is *engaging clients* in the diversion program and *negotiating* with criminal justice stakeholders to enroll these clients. Program participation is often voluntary. To help potential clients determine whether they would like to participate, programs may provide information about the nature of the treatment and the effects that participation may have on their court proceedings. For instance, as part of the screening process, the Nathaniel Project will "educate the potential client about what they will be expected of them if they choose to be part of the Nathaniel Project. They also talk to the client about what their goals are, who the important people in their lives are, and how they think the program can best work with them and support their recovery" (National GAINS Center, 2002, pp. 1–2).

When agreement of a potential client has been obtained, a process of *negotiation* takes place between treatment providers and the relevant players from the criminal justice system, especially the defense attorney, prosecutor, and judge (National GAINS Center, 2007; Steadman, Morris, & Dennis, 1995). For instance, staff members of the Nathaniel Project provide education to attorneys and judges as part of the negotiation process and explain the positive outcomes that may result from diversion (National GAINS Center, 2002). It is typically the judge who decides whether a potential client will be accepted to the diversion program. For instance, this is the procedure followed in the jail-based diversion program in Hillsborough County, Florida (Boccaccini et al., 2005), and in the court-based program studied by Steadman and colleagues (1999). Program staff may present the proposed treatment plan to the final decision maker as part of the negotiation process, and with special attention paid to respecting the privacy and confidentiality of the client (Frisman et al., 2006).

Once clients have been formally accepted to diversion programs, the next important step is to connect them to mental health, substance abuse, or other appropriate services (National GAINS Center, 2007). Case management is frequently an essential element of diversion programs, and case managers connect clients to appropriate services in the community. Ensuring that diverted clients receive psychiatric services—including appropriate medication and counseling—is also a primary goal of diversion programs. Counseling services may include group and individual treatment and inpatient and outpatient services (Boccaccini et al., 2005). Many programs may connect clients with housing or residential care (Eleventh Judicial Circuit of Florida, 2010; Tyuse, 2005), particularly if homelessness is a concern. Some programs may help clients to obtain benefits or entitlements (e.g., AltaPointe Health Systems, 2011; Eleventh Judicial Circuit of Florida, 2010; Tyuse, 2005) and provide referrals to vocational programming or medical care (AltaPointe Health Systems, 2011; Broner et al., 2003). Certain programs offer their own unique services in addition to connecting clients to community-based care. For instance, the New River Valley Bridge Program requires diversion clients to "participate in the Program's signature six-part education and recovery group series" (New River Valley Community Services, 2014, p. 1). Peer support specialists or mentors may also play a role in service provision (e.g., Eleventh Judicial Circuit of Florida, 2010; Rowe et al., 2007).

Diversion programs are also diverse with respect to the legal alternatives or reduced sanctions offered to clients. For instance, in Maricopa County, Arizona, clients may be released on the condition that they participate in treatment; participate in summary probation with mandatory treatment; or be granted deferred prosecution, with charges dismissed if they complete the program (National GAINS Center, 1999; Shafer et al., 2004). Deferred sentencing is offered in other programs, as are charge reductions and conditional discharge (e.g., Broner et al., 2005). Several programs offer the dismissal of charges to clients who fulfill program requirements (e.g., Boccaccini et al., 2005). Some diversion programs have a monitoring or enforcement component (e.g., Mitton et al., 2007; National GAINS Center, 2002), although others do not have a formal method of monitoring compliance (e.g., Boccaccini et al., 2005; Broner et al., 2005). For clients who do not complete the conditions of the program, there often are not formal consequences; instead, the case may be returned to court for traditional criminal justice proceedings.

In addition to these important components of postbooking diversion program models, Steadman and colleagues (1995) identified key administrative components of successful diversion programs. These elements, which are still considered essential, are (1) the provision of integrated services and interagency collaboration, (2) regular meetings and involvement by stakeholders, including diversion program staff, mental health providers and agencies, and criminal justice players, (3) employing "boundary spanners," who serve as liaisons among the stakeholder groups, (4) effective leadership, (5) early identification of eligible clients (as described previously), and (6) case management services to identify and connect clients with appropriate services (National GAINS Center, 2007; Steadman, Morris, & Dennis, 1995).

CURRENT OPERATIONAL STATE OF SIM-GUIDED DECISION MAKING AND PLANNING

The current literature in this area strongly suggests that there is no single model of Intercept 2 diversion. Some programs are prebooking. Others are postbooking and jail-based, while yet others are postbooking and based outside the jail. It does not seem indicated to describe any of these models as "best practice" to the exclusion of others. Among other things, the needs and resources of the jurisdiction are important in determining which model provides the best fit.

However, there are some common elements of diversion programs (of different models) that can be identified as best practice in terms of their theoretical support. These include identification, screening/assessment, engaging clients and negotiating with criminal justice stakeholders, and connection of clients with services. In addition, key administrative components include integrated services/interagency collaboration, regular meetings with stakeholders, use of boundary spanners, effective leadership, early identification of eligible clients, and the use of case management. These common elements have been described through the review of successful diversion programs. The questions of how important each might be await empirical research designed to address such questions.

There is some evidence that the use of mandated treatment, including monitoring for compliance with prescribed conditions, is an effective component of jail diversion. Diversion itself may reduce the costs associated with each participant, although the relevant evidence is mixed. Pending further research, we might describe these as promising practices in the area. We do not yet have sufficient research in this area to identify contraindicated practices.

IMPLICATIONS FOR RESEARCH

The first important implication of the review of existing research in this area involves the need for better-controlled studies. Randomized controlled trials are very difficult to implement in the area of alternatives to standard justice processing, so it is understandable that there is rarely this kind of evidence available. It is possible that the use of a "wait-list control condition" strategy could allow some investigators to implement more controlled designs. Even the addition of studies featuring some kind of control or comparison group, perhaps not randomly assigned but with differences controlled statistically, would provide valuable information beyond the more typical pre–post design used most often by investigators in this area.

The differences between jurisdictions are such that it would not be indicated to recommend a single model (prebooking, postbooking in the jail, or postbooking outside the jail). But research identifying the strengths and limitations of each model, particularly relative to a nondiverted comparison group, would offer valuable information to communities in selecting the model that might be the most effective (as well as the best fit) in that particular jurisdiction. Looking more specifically at the particular components of Intercept 2 programs—the screening/selection process and the intervention itself—may be difficult, but it would be extremely useful to know what procedures and interventions work best. Early work (e.g., Broner, Maryl, & Landsberg, 2005) suggests the importance of identifying the different aspects of programs that are related to overall effectiveness.

IMPLICATIONS FOR POLICY

The first implication for policy is that a jurisdiction should consider the various models of diversion at Intercept 2 in identifying the best fit—financially, resource-wise, and politically—for the particular community. The clearest conclusion to be drawn at this stage is that no particular model (prebooking, postbooking in the jail, postbooking outside the jail) can be called "best practice" relative to the others. Nonetheless, communities in the planning stages are also well advised to review the research that does exist in the attempt to identify any particular features that appear empirically supported in connection with a particular model being considered.

The other clear implication involves the importance of identifying clients, negotiating with criminal justice stakeholders, and effectively communicating (through the use of regular meetings, effective leadership, and boundary spanners) regarding clients in the program. Diversion programs have the potential to reduce per-client costs; they certainly have the potential to better deliver services and provide housing. But the process of planning, designing, and implementing a program at Intercept 2 can also be greatly enhanced by the kind of cross-systems mapping described in Chapter 13.

NOTE

1. This actually appears closer to an Intercept 3 or Intercept 4 reentry model, although it is described by the author as diversion and presented as such.

REFERENCES

Allegheny County Department of Human Services (2010). *Allegheny County justice-related services for individuals with mental illness: From point of initial contact/diversion to specialty courts to re-entry from county and state correctional institutions*. Pittsburgh, PA: Allegheny County Department of Human Services, Office of Behavioral Health, Justice-Related Services. Accessed January 21, 2012, from http://www.naco.org/programs/csd/Documents/Criminal%20Justice/Jail%20 Diversion%20Forum%20Materials/Amy%20Kroll%20Presentation.pdf.

AltaPointe Health Systems (2011, Spring). Jail diversion prevents needless incarceration of SMI offenders. *Solutions, 1*, 2.

Boccaccini, M. T., Christy, A., Poythress, N., & Kershaw, D. (2005). Rediversion in two postbooking jail diversion programs in Florida. *Psychiatric Services, 56*, 835–839.

Broner, N., Lamon, S. S., Maryl, D. W., & Karopkin, M. G. (2002–2003). Arrested adults awaiting arraignment: Mental health, substance abuse, and criminal justice characteristics and needs. *Fordham Urban Law Journal, 30*, 663–721.

Broner, N., Lattimore, P. K., Cowell, A. J., & Schlenger, W. F. (2004). Effects of diversion on adults with co-occurring mental illness and substance use: Outcomes from a national multi-site study. *Behavioral Sciences & the Law, 22*, 519–541.

Broner, N., Maryl, D. W., & Landsberg, G. (2005). Outcomes of mandated and non-mandated New York City jail diversion for offenders with alcohol, drug, and mental disorders. *The Prison Journal, 85*, 18–49.

Broner, N., Nguyen, H., Swern, A., & Goldfinger, S. (2003). Adapting a substance abuse court diversion model for felony offenders with co-occurring disorders: Initial implementation. *Psychiatric Quarterly, 74*, 361–385.

Case, B., Steadman, H., Dupuis, S., & Morris, L. (2009). Who succeeds in jail diversion programs for persons with mental illness? A multi-site study. *Behavioral Sciences and the Law, 27*, 661–674.

Clark, J. (2004). *Non-specialty first appearance court models for diverting persons with mental illness: Alternatives to mental health courts*. Delmar, NY: Technical Assistance and Policy Analysis Center for Jail Diversion.

DePiano, L., & Rodriguez, M. L. (2010). *Palm Beach County Criminal Justice, Mental Health, and Substance Abuse Planning Project Partnership*. Presentation at the 2010 Reinvestment Act Conference, Palm Beach County, FL.

Draine, J., Blank, A., Kottsieper, P., & Solomon, P. (2005). Contrasting jail diversion and in-jail services for mental illness and substance abuse: Do they serve the same clients? *Behavioral Sciences and the Law, 23*, 171–181.

Eleventh Judicial Circuit of Florida (2010). *Frequently asked questions for County Court Jail Diversion program*. Miami, FL: Author.

Frisman, L. K., Lin, H., Sturges, G. E., Levinson, M., Baranoski, M. V., & Pollard, J. M. (2006). Outcomes of court-based jail diversion programs for people with co-occurring disorders. *Journal of Dual Diagnosis, 2*, 5–26.

GAINS TAPA Center for Jail Diversion. (2006). *Making jail diversion work in rural communities*. Presentation at the GAINS TAPA Center for Jail Diversion Easy Access Net/Teleconference, March 27, 2006. Accessed Jan. 22, 2012, from http:// www.gainscenter.samhsa.gov/html/resources/presentation_materials/ppt/ Rural_3_27_06.ppt.

Gordon, J. A., & Barnes, C. M. (2006). The dual treatment track program: A descriptive assessment of a new "in-house" jail diversion program. *Federal Probation, 70*, 9–18.

Hoff, R., Baranosky, M., Buchanan, J., Zonana, H., & Rosenheck, R. (1999). The effects of a jail diversion program on incarceration: A retrospective cohort study. *Journal of the American Academy of Psychiatry and the Law, 27*, 377–386.

Lamb, H. R., Weinberger, L. E., & Reston-Parham, C. (1996). Court intervention to address the mental health needs of mentally ill offenders. *Psychiatric Services, 47,* 275–281.

Lattimore, P, K., Broner, N., Sherman, R., Frisman, L., & Shafer, M. S. (2003). A comparison of prebooking and postbooking diversion programs for mentally ill substance-using individuals with justice involvement. *Journal of Contemporary Criminal Justice, 19,* 30–64.

Mitton, C., Simpson, L., Gardner, L., Barnes, F., & Mcdougall, G. (2007). Calgary Diversion Program: A community-based alternative to incarceration for mentally ill offenders. *The Journal of Mental Health Policy and Economics, 10,* 145–151.

Morris, J. (2007). Jail diversion initiatives CSB/DMHMRSAS. Presentation to the JCHC Joint Behavioral Healthcare Subcommittee, August 16, 2007. Accessed January 22, 2012, from http://leg5.state.va.us/user_db/frmjchc.aspx?viewid=565.

Naples, M., & Steadman, H. J. (2003). Can persons with co-occurring disorders and violent charges be successfully diverted? *International Journal of Forensic Mental Health, 2,* 137–143.

National Association of Mental Health Planning and Advisory Councils (2006). *Jail diversion strategies for persons with serious mental illness.* Rockville, MD: Center for Mental Health Services, Substance Abuse and Mental Health Services Administration.

National GAINS Center (1999). *Using management information systems to locate people with serious mental illnesses and co-occurring substance use disorders in the criminal justice system for diversion.* Delmar, NY: Author.

National GAINS Center (2002). *The Nathaniel Project: An alternative to incarceration program for people with serious mental illness who have committed felony offenses.* Delmar, NY: Author.

National GAINS Center (2004). *What can we say about the effectiveness of jail diversion programs for persons with co-occurring disorders?* Delmar, NY: Author.

National GAINS Center (2007). *Practical advice on jail diversion: Ten years of learnings on jail diversion from the CMHS National GAINS Center.* Delmar, NY: Author.

New River Valley Community Services (2014). The Bridge Program (Jail Diversion). Retrieved 9-28-14 from http://www.nrvcs.org/bridge/

Policy Research Associates (2007). *Franklin County, Washington: Transforming services for persons with mental illness in contact with the criminal justice system.* Delmar, NY: Author.

Policy Research Associates (2008). *Denver metro area counties: Transforming services for persons with mental illness in contact with the criminal justice system.* Delmar, NY: Author.

Rowe, M., Bellamy, C., Baranoski, M., Wieland, M., O'Connell, M. J., Benedict, P., Davidson, L., Buchanan, J., & Sells, D. (2007). A peer-support, group intervention to reduce substance use and criminality among persons with severe mental illness. *Psychiatric Services, 58,* 955–961.

Shafer, M., Arthur, B., & Franczak, M. (2004). An analysis of post-booking jail diversion programming for persons with co-occurring disorders. *Behavioral Sciences and the Law, 22,* 771–785.

Steadman, H. J., Barbera, S. S., & Dennis, D. L. (1994). A national survey of jail diversion programs for mentally ill detainees. *Hospital and Community Psychiatry, 45,* 1109–1113.

Steadman, H. J., Morris, S. M., & Dennis, D. L. (1995). The diversion of mentally ill persons from jails to community-based services: A profile of programs. *American Journal of Public Health, 85,* 1630–1635.

Steadman, H. J., Cocozza, J. J., & Veysey, B. M. (1999). Comparing outcomes for diverted and nondiverted jail detainees with mental illness. *Law and Human Behavior, 23,* 615–627.

Steadman, H., & Naples, M. (2005). Assessing the effectiveness of jail diversion programs for persons with serious mental illness and co-occurring substance use disorders. *Behavioral Sciences & the Law, 23,* 163–170.

Swanson, R. M., Ghokar, R., & Tolle, L. W. (2011). Arapahoe County Diverts the Mentally Ill to Treatment (ADMIT): A program evaluation. *Corrections & Mental Health: An Update of the National Institute of Corrections, 1,* 1–16.

Tolmie, E. C., Meyers, H. B., & Glesner, T. J. (2010). Windsor County Sparrow Project program evaluation: Final report of year one findings, June 1, 2009–June 30, 2010. Burlington, VT: The University of Vermont, James M. Jeffords Center for Policy Research. Accessed January 21, 2012, from http://www.uvm.edu/~jeffords/reports/pdfs/Windsor%20Sparrow%20Evaluation%20Year%201.pdf.

Tyuse, S. W. (2005). The effectiveness of a jail diversion program in linking participants to federal entitlements and stable housing. *Californian Journal of Health Promotion, 3,* 84–98.

Weisman, R. L., Lamberti, J. S. & Price, N. (2004). Integrating criminal justice, community healthcare, and support services for adults with severe mental disorders. *Psychiatric Quarterly, 75,* 71–85.

5

Intercept 3: Jails and Courts

SIYU LIU AND ALLISON D. REDLICH ■

Let us consider the case of Joe. Joe is a thirty-seven-year-old man with few ties to the community, no chance of employment, substance abuse problems, and a rap sheet as long as his arm. He has been diagnosed with several different mental health disorders ranging from Major Depressive Disorder, Not Otherwise Specified to Bipolar Disorder to Schizoaffective Disorder. Joe sometimes has a place to live and sometimes not. Most recently, Joe was arrested for stealing food from a neighborhood store, which is his fourth arrest for theft. In addition, Joe was belligerent when the police officer tried to handcuff him, and thus he incurred an additional charge of resisting arrest. Although Joe was a candidate for his community's diversion programs at the arrest and prebooking stages, he was not recognized as such. Joe is now at the courthouse door. What will Joe experience from this point forward? What are his options?

In this chapter, our focus is on the third intercept in the Sequential Intercept Model (SIM): jails and courts. This is a crucial intercept given that it is the last opportunity (in this model) to intervene prior to a conviction and possible sentence. In theory, although a large proportion of people with serious mental illness (SMI) can be diverted from standard prosecution at Intercepts 1 and 2 (see Chapters 3 and 4), there remain considerable numbers of individuals with SMI, like Joe, concentrated in our nation's courts and correctional facilities (Diamond, Wang, Thomas, & Cruser, 2001). Among male and female jail inmates, 14.5% and 31%, respectively, are estimated to have SMI (Steadman, Osher, Robbins, Case, & Samuels, 2009). Because people with SMI (especially those who are homeless) have been found to be more likely to spend longer time in confinement on similar charges compared to people without SMI (McNiel, Binder, & Robinson, 2005), community-based interventions become all the more important.

Targeting these considerations, the SIM offers a clear guide for points of intervention. Given the current demographic composition and the mental health condition of people involved in the criminal justice system, an efficient intervention at this step (jail/court) can be a powerful way to keep offenders with SMI from incarceration. Currently, community-based programs in the form of jail diversion and specialty court supervision speak to the needs of this population and have been promoted enthusiastically following the "deinstitutionalization" of offenders with mental illness at both the state and federal levels. The preceding chapter focused on jail diversion programs; in this chapter, we stress the role of problem-solving courts and other relevant community-based options.

Rehabilitation for this population encompasses two broad objectives: (1) treating the mental illness (e.g., mood disorder, anxiety, schizophrenia, possibly accompanied by other diagnoses such as substance use disorders) and (2) adjusting the court order, either through release or a reduced punishment. These are the ideal goals. Numerous factors play vital roles in the rehabilitation of these offenders so they can reenter society with lower chances of recidivism. Thus, the outcome for this population should be considered on both legal and clinical dimensions.

RELEVANT HISTORY

As a person with mental illness involved in the criminal justice system, Joe has several pathways in front of him. Traditionally, there have been four options: (1) treatment as usual, in which Joe would be processed through the system like people who do not have known mental disorders, (2) jail transfer, in which Joe would be sent for a period of time to a secure treatment facility and returned when his symptoms are improved, (3) a plea of not guilty by reason of insanity (NGRI), in which Joe's mental illness would be recognized as having contributed to the commission of the crime by preventing him from knowing right from wrong (and/or, in some jurisdictions, impairing his capacity to conform his conduct to the requirements of the law), and (4) incompetence to stand trial, in which Joe's mental illness would be recognized as contributing to deficits in understanding and appreciating legal decisions (e.g., pleading guilty) and meaningful participation in the legal system. Options 3 and 4 are not mutually exclusive, and certainly Joe could argue that his mental illness contributed to the commission of the crime, as well as lending itself to an unfair and unconstitutional adjudication. In recent years, a fifth option available to persons with mental illness in the justice system has been more formally developed: diversion from incarceration into community mental health treatment.[1] For our purposes, we focus on problem-solving courts: drug treatment courts, community courts, and mental health courts. First, we briefly describe the history of, and problems with, the four traditional options.

Option 1: Treatment as Usual

In a sense, most persons with mental illness are treated like people without mental illnesses at some point along the SIM continuum. Depending upon if and when the mental illness is recognized and on the severity of the illness, people with mental illness may never entertain a mental health defense, may never raise the question of competence, and/or may recognize the futility and low chance of success for either of these options. Treatment as usual can be considered as the "normal" processing of the criminal justice system. At its simplest level, a person is arrested, arraigned, possibly detained in jail, adjudicated, and if found guilty, sentenced to probation, jail, or prison.

In addition to the research that has determined that persons with mental illness are drastically overrepresented in the justice system (in comparison to the general population) (Bradley-Engen, Cuddeback, Morrissey, Gayman & Mancuso, 2010), research has also consistently found that compared to persons without mental illness, those with mental illness are (1) more likely to be arrested, (2) more likely to be detained in jail before trial (as opposed to having their cases dismissed or being released on their own recognizance), and (3) more likely to have lengthier stays in jail and to complete their full sentences. In jail, the potential for behavioral problems is exacerbated in that they may not get the treatment they need. Thus, arguably "treatment as usual" for persons with mental illness may be different than for those without mental illness.

Option 2: Jail Transfer

This option offers the equivalent of emergency mental health treatment in a secure setting in jurisdictions that provide it. For individuals who are experiencing active symptoms of SMI resulting in behavior that is potentially harmful to themselves (e.g., self-mutilation, suicide) or others (e.g., assault), it can be helpful to provide a brief period of hospitalization in a secure setting, particularly when the individual is incarcerated in a jail that has a limited capacity for treatment of those with SMI. Since the treatment goals are more limited than in hospitalization under options 3 or 4, the hospital stay can be briefer. However, this alternative should be viewed as a very limited intervention designed to improve the individual's functioning in the jail rather than as providing a broader, rehabilitative disposition.

Option 3: Insanity Defense

The insanity defense has a long history in U.S. law. Its most recent revision was after John Hinckley Jr. attempted to shoot President Ronald Reagan (see Steadman, McGreevy, Morrissey, Callahan, Robbins, & Cirincione, 1993). To be considered insane under the law, the person must demonstrate that he lacked the capacity to know wrongfulness (and/or, in some jurisdictions, that he cannot meet the additional prong involving conforming conduct to the requirements of the law). This is quite a difficult threshold to meet.

Seminal research conducted in the 1980s found that only about 1% of all tried cases raised an NGRI defense. Within that 1%, only about one quarter were successful (Callahan, Steadman, McGreevy, & Robbins, 1991). The NGRI defense is also believed to be raised only in serious cases, such as homicide. Certainly, the insanity cases highlighted in the media are of this nature, such as the Andrea Yates case. But the perception that a finding of NGRI is only for the most serious cases is a myth (Perlin, 1983). One comprehensive study found that only 13.6% of NGRI crimes involved murder charges (Callahan et al., 1991; see also Cirincione, Steadman, & McGreevy, 1995).

Because the NGRI defense is rarely used, is rarely successful, and does not typically involve the most serious of crimes (and thus the severest punishments), the NGRI defense may not be raised even when warranted. It is likely that most defendants, defense attorneys, and prosecutors would rather negotiate an acceptable plea bargain than play out an insanity defense in the courtroom. For these reasons, the NGRI option is not a prevalent one despite the probability that more individuals meet the requirement than utilize it.

Option 4: Incompetence to Stand Trial

It is unconstitutional to proceed against someone who does not meet the legal standard set in *Dusky v. United States* (1960). An estimated 50,000 to 60,000 persons a year undergo competency evaluations in the United States (Mossman et al., 2007; Poythress, Bonnie, & Oberlander, 1994). However, given the sheer number of persons with SMI arrested annually (an estimated 1 million), it is likely that many more could have questions about their competence raised. So, why do only 5% (50,000/1,000,000) of those who are potentially eligible to have deficits in competence raise the issue? To most, the answer lies in the practice of competency evaluations and restorations. The period of time to evaluate and possibly restore one's competence exceeds the time one would spend in jail (or even in the justice system more generally) in some cases (Pinals, 2005). In the late 1970s and 1980s, competency *evaluations* changed from inpatient to outpatient settings, but competency *restorations* did not (Miller, 2003). Thus, although most states have established outpatient pretrial evaluation systems for court-ordered defendants (Grisso, Cocozza, Steadman, Fisher, & Greer, 1994; Miller, 2003; Pinals, 2005), most states either have no mechanism for community restoration or underutilize it. Miller (2003) surveyed state forensic directors and found that eighteen states require judges to hospitalize persons found incompetent. Thirty-two states permit outpatient restoration, but of these states, half reported that outpatient restoration was not done and another eleven reported that 5% or fewer restorations were done in the community.

In summary, the traditional options available to Joe and those like him are each problematic in some important respects. Treatment as usual does not (sufficiently) take into account mental illness and all of the accompanying considerations (e.g., medications and treatment in jail, behavioral problems). Jail transfer, even if available, offers only a short-term solution to larger rehabilitative needs.

The insanity defense has a difficult-to-meet standard, is rarely successful, and is time-consuming. Raising issues of competence is also time-consuming, particularly when contrasted against probable outcomes of time served.

Today, depending on the community in which Joe resides, he has another viable option: diversion. Although diversion programs such as problem-solving courts were in part intended to overcome some of the problems with treatment as usual in the criminal justice system, to our knowledge, no one has suggested that diversion programs were intended to supplant the options of jail transfer, NGRI, and incompetence. This is an open, empirical question, however. In theory, criminal justice diversion for persons with mental illness should be considered separate and apart from these traditional mechanisms. That is, someone who was insane at the time of the crime and someone who lacks the understanding and appreciation to meaningfully participate in his or her case theoretically should not be in a drug treatment court, community court, or mental health court. Nevertheless, because of the shortcomings and ineffectiveness of the traditional pathways, it is not unfathomable that diversion is used as an option in lieu of the others.

RELEVANT LITERATURE

Formal diversion programs for persons with mental illness are growing in popularity, number, and governmental support. The President's New Freedom Commission on Mental Health recommended "widely adopting adult criminal justice and juvenile justice diversion . . . strategies to avoid the unnecessary criminalization and extended incarceration of non-violent adult and juvenile offenders with mental illness" (2003, pp. 43–44). As such, community-based approaches in the sentencing phase have been developed on a nationwide scale in the past two decades. One prominent form is the problem-solving court. The discussion in this chapter will center around three types of problem-solving courts that deal with persons with mental illness—drug treatment court, community court, and mental health court—to describe how community-based alternatives can be practicable outcomes for people with SMI involved in the criminal justice system.

Drug Treatment Courts

After many decades of traditional criminal courts being burdened by the overwhelming number of drug-related cases and being characterized as a "revolving door" for drug offenders, in 1989 the nation established its first drug treatment court in Miami, Florida. Since that time, nearly 2,500 additional drug courts have been established (Berman & Feinblatt, 2001; Huddleston & Marlowe, 2011; Senjo & Leip, 2001; see Fig. 5.1). Drug treatment courts represent a symbol of therapeutic jurisprudence, becoming an important part of the American

Figure 5.1 Drug Courts and Problem-Solving Courts in the United States (December 2009).

SOURCE: Huddleston, C. W., & Marlowe, D. B. (2011). *Painting the current picture: A national report on drug courts and other problem-solving court programs in the United States.* Alexandria, VA: National Drug Court Institute. Retrieved Sept. 21, 2012, from http://www.ojp.usdoj.gov/BJA/pdf/12902_PCP_fnl.pdf.

criminal justice system (Belenko, 2001); they are also considered to be the most significant criminal justice initiative in the twentieth century (Brown, 2011). They target the addiction and provide treatment services to offenders in addition to the judicial supervision (Huddleston & Marlowe, 2011). They are regarded as a "combined systems" approach for offenders due to the team effort involved in the resources from the district attorney's office, the public defender's office, and probation and service treatment professionals under the unified command of the judge (Finigan, Carey, & Cox, 2007). Considerable variation exists in the specific procedure used, but in general they closely monitor the defendant/participant's progress, conduct drug testing, and provide a range of treatment options for twelve to eighteen months until graduation (GAO, 2005; Senjo & Leip, 2001).

High-quality empirical research is needed to assess the long-term performance of treatment programs. A comprehensive review was prepared by the National Center on Addiction and Substance Abuse (CASA) at Columbia University, which included thirty-seven published and unpublished evaluations of drug treatment courts between 1999 and 2001 (Belenko, 2001). Compared to the previous reviews in the series conducted by the same author (in 1998 and 1999), the conclusions were consistent that these programs have ample support from the community and the government, offer stable long-term service provision, and average a 47% graduation rate. Participants were observed to have reduced criminal activity and drug use while in the program. However, most of the studies did not report long-term effects. Based on the studies covering thirty-six drug treatment courts in the country, Belenko (2001) reported that four of the six studies that examined recidivism rates after the program found a reduction, but its size varied. Surprisingly, none of the studies investigated drug use, employment, or other outcomes after program participation that would be important to evaluate to understand the long-term effects. Furthermore, although Belenko found mental health services to be emphasized in the goals of drug treatment courts, data on the services—both description and delivery—were almost nonexistent in the evaluation research.

In another report on the economic analysis of drug treatment courts, Belenko, Patapis, and French (2005) reviewed more than one hundred relevant studies and illustrated how investing modestly in substance abuse treatment would benefit society substantially. Even though these courts provide more intensive monitoring and services and more frequent supervision and court appearances, and are thus more expensive to operate than standard court processing, they produce net economic benefits in the form of reduced recidivism. Current adult drug treatment courts are estimated to produce about $2.21 in benefit for each $1 in costs, resulting in a net benefit of around $624 million (Bhati, Roman, & Chalfin, 2008).

From the above general reviews of effectiveness and cost analyses, the performance of drug treatment courts seems promising. However, the design of these evaluative studies has been called into question. For example, Merrall and Bird (2009) presented a statistical review on five studies of drug treatment courts with a detailed discussion on randomization: Only one had adequately described the randomization method used. Randomization in the criminal justice field has been a debated subject due to the context, which is quite distinct from medical and pharmaceutical ones (see review by Farrington & Welsh, 2006). Inadequate information about the prior crime history and drug use history between the treatment and control groups, vagueness on primary outcome, and inconsistent measurement of the outcome variable between groups are important methodological issues that have been cited as problematic (Merrall & Bird, 2009).

In summary, the current evaluative literature on the performance of drug treatment courts has been largely promising, with positive and significant results (for an overview, see Belenko, 2001), although it has also been critiqued for its lack of rigor. The model pioneered by the drug treatment courts has also been recommended for adaptation into other problem-solving courts, particularly for its community-based treatment and employment services (Sanford & Arrigo, 2005).

Community Courts

Building upon the philosophy of the drug treatment courts and the central theme of the "broken windows" theory, the community court began in 1993 in midtown Manhattan, targeting "quality of life" crimes (Hakuta, Soroushian, &

Kralstein, 2008; Malkin, 2003). Subsequently about 52 community courts were created across the world (including 32 in the United States), and another twenty-seven were planned by the year 2007 (Karafin, 2008; Fig. 5.2). However, according to Huddleston and Marlowe (2011), only twenty-five such courts were in existence as of year-end 2009, about a 20% reduction from two years prior. Aimed at low-level crimes with small court dockets, community courts take advantage of neighborhood collective efforts in identifying the defendant's underlying problems and reducing the likelihood of future offending by finding the cause of the illegal behaviors, such as substance abuse, mental illness, or lack of social resources (Karafin, 2008). The various alternatives in sentencing are also preferred in community courts; these include substance abuse treatment and community service mandates (Frazer, 2006). A new direction has emerged in some community courts (e.g., Portland, OR, and Memphis, TN), involving the innovative practices of holding court hearings at local community centers and targeting particular social issues (e.g., abandoned and neglected property)

Figure 5.2 Community Courts in the United States (end 2007).

Reprinted from Karafin, D. L. (2008). *Community courts across the globe: A survey of goals, performance, measures, and operations.* New York: Center for Court Innovations, with kind permission from the Open Society Foundation. Retrieved Sept. 20, 2011, from http://osf.org.za/wp/wp-content/uploads/2012/09/Community-Courts-Across-the-Gl obe-A-survey-of-goals-performance-measures-and-operations1.pdf.

(Berman & Feinblatt, 2001). A key characteristic of the community court setting is the "lack of specialization." This has been viewed as an advantage over
other specialized courts (Dorf & Fagan, 2003). The problem of the offender is
considered globally rather than in a way that is focused only on behavioral health
problems (e.g., substance abuse) and criminal conduct.

Unlike drug treatment courts, community courts have not been systematically
examined. The Red Hook Community Justice Center stands out as an exemplary
model and has been promoted and adopted in other countries like the United
Kingdom.[2] Established in 2000 in southwest Brooklyn, the Red Hook court
receives hundreds of participants each year, and the judge reviews thirty-five to
forty lower-level criminal cases per day (Frazer, 2006). This court model is considered to be successful because of the priority placed on integrating community
participation into local issues and courtroom operations: The judge becomes
a significant figure in the community (Malkin, 2003). Because it is located in
the community, the Red Hook court gives service providers easy access to the
courtroom and presents them with current issues and conditions in the community. As the SIM has clearly demonstrated, community-based linkage to the
legal process serves a key role in the offender rehabilitation process. A study on
defendants' perceptions of the Red Hook court has shown that providing them
with proper drug treatment has had a positive effect on opinion of the judge
and indirectly on the perception of fairness (Frazer, 2006). In the same study,
when the Red Hook court was compared to a traditional court, the community court was found to provide more interpersonal support and other assistance
in related life issues (e.g., health insurance and lack of job training). Although
clearly promising, more research on community courts is needed before their
adoption is expanded.

Mental Health Courts

Stemming also from therapeutic jurisprudence, a relatively new but promising court innovation, mental health courts, has developed rapidly (Fig. 5.3).
Targeting a specific proportion of the court dockets—persons with mental
health problems—these are criminal courts aimed at diverting defendants from
jails and prisons into community-based mental health treatment, followed by
court monitoring and possible sanctions for noncompliance (Redlich, Steadman,
Monahan, Robbins, & Petrila, 2006; Steadman, Davidson, & Brown, 2001).

Similar to drug treatment courts, the mental health court atmosphere is characterized as less adversarial between courtroom actors, with the defendant playing a rather significant role (Boothroyd, Poythress, McGaha, & Petrila, 2003).
The variety of solutions the court offers may be the advantage of its function,
fitting into the general criminal justice system for those who have these needs.
It also requires the defendant to willingly participate in the program. Further,
the court itself and the communities under its jurisdiction monitor closely the
client's performance, with rewards and sanctions for (non)compliance. For those

Figure 5.3 Mental Health Courts in the United States (2006).

From Redlich, A. D., Steadman, H. J., Monahan, J., Robbins, P. C., & Petrila, J. Patterns of practice in mental health courts: A national survey. *Law and Human Behavior, 30,* 347–362. (2006) American Psychological Association. Reprinted with permission.

who graduate from mental health court, the initial charges may be dropped or reduced or the conviction vacated. Sanctions are also available in cases of non-adherence, but how often they are invoked varies (see, e.g., Callahan, Steadman, Tillman, & Vesselinov, 2012; Griffin, Steadman, & Petrila, 2002; Redlich, Steadman, Monahan, Petrila, & Griffin, 2005).

Considering how new they are, mental health courts have attracted more intensive research attention than other forms of problem-solving courts, although research still lags far behind the research on drug treatment courts. A recent comprehensive study (Steadman, Redlich, Callahan, Robbins, & Vesslinov, 2011) has revealed that across four courts (San Francisco County, CA; Santa Clara County, CA; Hennepin County, MN; and Marion County, IN), mental health court participants had lower rearrest rates, fewer rearrests after eighteen months, and fewer reincarceration days after eighteen months compared to "treatment as usual" participants (a group of similarly situated defendants with mental illness who did not go through the mental health court). Other studies have arrived at similar conclusions for the effectiveness of mental health courts (McNiel & Binder, 2007; Moore & Hiday, 2006; Sarteschi, Vaughn, & Kim, 2010). These studies also echo the results from drug treatment courts that the treated groups are less likely to recidivate.

Similar to other problem-solving courts, there are concerns related to procedural protections (Miller & Pereman, 2009), including lack of formal procedure guidance, coercion, procedural right violations, and process efficiency. Studies have investigated the issue of possible coercion and involuntary treatment (Redlich, 2005). Redlich and colleagues (2010) examined 200 newly enrolled clients of two mental health courts for their levels of knowingness and legal competence. Consistent with findings from the Broward court (Poythress, Petrila, McGaha, & Boothroyd, 2002), a majority of the clients reported having chosen to participate in the mental health court programs. Yet Redlich and colleagues (2010) also reported indications that these decisions were not made knowingly, intelligently, and/or voluntarily (e.g., some clients have claimed they were not informed, erred on knowledge questions on the court, or did not know they had a choice to enroll or not enroll in the mental health court). Some clients (around 40%) also demonstrated impaired adjudicative competence, which indicates that a sizable minority may not have understood and appreciated pleading guilty and/or the requirements, procedures, and possible consequences of being in the court.

Another concern regarding the operations of these courts lies in their processing efficiency. New research (Redlich, Liu, Steadman, Callahan, & Robbins, 2012) has examined the swiftness of the diversion process, comparing mental health courts with traditional courts. A nationally representative sample of general defendants was found to have a median length of seventy-six days from initial arrest to disposition. However, data from three mental health courts pointed to a median length of seventy days. A matched sample of offenders with SMI collected from the same counties produced a median length of thirty-seven days. Thus, these findings do not support the swift diversion process that was intended at the founding of mental health courts (see also McNiel & Binder, 2007). The authors postulated that the delay might have resulted from assessment issues and community placement.

In summary, mental health courts appear to have promise in reducing recidivism among a population known to cycle in and out of the criminal justice system. Nonetheless, issues surrounding due process, swiftness in processing, and coercion need to be resolved in these nascent courts.

CURRENT OPERATIONAL STATE OF SIM-GUIDED
DECISION MAKING AND PLANNING

An appropriate next question is whether these three types of problem-solving courts operate using "evidence-based practice." Is there sufficient evidence to recommend general and broad adoption of these courts? We will categorize them using four groups: best practice (empirical research support, theoretical and practical support); promising practice (limited empirical research support, theoretical and practical support); unsupported practice (no empirical evidence one way or another; theoretical or practical support mixed, limited, or nonexistent); and contraindicated practice (empirical research reflects ineffective or even harmful outcomes; theoretical and practical evidence includes ineffective or even harmful outcomes).

There is evidence that drug treatment courts can decrease recidivism rates. However, many of the evaluative studies have been criticized, and thus we do not feel comfortable labeling them as a best practice; rather, we consider them a promising practice. Although some would disagree with this categorization, we believe more and better research is needed. Wilson, Mitchell, and MacKenzie (2006) conducted a comprehensive meta-analysis of drug court studies that included a comparison group and an outcome related to criminal activity. Overall, they noted a 14% to 26% reduction in recidivism favoring the drug treatment courts but ultimately concluded the following:

> It is unfortunate that this large collection of studies leads to an equivocal statement on the effectiveness of drug courts. This equivocation is due to the generally weak nature of the research designs. Only five of the 55 drug court-comparison contrasts were constructed using random assignment methods, and two of these contrasts were seriously degraded. Roughly half the quasi-experimental designs made no attempt to statistically control for differences between drug court and comparison participants. A common comparison group, offenders who declined participation, may have a bias favoring the drug court condition. (p. 479)

Although there are other indicators of success beyond recidivism, they have been less researched, which also supports our tentative rating.

In regard to community courts, there is little to no research, and thus we categorize them as an unsupported practice. Although they do not appear to be as prevalent or controversial as other problem-solving courts, nevertheless a significant amount of research is needed before they expand further. Research could follow much of the same paths of the research done on drug treatment courts and mental health courts, though with careful attention paid to lessons learned and critiques put forth.

Like drug treatment courts, the research on mental health courts has been more plentiful, but the results are also equivocal. To be sure, there is consistent evidence that mental health courts do decrease rearrest rates and number of jail days in comparison to treatment as usual. However, some could argue that the evidence is less than robust and that other important outcomes, such as access to and engagement in treatment, are lacking or unclear. Further, research on issues such as voluntariness, competence, and speed of processing demonstrates that these courts, while attempting to improve the lives of offenders with SMI, can ignore other important issues. Thus, we also label mental health courts as a promising practice.

IMPLICATIONS

Let us return to the example case of Joe. Given that Joe has mental health, substance abuse, and homelessness problems, he is likely to be eligible for any of these three problem-solving courts. We do not know enough about Joe to determine which will be most effective, or even if treatment as usual is the best course for him (although we suspect not). In this section, we address the implications for research, policy, and practice that community-based interventions—in our case, problem-solving courts—have for Joe and similar others.

The five options in front of Joe are treatment as usual, jail transfer, raising an insanity defense, raising issues of competence, and diversion. As reviewed above, generally problem-solving courts (particularly drug treatment courts and mental health courts) are viewed as better options than treatment as usual (in that recidivism is reduced, access to treatment is increased). Indeed, a major impetus for the creation of these courts was the recognition that traditional processing was simply not effective for offenders with mental illness (leading to such labels as "frequent flyers" and "revolving door"). An important research, policy, and practical question to pose and address, however, is whether problem-solving courts are being used in lieu of insanity defenses and as backdoors to override competence.

To exemplify these concerns, we describe the contents of a video a mental health court created in 2004 as a promotional tool to describe their court and the successes they had reducing in the criminal behaviors of offenders with mental illness. The video, which lasts 8 minutes and 50 seconds, portrays the case of Steve (name changed). Steve was diagnosed with a developmental disability (not a typical mental health court case, but also not unusual) and had cerebral palsy and behavioral health issues (e.g., depression). He had been charged with his third felony car theft and was reported to have been coerced into committing crimes by fellow gang members. In the video, Steve's public defender said, "We really felt that Steve was being used to commit criminal offenses and that he wasn't fully aware of the extent of what he was doing or why he was doing it for these other individuals." In addition, the public defender said, "Steve clearly didn't understand why he was here and what these proceedings were all about." In this video, it was suggested that Steve lacked awareness of the wrongfulness of his behavior at the time of the crime and that he was not competent to be adjudicated, but yet Steve was presented as an ideal mental health court candidate. Of course, whether Steve would have meet the difficult-to-meet threshold for either NGRI or incompetence to stand trial is unknown, but clearly within the span of this brief documentary the notion of both was raised, although not as problems.

There are several questions generated from this brief example, including whether offenders eligible for problem-solving courts are the "same" people who can claim legitimate consideration for insanity and incompetence. Although we have begun to chip away at how problem-solving courts fare in comparison to traditional justice processing (i.e., treatment as usual), researchers should also attempt to understand how these newer courts affect other court procedures, defenses, and legal policies.

Additionally, the creation of problem-solving courts did not appear to be accompanied by a contemporaneous discussion of legal policy. As such, legal policy questions abound, such as attention to due process and other constitutional rights, equality in referral and acceptance practices, and the questions raised above about insanity and competence. Berman and Feinblatt (2001) offer some answers for frequently asked questions about the position and function of problem-solving courts as an important intervention in the criminal justice process for people with special needs. They emphasize the reasonable concerns over issues during the development of problem-solving courts such as coercion, measurement of counsel effectiveness, power of the judges, impartiality, paternalism, and the blurry line in regard to separation of governmental power. The authors regard this current condition as a sign of adaptation and a catalyst of model court settings. They also clarify that the "team approach" is the key feature that problem-solving courts should preserve. A critical view on this approach is the tendency for due process of law to be violated because of the near absence of an adversarial tone (Dorf & Fagan, 2003). Berman and Feinblatt (2001) argue that due process protection is emphasized even though the adversarial setting is not present inside a courtroom. However, they acknowledge the tension existing between the conventional court and the problem-solving court, felt more strongly by defense counsel.

To conclude, for offenders with mental illness, the time of entry into the correctional and court systems is a key intercept. Although prior interventions at Intercepts 1 and 2 would be preferable, at Intercept 3, the path into a complex and often convoluted system looms large and the possibility of exiting unscathed is low. Community-based alternatives, like drug treatment, community, and mental health courts, are viable options if and when available in the jurisdiction. While it is generally accepted that these courts are "better" for offenders with mental health problems than shuttling through the traditional system, many unanswered and important questions remain.

NOTES

1. Diversion on a case-by-case basis has certainly always been an option. However, over the past two decades, formal diversion programs have been developed (see Steadman, Morris, & Dennis, 1995) with specific eligibility criteria and operating procedures.
2. *UK's Justice Secretary Visits Red Hook* (http://www.courtinnovation.org/research/uk%E2%80%99s-justice-secretary-visits-red-hook?url=research%2F4%2Farticle&mode=4&type=article); *British Government Plans Wider Application of Community Justice* (http://www.courtinnovation.org/research/british-government-plans-wider-application-community-justice?url=research%2F4%2Farticle&mode=4&type=article).

REFERENCES

Belenko, S. (2001). *Research on Drug Courts: A critical review 2001 update.* New York: The National Center on Addiction and Substance Abuse (CASA) at Columbia University. Retrieved Sept. 1, 2011, from http://www.drugpolicy.org/docUploads/2001drugcourts.pdf.

Belenko, S., Patapis, N., & French, M. T. (2005). *Economic benefits of drug treatment: A critical review of the evidence for policy makers.* University of Pennsylvania Treatment Research Institute. Retrieved Sept. 12, 2011, from http://www.tresearch. org/resources/specials/2005Feb_EconomicBenefits.pdf.

Berman, G., & Feinblatt, J. (2001). Problem-solving courts: A brief primer. *Law & Policy, 23*(2), 125–140.

Bhati, A. S., Roman, J. K., & Chalfin, A. (2008). *To treat or not to treat: Evidence on the prospects of expanding treatment to drug-invovled offenders.* Washington, D.C.: Urban Institute, Justice Policy Center. Retrieved Sept. 11, 2011, from http:// www.urban.org/UploadedPDF/411645_treatment_offenders.pdf.

Boothroyd, R. A., Poythress, N. G., McGaha, A., & Petrila, J. (2003). The Broward mental health court: Process, outcomes, and service utilization. *International Journal of Law and Psychiatry, 26,* 55–71.

Bradley-Engen, M. S., Cuddeback, G. S., Gayman, M. D., Morrissey, J. P., & Mancuso, D. (2010). Trends in state prison admission offenders with serious mental illness. *Psychiatric Services, 61*(12), 1263–1265.

Brown, R. (2011). Drug court effectiveness: A matched cohort study in the Dane county drug treatment court. *Journal of Offender Rehabilitation, 50,* 191–201.

Callahan, L. A., Steadman, H. J., McGreevy, M. A., & Robbins, P. C. (1991). The volume and characteristics of insanity defense pleas: An eight-state study. *Bulletin of the American Academy of Psychiatry and the Law, 19,* 331–338.

Callahan, L. A., Steadman, H. J., Tillman, S., & Vesselinov, R. (2012). A multi-site study of the use of sanctions and incentives in mental health courts. *Law and Human Behavior.* Advance online first publication, doi:10.1037/h0093989

Cirincione, C., Steadman, H. J., & McGreevy, M. A. (1995). Rates of insanity acquittals and the factors associated with successful insanity pleas. *Bulletin of the American Academy of Psychiatry and the Law, 23,* 399–409.

Diamond, P. M., Wang, E. W., Holzer, C. E., III, Thomas, C., & Cruser, D. A. (2001). The prevalence of mental illness in prison. *Administration and Policy in Mental Health, 29*(1), 21–40.

Dorf, M. C., & Fagan, J. A. (2003). Community courts and community justice. *American Criminal Law Review, 40*(4), 1501–1511.

Dusky v. United States, 362 U.S. 402 (1960).

Farrington, D. P., & Welsh, B. C. (2006). A half century of randomized experiments on crime and justice. *Crime and Justice, 35,* 55–132.

Finigan, M. W., Carey, S. M., & Cox, A. (2007). *The impact of a mature drug court over 10 years of operation: Recidivism and costs—Final report.* Portland, OR: NPC Research. Available at https://www.ncjrs.gov/pdffiles1/nij/grants/219224.pdf.

Frazer, M. S. (2006). *The impact of the community court model on defendent perceptions of fairness—A case study at the Red Hook Community Justice Center.* New York: Center for Court Innovation. Retrieved Aug. 12, 2011, from http://www. courtinnovation.org/sites/default/files/Procedural_Fairness.pdf.

Government Accountability Office (GAO). 2005. *Adult drug courts: Evidence indicates recidivism reductions and mixed results for other outcomes.* Report to Congressional Committees (GAO-05-219). Retrieved Sept. 3, 2011, from http://www.gao.gov/new. items/d05219.pdf.

Griffin, P. A., Steadman, H. J., & Petrila, J. (2002). The use of criminal charges and sanctions in mental health courts. *Psychiatric Services, 53*(10), 1285–1289.

Grisso, T., Cocozza, J. J., Steadman, H. J., Fisher, W. H., & Greer, A. (1994). The organization of pretrial forensic evaluation services. *Law and Human Behavior, 18*(4), 377–393.

Hakuta, J., Soroushian, V., & Kralstein, D. (2008). *Do community courts transform the justice response to misdemeanor crime?* New York: Center for Court Innovation. Retrieved Sept. 3, 2011, from http://www.courtinnovation.org/sites/default/files/ Midtown_Downtown.pdf.

Huddleston, C. W., & Marlowe, D. B. (2011). *Painting the current picture: A national report on drug courts and other problem-solving court programs in the United States.* Alexandria, VA: National Drug Court Institute. Retrieved Sept. 21, 2012, from http://www.ojp.usdoj.gov/BJA/pdf/12902_PCP_fnl.pdf.

Karafin, D. L. (2008). *Community courts across the globe: A survey of goals, performance, measures, and operations.* New York: Center for Court Innovations. Retrieved Sept. 20, 2011, from http://osf.org.za/wp/wp-content/uploads/2012/09/ Community-Courts-Across-the-Globe-A-survey-of-goals-performance-measures-an d-operations1.pdf.

Malkin, V. (2003). Communicty courts and the process of accountability: Consensus and conflict at the Red Hook Community Justice Center. *The American Criminal Law Review, 40*(4), 1573–1593.

McNiel, D. E., & Binder, R. (2007). Effectiveness of a mental health court in reducing criminal recidivism and violence. *American Journal of Psychiatry, 164*(9), 1395–1403.

McNiel, D. E., Binder, R. L., & Robinson, J. C. (2005). Incarceration associated with homelessness, mental disorder, and co-occurring substance abuse. *Psychiatric Services, 56*(7), 840–846.

Merrall, E. L. C., & Bird, S. M. (2009). A statistical perspective on the design of drug-court studies. *Evaluation Review, 33*, 257–280.

Miller, R. D. (2003). Hospitalization of criminal defendants for evaluation of competence to stand trial or for restoration of competence: Clinical and legal issues. *Behavioral Sciences & the Law, 21*(3), 369–391.

Miller, S. L., & Pereman, A. M. (2009). Mental health courts: An overview and redefinition of tasks and goals. *Law and Psychology Review, 33*, 111–123.

Moore, M. E., & Hiday, V. A. (2006). Mental health court outcomes: A comparison of re-arrest and re-arrest severity betweeen mental health court and traditional court participants. *Law and Human Behavior, 30*, 659–674.

Mossman, D., Noffsinger, S. G., Ash, P., Frierson, R. L., Gerbasi, J., Hackett, M., Lewis, C F., Pinals, D. A., Scott, C. L., Sieg, K. G., Wall, B. W., & Zonana, H. V. (2007). AAPL practice guideline for the forensic psychiatric evaluation of competence to stand trial. *Journal of the American Academy of Psychiatry and Law, 35*(Suppl.), S3–S72.

Perlin, M. L. (1983). Whose plea is it anyway? Insanity defense myths and realities. *Philadelphia Medicine, 79*, 5–10.

Pinals, D. A. (2005). Where two roads meet: Restoration of competence to stand trial from a clinical perspective. *New England School of Law, 31*(1), 81–108.

Poythress, N. G., Bonnie, R. J., & Oberlander, L. B. (1994). Client abilities to assist counsel and make decisions in criminal cases. *Law and Human Behavior, 18*(4), 437–452.

Poythress, N., Petrila, J., McGaha, A., & Boothroyd, R. (2002). Perceived coercion and procedural justice in the Broward County Mental Health Court. *International Journal of Law and Psychiatry, 25,* 517–533.

President's New Freedom Commission on Mental Health (2003). *Achieving the promise: Transforming mental health care in America.* Available at http://www.mental-healthcommission.gov/reports/FinalReport/toc.html.

Redlich, A., Liu, S., Steadman, H., Callahan, L., & Robbins, P. C. (2012). Is diversion swift? Comparing mental health court and traditional criminal justice processing. *Criminal Justice and Behavior, 39*(4), 420–433.

Redlich, A. D. (2005). Voluntary, but knowing and intelligent? Comprehension in mental health courts. *Psychology, Public Policy, and Law, 11*(4), 605–619.

Redlich, A. D., Hoover, S., Summers, A., & Steadman, H. J. (2010). Enrollment in mental health courts: Voluntariness, knowingness, and adjudicative competence. *Law and Human Behavior, 34,* 91–104.

Redlich, A. D., Steadman, H. J., Monahan, J., Petrila, J., & Griffin, P. A. (2005). The second generation of mental health courts. *Psychology, Public Policy, and Law, 11*(4), 527–538.

Redlich, A. D., Steadman, H. J., Monahan, J., Robbins, P. C., & Petrila, J. (2006). Patterns of practice in mental health courts: A national survey. *Law and Human Behavior, 30,* 347–362.

Sanford, J. S., & Arrigo, B. A. (2005). Lifting the cover on drug courts: Evaluation findings and policy concerns. *International Journal of Offender Therapy and Comparative Criminology, 49*(3), 239–259.

Sarteschi, C. M., Vaughn, M. G., & Kim, K. (2010). Assessing the effectiveness of mental health courts: A quantitative review. *Journal of Criminal Justice, 39,* 12–20.

Senjo, S., & Leip, L. A. (2001). Testing therapeutic jurisprudence theory: An empirical assessment of the drug court process. *Western Criminology Review, 3*(1), [online]. Retrieved Sept. 3, 2011, from http://wcr.sonoma.edu/v3n1/senjo.html.

Steadman, H. J., Davidson, S., & Brown, C. (2001). Mental health courts: Their promise and unanswered questions. *Psychiatric Services, 52*(4), 457–458.

Steadman, H. J., McGreevy, M., Morrissey, J., Callahan, L., Robbins, P. C., & Cirincione, C. (1993). *Before and after Hinckley: Evaluating insanity defense reform.* Guilford Press.

Steadman, H. J., Morris, S. M., & Dennis, D. L. (1995). The diversion of mentally ill persons from jails to community-based services: a profile of programs. *American Journal of Public Health, 85*(12), 1630–1635.

Steadman, H. J., Osher, F., Robbins, P. C., Case, B., & Samuels, S. (2009). Prevalence of serious mental illness among jail inmates. *Psychiatric Services, 60,* 761–765.

Steadman, H. J., Redlich, A., Callahan, L., Robbins, P. C., & Vesslinov, R. (2011). Effect of mental health courts on arrests and jail days. *Archives of General Psychiatry, 68*(2), 162–172.

Wilson, D. B., Mitchell, O., & MacKenzie, D. L. (2006). A systematic review of drug court effects on recidivism. *Journal of Experimental Criminology, 2,* 459–487.

6

Intercept 4: Reentry from Jails and Prisons

FRED OSHER AND CHRISTOPHER KING ■

Persons with mental illnesses are vastly overrepresented in the criminal justice system, from arrest to reentry. Researchers have documented serious mental illnesses in 14.5% of male jail inmates and 31% of female jail inmates (Steadman, Osher, Robbins, Case, & Samuels, 2009), rates in excess of three to six times those found in the general population (Kessler et al., 1996). Generalized to the finding that over 13 million jail admissions were reported in 2009 (Minton, 2010), this suggests that over 2 million bookings of persons with serious mental illnesses occur annually. The presence of so many people with mental illnesses in criminal justice settings represents an enormous burden on federal and state corrections, behavioral health systems of care, communities, families, and those with mental illnesses. Multiple factors contribute to this phenomenon, but none is more salient than the high rates of recidivism following release from jail and prison (Pew Center on the States, 2011).

For individuals with mental illnesses, contact with the criminal justice system often starts a cycle of arrest, incarceration, release, and rearrest that can pose nearly insurmountable challenges to recovery. With more serious charges, or failure to comply with conditions of probation and parole, prisons become the institutional homes for these individuals. However, most criminal justice personnel agree with community-based treatment providers that jail and prison environments are poor settings for individuals with mental illnesses.

The incarceration of high numbers of persons with mental illnesses is taking place in the context of expanding incarcerated populations in general. Over the past 25 years, the nation's prison and jail population has skyrocketed to an all-time high, with over 2 million people incarcerated and over 5 million on some form of correctional supervision. Between 1973 and 2009, the nation's prison population grew by 705%, resulting in the United States reaching the dubious landmark of having over one in every 100 adults in the nation behind bars (Pew Center, 2008). The United States has just 5% of the world's population but accounts for 23% of the world's prisoners (Pew Center, 2008). Despite some decrease in the rate of incarceration in the United States in the past three years, the overall rate of about 500 per 100,000 population is well above the rate of approximately 100 per 100,000 in countries comparable to the United States (Bureau of Justice Statistics, 2012).

Beyond the human costs associated with such a state of affairs, correctional spending has soared over the past 20 years to keep pace with rising prison populations. Annual state spending on corrections has grown 137% and is now over $50 billion (National Association of State Budget Officers, 2009). Only Medicaid has grown faster than corrections as a proportion of state spending (National Association of State Budget Officers, 2009). Reducing the number of persons with mental illnesses under correctional supervision would reduce costs at a time when state and local revenues are severely restricted.

As striking as the above statistics are, the underlying factors associated with high rates of incarceration are equally stark. More than four in ten prisoners are returned to state prisons in the three years following their release (Pew Center, 2011), and having a mental illness is associated with higher recidivism rates than those in released individuals without a mental illness (Baillargeon, Binswanger, Penn, Williams, & Murray, 2009; Messina, Burdon, Hagopian, & Prendergast, 2004). With respect to high rates of recidivism among persons with mental illnesses, as will be discussed, this seems attributable in large part to concomitant individual and contextual factors rather than mental illness symptoms per se.

This chapter will focus on the challenges to successful reentry from correctional settings for offenders with mental illnesses and/or co-occurring substance use disorders. Reentry has been defined as "the process by which a former inmate returns to the community and hopefully transitions into a law-abiding citizen" (Turner & Petersilia, 2012). This definition can be extended to individuals with mental illnesses by appending the additional process of successful illness management and recovery upon return to the community. The Sequential Intercept Model (Munetz & Griffin, 2006) has conceived of reentry as the fourth intercept point along a five-point continuum. Due in part to the sobering state of affairs summarized above, and in realization of the fact that 93% of offenders are eventually released back to the community (in 2008, approximately 12.7 million jail and prison inmates), reentry (and by extension Intercept 4) has received perhaps the most attention of all the intercept points in recent years in the public sphere (Turner & Petersilia, 2012).

The distinction between jails and prisons in the context of reentry is significant. Jails, unlike prisons, hold detained individuals who are awaiting court hearings and disposition of charges, as well as people serving short sentences. Shorter stays create a churning effect in which inmates are constantly coming and going, and the unpredictable nature of jail discharges can make reentry particularly challenging (Griffin, 1990). In contrast, prisons exclusively house inmates serving longer sentences; thus, the process of reentry can be more easily anticipated and thoughtfully designed.

Petersilia (2004) noted that two strands characterize the general reentry literature: one focuses on general principles, the other on program evaluations. The
same appears true for the reentry literature specific to individuals with mental
illnesses. Various models have been proposed to help conceptualize the reentry
process for offenders with mental illnesses and to guide service delivery (Draine
& Herman, 2007; Draine, Wolff, Jacoby, Hartwell, & Duclos, 2005; Osher,
Steadman, & Barr, 2003; Prins & Osher, 2009; Vogel, Noether, & Steadman,
2007). The more general Risk–Need–Responsivity (RNR) model of offender
assessment and treatment (Andrews & Bonta, 2010) is also of considerable value
and provides a theoretical framework for prioritizing supervision and services
(King, Brooks Holliday, & Heilbrun, 2013; Osher, D'Amora, Plotkin, Jarrett, &
Eggleston, 2012). Meanwhile, evidence from program evaluations is also beginning to accrue (Heilbrun et al., 2012). We describe both principles/models and
program outcomes in the sections that follow.

GENERAL PRINCIPLES OF EFFECTIVE OFFENDER
REHABILITATION AND THEIR APPLICATION TO
OFFENDERS WITH MENTAL ILLNESSES

The RNR Model

The RNR model asserts that the greatest reductions in criminal recidivism
result from the delivery of individually tailored (specific responsivity principle),
cognitive-behavioral or social-learning interventions (general responsivity principle) to higher-risk offenders (risk principle) that target modifiable offender
characteristics associated with the likelihood to recidivate (need principle). Risk
assessment for recidivism is a composite of static factors (e.g., current age, age
at first arrest, gender) that are immutable and dynamic factors (e.g., substance
abuse, antisocial cognitions) that can be affected by targeted interventions. These
dynamic risk factors that are directly linked to criminal behavior are termed
criminogenic needs. Researchers have identified seven central dynamic risk factors that predict recidivism among individuals under supervision: antisocial personality pattern, procriminal attitudes, antisocial associates, poor use of leisure
time, substance abuse, problematic marital or family circumstances, and problematic circumstances at school or work (Andrews & Bonta, 2010). Validated
risk assessment tools are effective in classifying justice-involved cohorts along a
low- to high-risk continuum.

The RNR model has been validated by meta-analyses for a variety of offender
populations (Andrews, 2012; Andrews & Bonta, 2010; Dowden & Andrews, 1999,
2000; Hanson, Bourgon, Helmus, & Hodgson, 2009; Lipsey, 2009) and is utilized increasingly in the reentry context (Serin, Lloyd, & Hanby, 2010; Turner
& Petersilia, 2012). It has been found to be effective across settings (probation,
parole, and prisons) and offender types (young and older, white and nonwhite,
women and men) (Andrews, 2012). The RNR model permits the identification of

priority populations for scarce reentry resources whenever the goal is to reduce recidivism. For instance, one study (Lowenkamp & Latessa, 2005) found that putting higher-risk individuals into community corrections programs reduced their offense rates, whereas placing low-risk individuals into these same programs actually increased their likelihood of reoffending. To decrease the occurrence of improper placements, risk assessments can help program planners identify the populations that are most likely to benefit from community supervision and treatment (per risk level).

As for the model's application to offenders with mental illnesses, a meta-analysis conducted by Bonta, Law, and Hanson (1998) found that offenders with and without mental illnesses share the same major risk factors. Moreover, clinical diagnosis was found to be a poor predictor of general and violent recidivism (in fact, it was negatively associated with both outcomes). However, justice-involved persons with mental illness have been found to have more risk factors than their counterparts without mental illness (Peterson, Skeem, Hart, Vidal, & Keith, 2010).

The behavioral health system has traditionally focused on providing care to people with the highest functional impairments attributable to a mental illness and/or substance use disorder. However, such an approach is not the only strategy for promoting public safety when concerned with individuals who are involved with criminal offending. If reducing recidivism is a programmatic objective, RNR research suggests that it is critical to address additional factors besides functional impairment. In addition, the RNR model represents a tenable general rehabilitation theory for conceptualizing non–justice-related behavioral health service delivery (King et al., 2013; Osher et al., 2012). Many of RNR's key principles are already consistent with contemporary behavioral health service values and evidence-based approaches; others are readily adaptable (King et al., 2013). An RNR model recalibrated for behavioral health outcomes that are not justice-related per se (e.g., behavioral health service utilization; shelter, engagement, and connection; fear; nonpremature death) is consistent with the behavioral healthcare system's normative values (e.g., respect for the person and his or her context, strengths-focused, community-based, continuity of services and linkages) and potentially offers clarity, unification, cost-effectiveness, and a research agenda. Such an adaption has the potential to do for effectiveness in living what clinical interventions do for symptom reduction, and it broadens the scope from service systems to the person's psychosocial environment and the effectiveness of principles (King et al., 2013). Both justice-focused and non–justice-focused RNR models are readily dovetailed (Osher et al., 2012), although such a unified approach is in need of research.

The Criminalization Hypothesis

The criminalization hypothesis (Abramson, 1972) attributes the large number of persons with mental illnesses found in the criminal justice system to deinstitutionalization and inadequate community mental health services. Lacking proper resources and care in the community, many individuals with serious mental illnesses decompensate. Arrest then becomes commonplace as these individuals engage in substance misuse and/or disturbed behavior of varying severity and legality. Many of these individuals repeatedly cycle through the criminal justice system, following a pattern of community decompensation, arrest/jail stabilization, community release, and subsequent decompensation. The hypothesis presupposes that proper mental health treatment will alleviate the pattern of criminal justice involvement for such individuals. In other words, symptoms of mental illness are presumed to have a causal connection to offending rather than being a "consequence" of offending or an unrelated "concomitant" (Monahan & Steadman, 2012).

At least two studies have directly tested the criminalization hypothesis using offense classification methodologies. Utilizing jail diversion (Junginger, Claypoole, Laygo, & Crisanti, 2006) and parolee (Peterson et al., 2010) samples, both studies found that the vast majority of crimes committed by offenders with mental illnesses could not be directly or indirectly attributed to mental illness. However, each study identified an important subset (7% to 8%) of individuals whose criminal justice involvement did appear to be directly related to their mental illnesses.

This pattern of results is consistent with the findings from the meta-analysis by Bonta and colleagues (1998) that offenders without mental illness and offenders with mental illness share many of the same risk factors for recidivism. Additional support comes from the prospective MacArthur Violence Risk Assessment study: Only 11% (sixty-seven of 608) of the total incidents of community violence committed by people with mental illnesses returning from hospitalization to the community were attributable to delusional or hallucinatory symptoms; risk factors such as substance abuse, anger, and psychopathy were much stronger (Monahan et al., 2001). Also, there is limited evidence that the elevated numbers of individuals with mental illnesses in the criminal justice system are explained by a bias in arresting practices exhibited by police officers (specifically, that police officers are more inclined to arrest individuals with apparent mental illnesses because they are perceived as a threat to public safety). In contrast to an earlier study (Teplin, 1984), Engel and Silver's (2001) large, multisite study revealed no evidence of an arrest bias.

Discussion

Traditionally, both criminal justice and behavioral health practitioners believed that mental illnesses are the direct cause of criminal justice involvement (via displays of psychiatric symptoms in public or symptom-driven illegal behavior), and many local programs targeting justice-involved people with behavioral disorders were designed with this rationale in mind. The criminalization hypothesis is probably true for only a small subset of persons with mental illnesses, and even among individuals for whom it may be applicable, it is only one risk factor among many more potent ones (Monahan & Steadman, 2012). Importantly, the data also suggest that offenders with mental illnesses are likely to have criminogenic needs commonly associated with severe mental illnesses (e.g., antisocial peers, substance abuse, unstable housing/homelessness, school/work problems, and family/marital deficits). Moreover, pursuant to the RNR need and breadth principles, and consistent with holistic, multisystemic, and even ecological intervention approaches, greater reductions in recidivism can be expected when more criminogenic needs are addressed (Andrews & Bonta, 2010). The implication of these findings is that interventions to reduce recidivism among justice-involved persons with mental illnesses need to be multifaceted, integrating behavioral health and legal/correctional interventions, and target dynamic risk factors whenever present. Such dynamic risk factors may include the symptoms and criminogenic risk factors associated with mental illness. A recent study (Van Dorn, Desmarais, Petrila, Haynes, & Singh, 2013) used claims data for prescriptions and treatments to describe patterns and costs of outpatient services between 2005 and 2012 for 4,056 adult Florida Medicaid enrollees with schizophrenia or bipolar disorder after discharge from hospitalization. They reported that monthly medication possession and receipt of outpatient services reduced the likelihood of any arrest (misdemeanor or felony). Possession of medications for 90 days after hospital discharge also reduced the likelihood of arrest.

In keeping with the RNR model, mental illnesses and co-occurring substance use disorders often cause associated impairments that can significantly affect an individual's responsivity to interventions targeting criminogenic risk factors. For example, a person with a major depressive disorder may not benefit from participating in treatment to reduce criminogenic thinking until the symptoms of depression (e.g., hopelessness, lack of energy, and poor concentration) are addressed. Even though depression is not considered a criminogenic need (in the sense that it is not statistically correlated with increased criminal behavior), case planners must be aware of symptoms or disorders that might impede an individual's ability to adopt new skills when developing a case plan for a client with behavioral health needs. As is the case with criminogenic needs, case plans should address as many responsivity issues as possible to improve the potential for positive outcomes. However, these responsivity factors cannot be the focus of interventions in lieu of dynamic risk factors if successful community tenure is the principal objective.

Accordingly, to achieve positive public safety outcomes, the RNR model is useful regardless of whether an offender with mental illness presents with a clear link between his or her mental illness and offense, or (rather) appears at risk for offending because of more general criminogenic needs. It can be applied to identify priority populations in the allotment of scarce reentry resources (Osher et al., 2012). For the reasons discussed, and given the heterogeneity of justice-involved persons with mental illnesses, successful reentry will be more likely when both a person's mental health issues and his or her criminogenic needs are addressed.

REENTRY MODELS SPECIFIC TO OFFENDERS WITH MENTAL ILLNESSES

In addition to the more generalist RNR model, at least six reentry models specific to offenders with mental illnesses leaving jails and/or prisons have been proposed. These include efforts that focus on systems integration to address the comprehensive needs of these individuals, including the Assess, Plan, Identify, Coordinate (APIC) model (Osher et al., 2003), the Shared Responsibility and Interdependent (SRI) model (Draine et al., 2005), and the ACTION approach (Vogel et al., 2007). Reentry models that have specific service components have also been developed, such as the Critical Time Intervention (CTI) model (Draine & Herman, 2007), the Sensitizing Providers to the Effects of Correctional Incarceration on Treatment and Risk Management (SPECTRM) model (Rotter, McQuistion, Broner, & Steinbacher, 2005), and specialized community corrections caseloads (Skeem & Manchak, 2008).

System Integration Approaches

The APIC model. Osher and colleagues (2003) drew upon "multisite studies of the organization of jail mental health programs" (in lieu of outcome studies) and a stakeholder workgroup to construct a best practice approach for jail-to-community reentry for inmates with mental illnesses and/or co-occurring substance use disorders. The resulting APIC model calls first for systems integration among jail- and community-based criminal justice, mental health, and substance abuse providers. Indeed, the model's originators preferred the term *transition* over *reentry* as it implies bidirectionality and cooperation among providers.

The hierarchical model beings with an *assessment* of an offender's clinical and social needs, as well as the risk he or she poses to public safety. Treatment and services *planning* follows, which entails preparations for needs such as integrated psychological and substance abuse treatment, medication and medical care, housing, financial assistance, food and clothing, transportation, and childcare. Obtaining income supports and entitlements, including veterans' benefits, is an important component to gaining access to necessary housing, treatment, and support in the community. With the advent of the Affordable Care Act and its expansion of Medicaid eligibility, the opportunity for states to offset the cost of healthcare interventions has never been greater. Collaborative criminal justice and behavioral health oversight groups can help to overcome some common services barriers.

The specific correctional and community programs that will actually deliver the services are then *identified*. This stage of the model also entails matching the intensity of supervision and treatment with an offender's risk and needs; incorporating cultural, gender, and age considerations in service decisions; addressing confidentiality and information sharing issues; and documenting the transition plan. Finally, the transition plan needs to be *coordinated* between jail providers and community agencies to ensure continuity of care, proper implementation, and monitoring. A variety of system linkage mechanisms are available, including the use of case managers, assertive community treatment (ACT) teams (discussed later in this chapter), in-reach by community providers (i.e., community providers who begin service delivery while an offender is still jailed), and multidisciplinary oversight groups.

The APIC model has been implemented in communities across the country. Its focus on jails as the point of reentry required accommodation to the reality that episodes of incarceration can be quite short and discharges are unpredictable. Also, arrest can afford a public health opportunity for screening, assessment, and identification of mental illnesses. For some individuals, this may represent the first time they can address the impact of mental illness on their lives. For those individuals already connected to mental healthcare, the short-term jail stay makes it less likely that they will lose contact with their community providers.

The SRI model. Characterizing other models as "systems-centric," and, in turn, neglectful of many important individual–community dynamics, Draine and colleagues (2005) proposed a prison/long-term-jail reentry model for offenders with mental illnesses that puts more weight on underpinning social processes while still incorporating the role of professional services stressed by other models. An interdisciplinary team of researchers initially constructed the SRI model; stakeholder focus groups and interviews were then utilized to refine and validate the model. Central to the model is the dynamism between the individual and the community: "[s]uccessful community reintegration is an interdependent process. It depends upon the individual's willingness and ability to act in accordance with specific social norms as well as the community's willingness and capacity to support the individual's prosocial efforts" (Draine et al., 2005).

This interdependence is conceptualized in terms of resource exchanges between the individual and the community. Individuals are regarded as consumers of numerous social, cultural, and economic resources to be supplied by the community, including "housing, grocery stores, employment or meaningful activity options, health care providers, recreational opportunities, schools, childcare, religious and spiritual connections, . . . social services," and public transportation (Draine et al., 2005). The community also has needs, including security and public safety, to which the offender should contribute in the form of human capital (e.g., labor) and prosocial pursuits (e.g., law abidance, community involvement).

While offenders with and without mental illnesses share many reentry barriers, the SRI model accounts for many barriers unique to offenders with mental illnesses. These individuals may be viewed as undesirable clients by services agencies and their communities because they may be or are perceived to be at high risk for recidivism, substance relapse, and violence; indigent; disheveled; disorganized; and noncompliant. It is in overcoming reentry barriers that the model recognizes the importance of services agencies:

Barriers may be overcome in several ways. They may be scaled by persis-
tence of individuals and supportive family and social service workers. They
may be torn down (e.g., laws restricting the provision of services may be
changed). They may be circumvented (e.g., substitute services may be created or found). They may be tunneled through (e.g. well connected, motivated human service workers and criminal justice officers may arrange
for services by cooperative providers, despite structural obstacles). These
metaphors for strategies to obtain needed services highlight the important role played by probation, parole, and social service workers in helping
re-entering offenders negotiate the complicated resource structure of every
community.

—DRAINE ET AL., *2005*

While formal access to resources provided by public agencies is considered important in the SRI model, so too is informal access supplied by community connections like family and friends. The resources capital and social
policy of the community (i.e., the ability and willingness by governmental and
social service stakeholders to afford assistance to, and community members'
willingness to live near and employ, returning offenders) are also important
components of the dynamism between the returning individual and the community. If the match between an individual's resources and needs and community resources, needs, and attitudes is poor, reintegration is unlikely to be
successful. With its emphasis on individual and community-level factors and
their interplay in the context of professional services, the SRI model is rife
with research potential.

The ACTION approach. The ACTION approach (Vogel et al., 2007) was developed to address the common problem of disconnection among the criminal justice, mental health, substance abuse, and social services systems. (Its evolution is
discussed in more detail in Chapter 13.) Because offenders with mental illnesses
regularly cycle through these often-disjointed systems on account of their complex treatment needs, Vogel and colleagues (2007) (and his GAINS Center/Policy
Research Associates colleagues with whom he worked on this over a number of
years) recognized a need to promote better partnerships across systems to allow
for more integrated services. Doing so, they suggested, would result in more efficient and effective services that benefit both the offenders with mental illnesses
and the communities they are returning to (e.g., by increasing cost-effectiveness,
quality of life, and public safety).

To aid jurisdictions in their systems-linkages efforts, Vogel and colleagues
(2007) devised and assessed a two-day, five-module cross-training curriculum,
the Adult Cross-Training Curriculum (AXT) Project. The curriculum is currently
known as the ACTION approach—a multidisciplinary approach based upon the
Sequential Intercept Model that promotes formal and systematic (as opposed to
informal and sporadic) communication, collaboration, and cooperation among
systems; evidence-based and best-practices service; and jurisdiction-specific

assessment of currently available and needed services and local resources. The ACTION approach consists of *educating* providers at all levels across relevant systems about the "fundamental principles and culture" of each system and providing *facilitated strategic planning* for the development of a clear implementation plan for local system blending; follow-up *technical assistance* is optionally available (Vogel et al., 2007).

The specific modes by which the ACTION approach intervenes are threefold. First, providers are educated about the experiences and service needs of individuals with mental illness and/or substance use disorders who come into contact with the criminal justice system. A local cross-systems map is then constructed that diagrams (1) the flow of individuals through the criminal justice system and (2) juncture points among the criminal justice, mental health, substance abuse, and social services systems. This map allows for the identification of "critical gaps and untapped resources in the service delivery systems at each intercept" and identifies loci at which cross-systems linkages (i.e., intervention and diversion) are to be facilitated (Vogel et al., 2007). Finally, a clear and dynamic action plan is constructed that guides the implementation of such linkages.

The AXT Project involved an evaluation of process and outcome variables at five different levels related to cross-systems linkages—reaction, learning, behavior, results, and needs (i.e., community barriers). Nine sites participated in the process evaluation; eight participated in the outcome evaluation. Although results (and the adopted strategies) varied among the sites, the AXT cross-trainings were generally associated with a variety of positive process and outcome changes at both the systems and individual levels. Such early mapping work provides a model for planning improvements to reentry processes and systems. It is not reentry-specific and can be applied to other intercepts as well.

Reentry Service Approaches

The CTI model. Based upon their work with the CTI, Draine and Herman (2007) formulated a theoretical model to help appraise CTI outcome results for offenders with mental illnesses and/or co-occurring substance use disorders. CTI involves the provision of problem-solving training, motivational coaching, and services advocacy for a limited time at the point of release to strengthen a returning offender's ties to community services and interpersonal supports.

The CTI model is designed to connect correctional institutions and the community. Individual factors before incarceration (e.g., employment history, criminal history, substance abuse history, housing history, race and ethnicity) and at the outset of reentry (e.g., education and age, duration of incarceration, intensity of release supervision, mental illness, social support) are first considered. CTI services are then provided to individuals with mental illness as they are exiting the site of incarceration. It is thought that its effect on offender outcomes is mediated by increases in supportive community ties (i.e., increases in resources derived from supportive connections made in the community) that sustain the positive effects of CTI once the intervention ceases. Community-level factors are also regarded as potential moderators.

Much of the extant research of CTI has been conducted with non–justice-involved individuals with mental illnesses (at least at the time of study enrollment; see http://www.criticaltime.org/publications/). To date, only a single study of CTI with persons with mental illnesses reentering the community from incarceration (versus psychiatric hospitals or shelters) has been published (although there are studies under way with justice-involved samples; see http://www.criticaltime.org/training/). Jarrett and colleagues (2012) utilized a randomized controlled design to examine whether CTI delivered for four to six weeks during the transition to the community from three prisons in the United Kingdom was associated with increased service utilization and community connectivity compared to treatment as usual (i.e., prison in-reach that included discharge planning and arrangements) among prisoners with mental illnesses. The authors reported preliminary results for 23 participants (15 of whom were in the CTI group versus eight in the treatment-as-usual group) at four to six weeks after discharge. Significantly more CTI recipients were found to be registered with a general practitioner and receiving medication at follow-up than were treatment-as-usual participants. However, no significant group differences were found for contact with mental health services, contact with substance abuse services, contact with family, receipt of benefits, or housing.

The SPECTRM model. Rotter and colleagues (2005), in presenting their SPECTRM model, construed other models as linkage rather than treatment models. In contrast to linkage models, the SPECTRM model is much narrower, being developed to address the particular issue of incarceration acculturation and its impact on the attitudes and behaviors of offenders with mental illness during reentry. Community providers first participate in a half-day training workshop designed to educate them about behaviors and beliefs that are deemed adaptive in jail or prison (e.g., those stemming from the inmate code, such as aggression, isolation, stonewalling, and no snitching) but that prove problematic and are often misinterpreted in the community. Then, utilizing this cultural competence, providers engage recipients in a group treatment program named Re-entry After Prison/Jail (RAP). To date, the SPECTRM model has been tested in a state hospital and two homeless shelters (see Rotter et al., 2005).

The RAP program involves psychoeducation and social skills training and utilizes cognitive-behavioral intervention strategies. Providers help patients understand how certain attitudes and beliefs acquired during incarceration may be affecting their interactions with providers and others in the community, and help patients to develop effective coping strategies for dealing with emotional triggers and challenges faced in the community. That the SPECTRM model can be readily incorporated into the RNR framework is a particular strength. The effects of incarceration acculturation can be seen as specific responsivity considerations and, depending on how those effects are experienced and expressed, may also represent criminogenic needs. Moreover, the RAP component, utilizing cognitive-behavioral and social-learning strategies, adheres to the general responsivity principle.

Specialized community correction caseloads. The number of people with mental illnesses under correctional supervision has reached unprecedented levels and the majority of these persons are supervised in the community (Glaze, Bonczar, & Zhang, 2010). With incredibly high caseloads and little access to community resources, probation and parole officers are often left with revocation to jail or prison as a punishment for failing to meet conditions of probation (see Louden, Skeem, Camp, & Christensen, 2008). These *technical violations*, where a new crime has not been committed but rather a condition of supervision violated, are a major contributor to ballooning correctional populations. Community corrections officers may also have inaccurate perceptions about mental illness and its relation to risk level (Louden & Skeem, 2012; see Chapter 7 for a more detailed discussion).

In this context, specialized community corrections caseloads have been developed and are emerging as a best practice approach to improve outcomes for persons with mental illnesses under community supervision (Skeem & Manchak, 2008). The key features of this programmatic response are community corrections officers with smaller caseloads composed exclusively of persons with mental illnesses, significant officer training on mental health issues, the application of problem-solving strategies, and extensive collaboration with community-based providers (Prins & Draper, 2009). Studies support this model as effective in reducing violations and rearrests among persons with mental illnesses under community corrections supervision (Louden, Skeem, Camp, Vidal, & Peterson, 2010; Skeem, Louden, Manchak, Vidal, & Haddad, 2009). The use of specialized community corrections caseloads is also not back-end specific (reentry and parole) but can be applied to populations sentenced to community supervision (probationers) in lieu of incarceration. However, with states facing the reality of enormous budget shortfalls, the resources to fund effective transition strategies like specialized community corrections supervision and other effective mental health and co-occurring substance abuse treatments may be wanting.

Discussion

All of these models can be integrated into a unified framework. At the outset, the ACTION approach aids jurisdictions with the task of establishing cross-systems linkages at the macro level. For the necessary linkages to be made, an assessment of community resources, needs, and attitudes (i.e., SRI model considerations) should be undertaken upon the receipt of ACTION training. At the intermediate (program or agency) and individual levels, the APIC model guides the services process from individual assessment through the actual delivery of needed services, and the CTI model can be utilized to evaluate a time-limited programmatic set of interventions delivered upon transition to the community.

Specialized community corrections supervision prioritizes probation and parole agency resources for individuals with mental illnesses who present a high risk of recidivating. At the individual level, SPECTRM provides specific cognitive-based interventions to assist offenders with mental illnesses in the successful transition from prison to the community.

EMPIRICAL EVIDENCE REGARDING THE EFFICACY OF REENTRY STRATEGIES EMPLOYED WITH OFFENDERS WITH MENTAL ILLNESSES

The reentry models described above inform the range of interagency collaboration, sets of providers, and types of services required for successful reentry. Matching these variables to the justice-involved individuals with mental illnesses and putting an effective case plan together are tasks that require the provision of case management. Because of these clients' diverse and complex needs, case management may entail a multidisciplinary team effort. Such teams can exist in a variety of programmatic structures but are connected by their criminal justice sophistication and capacity to provide, or broker, a wide array of services.

Outcome evidence is accruing for reentry services delivered to the general offender population (Drake, Aos, & Miller, 2009; Seiter & Kadela, 2003; Wormith et al., 2007) and offenders with mental illnesses in particular (Heilbrun et al., 2012). Here we review the empirical literature specific to offenders with mental illnesses, in which three types of case management strategies have emerged in recent years: ACT-based programs, intensive case management (ICM)-based program, and more traditionally styled correctional reentry programs (Heilbrun et al., 2012).

ACT-Based Programs

The ACT approach (Mendota Mental Health Institute, 1974) was conceived of to help decrease instances of homelessness and hospitalization common among persons with severe mental illness (Dixon, 2000). This labor-intensive mode of service delivery involves the active and persistent provision of comprehensive community-based services to high-need individuals by coordinated, mobile teams. Interdisciplinary service teams drawn from psychiatry and psychology, nursing, and social work avail themselves 24/7 to a small caseload of challenging clients. Research has demonstrated that ACT is associated with improvements in its targeted domains of housing and community tenure (Coldwell & Bender, 2007) but that it is mostly ineffective at reducing criminal justice involvement and substance abuse (Bond, Drake, Mueser, & Latimer, 2001). The ACT approach is also relatively expensive compared to ICM, although it is less costly than housing an individual in a correctional facility (Hartwell, 2010; Morrissey & Meyer, 2008; Morrissey, Meyer, & Cuddeback, 2007).

Attempts have been made to modify ACT to increase its effect on criminal outcomes; these modifications are collectively termed Forensic Assertive Community Treatment (FACT; Jennings, 2009; Lamberti, Weisman, & Faden, 2004; Morrissey et al., 2007). According to Lamberti and colleagues (2004), FACT programs are those that exclusively serve offenders with mental illnesses referred by a criminal justice agency, and that do so in close connection with the referring agency. They further proposed that the key distinction between ACT and FACT is the degree to which the focus of service is on reducing criminal recidivism. While ACT teams must frequently interface with the criminal justice system, given the characteristics of their challenging clientele, criminogenic issues are low in treatment priority. In contrast, reducing criminogenic potential is the primary target of FACT.

A recent review (Heilbrun et al., 2012; see also Morrissey et al., 2007) identified outcome reports for four individual FACT programs (Cosden et al., 2003; McCoy, Roberts, Hanrahan, Clay, & Luchins, 2004; Smith, Jennings, & Cimino, 2010; Thresholds State County Collaborative Jail Linkage Project Chicago, 2001; Weisman, Lamberti, & Price, 2004) and one grouping of California programs (California Board of Corrections, 2005). Individual FACT programs were quite variable in implementation (see Lamberti et al., 2004, for a discussion of these variations), but all purported to be FACT-based.[1] Although the evaluations varied with respect to methodological rigor (only two utilized a control, treatment-as-usual group), three individual programs and the aggregate California programs were found to be associated with improvements in both quality of life (e.g., hospitalizations, substance abuse) and criminal justice outcomes (e.g., arrests and bookings, mean jail days). The California evaluation also found that higher-fidelity programs were generally associated with better outcomes than low-fidelity programs.

Findings from the randomized controlled trial by Cosden and colleagues (2003) of a FACT-modeled diversion court were more mixed with respect to criminal justice outcomes. Both the diverted and treatment-as-usual groups experienced quality of life improvements, but no significant differences in number of arrests or mean jail days were found. Also, diverted participants had fewer convictions overall but more bookings and more convictions for probation violations than those in the treatment-as-usual condition. Like some of the California programs, however, the study by Cosden and colleagues (2003) may be better classified as forensic intensive case management (see Morrissey & Meyer, 2008; Morrissey et al., 2007).

ICM-Based Programs

The ICM approach likewise originated outside of the criminal justice context, serving homeless persons with mental illness (Rog, Andranovich, & Rosenblum, 1987). Adaptations for justice-involved individuals with mental illnesses are termed forensic intensive case management. Forensic intensive case management is similar to FACT in that it involves the delivery of "assertive, in-vivo, and time-unlimited services, but it [differs insofar as it] uses case managers with individual caseloads, has no self-contained team, lacks 24/7 capacity, and brokers access to psychiatric treatment rather than providing it directly" (Morrissey et al., 2007). Because of these differences, forensic ICM is less resource-intensive than FACT, although the cost of brokered services must also be factored into total expense calculations (Morrissey & Meyer, 2008; Morrissey et al., 2007).

Steadman and Naples (2005) reported results from a large, multisite, non-random comparison group study of jail inmates with mental illness diverted to forensic ICM in the community (see also Broner, Lattimore, Cowell, & Schlenger, 2004). They found that diverted participants spent significantly more time in the community before rearrest and were significantly more likely to report medication compliance and counseling attendance. Forensic ICM recipients were also significantly more likely to report hospitalizations and emergency room visits and significantly less likely to report residential treatment for substance abuse. No significant differences were found with respect to mental health outcomes. Other forensic ICM studies (using a variety of methodological designs) have obtained similarly positive criminal justice outcomes (Godley, Finch, Dougan, McDonnell, & McDermeit, 2000; Ventura, Cassel, Jacoby, & Huang, 1998; Wilson, Tien, & Eaves, 1995), in addition to substance abuse and quality of life improvements (Godley et al., 2000).

Results from two randomized controlled trials (Cosden et al., 2003; Solomon & Draine, 1995), however, were not as promising. As was noted above, Cosden and colleagues (2003) found null or mixed results as to criminal justice outcomes. In addition, Solomon and Draine (1995) compared recipients of FACT, forensic ICM, and usual care on a variety of psychosocial and clinical outcomes. No differences were found among the groups except that FACT recipients were more likely to be rearrested. The authors attributed this to the inclusion of probation officers in the FACT teams and, in turn, the heightened behavioral scrutiny to which all recipients were thereby subjected.

Correctional Reentry Programs

Although roughly comparable to ICM-based approaches (in that it utilizes release planning and case manager advocacy), the forensic transition team approach (Hartwell, 2010; Hartwell & Orr, 1999) is unique in that it counts a significant number of offenders with mental illnesses reentering from Massachusetts state prisons (as opposed to just country jail facilities) among its clientele. Given the numerous differences between jails and prisons discussed earlier, the forensic transition team is positioned to provide a unique look at how ICM-type service delivery affects offenders with mental illnesses reentering the community following longer periods of incarceration. Although not all felony offenders ($n = 436$) in the most recently reported forensic transition team dataset ($N = 966$) necessarily served prison sentences, it is conceivable that a fair proportion may have, given that a felony conviction permits prison incarceration. Using felony convictions, then, as a crude signal of prison-positioned reentry, Hartwell (2010) reported that 43% of felons with mental illnesses were engaged in the community, 26% were hospitalized, 20% were reinvolved with the criminal justice system, and 10% were lost at a three-month follow-up. Unfortunately, the absence of a pretest or comparison group makes these results impossible to interpret.

In a 2008 analysis of Wisconsin's large prison population (Council of State Governments, 2008), a principal driver of growth was identified as, unsurprisingly, the high failure rate among people released from prison to desist from crime. Recidivism rates were especially high among people with serious mental illnesses. To reduce recidivism in this target population (i.e., prison inmates), lawmakers launched a pilot program called Opening Avenues to Reentry Success (OARS). OARS is an effort to demonstrate and document the impact of a comprehensive release program for prison inmates with serious mental illnesses. The program targets a group of individuals who (1) have high mental health needs, determined by a diagnosis of a serious mental illness that causes a moderate to high level of impairment, (2) have a moderate to high risk of recidivism based on an assessment of criminogenic risk factors, (3) are returning to counties in Fox Valley and southeastern Wisconsin, (4) are subject to at least six months of postrelease supervision, and (5) are willing to voluntarily participate in the OARS program. OARS addresses known barriers to successful community reentry through system collaboration, transition planning, and integrated treatment and supervision.

The OARS program has two distinct phases: institutional prerelease and postrelease. During the prerelease phase, participants are introduced to their OARS team and begin to build a relationship with them, partake in prerelease planning, consent to an individualized case plan, and have applications for benefits made on their behalf. During the postrelease phase, clients continue to work with their OARS team through regular appointments with their community corrections agent and case manager.

The OARS program's first participants were enrolled in 2010 and released in 2011. Program planners met their enrollment goal of 88 participants during their first year of operation. While the planned follow-up period is not yet complete, early results are promising: Less than 5% of program participants had returned to prison at the nine-month follow-up.

Discussion

These studies provide promising, preliminary support for the value of identifying, and delivering tailored reentry services to, offenders with mental illnesses. However, of the thirteen studies reviewed by Heilbrun and colleagues (2012), over half lacked a comparison group, and roughly a third did not test for significance. Moreover, none of the studies stratified samples according to criminogenic risk. To permit anything more than tentative conclusions to be drawn (or, sometimes, any conclusions at all), more rigorous study designs (e.g., randomized controlled trials, comparisons involving pre–post functioning or with a treatment-as-usual group) and statistical analyses (significance testing and effect size calculations) are sorely needed. In addition, it would be helpful if studies were designed so that outcomes for participants located at different intercepts could be compared.

CONCLUSIONS

In many states, a return to jail or prison, principally for violating conditions of release, is a significant event in light of the rising incarceration rate of people with serious mental illnesses. When this occurs, both public safety and recovery goals are compromised. Efforts to address this phenomenon have been implemented and promising practices to slow this revolving door have been identified. These practices include:

- Accurate assessment of individuals' risk of criminogenic and behavioral health recidivism (level of services need), criminogenic and behavioral health needs (specific services needs), and anticipated responsiveness to interventions (service style needs)
- Effective programming that includes structured cognitive-behavioral and skill-building interventions, and the provision of psychiatric medication when indicated
- Coordinated services before and after release to provide continuity of treatment and linkages to community supports. Monahan and Steadman (2012; citing Council of State Governments [2008] and Osher & Steadman [2007], among others) recently summarized promising services for justice-involved persons with mental illnesses. In addition to general cognitive-behavioral and social-learning change strategies (above) and case-management–type service delivery models (below), their listing consisted of illness self-management and recovery, integrated mental health and substance abuse services, supported employment, psychopharmacology, family psychoeducation, supported housing, and trauma interventions (Monahan & Steadman, 2012, pp. 248–249).
- A balanced (i.e., not overly punitive) approach to community supervision making effective and ethical use of leverage afforded by the corrections context
- Case management delivered by multidisciplinary teams consisting of team members who strive to establish and maintain positive, structured relationships with service recipients
- Information exchange systems between correctional and behavioral health agencies

- Regular process and outcome evaluations, and reviews of provider-, program-, and system-level integrity to evidence-based (or at least promising or recommended) programming and practices (Andrews, 2012; Turner & Petersilia, 2012). Brokeraged service providers should be able to demonstrate in their proposals that the services they offer reach the appropriate threshold of acceptability. Outcome evaluations of their services should also evince positive results.
- Education of community partners and members about the reentry process and its goals and involvement in reentry efforts (Turner & Petersilia, 2012)

The programmatic home for these practices will vary from jurisdiction to jurisdiction. What works, for whom, and under what circumstances for offenders with mental illnesses in the context of reentry are questions in need of a robust research agenda (see Monahan & Steadman, 2012). Yet if we have learned anything from our models and programmatic efforts, it is that the solution to successful reentry and the prevention of subsequent justice involvement resides in the collaborative, open-minded, and crime-prevention–focused efforts of the behavioral health and criminal justice systems and their community partners, the people they serve, and the local and greater communities in which they all reside.

NOTE

1. Morrissey and colleagues (2007) regarded many of the California programs as more similar to ICM programs than FACT programs.

REFERENCES

Abramson, M. F. (1972). The criminalization of mentally disordered behavior: Possible side-effect of a new mental health law. *Hospital & Community Psychiatry, 23*, 101–105.

Andrews, D. A., & Bonta, J. (2010). *The psychology of criminal conduct* (5th ed.). New Providence, NJ: LexisNexis.

Andrews, D. A. (2012). The Risk-Need-Responsivity (RNR) model of correctional assessment and treatment. In J. A. Dvoskin, J. L. Skeem, R. W. Novaco, & K. S. Douglas (Eds.), *Using social science to reduce violent offending* (pp. 127–156). New York: Oxford University Press. doi:10.1093/acprof:oso/9780195384642.001.0001

Baillargeon, J., Binswanger, I. A., Penn, J. V., Williams, B. A., & Murray, O. J. (2009). Psychiatric disorders and repeat incarcerations: The revolving prison door. *American Journal of Psychiatry, 66*, 103–109. doi:10.1176/appi.ajp.2008.08030416

Bond, G. R., Drake, R. E., Mueser, K. T., & Latimer, E. (2001). Assertive community treatment: Critical ingredients and impact on patients. *Disease Management and Health Outcomes, 9*, 141–159. doi:10.2165/00115677-200109030-00003

Bonta, J., Law, M., & Hanson, K. (1998). The prediction of criminal and violent recidivism among mentally disordered offenders: A meta-analysis. *Psychological Bulletin*, *123*, 123–142. doi:10.1037/0033-2909.123.2.123

Broner, N., Lattimore, P. K., Cowell, A. J., & Schlenger, W. E. (2004). Effects of diversion on adults with co-occurring mental illness and substance use: outcomes from a national multi-site study. *Behavioral Sciences & the Law*, *22*, 519–541. doi:10.1002/bsl.605

Bureau of Justice Statistics (2012). Prisoners in 2011. Washington, D.C.: Department of Justice. Retrieved 11-3-14 from http://www.bjs.gov/content/pub/pdf/p11.pdf

California Board of Corrections (2005). Mentally ill offender crime reduction grant program: Overview of statewide evaluation findings. Retrieved January 8, 2011, from California Department of Corrections and Rehabilitation website: http://www.cdcr.ca.gov/CSA/CPP/Grants/MIOCR/Docs/miocrg_report_presentation.pdf

Coldwell, C. M., & Bender, W. S. (2007). The effectiveness of assertive community treatment for homeless populations with severe mental illness: A meta-analysis. *American Journal of Psychiatry*, *164*, 393–399. doi:10.1176/appi.ajp.164.3.393

Cosden, M., Ellens, J. K., Schnell, J. L., Yamini-Diouf, Y., & Wolfe, M. M. (2003). Evaluation of a mental health treatment court with assertive community treatment. *Behavioral Sciences and the Law*, *21*, 415–427. doi:10.1002/bsl.542

Council of State Governments (2008). *Improving responses to people with mental illnesses: The essential elements of a mental health court.* New York: Council of State Governments Justice Center.

Dixon, L. (2000). Assertive community treatment: Twenty-five years of gold. *Psychiatric Services*, *51*, 759–765. doi:10.1176/appi.ps.51.6.759

Dowden, C., & Andrews, D. A. (1999). What works for female offenders: A meta-analytic review. *Crime & Delinquency*, *45*, 438–452. doi:10.1177/0011128799045004002

Dowden, C., & Andrews, D. A. (2000). Effective correctional treatment and violent reoffending: A meta-analysis. *Canadian Journal of Criminology*, *42*, 449–467.

Draine, J., & Herman, D. B. (2007). Critical time intervention for reentry from prison for persons with mental illness. *Psychiatric Services*, *58*, 1577–1581. doi:10.1176/appi.ps.58.12.1577

Draine, J., Wolff, N., Jacoby, J. E., Hartwell, S., & Duclos, C. (2005). Understanding community re-entry of former prisoners with mental illness: A conceptual model to guide new research. *Behavioral Sciences and the Law*, *23*, 689–707. doi:10.1002/bsl.642

Drake, E. K., Aos, S., & Miller, M. G. (2009). Evidence-based public policy options to reduce crime and criminal justice costs: Implication in Washington State. *Victims and Offenders*, *4*, 170–196. doi:10.1080/15564880802612615

Engel, R. S., & Silver, E. (2001) Policing mentally disordered suspects: A reexamination of the criminalization hypothesis. *Criminology*, *39*, 225–252. doi:10.1111/j.1745-9125.2001.tb00922.x

Glaze, L. E., Bonczar, T. P., & Zhang, F. (2010). *Probation and parole in the United States, 2009.* (BJS Special Bulletin NCJ 2231674). Washington, D.C.: U.S. Department of Justice. Retrieved from http://www.bjs.gov/content/pub/pdf/ppus09.pdf

Godley, S. H., Finch, M., Dougan, L., McDonnell, M., & McDermeit, M. (2000). Case management for dually diagnosed individuals involved in the criminal

justice system. *Journal of Substance Abuse Treatment, 18,* 137–148. doi:10.1016/
S0740-5472(99)00027-6

Griffin, P. A. (1990). The backdoor of the jail: Linking mentally ill offenders to community mental health services. In H. J. Steadman (Ed.), *Jail diversion for the mentally
ill: Breaking through the barriers* (pp. 91–107). Boulder, CO: National Institute of
Corrections.

Hanson, R. K., Bourgon, G., Helmus, L., & Hodgson, S. (2009). The principles of effective correctional treatment also apply to sexual offenders: A meta-analysis. *Criminal
Justice and Behavior, 36,* 865–891. doi:10.1177/0093854809338545

Hartwell, S. (2010). Ex-inmates with psychiatric disabilities returning to the community from correctional custody: The forensic transition team approach after
a decade. In M. Peyrot & S. Burns (Eds.), *Research in social problems and public
policy: Vol. 17. New approaches to social problems treatment* (pp. 263–283). Bingley,
United Kingdom: Emerald Group.

Hartwell, S. W., & Orr, K. (1999). The Massachusetts forensic transition team for mentally ill offenders re-entering the community. *Psychiatric Services, 50,* 1220–1222.

Heilbrun, K., DeMatteo, D., Brooks-Holliday, S., Shah, S., King, C., Bingham, A., &
Hamilton, D. (2012). Community-based alternatives for justice-involved individu-
als with severe mental illness: Review of the relevant research. *Criminal Justice and
Behavior, 39,* 351–419. doi:10.1177/0093854811432421

Jarrett, M., Thornicroft, G., Forrester, A., Harty, M., Senior, J., King, C., & . . . Shaw, J.
(2012). Continuity of care for recently released prisoners with mental illness: A pilot
randomised controlled trial testing the feasibility of a Critical Time Intervention.
Epidemiology and Psychiatric Services, 21, 187–193.

Jennings, J. L. (2009). Does assertive community treatment work with forensic populations? Review and recommendations. *The Open Psychiatry Journal, 3,* 13–19.
doi:10.2174/1874354400903010013

Junginger, J., Claypoole, K., Laygo, R., & Crisanti, A. (2006). Effects of serious mental
illness and substance abuse on criminal offenses. *Psychiatric Services, 57,* 879–882.
doi:10.1176/appi.ps.57.6.879

Kessler, R. C., Nelson, C. B., McKinagle, K. A., Edlund, M. J., Frank, R. G., & Leaf,
P. J. (1996). The epidemiology of co-occurring addictive and mental disor-
ders: Implications for prevention and service utilization. *American Journal of
Orthopsychiatry, 66,* 17–31. doi:10.1037/h0080151

King, C., Brooks Holliday, S., & Heilbrun, K. (2013, August). *Absent crime:
Risk-Need-Responsivity (RNR) as a tenable meta-model for non-justice related behav-
ioral health service delivery.* Presented at the annual convention of the American
Psychological Association, Honolulu, HI.

Lamberti, J. S., Weisman, R., & Faden, D. I. (2004). Forensic assertive community
treatment: preventing incarceration of adults with severe mental illness. *Psychiatric
Services, 55,* 1285–1293. doi:10.1176/appi.ps.55.11.1285

Lipsey, M. W. (2009). The primary factors that characterize effective interventions with
juvenile offenders: A meta-analytic overview. *Victims and Offenders, 4,* 124–147.
doi:10.1080/15564880802612573

Louden, J. E., & Skeem, J. L. (2012). How do probation officers assess and manage recidivism and violence risk for probationers with mental disorder? An experimental

investigation. *Law and Human Behavior.* Advance online publication. doi:10.1037/
   h0093991

Louden, J. E., Skeem, J. L., Camp, J., & Christensen, E. (2008). Supervising probationers
   with mental disorder: How do agencies respond to violations? *Criminal Justice and
   Behavior, 35,* 832–847. doi:10.1177/0093854808319042

Louden, J. E., Skeem, J. L., Camp, J., Vidal, S., & Peterson, J. (2010). Supervision practices in specialty mental health probation: What happens in officer-probationer
   meetings? *Law and Human Behavior, 36,* 109–119. doi:10.1037/h0093961

Lowenkamp, C. T., & Latessa, E. J. (2005). Increasing the effectiveness of correctional
   programming through the risk principle: Identifying offenders for residential placement. *Criminology and Public Policy, 4,* 263–290. doi:10.1111/j.1745-9133.2005.00021.x

McCoy, M. L., Roberts, D. L., Hanrahan, P., Clay, R., & Luchins, D. J. (2004). Jail linkage assertive community treatment services for individuals with mental illnesses.
   Psychiatric Rehabilitation Journal, 27, 243–250. doi:10.2975/27.2004.243.250

Mendota Mental Health Institute. (1974). The 1974 APA achievement award winners.
   Gold award: A community treatment program (Madison, Wisconsin). *Hospital and
   Community Psychiatry, 25,* 669–672.

Minton, T. D. (2010). *Jail inmates at midyear 2009–statistical tables* (NCJ No. NCJ
   230122). Retrieved from Bureau of Justice Statistics website: http://bjs.ojp.usdoj.gov/
   content/pub/pdf/jim09st.pdf

Messina, N., Burdon, W., Hagopian, G., & Prendergast, M. (2004). One-year return to
   custody rates among co-disordered offenders. *Behavioral Sciences & the Law, 22,*
   503–518. doi:10.1002/bsl.600

Monahan, J., & Steadman, H. J. (2012). Extending violence reduction principles to
   justice-involved persons with mental illness. In In J. A. Dvoskin, J. L. Skeem, R.
   W. Novaco, & K. S. Douglas (Eds.), *Using social science to reduce violent offending* (pp. 245–261). New York: Oxford University Press. doi:10.1093/acprof:
   oso/9780195384642.001.0001

Monahan, J., Steadman, H. J., Silver, E., Appelbaum, P. S., Robbins, P. C., Mulvey,
   E., . . . Banks, S. (2001). *Rethinking risk assessment: The MacArthur study of mental
   disorder and violence.* New York: Oxford University Press.

Morrissey, J., & Meyer, P. (2008). *Extending assertive community treatment to criminal
   justice settings.* Retrieved from SAMSHA National GAINS Center website: gain-
   scenter.samhsa.gov/pdfs/ebp/ExtendingAssertiveCommunity.pdf

Morrissey, J., Meyer, P., & Cuddeback, G. (2007). Extending assertive community treatment to criminal justice settings: Origins, current evidence, and future directions.
   Community Mental Health Journal, 43, 527–544. doi:10.1007/s10597-007-9092-9

Munetz, M., & Griffin, P. (2006). Use of the Sequential Intercept Model as an approach to
   decriminalization of people with serious mental illness. *Psychiatric Services, 57,* 544–549.

National Association of State Budget Officers. (2009). *State expenditure report 2008.*
   Washington, D.C.: Author.

Osher, F., D'Amora, D. A., Plotkin, M., Jarrett N., & Eggleston, A. (2012). *Adults with
   behavioral health needs under correctional supervision: A shared framework for reducing recidivism and promoting recovery.* New York: Council of State Governments
   Justice Center.

Osher, F., & Steadman, H. J. (2007). Adapting evidence-based practices for persons with mental illness involved with the criminal justice system. *Psychiatric Services, 58*, 1472–1478. doi:10.1176/appi.ps.58.11.1472

Osher, F., Steadman, H. J., & Barr, H. (2003). A best practice approach to community reentry from jails for inmates with co-occurring disorders: The APIC model. *Crime & Delinquency, 49*, 79–96. doi:10.1177/0011128702239237

Pew Center on the States (2008). *One in 100: Behind bars in America 2008.* Washington, D.C.: The Pew Charitable Trusts.

Pew Center on the States (2011). *State of recidivism: The revolving door of America's prisons.* Washington, D.C.: The Pew Charitable Trusts.

Petersilia, J. (2004). What works in prisoner reentry? Reviewing and questioning the evidence. *Federal Probation, 68*, 4–8.

Peterson, J., Skeem, J. L., Hart, E., Vidal, S., & Keith, F. (2010). Analyzing offense patterns as a function of mental illness to test the criminalization hypothesis. *Psychiatric Services, 61*, 1217–1222. doi:10.1176/appi.ps.61.12.1217

Prins, S. J., & Draper, L. (2009). *Improving outcomes for people with mental illnesses under community corrections supervision: A guide to research-informed policy and practice.* New York: Council of State Governments Justice Center.

Prins, S. J., & Osher, F.C. (2009). *Improving responses to people with mental illnesses: The essential elements of specialized probation initiatives.* New York: Council of State Governments Justice Center.

Rog, D., Andranovich, G., & Rosenblum, S. (1987). *Intensive case management for persons who are homeless and mentally ill: A review of CSP and Human Resource Development program efforts* (Vols. 1–3). Rockville, MD: National Institute of Mental Health.

Rotter, M., McQuistion, H. L., Broner, N., & Steinbacher, M. (2005). The impact of the "incarceration culture" on reentry for adults with mental illness: A training and group treatment model. *Psychiatric Services, 56*, 265–267. doi:10.1176/appi.ps.56.3.265

Seiter, R. P., & Kadela, K. R. (2003). Prisoner reentry: What works, what does not, and what is promising. *Crime & Delinquency, 49*, 360–388. doi:10.1177/0011128703049003002

Serin, R. C, Lloyd, C. D., & Hanby, L. J. (2010). Enhancing offender re-entry: An integrated model for enhancing offender re-entry. *European Journal of Probation, 2*, 53–75.

Skeem, J., Louden, J. E., Manchak, S., Vidal, S., & Haddad, E. (2009). Social networks and social control of probationers with co-occurring mental health and substance abuse problems. *Law and Human Behavior, 33*, 122–135. doi:10.1007/s10979-008-9140-1

Skeem, J., & Manchak, S. (2008). Back to the future: From Klockars' model of effective supervision to evidence-based practice in probation. *International Journal of Offender Rehabilitation, 47*, 220–247.

Smith, R. J., Jennings, J. L., & Cimino, A. (2010). Forensic continuum of care with ACT for persons recovering from co-occurring disabilities: Long-term outcome. *Psychiatric Rehabilitation Journal, 33*, 207–218. doi:10.2975/33.3.2010.207.218

Solomon, P., & Draine, J. (1995). One-year outcomes of a randomized trial of case management with seriously mentally ill clients leaving jail. *Evaluation Review, 19*, 256–273. doi:10.1177/0193841X9501900302

Steadman, H. J., & Naples, M. (2005). Assessing the effectiveness of jail diversion programs for persons with serious mental illness and co-occurring substance use disorders. *Behavioral Sciences & the Law, 23*, 163–170. doi:10.1002/bsl.640

Steadman, H. J., Osher, F. C., Robbins, P. C., Case, B., & Samuels, S. (2009). Prevalence of serious mental illness among jail inmates. *Psychiatric Services, 6*, 761–765. doi:10.1176/appi.ps.60.6.761

Teplin, L. A. (1984). Criminalizing mental disorder: The comparative arrest rate of the mentally ill. *American Psychology, 39*, 794–803. doi:10.1037/0003-066X.39.7.794

Thresholds State County Collaborative Jail Linkage Project Chicago (2001). Gold award: Helping mentally ill people break the cycle of jail and homelessness. *Psychiatric Services, 52*, 1380–1382. doi:10.1176/appi.ps.52.10.1380

Turner, S., & Petersilia, J. (2012). Putting science to work: How the principles of risk, need, and responsivity apply to reentry. In In J. A. Dvoskin, J. L. Skeem, R. Novaco, & K. S. Douglas (Eds.), *Using social science to reduce violent offending* (pp. 179–198). New York: Oxford University Press. doi:10.1093/acprof:oso/9780195384642.003.0055

Van Dorn, R., Desmarais, S., Petrila, J., Haynes, D., & Singh, J. (2013). Effects of outpatient treatment on risk of arrest of adults with serious mental illness and associated costs. *Psychiatric Services, 64*, 856–862. doi:10.1176/appi.ps.201200406

Ventura, L. A., Cassel, C. A., Jacoby, J. E., & Huang, B. (1998). Case management and recidivism of mentally ill persons released from jail. *Psychiatric Services, 49*, 1330–1337.

Vogel, W. M., Noether, C. D., & Steadman, H. J. (2007). Preparing communities for re-entry of offenders with mental illness: The ACTION approach. *Journal of Offender Rehabilitation, 45*, 167–188. doi:10.1300/J076v45n01_12

Weisman, R., Lamberti, J., & Price, N. (2004). Integrating criminal justice, community healthcare, and support services for adults with severe mental disorders. *Psychiatric Quarterly, 75*, 71–85. doi:10.1023/B:PSAQ.0000007562.37428.52

Wilson, D., Tien, G., & Eaves, D. (1995). Increasing the community tenure of mentally disordered offenders: An assertive case management program. *International Journal of Law and Psychiatry, 18*, 61–69. doi:10.1016/0160-2527(94)00027-1

Wormith, S. J., Althouse, R., Simpson, M., Reitzel, L. R., Fagan, T. J., & Morgan, R. D. (2007). The rehabilitation and reintegration of offenders: The current landscape and some future directions for correctional psychology. *Criminal Justice and Behavior, 34*, 879–892. doi:10.1177/0093854807301552

7

Applying the Sequential Intercept Model to Reduce Recidivism Among Probationers and Parolees with Mental Illness

JENNIFER ENO LOUDEN, SARAH MANCHAK, MEGAN O'CONNOR, AND JENNIFER L. SKEEM ■

The Sequential Intercept Model (SIM; Munetz & Griffin, 2006) is a conceptual guide to the stages at which persons with mental illness are involved in the criminal justice system. The utility of SIM lies in its identification of key entry points in standard criminal justice processing (e.g., police, courts, jails) where community alternatives to incarceration can be offered. These entry points may be conceptualized as series of filters, with each filter representing a later stage of criminal justice processing; the main goal at each filter is to decrease the unnecessary penetration of persons with mental illness further into the criminal justice system and to minimize the amount of time they spend in the system. According to the model, "an accessible, comprehensive, effective mental health treatment system focused on the needs of individuals with serious and persistent mental disorders is undoubtedly the most effective means of preventing the criminalization of people with mental illness;" in other words, mental health treatment is the ultimate intercept (Munetz & Griffin, 2006, p. 545). This chapter focuses on the fifth and final intercept of the SIM: community corrections. We first describe the unique challenges facing community corrections agencies in addressing the complex needs of persons with mental illness and then summarize evidence regarding the effectiveness of interventions seeking to address these needs. We conclude with recommendations for researchers, policymakers, and practitioners for integrating mental health treatment with principles of effective criminal justice practice to improve outcomes for people with mental illness under community corrections supervision.

COMMUNITY CORRECTIONS: THE FIFTH INTERCEPT

To best understand how the SIM can aid decision making in community corrections, it is necessary to understand the goals and nuances of both probation and parole. Whereas probation can be conceptualized as a form of diversion, in that offenders who would have been sentenced to prison are diverted to the less intensive punishment of community supervision on probation, parole is a period of supervision that occurs after a prison term. Both, however, function similarly in that they are settings in which supervising officers are tasked with both rehabilitating the offender and protecting community safety (see Klockars, 1972). At this community corrections intercept, offenders can "fail" supervision in one of two ways: by committing a new crime or by breaking the rules of community supervision (e.g., failure to maintain employment, association with known felons, or another "technical violation") (Abadinsky, 2000).

Recidivism can put offenders with mental disorder into contact with several criminal justice agencies. Technical violations are most often discovered and processed by the supervising community corrections officer. If the offender commits a new offense while on community supervision, this could be detected either by the community corrections agency or another criminal justice agency, such as the police; thus, the offender could be in contact with multiple intercepts of the SIM. In contrast to some of the earlier intercepts of the SIM (e.g., law enforcement), the goal at this stage is not to divert the person out of the criminal justice system entirely to mental health treatment. The person has already been found guilty of criminal conduct and is serving a sentence of community supervision. Thus, rather than diverting people who do not belong in the criminal justice system, the goal in community corrections is to decrease the likelihood that an individual will recidivate and move further into the criminal justice system—in essence, to divert individuals from further criminal justice involvement (see Munetz & Griffin, 2006).

SCOPE OF THE PROBLEM

The significance of parole and probation as an intercept point for decreasing criminal justice system involvement cannot be understated. The number of persons under correctional supervision in the United States has reached an all-time high of more than 7.3 million people, and most offenders (70%) are supervised in the community on probation and, to a lesser extent, parole (Bonczar & Glaze, 2009). Recent estimates suggest that approximately 14.5% of male offenders and

31.0% of female offenders have a serious mental illness such as schizophrenia, major depression, or bipolar disorder (Fazel & Danesh, 2002; Steadman, Osher, Robbins, Case, & Samuels, 2009)—meaning that approximately 1 million people with serious mental illness are currently supervised by community corrections agencies. As many as three quarters of these offenders have co-occurring substance abuse disorders (Hartwell, 2004; see also Abram & Teplin, 1991).

In general, persons with mental illness on community supervision are more likely to return to custody than are their relatively healthy counterparts, but there is somewhat mixed evidence regarding their likelihood of committing new offenses. For example, Porporino and Motiuk (1995) found that only 4.8% of parolees with mental disorder whom they followed for six months after release committed a new offense during that time, compared to 23.1% of parolees without mental disorder who committed a new offense (total $N = 72$). Other studies have similarly found that offenders with mental illness have equal or lower rates of rearrest than offenders without mental illness (e.g., Feder, 1991; Lovell, Gagliardi, & Peterson, 2002; McShane, Williams, Pelz, & Quarles, 2005). A few notable exceptions have found conflicting results. For example, Eno Louden and Skeem (2011) found that among more than 40,000 parolees in California followed for one year after release, those with mental illness were more likely than those without to return to custody for a new offense (45% to 78% increased likelihood, depending on offense type).

On the other hand, there is unequivocal evidence that technical offenses are a particular concern among offenders with mental illness. For example, Eno Louden and Skeem (2011) found that parolees with mental illness were 120% more likely than those without to commit a technical violation. Further, Porporino and Motiuk (1995) reported that parolees with mental disorder (who, as noted above, were *less* likely to have committed a new offense) were more likely to have their parole suspended than parolees without mental disorder (47.6% versus 38.5%). Thus, technical violations seem to be a primary mechanism by which offenders with mental disorder become further entangled in the criminal justice system.

Impetus for Change in the System

The problem of disproportionate recidivism for offenders with mental illness received national attention from the Council of State Governments (CSG) in its Criminal Justice/Mental Health Consensus Project report (2002). Until this time, there was scant research on the issue, save for an edited volume by Lurigio (1996) that presented descriptions of some novel community corrections programs. Based on input from policymakers and practitioners, the CSG report made a series of policy statements (recommendations) for alleviating this problem. Of particular relevance to community corrections was policy statement #16, which mirrored the sentiment of Lurigio's (1996) volume and suggested that agencies "assist offenders with mental illness in complying with conditions of probation." There were four recommendations for implementation:

1. Develop probation conditions that are realistic and address the relevant individual issues presented by the offender.
2. Streamline administrative procedures to ensure that federal and state benefits are reinstated immediately after a person with mental illness is released from jail.
3. Assign offenders with mental health conditions on probation to probation officers with specialized training and small caseloads.
4. Develop guidelines on compliance and violation policies regarding offenders with mental illness (CSG, 2002, pp. 120–124).

Although many agencies followed the CSG's recommendations by implementing specialty programs for offenders with mental illness, there was little research to inform the structure of such programs, and even less supporting their effectiveness (Skeem, Emke-Francis, & Eno Louden, 2006). Munetz and Griffin (2006) cited specialty probation and parole caseloads as key applications of the SIM in the fifth intercept. In addition, Lamberti and colleagues (2011) noted that many Forensic Assertive Community Treatment (FACT) programs interact with probation agencies, indicating that FACT is another application of the SIM in the fifth intercept. Specific evidence for the effectiveness of each of these interventions, and the extent to which mental health treatment is the mechanism for this effectiveness, are reviewed next.

EVIDENCE OF THE EFFECTIVENESS OF INTERVENTIONS IN INTERCEPT 5

Specialty Probation Caseloads

A national survey of ninety-one probation agencies identified five key features of a prototypic specialty mental health agency that distinguish specialty from traditional probation (Skeem et al., 2006):

- Caseloads are composed only of probationers with mental disorder.
- Officers have meaningfully reduced caseload size ($M = 48$, compared to over one hundred for traditional agencies).
- Efforts are made to provide ongoing training of officers in mental health-relevant issues.
- Internal and external resources are integrated (e.g., officers participated in treatment teams).
- Officers rely more heavily on problem solving (versus threats and sanctioning) as a supervision strategy (i.e., two-way discussions to identify

and troubleshoot obstacles to compliance; Skeem et al., 2006; see also Eno Louden, Skeem, Camp, & Christensen, 2008).

The research on the effectiveness of specialty mental health probation is sparse, and the methodological rigor of the extant studies varies. For example, Burke and Keaton's (2004) evaluation of San Diego's Connections program reported that the program had a positive impact on mental health functioning. However, 42% of probationers did not complete the program and were excluded from the analyses. These noncompleters were different in meaningful ways from those who completed the program (e.g., higher rates of homelessness, more prior criminal justice involvement), biasing the results.

The most extensive study of the effectiveness of specialty mental health caseloads in probation agencies was conducted by Skeem and colleagues (Skeem & Manchak, 2010). In this study, the researchers compared 176 probationers with mental illness on traditional probation supervision to 183 probationers with mental illness on specialty mental health supervision in a prototypical specialty agency. The agencies were similar in terms of population size, distribution of ethnic groups, and available mental health services. Because random assignment was not possible at this agency, participants were matched on age, gender, race, index offense, and time on probation, and propensity scores were employed to account for any additional preexisting differences between groups. Participants were interviewed at three time points during the course of a year (baseline, six months, twelve months), and official criminal justice outcomes (i.e., FBI arrest records, probation records) were collected for a minimum of two years after the beginning of the study. Preliminary results indicated that specialty probationers received more psychiatric services but not more substance use services, and they received more probation services (e.g., more frequent, longer meetings) than probationers in the traditional agency. Additionally, specialty probationers were 1.94 times less likely to be rearrested during the follow-up period than traditional probationers (Skeem & Manchak, 2010) but not more or less likely to have their probation term revoked.

There is more to learn about the mechanisms for the effectiveness of these caseloads, but there is some evidence about what these mechanisms might be. Informed from prior research and the larger literature, Skeem and colleagues embedded within their study several measures to assess three potential promising mediators, or mechanisms, of specialty probation's effectiveness: (1) officer compliance strategies, which examine whether officers tend to favor problem-solving or punitive, threat-oriented strategies to get supervisees to comply with probation terms and (2) the "dual role" officer–supervisee relationship that balances firmness with fairness and caring. Specialty probationers had officers with greater use of problem solving and lesser use of threats and sanctions and higher-quality "firm, fair, and caring" relationships than traditional probationers (Manchak, Skeem, & Vidal, 2007). In turn, these variables were related to improved criminal justice outcomes across both sites (e.g., lower incidence of probation violations and arrests; Manchak, Skeem, Kennealy, &

Eno Louden, 2014; Manchak, Vidal, Boal, & Skeem, 2008; Skeem, Manchak, Johnson, & Gillig, 2008). Most notably, the quality of the officer–probationer relationship fully mediated the effects of specialty probation (Skeem, Kennealy, & Manchak, 2010; Skeem & Manchak, 2010) on reducing arrests. Thus, the officer–probationer relationship appears to be an important mechanism that drives the effectiveness of specialty probation.

Just as research has helped to determine specialty probation's overall effectiveness and the potential mechanisms by which it can reduce recidivism, several studies have also helped identify programmatic elements that do not reduce recidivism. Psychiatric services, which are central to justice-based interventions for offenders with mental disorder (see Skeem, Manchak, & Peterson, 2011), do not appear to positively affect recidivism. For example, in a randomized controlled trial (N = 144) comparing Assertive Community Treatment (ACT), integrated treatment, and treatment as usual among homeless individuals with serious mental health and substance abuse disorders, Calsyn and colleagues (Calsyn, Yonker, Lemming, Morse, & Klinkenberg, 2005) found that none of the mental health treatment types had an effect on criminal justice outcomes. This is likely the case in probation settings as well. Similarly, Skeem and Manchak (2010) found that reductions in recidivism were unrelated to change in symptoms. There is relatively little evidence to suggest that mental health treatment has an effect on criminal justice outcomes in the community (although cf. Van Dorn, Desmarais, Petrila, Haynes, & Singh, 2013).

To date, specialty programs have been primarily evaluated as "packages" where the intervention as a whole is compared against treatment as usual. However, there is variability among specialty programs (Skeem et al., 2006), so the extent to which an individual program aligns with the features of a prototypical specialty agency may affect that program's level of effectiveness. As this research moves forward, it is likely to illuminate the effective ingredients of these programs: components that may be able to be used independently to address recidivism among offenders with mental disorder.

Specialty Parole Caseloads

Compared to specialty probation, there has been less research attention paid to specialty parole (see Skeem & Eno Louden, 2006). The evidence available suggests that these programs are structured similarly to typical specialty probation agencies. For example, the state of Kansas reportedly has five specialty parole officers who have backgrounds in mental health fields (e.g., social work) and supervise relatively small caseloads (forty to fifty offenders per officer; CSG Justice Center, 2007). It has been reported that parolees on these caseloads have lower rates of recidivism than parolees who received supervision as usual, but few details have been reported on the methodology of this study. In fact, there are no known randomized controlled trials of specialty parole caseloads, so only limited conclusions can be made about their effectiveness (see Skeem et al., 2011).

Perhaps the most extensive research on specialty parole caseloads has been done in California, which has a large mental health parole program. Parolees statewide who have serious psychotic symptoms and marked functional impairments—and thus are designated as in need of enhanced outpatient services—are supervised by parole agents with an average caseload of forty parolees compared to around seventy for regular agents (Farabee, Bennett, Garcia, Warda, & Yang, 2008). The main ingredients of this program are intensive supervision (via smaller caseloads for agents) and monitoring of treatment conditions, which is facilitated by parole outpatient clinics located at parole offices. As seen in specialty probation, increased services do not translate to better criminal outcomes in specialty parole. Based on data from more than 100,000 inmates released over a period of five years, Farabee and colleagues concluded that parolees receiving enhanced outpatient services were 1.13 times as likely as higher-functioning parolees with mental illness to attend at least one clinic appointment. However, they had higher recidivism rates for both new offenses and technical violations than parolees without mental disorders. For example, Eno Louden and Skeem (2011) examined all 44,987 persons released to a new term of parole in California during a one-year period and reviewed the outcomes of those parolees during their first year on parole. Compared to parolees without mental disorders, parolees receiving enhanced outpatient services were significantly more likely to return to custody (62.0% versus 33.0%, respectively; Eno Louden & Skeem, 2011). Because there have been no examinations using or replicating random assignment, the extent to which the use of enhanced outpatient services affects recidivism is unknown.

It is possible that the higher rate of technical violations for parolees receiving enhanced outpatient services may be related to the more intensive monitoring of these parolees. Frequent monitoring without effective services leads officers to discover misbehavior they otherwise would not have (Petersilia & Turner, 1993). Further, California's approach to handling technical violations is unique—parolees are routinely returned to custody solely for committing a technical violation, and often new offenses committed by parolees are handled by the parole board rather than criminal court (Petersilia, 2006). This directly affects recidivism rates for parolees with and without mental illness, which makes it difficult to determine the generalizability of findings from the state (see Eno Louden & Skeem, 2011).

Forensic Assertive Community Treatment

Forensic Assertive Community Treatment (FACT) is a variation of ACT, an intensive program that combines treatment, rehabilitation, and support services that are provided by an autonomous team composed of members from multiple fields (Morrissey & Meyer, 2005). Although FACT is not a mechanism of community supervision itself, it is sometimes used in conjunction with probation to facilitate mental health treatment (e.g., Cusack, Morrissey, Cuddeback, Prins, &

Williams, 2010). The main goal of FACT is to prevent future arrest and incarceration of clients. All clients admitted to the team have had past experience with the criminal justice system, and there is an emphasis on developing a supervised residential treatment particularly for clients with co-occurring substance use disorders (Morrissey & Meyer, 2005). Lamberti and colleagues (2004) described the characteristics of FACT programs. Key features include active partnership with judges, probation or parole officers and ensuring that clients adhere to treatment protocols though the use of legal mechanisms to maintain care as long as needed (Erickson et al., 2009). Further, Lamberti and colleagues (2011) report that the majority of programs have a probation officer as part of FACT teams on at least a part-time basis. However, there is considerable variability among programs, where programs may accept individuals with varying severity of mental illness and varying criminal justice histories. Thus, it is difficult to make generalizations about the outcomes of these programs (Cuddeback, Morrissey, & Cusack, 2008; Cusack et al., 2010; Lamberti et al., 2001, 2004).

As with the research on specialty caseloads, rigorous research on FACT is scarce. One randomized controlled trial (total $N = 132$) by Cusack and colleagues (2010) in California found reductions in jail contacts during the first twelve months after release from jail for FACT participants compared to probationers with mental illness receiving treatment as usual. Further, FACT clients received more mental health in the community and spent fewer days in the hospital than the comparison group. However, a review of FACT and similar programs concluded that FACT programs generally produce positive effects on mental health outcomes for clients but little reduction in recidivism (Jennings, 2009). Further, it is not known whether the promising effect of FACT on jail days found by Cusack and colleagues (2010) can be explained by symptom improvement. Given findings by Skeem and Manchak (2010) and others in jail diversion (Steadman, Dupius, & Morris, 2009) suggesting that symptoms improvement is unrelated to recidivism, this is a crucial question in FACT research. More broadly, it speaks to the need to know more about how and when mental health treatment can be used to reduce recidivism in community corrections.

MOVING FORWARD VIA THEORY

The lack of association between improvements in clinical outcomes and improvements in criminal justice outcomes in the interventions reviewed highlights the need to examine the theoretical underpinnings of these interventions. So far, researchers have employed a bottom-up approach by examining existing programs and attempting to parse out their effective ingredients. This has been guided by practitioners' and policymakers' reliance on mental health treatment as the primary, if not sole, mechanism for improving criminal justice outcomes for persons with mental illness (Munetz & Griffin, 2006). The 2002 CSG report described the perceptions of practitioners this way: "people on the front lines every day believe too many people with mental illness become involved in the criminal justice system because the mental health system has somehow failed. They believe that if many of the people with mental illness received the services they needed, they would not end up under arrest, in jail, or facing charges in court" (CSG, 2002, p. 26). Skeem, Manchak, and Peterson (2011) have articulated this belief as the unidimensional model, where one factor—mental illness—is viewed as the cause of most criminal behavior by persons with mental illness, and thus treating mental illness will logically prevent further criminal behavior by this group.

As described above, programs that implicitly rely on the unidimensional model and exclusively target mental illness as a means to prevent recidivism are ineffective. The reason for this is that most crimes committed by persons with mental disorder (as many as 90%) are not a direct result of symptoms. Separate research teams examined this issue among jail detainees in a diversion program (Junginger, Claypoole, Laygo, & Crisanti, 2006) and parolees with mental illness (Peterson, Skeem, Hart, Vidal, & Keith, 2010), and both teams concluded that symptoms such as hallucinations were the direct or indirect cause of offense in only about 10% of cases. These findings led scholars to wonder whether there is a subgroup of offenders with mental illness who consistently commit crimes because of symptoms, and whether this group could be identified (see Skeem et al., 2011). The prior studies (Junginger et al., 2006; Peterson et al., 2010) examined only the most recent crime for each offender they studied. Recently, Peterson (2012) interviewed 142 probationers and parolees with mental illness on their history of arrests and convictions and concluded that there was no identifiable group of offenders who primarily commit crimes that are caused by symptoms. These research findings together suggest that crimes that are caused by symptoms are rare (perhaps 10% of those offenses committed by persons with mental illness), so many offenders with mental illness will not have committed any crimes due to symptoms. Of those offenders who do commit some crimes because of symptoms, many of their crimes are unrelated to symptoms. As such, more than mental health treatment is needed to improve criminal justice outcomes for offenders with mental disorder (see Skeem et al., 2011, for a detailed argument). For clues on what specific interventions can be done, a top-down approach using theory is needed.

Given that offenders with mental disorder are similar to offenders without in the causes of their offenses, we can draw upon decades of research on general (without mental illness) offenders. This research has been distilled into concrete principles for correctional programming in the Risk–Need–Responsivity (RNR) model of correctional supervision (Andrews, Zinger, Hoge, Bonta, Gendreau, & Cullen, 1990; Bonta & Andrews, 2007). This model involves (a) targeting high-intensity supervision and services toward offenders at high risk of reoffense ("Risk"), (b) focusing supervision on reducing offenders' criminogenic needs, or changeable risk factors for recidivism like substance abuse ("Need"), and (c) delivering correctional interventions in a manner consistent with the offender's individual characteristics and learning style ("Responsivity"; Bonta & Andrews, 2007). The extent to which correctional programs align with the RNR principles relate directly to recidivism rates for offenders (Andrews & Dowden, 2005). The mechanisms of specialty caseloads that seem to reduce recidivism align with the RNR principles. For example, the notion that specialty officers may target criminogenic needs in addition to mental health during the course of supervision aligns with the "Need" principle (see Eno Louden, Skeem, Camp, Vidal, & Peterson, 2012). Here, an officer might monitor compliance with substance abuse treatment for an offender with identified substance abuse problems.

For offenders with mental illness, extant research suggests components of RNR where psychiatric treatment and, more broadly, the SIM best fit. In terms of the "Risk" principle, this is informed by meta-analyses such as the one conducted by Bonta and colleagues (1998), where data from sixty-four samples of offenders were analyzed to determine the best predictors of criminal behavior and violence. Clinical predictors (e.g., symptoms and functioning) had a near-zero ($r = -.02$) relationship with criminal behavior. The risk factors most strongly associated with offense were personal demographic and criminal history variables, commonly known as the "central eight": antisocial attitudes, antisocial cognitions, antisocial peers, a history of antisocial behavior, substance abuse, family problems, problems with employment, and low levels of involvement in anticriminal recreational activities (Andrews, Bonta, & Wormith, 2006). Thus, because mental disorder is not a robust risk factor for offense, offenders with mental disorder should not be automatically judged as being at high risk. Rather, they should be assessed via validated risk assessment tools to determine their level of risk as measured by robust risk factors. There is some evidence that offenders with mental disorder may be at higher risk than general offenders based on these risk factors (Skeem, Nicholson, & Kregg, 2008; see also Morgan et al., 2010).

The "Responsivity" principle includes both general and specific responsivity (Andrews & Bonta, 2010). General responsivity refers to the types of strategies officers employ to effect behavior change in offenders, which are rooted in cognitive and social-learning theories. Related to general responsivity is a set of practices known as core correctional practices, which refer to specific ways of interacting with offenders (Dowden & Andrews, 2004; see also the 2002 CSG report for a discussion). Core correctional practices emphasize the importance of officers' developing high-quality relationships with their supervisees, which will allow the officers to effect maximum behavior change (Andrews, 2011). The other aspect of responsivity is specific responsivity, which requires officers to tailor their interventions to the specific characteristics of the client. Andrews and Bonta (2010) suggest gender, ethnicity, and age as examples of such characteristics.

Andrews and Bonta (2010) have conceptualized mental illness as a "noncriminogenic" need in that it generally is not related to criminal behavior. Although symptoms of mental illness do seem to be related to about 10% of the crimes committed by offenders with mental illness, as described earlier (Junginger et al., 2006; Peterson et al., 2010), most offenders do not have consistent patterns of committing offenses only as the result of symptoms. Thus, mental health treatment is better conceptualized as a component of responsivity. In terms of general responsivity, officers may need to engage the offender in mental health treatment to increase the likelihood that the offender will respond to correctional interventions. Here, the SIM may be a mechanism to facilitate high-quality mental health treatment that can be used to improve symptoms and functioning, so that the offender can receive maximum benefit from core correctional practices (see Skeem et al., 2011). Further, this treatment is likely necessary to alleviate symptoms so that criminal behavior can be addressed; cognitive-behavioral programs that target criminal thinking (e.g., "Thinking for a Change," Bush, Glick, & Taymans, 1997) are unlikely to be effective with offenders with unmanaged mood or psychotic symptoms. Mental health treatment can also prevent the minority of offenses that may be caused by symptoms. In terms of specific responsivity, mental illness could be considered an individual characteristic relevant to tailoring correctional programming, such as including mental health treatment as one of many services the offender receives.

IMPLICATIONS FOR RESEARCH

A consistent theme among the research for all of the interventions discussed thus far is that rigorous research is needed that allows for causal inferences regarding the effectiveness in these programs. Ideally, this would include random assignment to interventions, or in lieu of that, sophisticated statistical procedures (e.g., propensity scores; Rosenbaum & Rubin, 1983) to account for the lack of random assignment (see Skeem & Manchak, 2010). Based on what we know about the interventions that have been tried, the most promising is specialty mental health caseloads. However, much more work needs to be done to parse out the effective ingredients of these caseloads—it is possible that some ingredients, such as problem-solving supervision strategies, can be used effectively as standalone interventions.

One factor that complicates research on these interventions is the lack of standardized models. Both FACT (Lamberti et al., 2004) and specialty community corrections caseloads (Skeem et al., 2006; Skeem & Eno Louden, 2006) vary in their implementation across agencies. Features that vary across agencies can directly affect the effectiveness of the intervention. For example, caseload size in specialty probation agencies is an important feature: Agencies that stray too much from the ideal small caseload size behave more like traditional agencies (Skeem et al., 2006). Further, more needs to be known about which features of these programs are the "active ingredients" so that we can isolate the components that may be able to be implemented individually for agencies that cannot commit to specialized caseloads (see Skeem et al., 2011). Thus, researchers must fully explore these features so that agencies wishing to implement such policies or programs can be informed about which features are crucial to success.

Beyond the research that has been done, it is important to draw from theory-driven research in general corrections. There is a wealth of data pointing to effective interventions, and these are being underutilized with offenders with mental illness. For example, Bonta and colleagues (2008) recently reported on the results of a program training probation officers in the principles of RNR. Here, eighty officers were randomly assigned to either receive the training or not. Analysis of audiotaped meetings between both groups of officers and their supervisees determined that officers who received the training were much more likely to utilize RNR principles in their supervision of these offenders, and probationers supervised by RNR-trained officers were less likely to recidivate. For research like this to be done with probationers and parolees with mental disorder, agencies must first implement these practices, then partner with researchers who can evaluate the effectiveness of these interventions with this group (Wolff & Gerardi, 2008, describe an example of such a partnership).

At the same time, it is important to determine the amount and quality of mental health treatment that is available to probationers and parolees. Draine, Wilson, and Pororzelski (2008) note that most reports of services for persons with mental disorder under community corrections supervision do not provide adequate detail on the nature of services provided. There is a large knowledge base regarding types of mental health treatment that improve clinical outcomes for persons with mental illness; however, this does not translate into widely available evidence-based mental health care in the community (Torrey, Drake, Dixon, Burns, Flynn, Rush, et al., 2001). To inform application of the SIM at the fifth intercept, we must know more about the mental health services that are available, with an emphasis on treatment modalities and applications that have demonstrated evidence of effectiveness in functional improvement and symptom reduction.

IMPLICATIONS FOR POLICY

Policies for supervising probationers and parolees with mental disorder should be informed by research on effective practices for these offenders. Although not yet "evidence-based" practice for offenders with mental disorder, the practices outlined by the RNR model can be implemented by agencies. In particular, mechanisms of recidivism reduction that have been used in specialty probation agencies are promising candidates. Beyond this, policy should discourage practices that are known to be detrimental to offenders' outcomes. This is crucial, as Eno Louden and colleagues (2008) found that most probation agencies (with and without mental health caseloads) lack specific policies for officers' supervision of offenders with mental disorder, especially in regard to response to technical violations. Agencies' policies should reflect a comprehensive approach to preventing recidivism for offenders with mental disorder—an approach that moves beyond the unidimensional model (Skeem et al., 2011).

This includes provision of both mental health treatment and evidence-based correctional practices—integration of RNR and the SIM. However, if mental health treatment is a condition of community supervision, nonadherence to treatment should be addressed with intermediate sanctions (e.g., community service, increasing supervision) rather than incarceration or probation revocation. As described earlier, offenders with mental disorder often return to custody for failing to attend treatment (Eno Louden & Skeem, 2011). Treatment, especially as conceptualized by the SIM, is intended to relieve symptoms and improve functioning, not to be another hurdle that offenders with mental disorder must clear to meet the requirements of community supervision.

IMPLICATIONS FOR PRACTICE

Practitioners are ideally guided by the principle of "evidence-based corrections" (see Eskridge, 2005). The research reviewed above does not point to specific practices that have met the threshold of an evidence-based practice (see Skeem & Eno Louden, 2006). However, it does point to programs and practices that are likely to be effective (and ineffective) in the supervision of offenders with mental illness in the community. Thus far, the practices most likely to be effective relate to principles of RNR, and those that focus on mental health treatment to the exclusion of all else are likely to be ineffective.

What Is Not Recommended

Although specialty probation caseloads are promising, we know that there is at least one key feature of them that can undermine their effectiveness: caseload size. Agencies that implement specialty caseloads but do not contain the size of these caseloads tend to differ little from traditional probation supervision (Skeem et al., 2006). Further, interventions that focus primarily on mental health treatment, such as FACT, are not effective at reducing recidivism, and thus not recommended for use toward this aim, unless the offender is committing crimes as a direct result of symptoms. Similarly, the provision of substance abuse treatment alone does not appear to have an effect on probationers' rates of recidivism (Perez, 2009). At the other end of the spectrum, interventions that focus only on surveillance, with no provision or services to reduce recidivism, are likewise ineffective: Frequent supervision increases the likelihood that minor transgressions will be discovered by the officer (Petersilia & Turner 1993).

What Is Recommended

One practice likely to reduce recidivism in offenders is focusing on criminogenic needs—changeable risk factors—during supervision. Prior research with general offenders has shown that the amount of time spent discussing these risk factors in meetings has a positive effect on recidivism (Bonta et al., 2008). In an examination of eighty-three audiotaped meetings between officers and probationers in a specialty agency, Eno Louden and colleagues (2012) found that officers in this agency spent a considerable amount of time discussing probationers' criminogenic needs. Although the most common topic in these meetings was general mental health concerns (e.g., side effects of medications), three quarters (75.9%) of the meetings included a discussion of at least one of the "central eight" risk factors (those most predictive of recidivism for offenders with and without mental illness; Bonta et al., 1998). These specialty officers were engaging in this evidence-based correctional practice, even though they were not specifically trained to do so. This suggests that officers in these agencies may intuitively follow principles of effective correctional practice in addition to focusing on the mental health needs of probationers.

To properly implement evidence-based correctional programming for probationers and parolees with mental disorder, a crucial component is thorough and ongoing training of line staff. Many of the key features of effective correctional supervision relate directly to what the supervising officer does with offenders. For example, using problem-solving strategies to foster compliance rather than threats of incarceration is a choice that officers make. Likewise, boundary spanning is a skill that officers can develop. The more that officers are aware of high-quality treatment resources and can obtain services for their clients, the more likely these clients are to respond to correctional supervision, and the more that officers target criminogenic needs in meetings, the more likely they are to effect change in these risk factors (see Bonta et al., 2008; Eno Louden et al., 2012).

Even more important is the relationship that officers establish with clients. This is related to skills that officers have. Dowden and Andrews (2004) noted that this is the most important ingredient in successful supervision. The more that officers can develop a warm, fair, and caring relationship with offenders, the more likely it is that the offender will avoid recidivism (Kennealy et al., 2012; Skeem et al., 2007). If officers respond more harshly to offenders with mental disorder out of frustration (see Skeem, Encandela, & Eno Louden, 2003), these offenders may be disproportionately more likely to return to custody.

Finally, officers' stigmatizing attitudes toward mental disorder may affect their supervision of these offenders. Eno Louden (2009) found that officers hold negative attitudes toward offenders with mental illness, particularly those with schizophrenia, and (incorrectly) believe that these offenders are at high risk of offense, particularly for violence. Further, officers seek to supervise these offenders in ways that increase the offenders' likelihood of returning to custody, particularly via closer monitoring and more frequent meetings. Officers should be provided with education regarding the relative utility of risk factors and effective supervision strategies. Further, their negative attitudes may be able to be softened via structured contact with individuals with mental illness (see Corrigan, River, Lundin, Penn, Uphoff-Wasowski, & Campton, et al., 2001) so that these attitudes do not guide their supervision of offenders.

In sum, much research remains to be done on effective practices in community corrections agencies to reduce the disproportionate rates of recidivism for offenders with mental illness. Promising practices can be distilled from research examining specialty mental health caseloads and research with general offenders, but implementation of these interventions, especially at the level of line staff, is key. As described in the SIM, mental health treatment is important, but this alone is unlikely to affect recidivism. Guided by the principles of RNR, agencies should (a) assign offenders to programs based on their level of risk while taking into account the overall weak predictive power of mental illness, (b) target changeable risk factors (which may be mental illness at times for some offenders), and (c) use mental health treatment as a tool to ensure that offenders with mental illness receive the most benefit from correctional programming (and prevent the 10% of crimes that are related to symptoms). With offenders who are at this deep level of the criminal justice system—the fifth intercept—a balance of mental health treatment and criminal justice interventions must be emphasized.

REFERENCES

Abadinsky, H. (2000). *Probation and parole: Theory and practice* (7th ed.). Upper Saddle River, NJ: Prentice Hall.

Abram, K. M., & Teplin, L. A. (1991). Co-occurring disorders among mentally ill jail detainees: Implications for public policy. *American Psychologist, 46,* 1036–1045. doi :10.1037/0003-066X.46.10.1036

Andrews, D. A. (2011). The Risk-Need-Responsivity (RNR) model of correctional assessment and treatment. In J. Dvoskin, J. Skeem, R. Novaco, & K. Douglas (Eds.), *Applying social science to reduce violent offending* (pp. 127–156). New York: Oxford.

Andrews, D., & Bonta, J. (2010). Rehabilitating criminal justice policy and practice. *Public Policy and Law, 16,* 39–55. doi:10.1037/a0018362

Andrews, D. A., Bonta, J., & Wormith, S. J. (2006). The recent past and near future of risk and/or need assessment. *Crime and Delinquency, 52,* 7–27. doi:10.1177/0011128705281756

Andrews, D. A., & Dowden, C. (2005). Managing correctional treatment for reduced recidivism: A meta-analytic review of programme integrity. *Legal and Criminological Psychology, 10,* 173–187. doi:10.1348/135532505X36723

Andrews, D. A., Zinger, I., Hoge, R. D., Bonta, J. L., Gendreau, P., & Cullen, F. T. (1990). Does correctional treatment work? A clinically relevant and psychologically informed meta-analysis. *Criminology, 28,* 369–404. doi:10.1111/j.1745-9125.1990. tb01330.x

Bonczar, T. P., & Glaze, L. E. (2009). *Probation and parole in the United States, 2008.* Washington, D.C.: Bureau of Justice Statistics.

Bonta, J., & Andrews, D. A. (2007). *Risk-need-responsivity model for offender assessment and treatment* (User Report No. 2007-06). Ottawa, Ontario: Public Safety Canada.

Bonta, J., Law, M., & Hanson, R. K. (1998). The prediction of criminal and violent recidivism among mentally disordered offenders: A meta-analysis. *Psychological Bulletin, 123,* 123–142. doi:10.1080/10509670802134085

Bonta, J., Rugge, T., Scott, T. L., Yessine, A. K., & Bourgon, G. (2008). Exploring the black box of community supervision. *Journal of Offender Rehabilitation, 47*, 248–270. doi:10.1080/10509670802134085

Burke, C., & Keaton, S. (2004). *San Diego County's Connections program: Board of Corrections Final Report.* San Diego, CA: SANDAG.

Bush, J., Glick, B., & Taymans, J. (1997). *Thinking for a Change: Integrated cognitive behavior change program.* Washington, D.C.: National Institute of Corrections, US Department of Justice. Retrieved from Google Scholar.

Calsyn, R. J., Yonker, R. D., Lemming, M. R., Morse, G. A., & Klinkenberg, W. D. (2005). Impact of assertive community treatment and client characteristics on criminal justice outcomes in dual disorder homeless individuals. *Criminal Behaviour and Mental Health, 15*, 236–248. doi:10.1002/cbm.24

Corrigan, P. W., River, L. P., Lundin, R. K., Penn, D. L., Uphoff-Wasowski, K., Campton, J., Mathisen, J., Gagnon, C., Bergman, M., Goldstein, H., & Kubiak, M. A. (2001). Three strategies for changing attributions about severe mental illness. *Schizophrenia Bulletin, 27*, 187–195.

Council of State Governments (2002). Criminal Justice/Mental Health Consensus Project. Retrieved from http://www.consensusproject.org

Council of State Governments Justice Center (2007). *Increasing collaboration between corrections and mental health organizations: Kansas case study.* New York: Council of State Governments Justice Center.

Cuddeback, G. S., Morrissey, J. P., & Cusack, K. J. (2008). How many forensic assertive community treatment teams do we need? *Psychiatric Services, 59*, 205–208. doi:10.1176/appi.ps.59.2.205

Cusack, K. J., Morrissey, J. P., Cuddeback, G. S., Prins, A., & Williams, D. M. (2010). Criminal justice involvement, behavioral health service use, and costs of forensic assertive community treatment: A randomized trial. *Community Mental Health Journal, 46*, 356–363.

Dowden, C., & Andrews, D.A. (2004). The importance of staff practice in delivering effective correctional treatment: A meta-analytic review of core correctional practice. *International Journal of Offender Therapy and Comparative Criminology, 48*, 203–214. doi:10.1177/0306624X03257765

Draine, J. Wilson, A., Pogorzelski, W. (2007). Limitations and potential in current research on services for people with mental illness in the criminal justice system. *Journal of Offender Rehabilitation, 45*, 159–177.

Eno Louden, J. (2009). *Effect of mental disorder and substance abuse stigma on probation officers' case management decisions.* Unpublished doctoral dissertation, University of California, Irvine.

Eno Louden, J., & Skeem, J. (2011). Parolees with mental disorder: Toward evidence-based practice. *Bulletin of the Center for Evidence-Based Corrections, 7*, 1–9.

Eno Louden, J., Skeem, J., Camp, J., & Christensen, E. (2008). Supervising probationers with mental disorder: How do agencies respond to violations? *Criminal Justice and Behavior, 35*, 832–847. doi:10.1177/0093854808319042

Eno Louden, J., Skeem, J., Camp, J., Vidal, S., & Peterson, J. (2012). Supervision practices in specialty mental health probation: What happens in officer-probationer meetings? *Law and Human Behavior, 36*, 109–119. doi:10.1037/h0093961

Erickson, S., Lamberti, J. S., Weisman, R., Crilly, J., Nihalani, N., Stefanovics, E., & Desai, R. (2009). Predictors of arrest during forensic assertive community treatment. *Psychiatric Services, 60*, 834–837.

Eskridge, C. W. (2005). The state of the field of criminology: Brief essay. *Journal of Contemporary Criminal Justice, 21*, 296–308.

Farabee, D., Bennett, D., Garcia, D., Warda, U., & Yang, J. (2008). *Final report on the Mental Health Services Continuum Program of the California Department of Corrections and Rehabilitation—Parole Division.* Sacramento, CA: CDCR Division of Adult Parole Operations.

Fazel, S., & Danesh, J. (2002). Serious mental disorder in 23000 prisoners: A systematic review of 62 surveys. *Lancet, 359*, 545–555. doi:10.1016/S0140-6736(02)07740-1

Feder, L. (1991). A comparison of the community adjustment of mentally ill offenders with those from the general prison population. *Law and Human Behavior, 15*, 477–493.

Hartwell, S. (2004). Triple stigma: Persons with mental illness and substance abuse problems in the criminal justice system. *Criminal Justice Policy Review, 15*, 84–99. doi:10.1177/0887403403255064

Jennings, J. L. (2009). Does assertive community treatment work with forensic populations? Review and recommendations. *The Open Psychiatry Journal, 3*, 13–19.

Junginger, J., Claypoole, K., Laygo, R., & Crisanti, A. (2006). Effects of serious mental illness and substance use on criminal offenses. *Psychiatric Services, 57*, 879–882. doi:10.1176/appi.ps.57.6.879

Kennealy, P. J., Skeem, J. L., Manchak, S., & Eno Louden, J. (2012). Relationships matter: The role of offender-officer relationship quality in supervision failure. *Law and Human Behavior, 36*, 496–505.

Klockars, C. (1972). A theory of probation supervision. *The Journal of Criminal Law, Criminology, and Police Science, 63*, 550–557. http://www.jstor.org/stable/1141809

Lamberti, J. S., Deem, A., Weisman, R. L., & LaDuke, C. (2011). The role of probation in forensic assertive community treatment. *Psychiatric Services, 62*, 418–421. doi:10.1176/appi.ps.62.4.418

Lamberti, J. S., Weisman, R., & Faden, D. I. (2004). Forensic assertive community treatment: Preventing incarceration of adults with severe mental illness. *Psychiatric Services, 55*, 1285–1293. doi:10.1176/appi.ps.55.11.1285

Lamberti, J. S., Weisman, R. L., Schwarzkopf, S. B., Price, N., Ashton, R. M., & Trompeter, J. (2001). The mentally ill in jails and prisons: Towards an integrated model of prevention. *The Psychiatric Quarterly, 72*, 63–77.

Lovell, D., Gagliardi, G. J., & Peterson, P. S. (2002). Recidivism and use of services among persons with mental illness after release from prison. *Psychiatric Services, 53*, 1290–1296.

Lurigio, A. J. (1996). Responding to the mentally ill on probation and parole: Recommendations and action plans. In A. J. Lurigio (Ed.), *Community corrections in America: New directions and sounder investments for persons with mental illness and codisorders* (pp. 166–171). Seattle, WA: National Coalition for Mental and Substance Abuse Health Care in the Justice System.

Manchak, S., Skeem, J., Kennealy, P., & Eno Louden, J. (2014). High fidelity specialty mental health probation improves officer practices, treatment access, and rule compliance. *Law and Human Behavior*, advance online publication. doi:10.1037/lhb0000076

Manchak, S., Skeem, J., & Vidal, S. (2007). Care, control, and mental disorder: Comparing practices and outcomes in prototypic specialty vs. traditional probation. *Crime Scene, 14*, 29–31.

Manchak, S., Vidal, S., Boal, A., & Skeem, J. (2008, March). *Six month outcomes for probationers with mental illness.* Paper presented at the American Psychology and Law Society (AP-LS) Annual Conference, Jacksonville, FL.

McShane, M. C., Williams, F. P., Pelz, B., & Quarles, T. (2005). The role of mental disorder in parolee success. *Southwest Journal of Criminal Justice, 2*, 3–22.

Morgan, R. L., Fisher, W. H., Duan, N., Mandracchia, J. T., & Murray, D. (2010). Prevalence of criminal thinking among state prison inmates with serious mental illness. *Law and Human Behavior, 34*, 324–336. doi:10.1007/s10979-009-9182-z.

Morrissey, J., & Meyer, P. (2005, February). *Extending assertive community treatment to criminal justice settings.* Paper presented at the National GAINS Center for Evidence-Based Programs in the Justice System expert panel meeting, Bethesda, MD.

Munetz, M. R., & Griffin, P. A. (2006). Use of the Sequential Intercept Model as an approach to decriminalization of people with serious mental illness. *Psychiatric Services, 57*, 544–549. doi:10.1176/appi.ps.57.4.544

Perez, D. (2009). Applying evidence-based practices to community corrections supervision: An evaluation of residential substance abuse treatment for high-risk probationers. *Journal of Contemporary Criminal Justice, 25*, 442–458. doi:10.1177/1043986208344557

Petersilia, J. (2006). *Understanding California corrections.* Berkeley, CA: University of California. California Policy Research Center.

Petersilia, J., & Turner, S. (1993). Intensive probation and parole. *Crime and Justice, 17*, 281–335.

Peterson, J. (2012). *Untangling mental illness and criminal behavior: Exploring direct and indirect pathways between symptoms and crime.* Unpublished doctoral dissertation, University of California, Irvine.

Peterson, J., Skeem, J., Hart, E., Vidal, S., & Keith, F. (2010). Typology of offenders with mental disorder: Exploring the criminalization hypothesis. *Psychiatric Services, 61*, 1217–1222. doi:10.1176/appi.ps.61.12.1217

Porporino, F. J., & Motiuk, L. L. (1995). The prison careers of mentally disordered offenders. *International Journal of Law and Psychiatry, 18*, 29–44.

Rosenbaum, P. R., & Rubin, D. B. (1983). The central role of the propensity score in observational studies for causal effects. *Biometrika, 70*, 41–55.

Skeem, J., Emke-Francis, P., & Eno Louden, J. (2006). Probation, mental health, and mandated treatment: A national survey. *Criminal Justice and Behavior, 33*, 158–184. doi:10.1177/0093854805284420

Skeem, J., Encandela, J., & Eno Louden, J. (2003). Perspectives on probation and mandated mental health treatment in specialized and traditional probation departments. *Behavioral Sciences & the Law, 21*, 429–458. doi:10.1002/bsl.547

Skeem, J., & Eno Louden, J. (2006). Toward evidence-based practice for probationers and parolees mandated to mental health treatment. *Psychiatric Services, 57*, 333–352. doi:10.1176/appi.ps.57.3.333

Skeem, J., Eno Louden, J., Polasheck, & Camp, J. (2007). Relationship quality in mandated treatment: Blending care with control. *Psychological Assessment, 19*, 397–410. doi:10.1037/1040-3590.19.4.397

Skeem, J., Kennealy, P., & Manchak, S. (2010, March). *Do "firm but fair" relationships mediate the effect of specialty mental health supervision on recidivism?* Paper presented at the American Psychology and Law Society (AP-LS) Annual Conference, Vancouver, BC, Canada.

Skeem, J., & Manchak, S. (2010, October). *Final outcomes of the longitudinal study: "What really works!" for probationers with serious mental illness.* Paper presented at the final meeting of the Macarthur Research Network on Mandated Community Treatment, Tucson, AZ.

Skeem, J., Manchak, S., Johnson, T., & Gillig, B. (2008, March). *Comparing specialty and traditional supervision for probationers with mental illness.* In S. Manchak (Chair), *Offenders with mental illness in community corrections.* Symposium presented at the meeting of the American Psychology-Law Society Annual Conference, Jacksonville, FL.

Skeem, J., Manchak, S., & Peterson, J. (2011). Correctional policy for offenders with mental disorder: Creating a new paradigm for recidivism reduction. *Law and Human Behavior, 35,* 110–126. doi:10.1007/s10979-010-9223-7

Skeem, J., Nicholson, E., & Kregg, C. (2008, March). *Understanding barriers to re-entry for parolees with mental disorder.* In D. Kroner (Chair), *Mentally disordered offenders: A special population requiring special attention.* Symposium conducted at the American Psychology-Law Society Annual Conference, Jacksonville, FL.

Steadman, H., Dupius, S., & Morris, L. (2009, March). *For whom does jail diversion work? Results of a multi-site longitudinal study.* Paper presented at the American Psychology-Law Society Annual Conference, San Antonio, TX.

Steadman, H. J., Osher, F. C., Robbins, P. C., Case, B., & Samuels, S. (2009). Prevalence of serious mental illness among jail inmates. *Psychiatric Services, 60,* 761–765. doi:10.1176/appi.ps.60.6.761

Torrey, W., Drake, R., Dixon, L., Burns, B., Flynn, Rush, A., Clark, R., & Klatzker, D. (2001). Implementing evidence-based practices for persons with severe mental illnesses. *Psychiatric Services, 52,* 45–50. doi:10.1176/appi.ps.52.1.45

Van Dorn, R., Desmarais, S., Petrila, J., Haynes, S., & Singh, J. (2013). Effects of outpatient treatment on risk of arrest of adults with serious mental illness and associated costs. *Psychiatric Services, 64,* 856–862. doi:10.1176/appi.ps.201200406.

Wolff, N., & Gerardi, D. (2008). Building evidence on best practice through corrections-academic partnerships: Getting to successful practice. *Crime and Justice International, 23,* 13–22.

8

From Resource Center to Systems Change

The GAINS Model

HENRY J. STEADMAN, BRIAN CASE, CHANSON NOETHER,
SAMANTHA CALIFANO, AND SUSAN SALASIN ■

In 1995, Google was in its infancy. Information for program design, development, and implementation was commonly found in printed materials. Libraries and personal copies were the options of choice. Fax was often used to share key printed material, as was "snail mail" or, when time-sensitive, overnight or two-day mail services such as Federal Express and UPS. In that era, the federal government operated or funded many centralized information centers with toll-free numbers. These centers archived the printed material and forwarded it to their customers. The centers were often called "resource centers."

In the early and mid-1990s, there was little emphasis on mental health, co-occurring substance use disorders, and criminal justice issues in these resource centers. People interested in finding research or program data on these issues relied on their personal skills at finding published and unpublished products and using various references services, such as Current Contents or MEDLINE.

In that world of pre-Internet knowledge, a team from Policy Research Associates conducted the first national study of jail diversion programs (Steadman, Morris, & Dennis, 1995). What became evident in that research was that many interesting and promising jail diversion models for persons with mental illnesses and co-occurring substance use disorders had been developed at the local level. Most did not yet have quantitative outcome data, but they often reflected high levels of integration across organizations, highly diverse groups of committed stakeholders, and on-the-ground coordination of information and services. For the most part, each community had "reinvented the wheel." Based on commitment, political will, and creative thinking, huge progress had been made (National GAINS Center & Open Society Institute, 1999). Yet few of these accomplishments were apparent to other communities thinking about starting their own jail diversion programs. These promising practices, these accomplishments, these "gains" were not figurative pebbles tossed into a pond producing ever-expanding ripples of broader impact; because they existed in isolation, they could not serve as "lessons learned" for other communities.

In this context, a federal Health and Human Services agency, the Substance Abuse and Mental Health Services Administration (SAMHSA), through its Center for Mental Health Services (CMHS) and its Center for Substance Abuse Treatment, created the National GAINS Center for Persons with Co-Occurring Disorders in the Justice System. The concept was to make visible the achievements in jail diversion, in-jail services, and reentry linkages for community corrections at the local level and to work with communities and states to turn this knowledge into systemic change through targeted technical assistance products and direct technical assistance built on both program and research data.

The federal concept developed by Susan Salasin was for a national prototype center for the creation and application of the best available knowledge about how to optimally structure and provide services for a given topical domain. Planned as a federally sponsored research into practice center, which emphasizes an overarching grasp of a given topical domain—including the integration of grassroots and consumer groups in the collection, assessment, and planned use of the extant knowledge base, and aggressive collaboration between center staff and potential users in the actual application of the knowledge—the center concept enlarges upon each of the existing elements typically found in government-funded technical assistance activities. It would link these elements with all of the affected constituencies into strategic and collaborative alliance toward improving policy, practice, and outcomes at the service delivery level.

The origin of the concept for this national prototype center was derived from about fifteen years of federally funded mental health services research about the knowledge into application process. Building upon the truism that emerging new knowledge does not automatically find its way into practice, and that local needs for knowledge must be brokered and matched with available and soundly evaluated knowledge, the concept for this center was a response to congressionally driven mandates conveying the belief that the responsibility for and management of this knowledge into practice brokerage responsibility was to be discharged by federal agencies.

A premise for such a center is that "not every piece of information is created equal" in the eyes of potential users. When carefully examined, some "facts" are better (i.e., more valid or useful) than others and require the use of different routes into practice in different settings for different outcomes. Through a continuing relationship between the center's core researchers, analysts, and expert consultants with frontline practitioners, administrators, consumers/survivors, and family members, an interactive process can be developed and replicated to build and share knowledge within and across existing networks. For these purposes, it is essential to go beyond identifying evidence-based or model practices that are not necessarily transportable from one type of setting to another without significant variation in format, and to focus on principles and guidelines that can facilitate the adaptation of these evidence-based or model practices to local settings and conditions. The assessment, interpretation, and networking functions are at the heart of this type of innovation and social change.

MAJOR FUNCTIONS OF THE GAINS CENTER

GAINS represents an acronym for the following:

- **G**ather empirical research, program descriptions of promising practices, rosters of expert consultants (individuals and organizations), meta-analyses, state-of-the-art summaries, and so on.
- **A**ssess the quality and utility of the knowledge base as it now exists through a variety of means of quantitative and structured expert and consumer interactions that represent a range of input from each of the relevant stakeholders in the process.
- **I**nterpret and integrate the results to produce guidelines for users that are geared to particular stakeholder perspectives through such means as targeted fact sheets or briefs, brochures, workshops, technical assistance protocols for in-person, computer, or email consultation, specifically designed trainings, and the like—and through the cultivation of the press, behavioral science writers, legislators and elected officials, and other relevant individuals and groups.
- **N**etwork with all relevant constituencies through a variety of approaches that build linkages not only within a given constituency group but also between each of the groups at both the policy and practice levels in order to distribute existing knowledge, to refine that knowledge and create optimal modes for application, and to stimulate networking supports, informal knowledge sharing and problem solving, and effective leadership strategies.
- **S**timulate applications of principles derived from the earlier stages of activity by creating technical assistance teams and identifying evidence-based practice sites that represent both the pure and the adapted versions of these practices to serve as learning laboratories, onsite, hands-on training at these learning laboratories, and the derivation of new ideas, research, programs, and policies in service of what will become a unified constituency for further support and development of this topical domain. In other words, stimulate community-level systemic change.

Using this model between 1995 and 2012, the GAINS Center provided onsite consultation to 404 U.S. communities and telephone consultation to 64,000 individuals across the United States to plan, implement, and operate community-based diversion and reentry programs. The GAINS Center developed eighty-nine publications that include one-page fact sheets, two- to four-page program and issue briefs, twenty- to fifty-page monographs, and a variety of e-newsletters. Nearly 135,000 requests for hard copies of publications have been filled.

While the GAINS Center was not funded until 1995, its genesis is really the 1992 legislation that established SAMHSA. That legislation required the agency to provide Congress with a report on services for persons with mental illnesses and substance use disorders in the criminal justice system. That report was *Double Jeopardy: Persons with Mental Illnesses in the Criminal Justice System—A Report to Congress* (CMHS, 1995). Subsequently the GAINS Center's mission evolved to meet the changing needs of the field:

I. **1992–1995** *Shaping the* Double Jeopardy *Report*
    SAMHSA's beginning focus on criminal justice was organized around a specific mandate in the SAMHSA enabling legislation to develop a report to Congress on addressing the needs of people in need of mental health services in contact with the criminal justice system. This pre-GAINS era focused on the conceptualization, development, and dissemination of the *Double Jeopardy* report to Congress.

II. **1995–1999** *Defining the Field and Developing a Shared Vocabulary*
    This era centered on creating the GAINS Center and new partnerships with SAMHSA and the CMHS and the Center for Substance Abuse Treatment around funding the GAINS Center and externally with the first memorandum of understanding between the Department of Justice (National Institute of Corrections and National Institute of Justice) and the Department of Health and Human Services (SAMHSA).

    A major focus was creating a shared set of concepts such that "co-occurring disorders" were substance use disorders and mental illnesses and such shared criminal justice–mental health terms as prebooking and postbooking diversion and boundary spanners.

III. **2000–2005** *New Partnerships and More Sophisticated Services and Models*
     Work at this stage was characterized by an emphasis on more sophisticated models for services and organization integration with the development of such ideas as the Sequential Intercept Model (Munetz & Griffin, 2006), trauma-informed care, and the Assess, Plan, Identify, and Coordinate (APIC) model for discharge planning (Osher, Steadman, & Barr, 2002).

IV. **2005–2010** *Using and Adapting Evidence-Based Practices in Criminal Justice Settings*
    This period highlighted the infusion of evidence-based practices into the criminal justice arena. A major set of issues involved how the various sets of evidence-based practices fit the worlds of justice-involved persons with co-occurring disorders, the high rates of physical and sexual abuse among justice-involved people with co-occurring disorders, and how evidence-based practices could be adapted to be effective within this context.

V. **2011–2014** *Behavioral Health Reform and Justice-Involved Persons*
As the Affordable Care Act is refined via regulation and rules and is
fully implemented in 2014, a wide array of opportunities are expected
to expand coverage for all types of healthcare for justice-involved
persons. It will be crucial to establish a locus for mapping these
changes, to determine how they could present opportunities, and to
work with states and localities to understand and take advantage of
these opportunities. The following seem to be good candidates for
future activity:

1. *Behavioral Health Services for Justice-Involved Persons Under the
   Affordable Care Act.* There is likely to be a major shift in the partnerships
   and forms of integration between the criminal justice system and the
   evolving behavioral health systems. With pretrial detainees eligible
   for Medicaid services, will there be an incentive for not-for-profit
   community providers to come into jails, or will private correctional
   companies expand? If there are new arrangements between hospitals
   and private providers, how will they play out? Who becomes eligible for
   Medicaid with the eligibility standard being 133% of the poverty level
   for those states that choose to expand Medicaid—and will this increase
   interest in providing services to justice-involved persons?

2. *Screening and Trauma.* As eligibilities change and possibly increase the
   incentives for community providers, how will more effective screenings
   for behavioral health disorders be introduced? How will trauma issues
   be central to these protocols where traditional psychiatric diagnostic
   data have usually been deemed the essential pieces of information?

3. *Veterans and Their Families as a Priority Population.* As the healthcare
   system undergoes radical change and has numerous and uncertain
   impacts on justice-involved persons, a group with special needs and
   discrete trauma issues includes veterans from all eras, but especially
   those returning from Iraq and Afghanistan with combat experiences.
   Related to this, but largely left out of the conversation, is the huge
   collateral impact of veterans' contact with the justice system on their
   families (Tanielian & Jaycox, 2008).

The remainder of this chapter details activities in each of the part of the
GAINS model to show how it can contribute to fundamental social change in
the key areas and can be adapted elsewhere at the state level to consolidate and
enhance best practices for justice-involved persons with behavioral health needs.

GATHER

Since 1995 the GAINS Center has been an agent for transforming behavioral
health services for justice-involved individuals in America by *translating* the
best available science and emerging knowledge in the field and *disseminating*

practices that ensure access to services. "Gather" speaks directly the first and most important element—locating key, relevant research findings and best and promising practices. Properly refined in the hands of change agents, this information has huge potential to improve the nature of behavioral health services provided in jails, prisons, and community-based settings, as well as the manner in which these services are provided.

The overall goal of the GAINS Center is to improve the treatment and management of individuals with mental illness and substance use disorders who are in contact with all segments of the adult criminal justice system (i.e., law enforcement, courts, jails, prisons, and community corrections). The GAINS Center staff routinely works with national experts, policymakers, practitioners, researchers, consumers, and family members to gather the best available information on the coordination of behavioral health services for this population. The GAINS staff uses this information to promote effective solutions that can be put to immediate use.

Typically, efforts to disseminate research findings target professional, peer-reviewed and/or trade publications. While these are important outlets, these issues go beyond the traditional readership of these publications. If these multiple and complex needs are to be addressed, efforts must involve a collaboration among mental health, substance abuse, and corrections personnel, local and state officials, and consumers and family members—the majority of whom are *not* "typical" consumers of peer-reviewed, technical publications.

No one discipline or profession has all the crucial information. To reach *all* critical stakeholders, new vehicles of dissemination must be developed. Information from the entire field needs to be gathered, critically and creatively analyzed, distilled into useful and practical formats, and disseminated in a broad but targeted manner. The information-gathering activities of the GAINS model involve surveying the criminal justice and behavioral health landscape to identify cutting-edge research, innovative approaches, and promising and evidence-based practices. The GAINS model accomplishes this task through a combination of methods, including the following:

- Systematic review of relevant peer-reviewed journals and trade publications
- Subscription to listservs of relevant trade organizations, advocacy groups, other national technical assistance centers, and other sources, with a systematic and targeted review of their content
- Attending webinars on relevant topics
- Offering technical assistance to the field, both in person and by other means. This provides a unique learning opportunity for staff to identify promising programs and practices at local/state levels.
- Program surveys and other programmatic data-gathering activities

The GAINS Center staff maintains a comprehensive database of the information gathered, providing easy access to empirical research, descriptions of innovative programs, and other key resources at a moment's notice.

The GAINS model for encouraging interagency collaboration and fostering systemic change distinguishes it from other technical assistance models. Rather than relying upon the traditional clearinghouse or knowledge transfer methods used by other technical assistance centers, the GAINS model involves working interactively with policymakers, frontline practitioners, administrators, consumers, and families to promote systems change.

The GAINS model targets key organizations, such as advocacy groups and national professional associations interested in fostering systemic change in the field, to more effectively spread its message. If funding is available, these efforts can be augmented by extending support to convene meetings of key constituents to address issues facing people with behavioral health issues in the justice system. This method can serve as a particularly valuable tool to gather cutting-edge information from key players in the field on a particular topic in a concentrated manner. The GAINS Center has used this model to gather information that led to the development of several cornerstone products, including the GAINS *Adapting Evidence-Based Practices for Justice-Involved Populations Fact Sheet Series* (http://gainscenter.samhsa.gov/topical_resources/ebps.asp) and the *Ending an American Tragedy: Addressing the Needs of Justice-Involved People with Mental Illnesses and Co-occurring Disorders* report, a joint publication with the National Council for Community Behavioral Healthcare (http://gainscenter. samhsa.gov/topical_resources/nlf.asp).

ASSESS

The second stage of the GAINS model is to assess the evidence. The emphasis on evidence as the driver of practice established the National GAINS Center as a bridge between the communities of researchers and practitioners. This "what works" approach serves as a filter for the material gathered in the first stage of the model. As a result, the center's products can point out gaps in the research, identify exemplary programs and practices, and translate research findings into recommendations for practice. Perhaps most importantly, this stage prepares for later-stage work by pointing to practices where implementation has outpaced the evidence and drilling down to the core principles for practices.

The assessment of evidence is important for several reasons. Policymakers require valid and reliable evidence to advance legislation. Even in a good fiscal climate, most communities cannot afford the risk of a new program or a change in practice unless there is evidence of its effectiveness in achieving public health and safety objectives and reducing net public expenditures. Products that highlight effective practices can help communities to avoid ineffective programming.

The focus of the GAINS Center has been to improve the lives of people with mental and substance use disorders in contact with the justice system through systems and services integration, attention to individual needs, and access to comprehensive and appropriate services. Therefore, any inquiry into the effectiveness of a given practice is not "Does the practice work for people with mental disorders?" but "Does this practice work for justice-involved people with mental disorders?" For example, in 2004 the center launched an initiative that examined the effectiveness for justice-involved persons with behavioral health needs of the evidence-based practices identified by the SAMHSA CMHS. Over the course of a year, the center convened six expert panels where an expert presented a paper to a review panel on the empirical evidence that each practice was effective when adapted for individuals in the justice system. The panels considered four of the practices identified as evidence-based practices by the CMHS and two promising practices. For the most part, the lack of published research on these practices when adapted for justice-involved individuals stood in contrast to the wealth of data on the practices for the general population of people with mental and substance use disorders. In many ways, these meetings and papers were a catalyst to the subsequent literature pointing out the need for evidence-based practices targeting criminogenic risk factors if treatment was expected to achieve public safety outcomes. As they stood at the time, the accepted evidence-based practices had been validated on improvements in symptom reduction, increased functioning, higher quality of life, successful employment, and the like rather than arrests and jail days (Bond, 2004; Bond, Drake, & Becker, 2008; Coldwell & Bender, 2007; Drake, Mercer-McFadden, Mueser, McHugo, & Bond, 1998; Drake, Mueser, Brunette, & McHugo, 2004; Marshall & Lockwood, 1998; McFarlane, Dixon, Lukens, & Lucksted, 2003; Miklowitz, George, Richards, Simoneau, & Suddath, 2003; Mueser et al., 2002; Pitschel-Walz, Leucht, Bauml, Kissling, & Engel, 2001).

Several types of evidence are employed during the assessment phase. In general, the first step is to conduct a literature review of articles published in peer-reviewed journals. Research reports from government agencies, foundations, and private evaluation firms are also considered. However, published research is often insufficient. It often avoids drawing meaningful conclusions about proposed changes in practice; what is often needed is a good idea of how to apply the results. Program case studies and the testaments of key informants, from administrators to clinicians to consumers, are important for obtaining the full picture.

Depending on the practice and the intended product, the center uses a number of methods for assessing the evidence. The methods range from staffers whose work is reviewed by independent experts, to experts whose work is then sent out for review by other experts, to work groups.

Particular topics lend themselves to development by content-area experts with independent review by other experts. One product developed in this fashion was the monograph *Screening and Assessment of Co-Occurring Disorders in the Justice System* (Peters, Bartoi, & Sherman, 2008). It offered guidance in addressing challenges and implementing state-of-the-art practices in the screening and assessment of persons with co-occurring disorders involved in the criminal justice system.

Work groups can be used to start or conclude the assessment phase. Work groups on combat veterans in the justice system and backlogged competency restoration systems, for example, provided direction for the remainder of the assessment phase. Work group members helped to define the problem, identify the objectives, nominate best practices, and delineate criteria for reviewing the published evidence. One product developed through this process was the 2008 consensus report *Responding to the Needs of Justice-Involved Combat Veterans with Service-Related Trauma and Mental Health Conditions* (CMHS National GAINS Center, 2008).

Work groups at the end of the assessment phase are valuable for the product from multiple perspectives. For example, the center developed a guide, *Practical Advice on Jail Diversion* (CMHS National GAINS Center, 2007), in 2006 and 2007. The experts invited to participate in the work group included jail diversion coordinators, public defenders, psychiatrists, peer specialists, graduates of jail diversion programs, state mental health administrators, and law enforcement personnel. In addition, to test the value of the guide, three communities (Missoula, MT; Charlottesville, VA; Somerset County, ME) pilot-tested the guide for six months and provided feedback.

An essential element of this phase is the use of people with different perspectives—differences in background, lived experience, and profession—to evaluate the evidence. In the example above, the center gathered people who were experts in the practice of jail diversion, but each person had a different perspective. A wide breadth in perspective is important because the center's activities are intended to have practical value for every individual interested in criminal justice/behavioral health initiatives, from program participants to program evaluators to program funders. This process may not result in the most efficient assessment phase, as the diversity of opinion extends the process of determining what constitutes evidence and assessing its quality, but it leads to a product truer to the diverse perspectives of community members.

The "A" in the GAINS model serves as a filter for the material gathered in the first phase. The assessment phase is driven by a "what works" approach, but it is more specific: "What works, for whom, in what context?" The center has employed multiple strategies to assess the evidence for a particular practice or program model. In the end, the goal is provide communities with straightforward guidance on how to meet the needs of justice-involved people with mental and substance use disorders.

INTEGRATE

As promising models for persons with co-occurring disorders involved in the justice system develop, few accomplishments were evident to other communities initiating diversion programs. For the research, knowledge, and "lessons learned" to be turned into systemic change in other communities, targeted program and research data must be distilled into comprehensible and practical units. The "I" in the GAINS acronym represents two facets that the center strives to achieve: integrating the research and data into useable, targeted products and integrating the products into direct technical assistance events.

Once all relevant program and research data on services and strategies for responding to the needs of people with co-occurring disorders who come in contact with the justice system have been gathered and assessed, the GAINS Center works to integrate the various results into understandable and practical products—and works with communities to turn these results into transferable principles, practices, and procedures that other communities can use. The GAINS Center transforms projects' models, strategies, tools, and lessons learned into technical assistance products and events building on research. These targeted products help communities identify gaps in services and develop integrated approaches to respond more effectively to people with co-occurring disorders in the justice system.

The GAINS Center has developed eighty-nine publications that include factsheets, program/issue briefs, monographs, and a variety of e-newsletters. These publications and resources document the prevalence, characteristics, needs, and treatment interventions for justice-involved individuals with co-occurring disorders. Publications and resources available include program briefs (*The EXIT Program: Engaging Diverted Individuals Through Voluntary Services*), clinical interventions (*Motivational Interviewing*), community guides (*Practical Advice on Jail Diversion: Ten Years of Learning on Jail Diversion from the CMHS National GAINS Center*), transition planning models (*A Best Practice Approach to Community Re-entry from Jails for Inmates with Co-occurring Disorders: The APIC Model*), transition planning instruments (*The Re-Entry Checklist*), and education tools (*Consumer Perspective Exhibit*). These products are available from the GAINS Center's website at http://gainscenter.samhsa.gov.

Program/Issue Briefs and Monographs: These briefs and monographs describe particular models and programs while reporting on the key outcome research and data and offer transferable ideas and practices to other communities. Monographs also provide detailed information on the implementation and integration of these models and programs into communities.

Evidence-Based Practice Factsheets: Too few people with serious mental illness who are involved in the justice system receive comprehensive and appropriate services. The GAINS Center's evidence-based practices initiative is intended to help close this treatment gap by promoting the adaptation and use of these practices with people involved in the criminal justice system. The GAINS Center has turned the results of a series of expert panel meetings into eight factsheets that examine the adaptation and implementation of evidence-based practices with justice-involved individuals, review the research evidence base, and highlight initiative programs.

E-Newsletters: The GAINS Center publishes monthly e-newsletters and periodic news flashes to a distribution list of 5,500 email addresses regarding upcoming events or opportunities and new resources. The monthly e-newsletters feature new and/or innovative programs on behavioral health/criminal justice initiatives throughout the nation.

Along with integrating data and research into useable products, the GAINS Center uses national and local experts to refine the research into targeted technical assistance to communities. As discussed previously, the GAINS Center has provided technical assistance to many communities across the United States who wish to design, plan, implement, and evaluate interventions such as uniform screening and assessment procedures, jail diversion and reentry programs, and cross-training strategies such as Sequential Intercept Mapping, consumer integration training, and trauma-informed criminal justice systems training.

As technical assistance providers for the 2002–2007 CMHS Targeted Capacity Expansion grantees and the 2008–2010 CMHS Jail Diversion and Trauma Recovery—Priority to Veterans grantees, the GAINS Center has provided support to these jail diversion grantees in infrastructure development, incorporating consumer/veterans' voices into program development and implementation, organizing and assessing how the mental health and criminal justice systems interact with persons with mental illness, and providing expert advice and guidance on sustainability. Trainings provided by the GAINS Center include but are not limited to the following:

Sequential Intercept Mapping: The focus of this workshop is to improve criminal justice and behavioral health collaboration, to promote increased jail diversion opportunities for justice-involved persons with mental illness and justice-involved veterans, and to strengthen reentry service linkages from jail and prison. Sequential Intercept Mapping facilitates cross-system communication and helps identify resources, gaps, and barriers in the existing system. The essential ingredient to its success is gathering twenty-five to forty-five people representing the full array of local systems and organizations needed to provide integrated services to justice-involved persons with behavioral health disorders. A local map is created using the Sequential Intercept Model based on input from all the participants. Often it is the first time many of them have grasped the full picture of services available in their community across the five criminal justice system intercept points.

Consumer Integration Training: This training involves partnering with people in recovery to guide the behavioral health system, promote system transformation, increase supports, reduce barriers, and support the vision that all persons with mental illness can recover. To effect system transformation, consumers of mental health services must be integral to the planning process, including development of policies and procedures. This training provides:

- Administrators and policymakers with information and direction to facilitate the integration of consumers into policy and program development
- Consumers with information and skills to become effective partners and participants in this process

- Communities with assistance in developing a strategic plan for community-based systems change.

Trauma-Informed Criminal Justice Systems Training: Although prevalence estimates vary, there is consensus that high percentages of justice-involved women and men have experienced serious trauma throughout their lifetime (Browne, Miller, & Maguin, 1999; Policy Research Associates, 2011). The reverberating effects of trauma can challenge a person's capacity for recovery and pose significant barriers to accessing services, often resulting in an increased risk of coming into contact with the criminal justice system. *How Being Trauma-Informed Improves Criminal Justice System Responses* is a half-day training for criminal justice professionals; the goals are to increase their understanding and awareness of the impact of trauma, develop trauma-informed responses, and provide strategies for developing and implementing trauma-informed policies.

Trauma-informed criminal justice responses can help to avoid retraumatizing individuals and thereby increase safety for all, decrease recidivism, and promote and support recovery of justice-involved people with serious mental illness. Partnerships across systems can also help to link individuals to trauma-informed services and treatment.

Identifying the best practices and applying research and knowledge to program development is critical to communities developing jail diversion and reentry programs for individuals with co-occurring disorders. As a national locus for collection and dissemination of information about effective services for people with co-occurring disorders in contact with the justice system, the GAINS Center interprets and integrates the research and knowledge that has been gathered and assessed into useable products and distills the results into direct technical evidence that can be provided to communities.

NETWORK

The next stage focuses on getting the products into the hands of people who can be change agents. One of the fundamental principles for networking activities is that anyone can be a change agent: Over sixteen years, we have seen judges, family members, consumers, behavioral health program administrators, police officers, jail administrators, clinicians, elected officials, defense attorneys, and many others become successful change agents, aided greatly by GAINS products.

One major mechanism for networking has been five national GAINS conferences. Beginning in 2000 in Miami with 400 attendees through 1,100 attendees in Washington, D.C. in 2010, an interdisciplinary gathering of dedicated change agents sharing information on their programs and using GAINS products has had a huge impact at the local level in shaping new programs. It has exposed

GAINS staff to innovations in practice and policy that can then be mined using the GAINS model to produce further materials to effect radical change.

Another type of activity has been a partnership with the Council of State Governments Justice Center to develop the Judges' Criminal Justice/Mental Health Leadership Initiative. Having jointly recognized the powerful role judges were playing in developing community-based alternatives to incarceration for persons with behavioral health needs, GAINS and the Council of State Governments brought together the twenty judges attending the 2004 GAINS Conference to determine whether an informal group of judges working on these issues would be useful to support their peers and to encourage judges new to this area to be active, productive change agents. Currently there are approximately 350 on the Judges Leadership Initiative email listserv. Nearly seventy-five judges met while attending the alternate-year GAINS and Council of State Governments national conferences. Working with the Judges' Leadership Initiative national advisory board, we have created three widely distributed products, the *Judges' Guide to Mental Health Jargon* (Judges' Criminal Justice/Mental Health Leadership Initiative, 2007; revised 2012), the *Judges' Guide to Mental Health Diversion* (Judges' Criminal Justice/Mental Health Leadership Initiative, 2010), and the *Judges' Guide to Mental Health Jargon in Juvenile Justice* (Judges' Criminal Justice/Mental Health Leadership Initiative, 2012). Just over 14,000 copies of the first guide have been distributed.

Networking takes many different forms in addition to the two examples mentioned above. Sometimes it is the GAINS Center sending materials to local or regional advocacy groups convening work groups or lobbying meetings. Sometimes it is presenting a webinar with 150 to 800 phone lines involving an unknown number of people. Sometimes it is presenting a panel of researchers, clinicians, and consumers at annual professional meetings. Regardless of the event, it would not happen without the successful work at the prior three GAINS model stages.

STIMULATE SYSTEMIC CHANGE

Without the final stage of the GAINS model, all is for naught. The model is predicated on creating community-based comprehensive and appropriate services for justice-involved persons with behavioral health needs. The model is not one of direct advocacy; rather, it is based on equipping (maybe "empowering" in today's mental health advocacy language) those in positions in their communities to directly produce change to do what only they can do. There is no one template for how this happens.

One example is the *Brief Jail Mental Health Screen* (Policy Research Associates, 2005). With National Institute of Justice funding, the project developed a screening instrument for mental disorders for booking officers in local jails to support universal screening for mental disorders at the booking stage in local jails. After the empirical basis for this eight-question, 2.5-minute screening instrument was established, the 5,500-person email listserv was informed of its availability, and it was advertised at the biannual GAINS conference. As a result, the GAINS Center estimates that more than 200 U.S. jails are using the screening instrument—and there is legislation in North Carolina mandating its use in every local jail. Moreover, it is used in some communities to screen for eligibility in jail diversion and in at least one day-reporting program in New York City to screen for mental illness.

Another example is the development in the past decade of a comprehensive, community-based system for justice-involved persons with behavioral health disorders. At the 2000 National GAINS Conference in Miami, two GAINS Center staff members—at the request of the Honorable Steven Leifman—met in his chambers with key court staff to give them an overview of options for jail diversion for the county misdemeanor court. This meeting was followed by having three GAINS consultants meet with a twenty-five-person stakeholder group to map the Miami-Dade criminal justice system to identify its current capacities and gaps. What evolved was the 11th Judicial Circuit Criminal Mental Health Project (Leifman, 2011; Leifman & Coffey, 2010). The project currently operates a prebooking crisis intervention team (CIT) training program, which teaches law enforcement officers to respond more effectively to psychiatric emergencies in the community, two postbooking jail diversion programs targeting individuals charged with misdemeanor and felony offenses, a postbooking forensic hospital diversion program targeting individuals adjudicated incompetent to proceed to trial, and a program that works to expedite access to federal entitlement benefits using the SSI/SSDI, Outreach, Access, and Recovery (SOAR) approach (http://www.prainc.com/SOAR).

To date, more than 4,300 law enforcement officers representing every municipality in the county, the county jail, and the county school system (a total of thirty-six agencies) have completed the forty-hour CIT training. Since implementing CIT seven years ago, officers from a single police force—the Miami-Dade Police Department—have responded to approximately 25,000 calls involving people with mental illnesses. During the first six months of 2011 alone, CIT officers from this agency responded to a total of 2,321 mental health calls, resulting in 751 diversions to crisis stabilization units and only one individual being arrested and booked into the county jail. Overall, criminal justice recidivism rates among program participants have decreased by 75% for felony diversions. Owing in part to the success of the felony jail diversion and forensic hospital diversion programs, admissions to state forensic treatment facilities from the county have dropped by 41% since 2006 (Leifman, 2011; Leifman & Coffey, 2010).

This project has also achieved remarkable success in obtaining federal entitlement benefits for participants, with 91% of applications submitted approved in fewer than sixty days. Since its creation, the project has received ongoing support from Miami-Dade County and the Florida Department of Children and Families, which helps to fund case management positions, housing, medications, and transportation for participants. Because most of the participants are homeless at the time of enrollment, the project has also partnered with the Miami-Dade County Homeless Trust, which has provided dedicated housing resources for individuals with mental illness coming out of the justice system. Together, these efforts have been credited with contributing to a reduction in the average daily jail census from over 7,200 inmates to 5,200, a reduction of nearly 2,000 individuals between 2009 and 2011, resulting in meaningful cost avoidance and dramatically improved public health and safety (Leifman, 2011; Leifman & Coffey, 2010).

Another area to which we contributed was assisting state "mini-GAINS" centers. The first was the Ohio Criminal Justice Coordinating Center of Excellence, followed by similar centers at the University of Massachusetts Medical School, the University of South Florida's Florida Mental Health Institute, the Pennsylvania Mental Health and Justice Center of Excellence, and recently the Illinois Center of Excellence for Behavioral Health and Justice. For each, we supported site visits to the GAINS Center, numerous telephone consultations, and shared resources. A full account of these centers, each powerful sources for systemic change, may be seen in Chapter 10.

CONCLUSION

The GAINS model, as implemented through the GAINS Center since 1995, has proven its value as a generalizable model for stimulating and supporting significant social change in an area often bereft of public support. It appears to be a model that has generalized application to programs at the interface of criminal justice, mental health, and substance abuse, but also to many other areas of public health and safety. Although there may not be rigorous evaluations of its outcomes, the eighteen years of activity with the examples included in this chapter strongly support the model's value.

REFERENCES

Bond, G. R. (2004). Supported employment: Evidence for an evidence-based practice. *Psychiatric Rehabilitation Journal, 27,* 345–359.

Bond, G. R., Drake, R. E., & Becker, D. R. (2008). An updated on randomized controlled trials of evidence-based supported employment. *Psychiatric Rehabilitation Journal, 31,* 280–290.

Browne, A., Miller, B., & Maguin, E. (1999). Prevalence and severity of lifetime physical and sexual victimization among incarcerated women. *International Journal of Law and Psychiatry, 22,* 301–322.

Center for Mental Health Services (1995). *Double jeopardy: Persons with mental illnesses in the criminal justice system.* Rockville, MD: Author. Available from http://gainscenter.samhsa.gov/pdfs/disorders/Double_Jeopardy.pdf

CMHS National GAINS Center (2007). *Practical advice on jail diversion: Ten years of learnings on jail diversion from the CMHS National GAINS Center.* Delmar,

NY: Author. Available from http://gainscenter.samhsa.gov/pdfs/jail_diversion/PracticalAdviceOnJailDiversion.pdf

CMHS National GAINS Center (2008). *Responding to the needs of justice-involved combat veterans with service-related trauma and mental health conditions: A consensus report of the CMHS National GAINS Center's forum on combat veterans, trauma, and the justice system.* Delmar, NY: Author. Available from http://gainscenter.samhsa.gov/pdfs/veterans/CVTJS_Report.pdf

Coldwell, C. M., & Bender, W. S. (2007). The effectiveness of assertive community treatment for homeless populations with severe mental illness: A meta-analysis. *Psychiatric Services, 164*, 363–399.

Drake, R. E., Mercer-McFadden, C., Mueser, K. T., McHugo, G. J., & Bond, G. R. (1998). Review of integrated mental health and substance abuse treatment for patients with dual disorders. *Schizophrenia Bulletin, 24*, 589–608.

Drake, R. E., Mueser, K. T., Brunette, M. F., & McHugo, G. J. (2004). A review of treatments for people with severe mental illnesses and co-occurring substance use disorders. *Psychiatric Rehabilitation Journal, 27*, 360–374.

Judges' Criminal Justice/Mental Health Leadership Initiative (2012). *Judges' guide to mental health jargon: A quick reference for justice system practitioners* (2nd ed.). Delmar, NY: Policy Research Associates.

Judges' Criminal Justice/Mental Health Leadership Initiative (2010). *Judges' guide to mental health diversion: A quick reference for justice system practitioners.* Delmar, NY: Policy Research Associates, CMHS National GAINS Center.

Judges' Criminal Justice/Mental Health Leadership Initiative (2012). *Judges' guide to juvenile mental health jargon: A quick reference for juvenile justice system practitioners.* Delmar, NY: Policy Research Associates.

Leifman, S. (2011, November). *Interplay between mental health and criminal justice system.* Presented to the Mental Health HOPE Symposium, Washington, D.C.

Leifman, S., & Coffey, T. (2010). Decriminalizing mental illness: Miami-Dade County tackles a crisis at the roots. *National Council Magazine, 1*, 18–22.

Marshall, M., & Lockwood, A. (1998). Assertive community treatment for people with severe mental disorders. *Cochrane Database of Systematic Reviews, 1998*, 2.

McFarlane, W. R., Dixon, L., Lukens, E., & Lucksted, A. (2003). Family psychoeducation and schizophrenia: A review of the literature. *Journal of Marital & Family Therapy, 29*, 223–245.

Miklowitz, D. J., George, E. L., Richards, J. A., Simoneau, T. L., & Suddath, R. L. (2003). A randomized study of family-focused psychoeducation and pharmacotherapy in the outpatient management of bipolar disorder. *Archives of General Psychiatry, 60*, 904–912.

Mueser, K. T., Corrigan, P. W., Hilton, D. W., Tanzman, B., Schaub, A., Gingerich, S., Essock, S. M., Tarrier, N., Morey, B., Vogel-Scibilia, S., & Herz, M. I. (2002). Illness management and recovery: A review of the research. *Psychiatric Services, 53*, doi:10.1176/appi.ps.53.10.1272. Full text available from http://ps.psychiatryonline.org/article.aspx?articleid=87149

Munetz, M. R., & Griffin, P.A. (2006). Use of the Sequential Intercept Model as an approach to decriminalization of people with serious mental illness. *Psychiatric Services, 57*, 544–549.

National GAINS Center & Open Society Institute (1999). *The courage to change: A guide for communities to create integrated services for people with co-occurring disorders in the justice system.* Delmar, NY: National GAINS Center. Available from http://gainscenter.samhsa.gov/pdfs/guides/CourageToChange.pdf

Osher, F., Steadman, H. J., & Barr, H. (2002). *A best practice approach to community re-entry from jail for inmates with co-occurring disorders: The APIC model.* Delmar, NY: National GAINS Center. Available from http://gainscenter.samhsa.gov/pdfs/reentry/apic.pdf

Peters, R. H., Bartoi, M. G., & Sherman, P. B. (2008). *Screening and assessment of co-occurring disorders in the justice system.* Delmar, NY: CMHS National GAINS Center. Available from http://gainscenter.samhsa.gov/pdfs/disorders/ScreeningAndAssessment.pdf

Pitschel-Walz, G., Leucht, S., Bauml, J., Kissling, W., & Engel, R. R. (2001). The effect of family interventions on relapse and rehospitalization in schizophrenia: A meta-analysis. *Schizophrenia Bulletin, 27,* 73–92.

Policy Research Associates (2005). *Brief jail mental health screen.* Delmar, NY: Author. Available from http://gainscenter.samhsa.gov/pdfs/disorders/bjmhsform.pdf

Policy Research Associates (2011). *Evaluation of the CMHS Targeted Capacity Expansion for Jail Diversion Programs: Final report.* Delmar, NY: Author.

Steadman, H. J., Morris, S. M., & Dennis, D. L. (1995). The diversion of mentally ill persons from jails to community-based services: A profile of programs. *American Journal of Public Health, 85,* 1630–1635.

Tanielian, T., & Jaycox, L. H. (Eds.). (2008). *Invisible wounds of war: Psychological and cognitive injuries, their consequences, and services to assist recovery.* Santa Monica, CA: RAND Center for Military Health Police Research. Available from http://www.rand.org/pubs/monographs/MG720.html

9

Using the Consensus Project Report to Plan for System Change

AMANDA BROWN CROSS, CAROL A. SCHUBERT,
AND KIRK HEILBRUN ■

This chapter addresses two important considerations relevant to diversion and the Sequential Intercept Model (SIM). First, we describe the Consensus Project, a product of the Council of State Governments (CSG), which offers a model for different points of intervention that is similar in some respects to the SIM. Readers should be aware of both models and of the Consensus Project more generally. Second, we describe the development and implementation of a diversion program in Bexar County (San Antonio), Texas, as an illustration of a program developed under the Consensus Project model. Bexar County's experience provides important (and concrete) guidance for communities seeking to develop diversion programs. We will describe Bexar County's experience with comments about the selection of various points of interception—and the ways in which other communities can use the Consensus Project and the SIM to help plan and implement diversion programs.

THE CSG CONSENSUS PROJECT

Recognizing many of the problems regarding the management and treatment of persons with mental illness involved in the criminal justice system, the CSG convened a group of stakeholders to create recommendations for improving response to persons with mental illness in the justice system. The two-year initiative included consultations from over one hundred state legislators, judges and other legal personnel, corrections personnel, mental health administrators, consumer advocates, and leaders in law enforcement. The findings were released in 2002 in the report *Criminal Justice/Mental Health Consensus Project*. The report was summarized in an article by Thompson, Reuland, and Souweine (2003).

The report explicitly incorporates political considerations. The Consensus Project initiative itself was implemented with the intent of providing bipartisan policy recommendations to public and private stakeholders in criminal justice and mental health. As such, the recommendations in the report are targeted toward "agents of change"—high-level policymakers whose decisions have broad impact, practitioners in management positions whose agencies deliver services in the community, and leading advocates.

The report is divided into two parts. In this chapter we summarize the first part, which describes the opportunities available in the criminal justice and mental health systems to identify individuals with mental illness and to respond in ways that respect individual rights while promoting public safety and accountability. These opportunities are identified at different points across the continuum of criminal justice processing, from community prevention of police involvement altogether to community prevention of rearrest after release from criminal justice monitoring. The report categorizes stages of mental health/justice involvement as (1) participation in the community mental health system, (2) initial contact with law enforcement, (3) pretrial issues, courts, and sentencing, (4) incarceration and reentry, and (5) continued involvement with the mental health system after completion of the criminal justice sentence. This categorization is similar to the intercepts described in the SIM, although the SIM does not use "participation in community mental health" as an intercept, and the Consensus Project describes SIM Intercepts 2 and 3 in a single stage (pretrial issues, courts, and sentencing). As the next section of this chapter will illustrate, there is value in considering the prebooking and postbooking diversion models separately from the courts, particularly since problem-solving courts (a widespread and growing form of specialized intervention) would share a single step with these prebooking and postbooking models under the Consensus Project description.

In the Consensus Project model, opportunities for diversion are emphasized heavily in the early phases of the continuum: community mental health participation, police contact, and pretrial detention. Recommendations for subsequent phases (incarceration and reentry) stress the fair accommodation and treatment of an individual's behavioral health needs. The recommendations at each stage assume that recommendations at earlier stages were followed. In this way, the Consensus Project model is not a series of discrete recommendations but rather a model for larger system reform, with recommendations for each stage related to those made at earlier stages. For example, the model's recommendations about diverting persons to mental healthcare when appropriate assume that the first recommendation, regarding the availability of suitable mental health services, is followed.

Within five broad stages of mental health and justice processing, the report identifies twenty-three specific events that provide an opportunity to improve the typical interaction between a person with mental illness and the criminal justice system. Each event is accompanied by a proposed improvement. For example, for the event "Pretrial release/detention hearing," the recommendation is "Maximize the use of pretrial release options in appropriate cases of defendants with mental illness so that no person is detained pretrial solely for the lack of information or options to address the person's mental illness." For each event–policy dyad, the report offers detailed recommendations for implementing the policy change, often including narrative examples of model programs already in place. Policy statements also include suggestions facilitating the provision of appropriate and effective treatment over time to support an individual progressing toward recovery.

The report identifies the following events during the law enforcement contact stage: dispatch, on-scene assessment (assessing contributing mental disturbance and its severity, determining the need for consultation from mental health personnel, determining whether a serious crime has been committed), on-scene response (jail diversion decision making and treatment referral), proper incident documentation, and evaluation of response (follow-up to determine the effectiveness of the response, including treatment involvement and rearrest). The report discusses how each of these could be improved to provide a more effective police response but does not endorse any particular model.

During the court stage of mental health/criminal justice processing, the report targets these action points for reform: appointment of counsel, consultation with victim, prosecutorial review of charges, modification of pretrial diversion conditions (to provide persons with mental illness assistance in complying with the terms of the diversion agreement), pretrial release/detention hearing, modification of pretrial release conditions, intake at detention facility, adjudication, and sentencing. Recommendations for improvement at this stage underscore the importance of sharing information by those providing and monitoring relevant services, particularly among mental health staff, court personnel, and attorneys. It is important that the court community be aware of the defendant's mental health condition, the nonjudicial options available for treatment, and applicable legal sources of authority.

While individuals are under correctional supervision, the report indicates, the following could be improved: receiving and intake of sentenced inmates, development of treatment plans, assignment to programs and classification/housing decisions, subsequent referral for screening and mental health evaluation, release decisions, development of transition plans, and modification of the conditions of supervised release. These recommendations stem from three major tasks for corrections administrators: identifying inmates with mental illness, providing appropriate housing and treatment, and preparing them for successful community reentry. Recommendations for the corrections stage focus on partnerships between community mental health providers and the prison and jail systems. Community mental health staff can assist with inmate mental health evaluations, service provision, and planning for indicated community-based treatment.

In the final stage, participation in community mental health after release from criminal justice supervision, the recommendation is very similar to the recommendation at the first stage. Persons with mental illness who have completed the requirements of their criminal sentence should have access to quality mental health services in the community as needed.

Recommendations for improvement address both the criminal justice and mental health systems, but apply largely to the mental health system. At the heart of the report is the notion that barriers to mental health services for those with the most severe and acute needs must be removed before the criminal justice system can meaningfully divert mentally ill subjects from arrest and incarceration.

The report points out that mentally ill persons with the highest risk of arrest are also the most likely to be turned away from community-based mental health clinics. Their erratic behaviors, criminal record, active psychosis or substance use, or lack of insurance can make them ineligible for treatment at some community mental health centers. To reduce the risk of mental health emergencies, such individuals must be engaged in appropriate mental health treatment *before* they have a crisis requiring police response. Also, effective mental health services must be available to persons who are diverted from jail or court, or upon reentry from incarceration. Without the capacity to provide appropriate services to those with urgent mental health needs and to engage them in such services, law enforcement and court officials will be faced with the ongoing problems that diversion is designed to address.

THE BEXAR COUNTY MODEL: ESTABLISHING AND OPERATING A JAIL DIVERSION PROGRAM

From 2002 to 2007, the Bexar County Jail Diversion Program was developed into a successful, coordinated delivery network that has had a significant impact on how those with behavioral health needs are handled in the criminal justice system in San Antonio. As we describe the development and operation of the program, we will note how the Consensus Project information proved useful. The SIM, which was developed somewhat later and published in 2006, may also describe ideas that can be influential in diversion programming—and we will use both the Consensus Project report and the SIM as sources of guidance for those interested in developing an integrated diversion program like Bexar County's.

Program Description

Bexar County's program integrates healthcare, law enforcement, and the judicial system to change how mental health services are delivered to offenders with mental illness who are charged with minor offenses. The program diverts an estimated 4,000 people with mental illness yearly from jail to a treatment facility, saving the county an estimated $5 million annually for jail costs and $4 million annually for inappropriate admissions to the emergency room (Evans, 2007).

Consistent with the spirit of the Consensus Project report, the program does not focus on a single point of interception. Instead, it has developed significant capacity for specialized police responding, prebooking and postbooking diversion, and reentry in a way that applies changes in policy and practice to multiple stages in the process described by both the report and the SIM. Diversion can occur at first contact with law enforcement (diverted to 24/7 crisis services, emergency transport to hospital, referred to community providers), postbooking (to community-based wraparound care), pretrial/jail, or probation/incarceration/parole.

The benefits of such a diversion program have been described broadly:

- Reduce monetary costs to community
- Improve quality of life for consumers arising from inadequate mental health services in corrections
- Offer judges and prosecutors alternatives for disposing of cases involving persons with mental illness
- Free up space for violent offenders

One important step was the establishment of crisis care centers in conjunction with diversion. Crisis centers reduce emergency room use, resulting in significant savings for the community and freeing up significant time for police officers transporting individuals to crisis care in lieu of arrest. Before the establishment of crisis care centers, the waiting time in Bexar County for police officers after transporting an individual to the hospital was more than nine hours—and more than twelve hours if psychiatric evaluation was needed in addition. As of 2009, the wait time for the former was forty-five minutes and the latter sixty to sixty-five minutes.

Establishing this program required significant upfront investment. Most of this investment involved hiring a full-time diversion director (a "boundary spanner," in Steadman's terms). Additional investment came from in-kind contributions from various stakeholders who donated time to attend planning meetings. The costs incurred by each agency varied depending on the type of diversion. As we discuss later in this chapter, the community mental health center bore a large proportion of prebooking diversion costs. When diversion was done at the postbooking stage through a bond, then the courts and pretrial services were responsible for most costs. For postbooking specialty docket diversion, the costs were about evenly split between the courts and the community mental health center.

Planning for Diversion

Planning diversion programs is similar to starting any new business (Evans, 2007). Important elements include vision, planning, partners, a gradual start, building product confidence, improving the product, staying close to customers, looking for new partners and funding, and building your case. Planning of the Bexar County program involved a variety of stakeholders:

- Jail diversion oversight committee (composed of thirty-four community agencies/stakeholders)
- Community medical directors roundtable

- Children's medical directors roundtable
- County children's diversion school district subcommittee
- County children's diversion child protective services subcommittee
- County children's diversion juvenile justice probation subcommittee
- Community co-location coalition (twenty-nine community agencies, including law enforcement, concerning homeless and public inebriation)

In addition, the planners included private sponsorship by working with AstraZeneca.

Planning incorporated a number of different strategies. In-person contact was a priority (an important point in this era of increased reliance upon indirect communications such as text messages and email). The information-gathering and planning stage facilitated relationships and trust among the various constituents whose participation would be needed. In addition, the project recruited "champions"—individual and organizational spokespersons who were widely perceived as credible and trustworthy. Securing such a champion helped to overcome barriers to information gathering stemming from security, privacy, and reluctance of some agencies because it might affect their funding. Finally, planning employed the strategy of involving individuals who could become effective supporters of the larger project once it was operational.

A number of "local considerations" went into planning and implementing this diversion program. One of the most important was a detailed description of current (or prediversion) policies and practices. What are the economic and demographic descriptors of this community? What are the size, structure, funding, and current interactions of important diversion stakeholders in the mental health system, legal system, law enforcement, and other public service agencies (e.g., Centers for Medicare and Medicaid Services, housing, labor, transportation)? What broader governmental organizations might be supportive, including local, state, and federal resources?

The next issue concerned the scale and scope of the planned diversion. What are current estimates of the impact of individuals with mental illness being processed "as usual" through the criminal justice system? Will the planned changes involve the development of new services, the better integration and tracking of existing services, or both? What are the gaps in the current system—and what are the opportunities?

The scope of any new program must reflect the community's needs and the commitment of its contributors. This may be affected by newsworthy crimes involving individuals with mental illness; serious offenses or tragedies may create an urgency that can affect both funding and timetables.

Operating the Program

The Bexar County program is structured around seven major initiatives:

- Establish training programs for mental health and law enforcement professionals and other stakeholders

- Encourage law enforcement involvement in the diversion process
- Form collaborative relationships with the community
- Establish pretrial services
- Establish posttrial services
- Ensure effective mental health treatment
- Identify outcomes

As noted earlier, this program uses interventions on multiple initiatives. In SIM terms, the only major intervention that the program does not offer is a problem-solving court. But it has targeted interventions on Intercepts 1, 2, 4, and 5.

Beyond these broad programmatic goals, a number of specific "building blocks" can be identified for the program. In particular, it sought to do the following:

- Implement crisis intervention teams and expand the deputy mobile outreach team for prearrest diversion
- Provide continuity of care by recording persons receiving prebooking services in the information system and following up with all individuals served to help gauge the system's impact
- Provide consistent and continuous cross-training to all law enforcement officers, court personnel, and mental health or social service providers
- Expand residential care components to include "no-refusal" crisis intervention drop-off centers for law enforcement officers
- Shift the pretrial diversion program to a postbooking intervention in the magistrate court, minimizing the need to transport eligible detainees to county jail and lessening the chance they will become "lost" within the criminal justice system
- Allow individuals with felony convictions to be eligible for postbooking services at the judge's discretion
- Create a team of partners and services to provide case management, community treatment, medication management and access, integrated mental health and substance abuse treatment, psychiatric rehabilitation, life skills training, job placement, healthcare, and gender-based and trauma-based services
- Add a peer support component
- Formalize linkage between consumers' families and support groups

The program is managed by an oversight committee, which evaluates the program and disseminates the model statewide. Of particular interest are the program's impacts on mentally ill individuals and their families in terms of consumers' functioning in the community, quality of life, family relations, and consumer and family satisfaction with treatment. Mental health outcomes of interest include crisis facility admissions, psychiatric inpatient admissions and hospitalization days, substance abuse crisis facility admissions, and involuntary treatment costs. Criminal justice outcomes of interest include criminal justice history and status, law enforcement contacts, rearrest, jail admissions and days, and community supervision revocation. Feedback is routinely provided to community stakeholders, including the county judge, city mayor, county sheriff, pretrial services representatives, Center for Health Care Services, district judges, probate judges, municipal judges, magistrates, district attorney, the National Alliance on Mental Illness chapter, police department, hospitals, Adult Protective Services, and Child Protective Services.

Funding the Program

The program employs 146 multidisciplinary staff, including physicians, nurses, licensed mental health practitioners, benefit specialists, caseworkers, and vocational and housing specialists. Yearly program funding is about $9 million. This is obtained through multiple sources, including federal grants, state and local support, Medicaid, Medicare, the University Health System, and a county initiative for residents without health insurance who are not eligible for federally funded programs.

Several important steps were taken to obtain funding at this level. The deputy mobile outreach team, which was originally jointly funded by the sheriff's department and the Center for Health Care Services, was ultimately taken over completely by the sheriff's department. In the program's early years, standard reimbursement mechanisms were used and minor offenders were screened for mental illness and Medicaid eligibility. This practice helped to secure Medicaid funds, which can cover 25% to 30% of the cost of diverting someone with mental illness from jail. The program also encouraged state hospital and other institutional practitioners to seek out panel inclusion (becoming a "participating provider" and therefore eligible for reimbursement of services) with all available payers in the area, including private insurance, Medicaid managed-care payers, and Veterans Affairs, as well as grant sources (Substance Abuse and Mental Health Services Administration, private foundations). In subsequent years, as the program became better established, it sought to increase the contribution provided by state funding.

A key to success in financing a diversion program has been described as blending, braiding, or integrating resources from local, state, and federal levels (Evans, 2009). But the Bexar County program is clearly a strong, stable diversion program operating across multiple intercepts that integrates health and behavioral health services and merges treatment for mental health and substance abuse. It can serve as a model for other communities seeking to promote systems change involving diversion. But many communities might decide on more modest goals, perhaps focusing on a single intercept and seeking funding that is less comprehensive. The needs of the community and the individuals receiving services should be primary considerations in seeking funding. Start where you can—and build up to what you need.

Evaluating the Program

One of the original objectives in developing the program was to provide stakeholders and funding sources with good information for judging the extent to which the program was reaching its goals. Part of this process involved a formal program evaluation funded jointly by the National Center for Behavioral Health Solutions and a private company (AstraZeneca). Program cost per service delivered is one of the most basic kinds of data provided as part of this program evaluation, which sought to determine the cost to the taxpayers of the program. (Subsequent additional domains were also addressed in program evaluation, including cost shifting between criminal justice and treatment, program cost-effectiveness, and program cost–benefit ratio).

The evaluation concluded that there are different costs for diversion at different stages. Prebooking diversion costs taxpayers about $370 per individual diverted. About 90% of this cost is borne by the Center for Health Care Services, mostly from short-term monitoring and initial screening.

When an arrestee has been booked but has not yet appeared on a court docket, and is diverted through a bond, the cost is less (about $238 per diverted individual). These costs are mostly borne by the courts (54%) and pretrial services (38%). After the individual has been booked but is diverted via a special court docket, the cost is even less (about $205 per diverted individual). The costs for this latter form of diversion are divided about equally between the Center for Health Care Services and the courts.

CONCLUSION

Both the Consensus Project and the SIM provide a conceptual basis for identifying the needs of a community and subsequently planning and implementing a program focusing on one or more of the intercepts at which individuals may be diverted from standard prosecution. The Bexar County Jail Diversion Program provides an example of a well-conceived, appropriately funded, well-evaluated, and multi-intercept diversion program that is consistent with the spirit of the Consensus Project regarding the interrelatedness of intercepts. This program provides a good example of the stages through which a good diversion program might pass during its development. However, the particular needs of communities may well differ from those in San Antonio, Texas, and communities should use this example and the guidance from the Consensus Project and SIM to identify their own needs and implement programs accordingly.

REFERENCES

Council of State Governments (2002). *Criminal Justice/Mental Health Consensus Project* (2002). Washington, D.C.: Council of State Governments.

Evans, L. (2007). *Blueprint for success: The Bexar County model.* San Antonio, TX: Bexar County Jail Diversion Program.

Evans, L. (2009, October). *Financing systems: Leveraging funds to support a comprehensive program.* Presented at the National Association of County Governments Jail Diversion Educational Forum.

Thompson, M., Reuland, M., & Souweine, D. (2003). Criminal Justice/Mental Health Consensus Project: Improving responses to people with mental illness. *Crime & Delinquency, 49,* 30–51.

10

State-Level Dissemination and Promotion Initiatives

Florida, Illinois, Massachusetts, Ohio, and Pennsylvania

DAVID DeMATTEO, MARK MUNETZ, JOHN PETRILA,
ALBERT GRUDZINSKAS, JR., WILLIAM FISHER,
SARAH FILONE, KATY WINCKWORTH-PREJSNAR,
AND MICHELLE R. ROCK ■

The overrepresentation of people with mental illness in the criminal justice system is a major concern in the United States. State departments of mental health, alcohol, substance use, and corrections are interested in diverting people with mental illness into treatment and out of the criminal justice system. From the mental health system's perspective, what can be viewed as the "transinstitutionalization" of people with mental illness is unacceptable. The large number of people with mental illness in jails and prisons may reflect a failure to provide adequate mental health services, particularly when many arrests are for non-violent misdemeanors. From the correctional perspective, their facilities have become the "new asylums." Caring for people with mental health disorders is difficult and expensive, and jails and prisons were not designed for this purpose. As such, there is often tension between the correctional staff charged with keeping order in the facility and the mental health staff's efforts to provide assessment and treatment.

Despite substantial state interest in reducing the number of individuals with severe mental illness in the criminal justice system, states are limited in what they can do directly to support jail diversion efforts. Jail diversion (which may also lead to diversion from prison) is largely a local effort implemented at the county or city level, although some states (e.g., Connecticut, Delaware) have state-operated jails. Regardless of the degree of authority a state may have over mental health and criminal justice programs, the implementation of jail diversion efforts is done at the local level and requires buy-in from relevant stakeholders. States may approach this by providing direction and resources at the state level that can be utilized with technical assistance at the local level.

The problem of having large numbers of people with mental illness in the criminal justice system is complex and multidetermined. Because there is no single solution, and different states and local jurisdictions are at different stages of readiness to tackle the problem at different points, some states and localities have found the Sequential Intercept Model (SIM; Munetz & Griffin, 2006) to be a useful framework for developing a state-level response. The SIM describes five points at which criminal justice processing can be interrupted and individuals can be diverted from standard prosecution: (1) law enforcement and emergency services; (2) post-arrest: initial detention/hearing and pretrial services; (3) after initial hearings: jails/prisons, courts, forensic evaluations, and commitments; (4) reentry from jails, prisons, and forensic hospitals; and (5) community corrections and community support (Munetz & Griffin, 2006).

Each intercept in the SIM provides an opportunity to intervene with offenders and break the costly and ineffective cycle of arrest, incarceration, release, and rearrest that has often characterized the criminal justice system's response to certain types of offenders, including those with severe mental illness and/or substance use problems. These interception points can prevent individuals from entering the criminal justice system or prevent further penetration for those already in the system. Departments of mental health recognize that the ultimate intercept—accessible and effective mental health services—is part of their primary mission. Depending on the particular state agency, available resources, and degree of collaboration across state agencies, addressing all five intercepts or selecting only one or two may lead to the evolution of jail diversion efforts at the state level, although this type of cross-system collaboration is more likely to occur at the county and local levels.

The idea for statewide efforts to address jail diversion most likely emerged from the substantial national efforts of the Substance Abuse and Mental Health Services Association's (SAMHSA) GAINS Center. Since 1995, the GAINS Center has operated as a national locus for the collection and dissemination of information about effective mental health and substance abuse services for people with co-occurring disorders who come into contact with the justice system. The GAINS Center consists of the Technical Assistance and Policy Analysis Center for Jail Diversion, funded by the Center for Mental Health Services (CMHS) in 2001, and the Center for Evidence-Based Programs in the Justice System, funded by CMHS in 2004.

GAINS Center Director Henry Steadman helped develop the SIM along with Munetz and Griffin and has used it as a framework for technical assistance offered to local communities interested in developing jail diversion programs. Taking a cue from the GAINS Center, several states recognized that they could more effectively promote jail diversion by creating technical assistance centers of their own to disseminate such diversion statewide. Funding for these efforts varied greatly, as did their structure and operation. Some funding came from departments of mental health and some from legislation addressing the criminal justice system. Some efforts used pooled funds from multiple state departments crossing the boundaries between mental health and criminal justice, and some used funds from grants awarded to local stakeholders (e.g., police departments, homeless outreach agencies) or the technical assistance centers themselves. Just as funding varied, the activities of these statewide efforts have varied, as will be described later in this chapter. What the initiatives have in common is using the SIM in some fashion to help communities reduce the number of people with mental illness in the criminal justice system.

STATE-LEVEL EFFORTS

Several states followed the lead of the National GAINS Center and developed their own centers to promote diversion in their state. Despite differences in operation and structure, they share the goal of reducing justice involvement for individuals with severe mental illness. In this section, we describe the efforts of five states that have developed centers that are active in providing technical assistance.

Ohio

At the end of the twentieth century, as deinstitutionalization had largely gone as far is it could go in Ohio, the Ohio Department of Mental Health developed a strategy for supporting the dissemination of evidence-based and emerging best practices across the state. Recognizing that Ohio is a highly decentralized state with a strong tradition of local control, it was clear that a purely top-down approach was unlikely to be successful. This led to the then-novel idea of creating Coordinating Centers of Excellence (CCoEs), which are often university-based organizations that provide expert technical assistance and consultation in an effort to improve quality by promoting best practices (Ohio Department of Mental Health, 2005). In creating the CCoEs, the Ohio Department of Mental Health used a theory of diffusion of innovation, suggesting that the most effective strategy was to combine elements of unplanned or spontaneous diffusion along with more directed and managed dissemination (Rogers, 2003). For the former, the state looked to communities or organizations that had embraced a particular innovation and had the energy to spread the model throughout the state. However, there was some uncertainty in 2000–2001 as to whether there were yet best practices to divert people with mental illness that warranted wide dissemination, and there was not a clear model for doing so.

Beginning in the late 1990s, Summit County (Akron), Ohio, began looking at the problem of the overrepresentation of people with mental illness in its jail. The Summit County Alcohol, Drug Addiction, and Mental Health Services (ADM)

Board received a technical assistance consultation from the GAINS Center in 1999 from Patricia Griffin, PhD, which established a relationship between the GAINS Center (especially Griffin) and the Summit County ADM Board (especially Mark Munetz, the board's chief clinical officer). Partly as a result of that consultation, Akron became the first community in Ohio to establish a Crisis Intervention Team (CIT) using the Memphis Model, and developed the first municipal mental health court in Ohio.

Seeing the energy behind these two emerging programs, the Ohio Department of Mental Health awarded the Summit County ADM Board a grant in 2001 to establish a Criminal Justice Coordinating Center of Excellence (CJ CCoE). The Center was to be operated by the Northeast Ohio Medical University (formerly known as Northeastern Ohio Universities College of Medicine). A mandate to the CJ CCoE in its first year was to develop a conceptual model for jail diversion. Inspired by Steadman and the GAINS Center, the Ohio Department of Mental Health's director at the time, Michael Hogan, wanted the CJ CCoE to be a "mini-GAINS Center" for Ohio. At the same time, Justice Evelyn Stratton of the Supreme Court of Ohio established the Advisory Committee on Mental Illness and the Courts, with dedicated staff to promote mental health courts in Ohio.

The development of the SIM Model was an outgrowth of the growing collaboration between Munetz and Griffin (2006), with substantial input from Steadman. The SIM became the framework for jail diversion work in Ohio. Eventually the CCoE largely focused on Intercept 1 (law enforcement and emergency services), and by 2011 it was known by the Ohio Department of Mental Health as the CIT CCoE. Other influences on the CCoE included the promotion of mental health courts by the Supreme Court of Ohio and a Transformation State Incentive Grant from SAMHSA to Ohio, which created a large statewide reentry project independent of the CJ CCoE.

Ohio's CIT dissemination has been described elsewhere (see Munetz, Morrison, Krake, Young, & Woody, 2006) and was initially driven by the mental health system. As a partnership among law enforcement, mental health, individuals with mental illness, and their families, CIT at its core is a grassroots program; meaningful community-level collaboration is difficult to mandate from a central authority. With modest resources but a great deal of commitment, the CJ CCoE has successfully disseminated these teams throughout Ohio. The Commonwealth Fund recognized its work as one of seventeen state-level behavioral health innovations, and the only one at the interface of the mental health and law enforcement systems (Perlman & Dougherty, 2006). Its success was attributed to multiple partners and CIT champions, including the Ohio chapter of the National Alliance on Mental Illness, Justice Stratton of the Supreme Court of Ohio, and the Court's Advisory Committee on Mental Illness and the Courts. The CJ CCoE maintains an active website (www.neomed.edu/ cjccoe) with its partners, provides ongoing technical assistance and resource material, and hosts biannual Ohio CIT Coordinators meetings. By mid-2011, Ohio had trained more than 4,500 CIT officers, representing 13% of all officers in the state. There are currently CIT-trained officers in seventy-six of Ohio's eighty-eight counties, representing 395 law enforcement agencies, sixty county sheriff's offices, forty-nine university or college police/security departments, as well as the State Highway Patrol, park rangers, corrections officers, probation and parole officers, police dispatchers, and hospital security.

In addition to continuing efforts to bring these teams to the remaining counties, the current focus of the Ohio CIT program is to ensure that each county operates a CIT program consistent with articulated core elements of a CIT program (Ohio CIT Coordinators Committee & Ohio Criminal Justice Coordinating Center of Excellence, 2004). The CJ CCoE is using a peer assessment process to ensure continued quality improvement of CIT programs at a time when increasingly tight resources threaten the integrity of existing CIT programs. It appears clear that ongoing support is needed for these teams to be sustained in communities; such support can be provided by a statewide organization like the CJ CCoE.

The CJ CCoE intends to expand its mission to become the technical assistance center for jail diversion in the state as was originally envisioned. The strategy is to use mapping to bring communities together at the county level. To achieve this, the center leadership believes that funding must be broadened from almost exclusively state mental health dollars to include a matching amount from criminal justice agencies within the state. The recent evolution of the Advisory Committee on Mental Illness and the Courts into an Attorney General Task Force on Criminal Justice and Mental Illness (co-led by Attorney General Mike DeWine) and interest in the mapping concept by the Ohio Office of Criminal Justice Services provide hope that the CCoE expansion may be successful. The SIM has been adopted as a structure for the task force's subcommittee work.

Massachusetts

The Massachusetts Mental Health Diversion and Integration Program (MMHDIP) began in early 2001 as a service of the Law and Psychiatry Program in the Department of Psychiatry at the University of Massachusetts Medical School (UMass). The project was conceptualized by then-recently-retired District Court Justice Maurice H. Richardson, working in conjunction with UMass researchers. Utilizing technical assistance from the National GAINS Center (the MMHDIP was modeled on the GAINS Center), they began with a planning conference for stakeholders in central Massachusetts focused on developing plans for diverting persons with mental illness involved in the criminal justice system. The initial idea was to create a Memphis-like CIT for the Worcester Police Department. The conference brought together local court, police, and mental health and substance abuse providers to hear about issues related to homelessness, criminal justice involvement of persons with mental illness, the prevalence of co-occurring substance use in persons with mental illness, and solutions implemented in other jurisdictions. Utilizing technical assistance from the GAINS Center, the conference keynote address given by Steadman addressed the need for collaboration and someone to "span boundaries between stakeholders."

The conference led to the formation of the Worcester Diversion Consortium, a group of criminal justice and social service agencies and providers dedicated to reducing the numbers of persons with mental illness in the criminal justice system. With assistance from GAINS, David Wertheimer, from the successful Seattle-based Harborview Medical Center diversion program, came to Worcester in July 2003 to map the course of people's penetration through the justice system and explore avenues for linking people to services as an alternative to criminalization. The resulting model built on the series of ad hoc procedures that had been developed for diverting offenders with mental health problems into a community-based system of care and evolved into a multifaceted diversion approach for the central Massachusetts area.

Intercept points were identified during the SIM session. As the group discussed solutions to divert persons from the criminal justice track, it became apparent that the Worcester police had no desire or need to create a CIT unit. The system mapped out demonstrated that a set of factors unique to central Massachusetts combined to create a functioning diversionary program. Worcester police were intercepting persons at the crisis or emergency services stage (SIM Intercept 1). They had been empowered since 1992 by the written policy of the department to utilize their discretion to ignore "non-serious criminal activity" (defined as not a felony and without injury to persons) if the perpetrator appeared to be someone with an "emotional disturbance." In such cases the officer could call for transportation to Emergency Mental Health Services at the UMass Medical Center. Working with the UMass police department and emergency room personnel, they could then help to initiate a procedure pursuant to Massachusetts law (MGL, c. 123, § 12(a))[1] for an evaluation regarding the person's potential for civil commitment. Even if not eventually committed, the emergency room was serving as a triage point for persons in crisis who might otherwise be arrested for nuisance-like behaviors (Clayfield, Grudzinskas, Fisher, & Roy-Bujnowski, 2005).

Since the development of a specialty unit would create an additional funding strain on the department, and the system was "not broken," the police opted out of the CIT model. They did, however, recognize the need for additional training to help them identify and deescalate persons in crisis. The MMHDIP sought funding from private foundations, including the Gardiner Howland Shaw Foundation, the George Harrington Trust, and the Boston Foundation, to develop and deliver training to all officers and dispatchers. The trainings sought to integrate crisis intervention and risk management training into the ongoing in-service and new recruit academy curriculums. These trainings remain ongoing and now also focus on suicide prevention, working with the elderly, working with children and adolescents, culturally competent communication, stress management and the human elements of policing, and understanding the community-based system of care. The trainers are drawn from the UMass faculty and the clinical staff of the UMass/Memorial Healthcare System.

Another outgrowth of the planning session was the development of the Worcester Diversion Consortium. The session demonstrated the need to identify the network of agencies providing services to encourage the development of

linkages to ensure continuity of care. That the court, police, and service providers were often dealing with different stages of people's behavioral issues had been
clearly demonstrated. Utilizing Ucinet 6.0 Social Network Analysis software, the
MMHDIP provided stakeholders with an accurate picture of the strength and
directionality of agency linkages and relationships. The analysis demonstrated
that while the court system was often a source of information regarding individuals, the information flow was unidirectional. As a result, linkages to the
probation department were developed and expanded. This permitted the court
to utilize existing laws (MGL, c. 276, § 87)[2] regarding pretrial probation (when
appropriate) and post-adjudication probation (for more serious offenses) to set
conditions mandating treatment for persons who had penetrated the system
without being diverted at the police intercept. This was done without establishing a dedicated court session and by utilizing probation officers who had experience working with persons with substance use problems. While mental health
court and specialty probation models were explored, the lack of a funding source
prompted stakeholders to modify existing protocols to meet the needs of persons
in the system.

The consortium, with technical assistance from the MMHDIP, has evolved
into an effective problem-solving partnership. Massachusetts law, for example,
permits judges to commit persons to either mental health or substance use treatment if they are deemed at risk to themselves or the community by reason of their
illness. It does not currently permit judges to order persons into co-occurring
disorder treatment. The consortium helped identify programs that can be mandated under conditions of probation to fill the gap. The court now utilizes this
tool without any new funding or modification of the law.

In 2008, the consortium collaborated with UMass researchers and the
Department of Mental Health to obtain funding from SAMHSA to create a
post-adjudication mental health diversion session in the Worcester District
Court to link veterans with trauma histories and substance use treatment needs
to peer support and case management services as conditions of probation. The
project, known as MISSION Direct-Vet, is ongoing and is part of a broader
SAMHSA study coordinated by the GAINS Center.

The Boston Police Department had no provision for allowing officers discretion to resolve mental health issues for persons who commit minor offenses.
There were, however, a number of service differences that permitted the development of a diversionary program. The MMHDIP worked in 2002 with the Boston
Police Department, the Boston Municipal Court, the Department of Mental
Health, and a consortium of community-based service providers to develop a
memorandum of understanding among the court system, police, Department
of Mental Health, and various other agency and contract service providers that
sought to develop three initiatives:

- To assist in the expansion of the training curriculum of the Boston
  police in the downtown area and the Massachusetts Bay Transportation
  Authority

- To develop a pilot crisis triage unit near the Boston Medical Center, which would operate as a "No Wrong Door" facility, modeled on the Harborview program from Seattle, as an alternative to arrest for the Boston police
- To consider with the Chief Justice of the Boston Municipal Court Department the development of a mental health court session or program for mentally ill criminal defendants arrested in downtown Boston

In addition, a planning session was held with the Boston Diversion Consortium in early 2002 to map intercept points and outcomes for persons with mental illness involved in the criminal justice system. The result was a modification of the goals of the memorandum of understanding. The Boston Police Department initiated a series of training protocols that eventually included obtaining funding in 2007 for the Boston Police Study from the Sidney R. Baer, Jr. Foundation to train and evaluate one shift of three precincts of the department. Officers in District B2 were given access to an onsite social worker funded by the Department of Mental Health to assist them with mental health and substance use issues that arose in their work. A cadre of officers in District A1 received forty hours of training to create a rapid response CIT-like unit. All officers in District D4 received a four-hour crisis intervention and risk management training. The comparisons of results before and after the intervention and of results among the precincts of outcomes of emergency calls for emotionally disturbed persons is ongoing but has been severely curtailed due to funding cutbacks. The ultimate model will depend in part on what the evaluation shows to be the impact of the training modes. The consortium helped develop the Boston Municipal Court Mental Health Session, which utilizes case management assistance (now funded by the Department of Mental Health) from the Boston Medical Center to help diverted individuals stay in probation-supervised treatment for one year. The triage unit proposal developed into a "virtual" triage service of the Boston Emergency Services Team that utilizes existing service providers as the diversion point.

The 2002 planning session also demonstrated a phenomenon that has not yet been discussed. The presence of various highly respected community leaders (and the allocation of competence to these individuals by other session participants) often leads to their "version" of how the system is functioning becoming the adopted consensus model (Anderson & Kilduff, 2009). Subsequent discussions revealed that not all participants agreed with the consensus model. As part of the Boston Police Study, researchers conducted a series of sessions with subgroups identified by similar functions, which demonstrated that the various parties had different understandings of how the system actually functioned. By "stacking" the versions, a somewhat more accurate picture emerged, including explanations for why persons did not flow smoothly through the hand-off points. The hand-offs were not occurring as system members believed they were, yet the parties each continued to act as if their version represented an accurate understanding. The court, for example, believed that persons in crisis who did not meet commitment criteria could be brought to homeless shelters for safety. Police officers were in fact utilizing the shelter system as a proxy for the crisis stabilization beds previously available. Funding issues had resulted in a practical redefinition of the severity of behavior necessary to qualify as being at a "substantial risk," the statutorily defined term for the dangerousness element for civil commitment. The shelters began "banning" persons who had engaged in predatory behavior during prior stays. The shelters have no legal authority to hold a person against his or her will and little capacity to offer treatment. Unless the person's behavior constitutes criminal activity, police are left with few options. Subsequent discussions among the parties led to modifications in the model.

Recent funding cutbacks, including the expiration of the Sidney R. Baer, Jr. Foundation grant, have curtailed further development of similar models. The MMHDIP, working with the Department of Mental Health, developed a pilot program funded by the latter to bring social work support to some municipal police departments. The funding, coupled with modeling sessions for community stakeholders and training for police officers, has created a different intercept model that appears to be gaining support as an alternative diversion model. To date, no evaluations of the programs other than Department of Mental Health performance compliance measures have been undertaken.

Florida

Statutory mission. In 2007, the Florida legislature enacted the Criminal Justice, Mental Health, and Substance Abuse Reinvestment Grant Program (Fla. Stat. § 394.656). This statute was based on the federal Mentally Ill Offender Treatment and Crime Reduction Act of 2002 (H.R. 5701). The statute established a grant program for qualifying counties so that they:

> can plan, implement, or expand initiatives that increase public safety, avert increased spending on criminal justice, and improve the accessibility and effectiveness of treatment services for adults and juveniles who have a mental illness, substance abuse disorder, or co-occurring mental health and substance abuse disorders and who are in, or at risk of entering, the criminal or juvenile justice system.
>
> —FLA. STAT. § 394.656(1)

Counties could apply for one-year planning grants or three-year implementation or expansion grants to demonstrate that investment in treatment "results in a reduced demand on the resources of the judicial, corrections, juvenile detention, and health and social services systems" (Fla. Stat. § 394.656(3)(a)).

Applicants for planning grants had to commit to creating cross-system collaboration that would result in a strategic plan for identifying and treating the target population. Implementation and expansion applicants could use grant funding for a variety of initiatives, including mental health courts; diversion programs; alternative prosecution and sentencing programs; CITs; treatment accountability services; specialized training for criminal justice, juvenile justice, and treatment services professionals; delivery of collateral services such as transitional housing and supported employment; and reentry services (Fla. Stat. § 394.658(b)(1)-(8)). Counties had to provide at least a 100% match for state funds, which could be up to $50,000 for a one-year planning grant and $300,000 for a three-year implementation grant.

Finally, the legislation created a technical assistance center and housed it at the Louis de la Parte Florida Mental Health Institute at the University of South Florida (FMHI). The legislation tasked the center with several obligations, including providing technical assistance to counties preparing a grant application; assisting an applicant in projecting the effect of the proposed intervention on the county jail's population; assisting a county in monitoring the effect of a grant on the county's criminal justice system; disseminating and sharing evidence-based practices among grantees; acting as a clearinghouse; and coordinating a state interagency justice, mental health, and substance abuse work group examining outcomes achieved by the grants. Finally, the center must submit an annual report to the governor and legislature on the grant program.

Four goals informed the initial development of the technical assistance center. First, the initial focus had to be on activities and products of specific use to the original twenty-three grantee counties. Second, a decision was made to create some products that would be potentially valuable to all sixty-seven Florida counties, not simply the original ones, and linked, if possible, to national concerns. Third, a decision was made to anticipate an eventual reduction or elimination of the initial $120,000 annual appropriation made available for the center. Finally, all activities had to be designed to meet the legislative statutory charge.

Working with the original grantee counties. Florida is a large state geographically and with nearly 19 million people is the fourth most populated state in the United States. The center had a limited budget and staff; it had a full-time administrative coordinator, a graduate student, and a senior faculty member who spent part of his time as director. Matching these limited resources to need was a significant issue. We focused on Sequential Intercept Mapping as the primary tool to engage counties with planning grants. This fit the legislative directive that the purpose of planning grants was to create cross-system strategic plans. To accomplish this, we asked the GAINS Center if it would provide a "train the trainer" approach to create a cadre of individuals qualified to conduct mapping under the auspice of the technical assistance center. The GAINS Center conducted a two-day training for seven people, including University of South Florida faculty. The technical assistance center paid for the training from funds secured from the JEHT Foundation.

Since then, mapping has been provided to more than twelve counties. Two counties asked to be mapped a second time, and mapping of the juvenile justice system was provided in two counties. Mapping has been the foundation of the technical assistance center's activities and is indispensable to counties as a planning tool. The mapping process itself has led to modest but important changes during the mapping. For example, in one small county, mental health providers noted that because inmates were often released from jail at night, they had little chance of accessing a pharmacy for prescriptions. On the second day of mapping, the sheriff stated that they would change their policy and offer inmates with mental illnesses the option of being released at times when the pharmacy was open. While the substantive policy change was important, the discussion about the issue and the spirit in which the offer was made was even more important.

In addition to mapping, consultation was offered on discrete topics of interest to a county. For example, consultation was provided in multiple counties on HIPAA and information sharing, housing and supported employment, and the provision of co-occurring treatment. These consultations were provided through faculty experts at the University of South Florida and like the mapping were made available to the counties for no charge.

"Statewideness." While the legislation creating the Reinvestment Grant Program focused on grantee counties, the issues faced by those counties were not unique. In addition, the technical assistance center hoped to gain traction with a broader constituency, in part anticipating a time when state funding for the center and grant program might be reduced or eliminated. There was also a desire to create a product that branded the center in a visible manner.

The center is housed by statute in FMHI. Over the years, FMHI had negotiated for access to statewide data systems to conduct various analyses. These datasets include the state's Medicaid claims, all civil commitment petitions, statewide arrest data, units of service data on behavioral health services provided throughout the state, and eventually juvenile justice data. A decision was made to create a website for the center with analyses for all sixty-seven Florida counties that would integrate arrest data, Medicaid claims data, and unit of service data. The website (www.floridatac.org) would also serve as a clearinghouse for information on a wide array of topics relevant to diversion.

Funding for website development was obtained from the JEHT Foundation, and a private developer was retained to develop the site, which took roughly one year. The website receives nearly 30,000 hits per year and data for each county are updated annually. For example, a county commissioner or judge can access the website and download a table showing how many people were arrested in the county, how many of them had used a Medicaid service for mental health or substance use treatment, and how many had been civilly committed. In a state in which 680,000 people are arrested each year, the website provides a way to focus on more targeted numbers of people. The center worked closely with the Justice Center at the Council of State Governments to make their websites interactive. As a result, when someone accesses data on a Florida county through the technical assistance center website, material about that county on the Justice Center's website is automatically displayed.

In addition to the website, myriad data available to the center through FMHI have been used in county-specific analyses. For example, in Miami-Dade County, an analysis showed that ninety-seven "heavy users" of the criminal justice system, who also had a serious mental illness, spent on average approximately 25% of each year, over five years, in a jail, psychiatric emergency room, or psychiatric hospital. This analysis became the basis for a successful grant application designed to create integrated services for these heavy users.

Anticipating reductions in funding. The initial appropriation for the center was $120,000 per year for the first three years of the grant program. However, funding for programs in Florida is notoriously fickle, so the question is whether the center can survive beyond grant funding. In fact, at the time of this writing, the funding had been reduced to $20,000 because of budget shortfalls. As a result, center staff searched from the beginning for additional funding. In addition to JEHT Foundation funding, FMHI has a contract with the state Medicaid office to do analyses using Medicaid data, and criminal justice-focused projects were written into that contract to provide supplemental funding for the center; those analyses, integrating Medicaid and arrest data, have begun to yield publications as well (e.g., Petrila et al., 2010).

Some counties have also begun writing the center into funding proposals, for example to the U.S. Bureau of Justice Assistance, to provide evaluations, and in two counties the center and associated faculty have partnered with counties on funding proposals to the National Institutes of Health and National Institute of Mental Health. In the future, it is likely that funding for center activities will rest on county-specific activities, either in direct contracts with counties or through grant and foundation funding obtained in partnership.

Meeting the legislative statutory directives. Each of these activities was designed not only to provide technical assistance but also to meet the statutory tasks assigned to the center. For example, the website serves as the clearinghouse mandated by the legislation, and the mapping assists counties in planning their intervention. Various data analyses assist in targeting a population for intervention, and the statewide datasets can be combined with local data to assess the impact of those interventions on jail stays and access to services.

While funding has been a significant and continuing issue, in some ways the most difficult legislative task has been preparation of the annual report to the governor and legislature. The legislation requires that this report include the following: a detailed description of each grantee's progress in meeting the goals in its application; a description of the effect of grant-funded initiatives on meeting the needs of adults and juveniles with mental disorders, thereby reducing the number of forensic commitments to state facilities; a summary of the effects of these initiatives on jail, correctional, and juvenile facility growth and expenditures; a summary of how grant-funded initiatives have increased access to community services and how expanded community diversion capacity has decreased jail incarceration and commitments to state treatment facilities; and how grantee counties leveraged grant funding with additional funding.

It is difficult to gauge the impact of legislative reports on program sustainability, but the legislation may have articulated goals for grant funding that were difficult to achieve. Grant funding is comparatively modest (even when supplemented by the mandatory county match) and many grant-funded programs initially targeted small caseloads of thirty-five to one hundred individuals. Although such initiatives can have impact over time, few initiatives will have immediate and measurable effects on "jail, correctional and juvenile facility growth and expenditures." In addition, many counties did not have the capacity to track outcomes, so locating good data relevant to the issues the report must address has sometimes been difficult. To remedy this problem in some counties, the center has created intervention-specific electronic databases for counties to log information about individuals enrolled in a grant-funded intervention. Those data can then be matched with the statewide databases available to the center to track individuals over time.

Pennsylvania

The Pennsylvania Mental Health and Justice CoE is a cooperative effort of Drexel University's Department of Psychology and the University of Pittsburgh Medical Center. The CoE has been jointly funded since 2009 by the Pennsylvania Commission on Crime and Delinquency and the Pennsylvania Department of Public Welfare's Office of Mental Health and Substance Abuse Services. CoE oversight is provided by the Pennsylvania Mental Health and Justice Advisory Committee, which was established in June 2009. The Mental Health and Justice Advisory Committee advises the Commission on Crime and Delinquency and works with counties on issues related to the intersection of mental health and criminal justice activities, such as jail diversion and reentry programs.

The CoE's broad purpose is to work with Pennsylvania communities to identify points at which individuals with severe mental illness can be prevented from entering or penetrating deeper into the criminal justice system. The CoE works collaboratively with the state at the state level and various counties at the local level in developing and implementing programs serving justice-involved adults with mental illness and co-occurring substance use disorders, providing information to promote their use of evidence-based practices, and serving as a resource for technical assistance and training. The CoE also hosts a repository for collected data and information on criminal justice/mental health responses throughout the state. The CoE utilizes the SIM as a broad organizing tool for the majority of its services, including cross-systems mapping workshops, the CoE website, and resource guides.

Cross-systems mapping workshops are an important component of the work of the CoE. This 1.5-day workshop is designed to bring key stakeholders together, identify barriers to service, develop a local map of each of the five intercepts, and create an action plan to address mutually identified priorities for the community. For more information on cross-systems mapping, see Chapter 14.

As of September 2014, thirty-four of Pennsylvania's sixty-seven counties have been mapped (thirty by the CoE and four by the GAINS Center prior to the development of the CoE), with several more counties tentatively scheduled to be mapped over the next year. Although each county has a unique set of challenges and opportunities—to be expected in a state that has a large mix of predominantly urban and predominantly rural counties—some common themes have emerged at each intercept (Table 10.1).

The cross-systems mapping workshops have also revealed multiple strengths throughout the state. Common opportunities for growth include collaborative efforts among systems (e.g., criminal justice advisory boards, problem-solving courts, forensic treatment teams), increased utilization of peer support services in forensic settings, and multisystem support for training at Intercept 1 (e.g., CIT training, Mental Health First Aid training).

Each county is encouraged to develop priorities based on its work during the mapping. Although the focus and scope of selected priorities vary by county, some commonly identified priorities include increased law enforcement training (Intercept 1), formal detoxification procedures (Intercept 1), continuity of care during reentry (Intercept 4), housing (Intercept 5), and increased information sharing across all intercepts.

The CoE offers resource guides for counties seeking to change their policies and practice regarding the diversion of individuals with severe mental illness and co-occurring substance use disorders from standard criminal prosecution. This resource guide is organized by intercept and provides information on several topics, including specialized police response and law enforcement/behavioral

Table 10.1 SEQUENTIAL INTERCEPTS AND ASSOCIATED CHALLENGES
TO DIVERSION IN PENNSYLVANIA

Intercept	Common Challenges in Pennsylvania
Intercept 1: Arrest	• Small/rural law enforcement agencies cannot spare officers for training. • Law enforcement officers often spend hours waiting with individuals with mental health/substance use treatment needs at local hospitals. • Significant lack of detoxification services
Intercept 2: Initial Detention/Initial Court Hearings	• Lack of pretrial services • Problems with video arraignment equipment
Intercept 3: Jails/Courts	• Many jail admissions require detoxification. • Lack of treatment staff in correctional facilities
Intercept 4: Reentry	• Difficulty with reactivation of medical assistance benefits • Continuity of care issues (e.g., jail versus community formularies, lag time between release and first psychiatric appointment) • Limited reentry planning
Intercept 5: Community	• Lack of housing options • Lack of public transportation

health collaboration, resources for improving reentry, community corrections, and forensic peer support services.

The CoE developed and maintains a website (www.pacenterofexcellence.pitt. edu) that includes relevant information organized by intercept. Visitors can browse resources organized by each of the intercepts and find examples of successful systems integration, promising programs, and emergent collaborations from within Pennsylvania and around the United States. There is also county-specific information designed to be useful for state- and county-level agencies and the general public. The website also provides presentations and videos, and information on available services, training, and funding opportunities. Data on website usage suggest a steady increase in use since the development of the CoE.

Illinois

History. In 2008, the Illinois Department of Human Services, Division of Mental Health embarked on a transformation initiative to better address the needs of individuals with mental illnesses and co-occurring substance use disorders who are involved with the criminal justice system. The primary goal of the initiative was to support the efforts of the Criminal Justice Transformation Workgroup led by the Division of Mental Health. This workgroup was convened to plan enhancements in the system of care for this population. System collaborators in this effort included the Illinois Department of Corrections, the Illinois Department of Alcohol and Substance Abuse, the Illinois Sheriff's Association, the Illinois National Alliance for Mental Illness, and a host of community providers and key stakeholders. Most significantly, a partnership was formed with the judiciary in Illinois, headed by Justice Kathryn Zenoff. The Illinois Department of Human Services, Division of Mental Health, with funding from the National Association of Mental Health Program Directors, contracted with Policy Research Associates of Delmar, New York, to provide technical assistance to inform its transformation efforts. "ACTION: Transforming Systems & Services" is the technical assistance initiative provided by Policy Research Associates. It is meant to serve as a catalyst for change to improve mental health and criminal justice collaboration for justice-involved persons with co-occurring disorders and to help transform fragmented systems. ACTION uses the Sequential Intercept Model to map the local criminal justice system; it identifies local resources, assesses gaps in services, and helps communities develop priorities for change. The process included planning telephone calls, an initial meeting of representatives from each of Illinois's five Department of Mental Health regions to introduce the initiative, strategic planning workshops in each region, an additional meeting to relate Policy Research Associates' findings and recommendations, and the final strategic report. The regional strategic planning workshops attempted to convene a diversified group representing all systems.

In April 2010, the Illinois Supreme Court named a Special Judicial Advisory Committee for Justice and Mental Health Planning. One of the charges for this committee is to consider how to maximize the use of court and community resources in aiding the rehabilitation and treatment of accused offenders with mental health and substance use issues. The Advisory Committee has studied, reviewed, and collaborated on issues and matters related to mental illness, substance use, and the justice system to make recommendations to the Illinois Supreme Court. One of the ideas discussed was a CoE for Illinois.

In December 2010, a multidisciplinary group of Illinois stakeholders was convened, consisting of representatives from the Department of Human Services, Division of Mental Health; Illinois Criminal Justice Information Authority; Treatment Alternatives for Safe Communities; the Mental Health Court Association of Illinois; the Administrative Office of the Illinois Courts; and members of the Special Supreme Court Advisory Committee on Justice and Mental Health Planning to discuss the purpose and feasibility of a CoE in Illinois. Hank Steadman of Policy Research Associates and the GAINS Center facilitated the initial meeting. After research, continued discussion, and meetings a consensus was reached regarding the mission, structure, and purpose of a CoE in Illinois.

Structure. An intergovernmental agreement dated December 22, 2011, established the Illinois Center of Excellence for Behavioral Health and Justice. Its board of directors consists of one member each from the Illinois Criminal Justice Information Authority, Illinois Department of Human Services, and County of Winnebago. The agreement also creates an advisory board with members from the original planning group, including members from the Second District Appellate Court; Criminal Division, Cook County Circuit Court; specialty courts, Cook County Circuit Court; juvenile and specialty courts, 17th Judicial Circuit Court; University of Illinois Rockford; 11th Judicial Circuit Court; TASC, Inc.; and the administrative office of the Illinois Courts. The role of the advisory board is to ensure that the CoE's mission statement is followed, to set priorities for the CoE, to ensure consumer involvement, and to make recommendations regarding hiring and overseeing the director. As the CoE moves forward, the advisory board will undertake to add members from law enforcement, consumer/National Alliance on Mental Illness, and other community treatment providers.

In April 2012, the CoE formally opened. Its mission is to equip communities to appropriately respond to the needs of persons with behavioral health disorders who are involved in the criminal justice system. To that end, the CoE provides technical assistance, resources, and training to improve systemic responses to persons with mental health and/or substance use disorders involved in the criminal justice system. It also compiles information about evidence-based practices and research and makes it available on its website (www.illinoiscenterofexcellence.org).

The CoE uses the SIM to identify strategies for linking individuals in need of treatment at each intercept within the criminal justice system. The CoE focuses on the first three intercepts (law enforcement, initial detention/initial court hearings, and jails/courts) to seek and disseminate information about evidence-based practices and to provide services such as training and technical assistance for problem-solving courts or other diversion models around the state. The CoE's target group of users is law enforcement, judges, courts, policymakers, consumers, families, and treatment providers.

The CoE serves the entire state through a partnership with the Winnebago County and the University of Illinois. The CoE is housed at the University of Illinois School of Medicine in Rockford, which has other sites within the University of Illinois system located in Chicago, Peoria, Springfield, and Urbana/Champaign. These multiple sites will allow expanded statewide access and convenience.

The staff includes a director and assistant director. The first six months of the CoE was devoted to the startup activities, including development of the website, review of statewide initiatives, a grand opening celebration with statewide dignitaries, and dissemination of information about the CoE throughout the state. All 102 counties were contacted and a presentation about the CoE was provided for the state's Conference of Chief Judges. In its first year, the CoE provided services to sixty-three counties, with individualized onsite training to thirty-one counties. Over 3,000 individuals participated in technical assistance or training sponsored by the CoE.

Funding. Funding for the CoE is provided through a Bureau of Justice Assistance Grant to Winnebago County through the Illinois Criminal Justice Information Authority.[3]

RELEVANT LITERATURE

Although progress has been made in statewide dissemination efforts in Florida, Illinois, Massachusetts, Ohio, and Pennsylvania, there is limited empirical evidence on the operations and effectiveness of these state-level initiatives. This virtual absence of research is likely attributable to the inherent challenges in studying the effects of these types of centers, which will be discussed later in this chapter. Although there is empirical support to varying degrees for some of the interventions promoted by these centers, including CITs, problem-solving courts (e.g., drug courts, mental health courts), and offender reentry initiatives (Heilbrun et al., 2012; see Chapter 1), the nature of the work done by the state centers makes outcome research particularly difficult. For example, it is difficult to quantify the effects of providing technical assistance, consultation, and training. Nevertheless, emerging evidence suggests that these centers may be producing positive outcomes in several domains. To illustrate this point, some recent data from the Pennsylvania CoE relating to the effects of cross-systems mappings are discussed in detail in Chapter 13. Interviews reflect that the mappings have fostered increased collaboration and significant progress in each county's action plan. About 90% of the survey respondents felt that the mapping improved the county's ability/willingness to collaborate across systems.

Since 2009, the Pennsylvania CoE has implemented statewide dissemination of the SIM as a tool for diversion and community-based alternatives for individuals with mental illness and/or co-occurring substance use disorders. Through systematic mappings conducted in more than half of Pennsylvania's sixty-seven counties, many counties have gained tools and means for greater collaboration across systems, worked together to identify gaps at each of the five intercepts, and developed local action plans to address the community's behavioral health needs and build upon local opportunities.

IMPLICATIONS FOR RESEARCH

The types of state-level centers described in this chapter are ripe for research, although there are multiple challenges in studying their operations and effectiveness. State-level centers do not lend themselves readily to traditional methods of conducting research. The two hallmarks of a high-quality research study—a comparison group and relevant outcomes—are not available or are difficult to define/obtain when it comes to state-level centers. Moreover, much of the work of these centers is difficult to quantify, which means that traditional statistical analyses are often not an option. Although it is possible to collect data on various center activities, such as the number of technical assistance calls received, the resulting descriptive data provide limited information about the actual effectiveness of the centers. Furthermore, identifying relevant and measurable outcomes can be challenging, and the data that are of most interest to researchers, policymakers, and funders are often the most difficult to obtain. For example, it may be difficult to collect valid and reliable data on the number of individuals with severe mental illness who are diverted from standard prosecution, and even more challenging to gauge whether such diversion can be attributed to the center's activities.

Despite these challenges, it has become increasingly important for state-level centers to collect data on their processes and outcomes. Obtaining initial and ongoing funding can be difficult, and funding sources are becoming more results-oriented regarding the types of state-level initiatives described in this chapter. As such, obtaining relevant and meaningful data has become a priority. To effect meaningful state and local policy changes aimed at reducing the number of people with mental illness in the criminal justice system, it is important to have data demonstrating the effectiveness of various diversion efforts at different points in the SIM, and the roles played by state-level centers in facilitating those diversion efforts.

As discussed, there is little research examining the operations and effectiveness of the types of state centers described in this chapter, leaving many empirical questions. In this section, we highlight several research avenues, focusing on the broad areas of process and outcome while recognizing that the work of these centers differs in scope. We hope this discussion will spark a dialogue among researchers and help establish a research agenda.

Several aspects of the operation of state-level centers can be studied. For example, it is possible to keep track of the provision of technical assistance, consultation, and training (although studying the effects of these efforts is more challenging, as will be discussed). If all incoming calls and emails to the center are received in a central location, a simple Excel spreadsheet can be a useful data-tracking tool. Relevant variables to track might include the nature of the request (e.g., technical assistance, consultation, training, systems mapping), the location from which the request is made (e.g., county, city), the date of the request, and the nature of the assistance provided. The types of operations data collected will differ depending on the work being done by the centers. Although these data are simply descriptive, when aggregated across all such requests they can be used to justify the continued existence of the centers; a high volume of requests suggests the need for such a center and the ability of the center to meet those needs, which would be useful information when seeking additional funding.

When it comes to evaluating implementation, there is a developing literature regarding how to examine the development, implementation, adaptation, and quality improvement of exemplary service models, evidence-based programs and practices, and strategies for effective scale-up and systems change. Fixsen and colleagues (2005) identified several core components among successful implementing practices at practitioner, organizational, and national levels, including staff selection, preservice and in-service training, ongoing consultation and coaching, staff and program evaluation, facilitative administrative support, and systems interventions. These components provide a concrete foundation for any successful statewide implementation and a model for the assessment of state-level efforts.

Outcome data are more varied and difficult to obtain. If the ultimate goal of these centers is to reduce the number of people with mental illness in the criminal justice system, then data on the number of individuals diverted would be the gold standard. These data may be difficult to obtain, as locales vary greatly in terms of the type and quality of the data they collect. Moreover, even if such data are available, it would be difficult to determine whether offenders were diverted as a direct result of the center's activities. It may be that the center has a modest effect that is mediated by the locality's implementation of a plan developed using the SIM. Even in these instances, however, the center's actual impact on diversion would be difficult to discern. It is likely that the SIM is functioning as a tool for system change, facilitated in its use by the centers. Other potential outcome variables include the number of people trained and the effects of the training, again recognizing that state centers differ in the types of trainings being offered.

IMPLICATIONS FOR POLICY

These state-level centers, and the use of systems mapping as a primary strategic planning tool, have several implications for policy. Four are worth noting here. First, the SIM is an ideal vehicle to bring together local stakeholders, including practitioners, policymakers, criminal justice officials, and others. One of the most striking occurrences at many mappings is that some individuals from the local jurisdiction are meeting in person for the first time. As a result, mapping can have an impact on policy, not only as a planning tool but as a way to create productive working relationships among stakeholders that in turn may yield policy initiatives. Steadman (1992) has written about "boundary spanners," and mapping is a process that by definition spans boundaries.

Second, the centers have the potential to create data-informed policy. It is important for even the most policy-savvy researchers and consultants to understand the limits of data in influencing policy creation. However, technical assistance centers, by focusing on "small wins" with the use of data, can gradually instruct policymakers about the utility of data in creating policy initiatives. Systems mapping can facilitate this as well. For example, a commonly asked question in the course of mappings involves "how many individuals" can be found at the various intercept points. Often, the answer is not available, or the numbers are ambiguous or sometimes conflicting, depending on the source. In addition, mappings raise further questions such as "What happens to these individuals?" or "What would happen if we tried that?" These create opportunities for the use of data (if available) or the suggestion to collect them (if not).

Third, the centers—through the use of mapping and other tools—can influence policy by emphasizing two issues. First, treatment resources, judicial resources, and virtually all human services resources have shrunk in many jurisdictions over the past few years. The diminution of resources will not be news to any policymaker or practitioner at a state or local level. However, the second point, perhaps less obvious, is that there are subgroups of individuals within the larger cohort of individuals with mental illness entering the criminal justice system. Technical assistance centers can assist in identifying these subgroups, which can promote the policy-relevant outcome of a more judicious matching of limited resources with more carefully identified need. The matching of resources with need is a fundamental policy decision and represents an area where a technical assistance center can play a useful role.

Finally, these emerging centers can influence policy by using different tools that can affect the immediate debate and long-term priorities of policymakers. If a community finds that mapping improves local communication because it has introduced individuals to each other personally and caused them to spend a day or two together focused on diversion issues, that may have some lasting effect. If a community adopts the use of data even in limited fashion, and finds that it improves its vision of what it is implementing even if it does not immediately show improved outcomes, that can alter habits of decision making and in turn change the way policy is made.

These suggestions may strike some as too limited in scope. But dramatic policy changes—whether at a local, state, or national level—are rare. Rather, incremental change is generally the rule, if change is to occur at all, and technical assistance centers can play a significant role in setting the stage for incremental policy change at a local level, aligned with practices and initiatives that are occurring in jurisdictions across the United States.

IMPLICATIONS FOR PRACTICE

The centers described here have taken different paths to diverting persons with mental illness from the criminal justice system. Even within the same state, a number of influences (e.g., local differences in resources, relationships among providers, relationships of providers to the criminal justice system) can result in very different systems. No single method or template can address the myriad possibilities for how these systems react to the persons they serve. Understanding how the system actually functions is critical to affecting the system in a positive fashion. It is also essential to understand that the forces that influence a person's interaction with the system may not be those traditionally identified in diversion efforts. For example, in many states, persons with mental illness interact with the civil justice system as much or more than they do with the criminal justice system. Ignoring the impact of civil commitment proceedings and housing court proceedings can begin the path to increased involvement with the criminal justice system for persons with mental illness. When developing any response, persons guiding the development must make themselves familiar with the players and the nature of their interactions. The use of sequential intercept modeling can help create the institutional change that may result in improved integration of care.

The use of tools like sequential intercept modeling and network analysis help provide evidence on which to base practice development. Collecting and disseminating data are critical roles for technical assistance centers. The nature of data exchange and the directionality of that exchange are also important. Too often, barriers to exchange of information inhibit the ability of the system to function at optimal levels. Planning early to accommodate the exchange of such data can lead to far more positive outcomes for individuals.

The process of modeling system function should also consider that funding, legal decisions, legislation, and other factors are a constant influence on systems. A method for frequently updating the information on which policy and practice determinations are made should therefore be built into any program from the outset. Funding cuts to social service programs have resulted in other social support structures needing to fill the resulting service gaps. Learning to adapt existing systems to deliver services without increases in funding has become a necessity for state and local governments. Utilizing modeling to identify pressure points and relieve service delivery backlog can permit community-based providers and state mental health service providers to continue to meet the demands placed on them by the persons and communities they serve.

Finally, diversion programs should be willing to address persons with more than minor misdemeanor charges. The need to involve prosecutors and the criminal defense bar in the development of diversion programs may appear so obvious that it does not need mentioning. However, our experience suggests that some diversion programs fail to meet their goals because they offer far more involvement for persons with mental illness in the justice system than a simple guilty plea and a short jail sentence would bring. Considering this, it is often the case that short, unsupervised sanctions may be far more desirable to defendants than attempts at mandated treatment—so implementing the latter will require agreement by both the prosecution and the defense. Keeping the focus on achievable goals that can be documented will better serve all stakeholders involved.

NOTES

1. Section 12(a): Any physician who is licensed pursuant to section 2 of chapter 112 or qualified psychiatric nurse mental health clinical specialist authorized to practice as such under regulations promulgated pursuant to the provisions of section 80B of said chapter 112 or a qualified psychologist licensed pursuant to sections 118 to 129, inclusive, of said chapter 112, or a licensed independent clinical social worker licensed pursuant to sections 130 to 137, inclusive, of chapter 112 who, after examining a person, has reason to believe that failure to hospitalize such person would create a likelihood of serious harm by reason of mental illness may restrain or authorize the restraint of such person and apply for the hospitalization of such person for a 3-day period at a public facility or at a private facility authorized for such purposes by the department. If an examination is not possible because of the emergency nature of the case and because of the refusal of the person to consent to such examination, the physician, qualified psychologist, qualified psychiatric nurse mental health clinical specialist or licensed independent clinical social worker on the basis of the facts and circumstances may determine that hospitalization is necessary and may apply therefore. In an emergency situation, if a physician, qualified psychologist, qualified psychiatric nurse mental health clinical specialist or licensed independent clinical social worker is not available, a police officer, who believes that failure to hospitalize a person would create a likelihood of serious harm by reason of mental illness may restrain such person and apply for the hospitalization of such person for a 3-day period at a public facility or a private facility authorized for such purpose by the department. An application for hospitalization shall state the reasons for the restraint of such person and any other relevant information which may assist the admitting physician or physicians. Whenever practicable, prior to transporting such person, the applicant shall telephone or otherwise communicate with a facility to describe the circumstances and known clinical history and to determine whether the facility is the proper facility to receive such person and also to give notice of any restraint to be used and to determine whether such restraint is necessary.
2. Section 87. The superior court, any district court and any juvenile court may place on probation in the care of its probation officer any person before it charged with an offense or a crime for such time and upon such conditions as it deems proper, with the defendant's consent, before trial and before a plea of guilty, or in any case after a finding or verdict of guilty; provided, that, in the case of any child under the

age of seventeen placed upon probation by the superior court, he may be placed in the care of a probation officer of any district court or of any juvenile court, within the judicial district of which such child resides; and provided further, that no person convicted under section twenty-two A, 22B, 22C or twenty-four B of chapter two hundred and sixty-five or section thirty-five A of chapter two hundred and seventy-two shall, if it appears that he has previously been convicted under said sections and was eighteen years of age or older at the time of committing the offense for which he was so convicted, be released on parole or probation prior to the completion of five years of his sentence.

3. This project was supported by Grant #2010-DJ-BX-0015, awarded by the Bureau of Justice Assistance, Office of Justice Programs, U.S. Department of Justice, through the Illinois Criminal Justice Information Authority. Points of view or opinions contained within this document are those of the author and do not necessarily represent the official position or policies of the U.S. Department of Justice, or the Illinois Criminal Justice Information Authority.

REFERENCES

Anderson, C., & Kilduff, G. J. (2009). Why do dominant personalities attain influence in face-to-face groups? The competence-signaling effects of trait dominance. *Journal of Personality and Social Psychology, 96,* 491–503.

Clayfield, J. C., Grudzinskas, A. J., Fisher, W. H., & Roy-Bujnowski, K. (2005). E Pluribus Unum: Creating a multi-organizational structure for serving arrestees with serious mental illness (pp. 27–49). In S. W. Hartwell (Ed.), *Research in social problems and public policy; Volume 12: The organizational response to persons with mental illness involved with the criminal justice system.* Oxford, UK: Elsevier.

Fixsen, D. L., Naoom, S. F., Blase, K. A., Friedman, R. M. & Wallace, F. (2005). *Implementation research: A synthesis of the literature.* Tampa, FL: University of South Florida, Louis de la Parte Florida Mental Health Institute, National Implementation Research Network (FMHI Publication #231).

Fla. Stat. § 394.656.

Fla. Stat. § 394.658.

Heilbrun, K., DeMatteo, D., Yasuhara, K., Brooks-Holliday, S., Shah, S., King, C., Bingham DiCarlo, A., Hamilton, D., & LaDuke, C. (2012). Community-based alternatives for justice-involved individuals with severe mental illness: Review of the relevant research. *Criminal Justice and Behavior, 39,* 351–419.

MGL, c. 123, § 12(a).

MGL, c. 276, § 87.

Mentally Ill Offender Treatment and Crime Reduction Act of 2002 (H.R. 5701).

Munetz, M. R., & Griffin, P. A. (2006). Use of the Sequential Intercept Model as an approach to decriminalization of people with severe mental illness. *Psychiatric Services, 57,* 544–549.

Munetz, M. R., Morrison, A., Krake, J., Young, B., & Woody, M. (2006). Statewide implementation of the Crisis Intervention Team Program: The Ohio Model. *Psychiatric Services, 57,* 1569–1571.

Ohio CIT Coordinators Committee & The Ohio Criminal Justice Coordinating Center of Excellence. (2004, September). *Expert consensus document: Core elements for effective crisis intervention team (CIT) programs*. Retrieved on August 12, 2011, at http://cjccoe.neoucom.edu/uploads/CIT Background/Core Elements for CIT.pdf.

Ohio Department of Mental Health (2005, Spring). *Tools for transformation: A guide to Ohio's coordinating centers of excellence and networks*. Ohio: Office of the Medical Director.

Perlman, S. B., & Dougherty, R. H. (2006, August). *State behavioral health innovations: Disseminating promising practices*. Ohio: The Commonwealth Fund.

Petrila, J., Haynes, D., Guo, J., Fisher, W., Dion, C., & Springer, N. (2010). Medicaid enrollment rates among individuals arrested in the State of Florida prior to and at the time of arrest. *Psychiatric Services, 62*, 93–96.

Rogers, E. M. (2003). *Diffusion of innovations* (5th ed.). New York: Free Press.

Steadman, H. (1992). Boundary spanners: A key component for the effective interactions of the justice and mental health systems. *Law and Human Behavior, 16*, 75–86.

11

Rethinking Mental Health Legal Policy and Practice

History and Needed Reforms

STEVE LEIFMAN AND TIM COFFEY ■

> We cannot solve problems by using the same kind of thinking we used
> when we created them.
>
> —ALBERT EINSTEIN

According to the most recent prevalence estimates of jail detainees at intake, roughly 16.9% (14.5% of men and 31.0% of women) experience serious mental illnesses (SMI) (Steadman, Osher, Robbins, Case, & Samuels, 2009). Considering that roughly 13 million bookings into local jails occur in the United States annually (Minton, 2011), this suggests that nearly 2.2 million involve people with SMI. Roughly three quarters of these individuals also experience co-occurring substance use disorders, which increase the likelihood of becoming involved in the justice system (Abram, Teplin, & McClelland 2003; National GAINS Center, 2005).

The challenge of combining rehabilitation with other priorities in contemporary justice-related contexts is substantial. In this chapter, we first review the relevant history involving the prosecution, incarceration, and treatment (or lack thereof) of individuals with SMI in the criminal justice system, primarily from a legal perspective. We then address more contemporary approaches to this problem and draw conclusions regarding needed reforms that are based on this historical consideration and contemporary analysis.

Because of the disproportionate representation of people with behavioral health disorders among criminal justice populations, criminal justice personnel such as law enforcement, correctional, and judicial stakeholders (who are often untrained to respond to individuals in acute psychiatric distress) must navigate an increasingly impoverished and fragmented system of community-based care. Unfortunately, the services typically available in the traditional community mental health marketplace tend to be insufficient in scope and intensity to address the complex needs of individuals who experience the most severe and persistent forms of mental illnesses, and who are at highest risk for involvement in the justice system. Part of the reason existing services tend to fall short is that many of the unique needs of this population fall outside of traditional behavioral health services. For example, many services currently available do not address the environmental needs and criminogenic risk factors that are among the strongest predictors of justice system involvement among people with and without mental illnesses.

As a result, jails have become places where a disproportionate number of people with behavioral health disorders spend significant amounts of time—their ties to the community severed, their treatment needs unmet, and their illnesses made worse. Upon release, many have little access to the services and supports necessary to facilitate adaptive community reentry and minimize the likelihood of reoffending. In addition, because services currently available in the community tend to be poorly coordinated and difficult to access, many individuals do not have the opportunity to receive treatment. The results are high rates of criminal recidivism, compromised public health and safety, disproportionate use of costly and inefficient acute care services, chronic homelessness, and unnecessary suffering for individuals, families, and communities.

To complicate matters, the basis of most current mental health laws and policies reflects legislation passed in the 1960s and 1970s designed to address a different set of needs and circumstances. At that time, the mental health system was under intense scrutiny for being overly coercive and subjecting individuals to horrendous abuses and experimentation under the guise of treatment. Clearly, there was a need for laws that would prevent people from being arbitrarily deprived of their rights and freedom, or being subject to invasive interventions that had proven neither safe nor effective. The result, however, was a dramatic shift in the locus of authority from the professional discretion of the medical community to the legal discretion of courts. In doing so, the concept of individual *rights* came to replace the concept of *need for treatment* as the central criterion governing authorization of involuntary treatment (McSherry & Weller, 2010). In this sense, the courts ruled that, provided an individual is not dangerous, he or she is entitled to refuse treatment that otherwise may be deemed necessary by a medical professional. While this provided legal protections to allow a person to refuse treatment, it removed any entitlement to receive treatment in times of psychiatric crisis when judgment and reasoning may be impaired.

Today, the mental health system is under renewed scrutiny for being overly fragmented, underresourced, and unresponsive to the needs of those most vulnerable. While the conditions that necessitated the creation of our current mental health laws no longer exist for the most part, this legislation and its effects on access to care, particularly in times of crisis, continue. Ironically, while most communities have safeguards to ensure that people with mental illnesses are not inappropriately forced into treatment, few communities employ safeguards to ensure that people with mental illnesses are not inappropriately forced into the criminal justice system.

To illustrate the inefficient consequences of the system, researchers from the Florida Mental Health Institute at the University of South Florida examined arrest, incarceration, acute care, and inpatient service utilization rates among ninety-seven individuals with SMI in jail diversion programs in Miami-Dade County, Florida. Individuals were selected based on having been referred for diversion from jail to acute care crisis units on four or more occasions as the result of four or more arrests. Total number of referrals for diversion services per person ranged from four to seventeen, with an average of 7.1. Total number of lifetime bookings into the county jail ranged from eight to 104, with an average of 36.6. Over a five-year period, these individuals accounted for nearly 2,200 arrests, 27,000 days in jail, and 13,000 days in crisis units, state hospitals, and emergency rooms, at a cost to taxpayers of nearly $13 million (Florida Mental Health Institute, 2010).

These findings are not unique to Miami-Dade County: Individuals ordered into forensic commitment are the fastest-growing segment of the publicly funded mental health marketplace in Florida. Between 1999 and 2007, forensic commitments increased by 72%, including an unprecedented 16% increase between 2005 and 2006 (Florida Department of Children and Families, 2007). In 2006, Florida experienced a constitutional crisis when demand for state hospital beds among people with mental illnesses involved in the justice system outpaced the number of beds in state treatment facilities. With an average waiting time for admission of three months, the Secretary of the Department of Children and Family Services was found in contempt of court. The state was forced to allocate $16 million in emergency funding and $48 million in recurring annual funding to create 300 additional forensic treatment beds. According to its Department of Children and Family Services, Florida currently spends more than $210 million annually—one third of all adult mental health dollars and two thirds of all state mental health hospital dollars—on 1,700 beds serving roughly 3,000 individuals under forensic commitment.

People with mental illnesses are the fastest-growing population within Florida's prison system. Data published in annual reports released by the Florida Department of Corrections between 1996 and 2013 reveal that the inmate population increased by 57% over this time. By contrast, the number of inmates receiving ongoing mental health treatment in state prisons increased by 153%, and those with moderate to severe mental illnesses increased by 170%. Based on historic growth rates, the number of beds serving inmates with mental illnesses is projected to more than double in the next decade from roughly 17,000 to nearly 30,000 beds. This represents an increase of over 1,300 beds—or one prison—per year. Based on the same annual report data and the average annual cost per inmate, it is estimated that in the next decade operating costs for prison beds housing inmates with mental illnesses will reach nearly 700 million dollars annually. Additional costs will result from the need to construct additional prison capacity to absorb the increase in the number of inmates and to provide adequate housing for people with mental illnesses in acute distress.

Clearly, these figures represent a failure of policy, practice, and law, as well as a terrible misuse of both criminal justice and community behavioral health resources. Frequent recidivism to criminal justice and acute care settings is due, in part, to gaps in the availability and coordination of high-quality services targeting the unique needs, risk factors, and experiences of justice-involved individuals. However, it is also due to policies reflecting the assumption that there is a direct, causal relationship between untreated mental illnesses and behavior leading to involvement in the criminal justice system. Recent research suggests that this relationship may not be as straightforward as once thought, and that drivers of criminal justice system involvement are much are more complex, involving risk factors and environmental influences attendant to people both with and without mental illnesses (Junginger, Claypoole, Laygo, & Crisanti, 2006; Peterson, Skeem, Hart, Vidal, & Keith, 2010; Skeem, Manchak, & Peterson, 2011).

Effectively designing, implementing, and reimbursing treatment providers for delivering high-quality services targeting specialized treatment needs, and ensuring that existing policies and laws facilitate appropriate access to needed care, are critical to establishing an effective community-based system of care for people with SMIs involved in or at risk of becoming involved in the justice system. In the absence of such specialty care, people will continue to be forced into more costly services provided in acute care settings such as hospitals, crisis centers, emergency rooms, and the justice system. To achieve these goals and better understand where opportunities and obstacles may arise, it is helpful to first consider where behavioral health and criminal justice policies reside within the broader domain of public policy (Goldman, Glied, & Alegria, 2008).

Employing the Sequential Intercept Model (SIM; Munetz & Griffin, 2006) to prevent unnecessary penetration into the justice system among people with behavioral health disorders is contingent upon having a broad public policy framework that creates incentives within the mental health and criminal justice systems to provide accessible, timely, and effective interventions. This framework must reflect the contemporary landscape of civil liberties and human rights with regard to the administration of mental health treatment services, without inadvertently creating barriers to care that may prolong episodes of untreated mental illnesses and frustrate opportunities for recovery, potentially contributing to even greater threats to public health and safety.

In this chapter, we provide a brief historical overview of factors that have helped shape current policy and practice in community behavioral health. This will highlight the politically temperamental relationship that has existed between the behavioral health and criminal justice systems as unwitting, yet undeniable, partners in administering the public health safety net for people with SMIs. Consideration of these issues is important if we are to design a more responsive system of care that promotes recovery and resiliency. We also provide a discussion of current policy and the need to reexamine assumptions about the relationship between untreated mental illnesses and involvement in the criminal justice system. Based on this discussion, we offer recommendations for enhanced services and service coordination targeting the needs of people with SMIs in the justice system, and for the reconsideration of current mental health laws.

RELEVANT HISTORY: AN OVERVIEW

The current problems of the community mental health system can be traced to historical events that shaped public policy and attitudes toward people with mental illnesses for more than two centuries. Pressure to impose social control over behaviors deemed inconsistent with social norms within mainstream social institutions is longstanding (Abramson, 1972; Fisher & Drake, 2007; Klerman, 1977). Two hundred years ago, people with severe mental illnesses who could not be cared for by family members were often confined under cruel and inhumane conditions in jails and almshouses. Because no effective treatments or alternative system of care existed, these placements tended to serve exclusively custodial functions (Goff & Gudeman, 1999).

During the early 1800s, a movement known as *moral treatment* began. It sought to hospitalize and treat individuals who were acutely symptomatic, rather than incarcerating and warehousing them. By 1900, every state had a psychiatric hospital (Goff & Gudeman, 1999). Unfortunately, the conditions of such hospitals—overcrowding, inadequate staff, and lack of effective treatments—resulted, once again, in the provision of little more than custodial care. Physical and mental abuses were common, and the widespread use of physical restraints deprived patients of their dignity and freedom. Asylums intended to be humane refuges from suffering had instead turned into houses of horrors (Florida Supreme Court, 2007).

By the late 1800s, mental health treatment took the form of more somatically based models of psychiatric illnesses and care (Braslow, 1997). To justify psychiatry as a bona fide medical profession, more medically based interventions were developed. As such, the body became the focus of new interventions. While the aspirations of professional development refocused attention on physical processes, they did so at substantial cost to human rights and suffering (Scull, 2005; Whitaker, 2002). Experimental procedures included surgeries to remove teeth, tonsils, gallbladder, uterus, ovaries, fallopian tubes, thyroid glands, spleen, and stomach. Individuals were injected with various substances to induce severe fever, coma, or convulsions believed to be therapeutic for mental illnesses. These included typhoid, tuberculosis, malaria, arsenic, insulin, strychnine, and other chemical convulsants. There was also the widespread use of prefrontal lobotomy and primitive applications of electroconvulsive therapy.

By the early 1900s, forms of physical restraint that could not be masked as therapeutic were regarded as barbaric, with many states moving to ban the use of restraint except as a necessary measure of last resort (Braslow, 1997). Ironically, many of the new more invasive procedures being experimented with were justified, in part, on the basis that they were therapeutic alternatives to the purely custodial restraint that had become so prevalent. Despite the so-called medical justifications for the use of these interventions, historical records indicate that their value was primarily in controlling behavior among disruptive individuals.

By the mid-1900s, more than a half-million people were housed in state hospitals across the country. With increasing public awareness of abuses, and systems stretched beyond capacity, states desperately needed an alternative to address the costly, expanding crisis of asylums. Around this time, the first effective psychotropic medications were developed, lending support to the idea that people with mental illnesses could be treated more effectively, safely, and humanely in the community.

In 1963, Congress passed the Community Mental Health Centers Act, which was intended to create a network of community-based mental health providers that would replace failing and costly state hospitals and integrate people with mental illnesses back into their communities with comprehensive treatment and support services in place. Under this legislation, the country was to be divided into roughly 3,000 catchment areas, with one community mental health center responsible for providing services for a population of 75,000 to 200,000 people (Gronfein, 1985; Sharfstein, 2000). Each center was to provide five essential services: inpatient care, outpatient care, partial hospitalization, emergency services, and education and consultation.

On October 31, 1963, in what would be his last public bill signing, President Kennedy authorized Congress to spend up to $3 billion to support the movement from institutional to community-based treatment in the coming decades (Earley, 2007). The goal at the time was to have every catchment area in the country covered by a community mental health center within the next decade. Unfortunately, due to competing domestic and international priorities, the political enthusiasm and humanitarian intentions that accompanied the signing of the act soon began to fade (Sharfstein, 2000). Tragically, following President Kennedy's assassination and the escalation of the Vietnam War, which placed a significant strain on national resources, not one penny of this authorization was ever appropriated (Earley, 2007).

As it became clearer that the conditions in state psychiatric hospitals were often problematic, and advances in psychotropic medication offered more hope for independent living, a flurry of federal lawsuits were filed against states beginning in the 1960s and continuing for several decades that ultimately resulted in the deinstitutionalization of public mental health care by the courts. Unfortunately, while state hospital beds were shut down by the thousands, comprehensive community-based services and supports needed for people who experience the most severe, acute, and disabling forms of mental illnesses were never developed. In fact, by the early 1980s only about half of the population in the United States was covered by a community mental health center and only about one quarter of the centers originally envisioned had been established (Gronfein, 1985).

The community mental health system that developed in the wake of deinstitutionalization failed to respond to the problem it was envisioned to address. Rather than creating a system of care to support community reentry and ongoing treatment for people residing in state hospitals at the time, the system instead prioritized decreasing unnecessary admissions and reducing lengths of stay in state institutions. As such, funding and policy development for the community mental health system tended to favor individuals with more moderate and episodic treatment needs and failed to address the community-based treatment needs of individuals with more severe and persistent psychiatric illnesses.

In its early stages, this system proved to be effective for many, as most people who were discharged from state hospitals tended to be those who experienced less severe psychiatric impairment and required less intensive community-based services. However, as states began to recognize that community placement was a viable option for people with mental illnesses, and that substantial cost-avoidance could be achieved by closing state hospital beds, political and financial pressures further reduced hospital censuses and decreased lengths of stay for those admitted. Over time, as more individuals with intensive treatment needs have come to reside in the community, the gaps in the community mental health system have become more apparent.

With long-term stays in state hospitals no longer an option, other systems have been forced to assume responsibility for the treatment needs of people who lack sufficient social and/or financial resources to live independently in the community. But few of these other systems are equipped to provide long-term support. The result has been a recycling of individuals between jails, prisons, shelters, short-term hospitalizations, and homelessness—with staggering public health, public safety, and public policy implications.

There has been a fundamental failure to achieve the goals of the community mental health movement; consequently, history has repeated itself in costly and unnecessary ways. There are two ironies here. First, despite enormous scientific advances, treatment for severe and persistent mental illnesses was never deinstitutionalized, but rather "transinstitutionalized" from state psychiatric hospitals to jails and prisons. Second, jails and prisons once again function as de facto mental health institutions for people with severe and disabling mental illnesses. In two centuries, we have come full circle, and today our jails are once again psychiatric warehouses.

MENTAL HEALTH AND PUBLIC POLICY

Wicked Problems

In 1973, design theorist Horst Rittel and urban planner Melvin Webber developed the concept of "wicked problems" to describe complex challenges of social planning and policy that encompass multiple causes and effects across disparate but interconnected systems. Decisions about education policy, where to build a new highway, and environmental planning are examples of this class of problems, as are homelessness, poverty, crime, and untreated mental illnesses.

Wicked problems tend to be cumbersome, unwieldy, and open to interpretation based on individual perspective. Because these problems tend to reside in multiple systems, it is difficult to determine where the problem originates or to distinguish between causes and effects. Furthermore, attempts to address the problem in one context will invariably result in repercussions across systems and over time, possibly yielding unintended outcomes that may be worse than the problem originally targeted. Solutions to wicked problems involve tradeoffs and compromises and cannot be right or wrong, only better or worse (Rittel & Webber, 1973).

Part of the reason wicked problems are so difficult is that they tend to defy ownership, thereby diffusing responsibility and accountability across stakeholders who may have very different opinions of what the problem is, where it resides, and what should be done about it. As such, one of the biggest challenges is not necessarily arriving at solutions, but reaching consensus as to how to define the problem as accurately and dispassionately as possible.

Solutions to wicked problems tend to be costly. They also have substantial impact, sometimes unintended, as policymakers typically do not have the luxury of experimenting with different options, and solutions tend to result in long-term impacts that cannot be easily undone. For example, when considering sites for a new airport, a city cannot try one location and then move to another if unforeseen consequences arise. Similarly, strict drug-control policies implemented in the 1970s and 1980s are significant drivers of the unsustainable growth in correctional populations. It was not until relatively recently that the impact of these policies began to be acknowledged. While states are beginning to explore "smart justice" alternatives to counter the unintended consequences of the "war on drugs," this does little to compensate for the resources lost due to a failed policy—or for the millions of Americans whose lives were irreversibly altered.

Because of these pitfalls, solutions to wicked problems are generally not undertaken without considerable deliberation. Policymakers are often reticent to take bold steps, fearing public backlash if their decisions prove unpopular or wrong. Most treacherous is that solutions to wicked problems are largely dependent on political judgment and political will, which are typically guided, at least in part, by forces and ideologies unrelated to the problem at hand.

In contrast to wicked problems are what Rittel and Webber (1973) describe as "tame problems," which tend to be the focus of the natural sciences, medicine, and engineering, and exist within definable dimensions with a finite set of agreed-upon causes and concrete technical solutions that either work or do not work. Tame problems (e.g., curing a disease, discovering alternative energy sources) are not necessarily easy, but they are potentially solvable. Wicked problems, by contrast, are never fully solvable, only managed and re-solved over time as conditions change and the problem is redefined.

Application to Mental Health and Criminal Justice Policy

The shift in mental health policy that led to deinstitutionalization highlights the role of wicked problems and the political undercurrents they traverse. Part of the problem underlying the failures of the community mental health system as originally conceived is that it was driven by competing goals and motivations, some of which had little to do with mental health. While there were certainly valuable scientific advances to support movement toward community-based care, there were also political and bureaucratic forces promoting the move away from institutional care, which had become an enormous fiscal burden for states. As a result, this massive public health and welfare endeavor was launched without adequate planning or the completion of pilot programs demonstrating feasibility and effectiveness. Anticipating the consequences of shifts in mental health policy in a 1975 article in the journal *Science*, Ahrnoff noted:

> The political-public-policy process is such that, once a program of respectable size and political prescription is mounted, it is extremely difficult to change its course even if there is mounting evidence that its cost or its harmful effects far exceed its benefits. When the policies involve ideological issues, they may rather quickly pass through a process of "social validation" and acquire a life of their own, divorced from empirical validation or refutation. (p. 1277)

Ironically, the push to move people into institutional settings during the 1800s and the push to move them out beginning in the 1960s were driven by the same basic ideal: to provide more humane and effective treatment to people with mental illnesses who, it was generally agreed, were being abused by current practice at the time. Equally ironic, both movements suffered similar shortcomings. They were based on overly optimistic assumptions regarding infrastructure and resources, which were only weakly supported by research and practice. Nonetheless, these assumptions offered hope and were sufficiently seductive to lead policymakers to commit to strategies that overpromised what could be realistically delivered.

In addition, in both cases, supply and demand led to implementation of practices that were markedly different from the original vision of either movement (Campbell, 1984). Early advocates of moral treatment and the asylum movement never envisioned overcrowded, neglectful warehouses, and community mental health advocates never envisioned a fragmented system of care. However, policies and practices established in support of each movement, and shaped by social, political, and economic forces that often had nothing to do with mental health, led to a drift away from the original visions that made these outcomes all but inevitable.

The problems facing the behavioral health and criminal justice systems relate to the fact that the community-based treatment infrastructure and its policy foundation were developed at a time when people with SMIs tended to reside in state hospitals. While deinstitutionalization was intended to build a robust infrastructure capable of responding to individuals with wide-ranging psychiatric needs, the community mental health system that developed was designed for individuals with more moderate treatment needs. People who would have been hospitalized forty years ago due to compromised capacity for independent living are now forced to seek services from an inappropriate, fragmented, and unwelcoming system of community-based care.

When the current system of community-based care was developed, mental health services were considered specialty services, distinct from those provided by the mainstream healthcare system (Goldman et al., 2008). Despite the dramatic trend away from providing services in institutional settings over the past forty years, the tendency to conceptualize behavioral health services as distinct from mainstream healthcare persists. As such, behavioral health has long been poorly integrated with other facets of healthcare. While behavioral health services are becoming better recognized across mainstream public policy, there are barriers to integrating mental health services into the broader healthcare system. Similarly, conceptualizing behavioral healthcare from a framework including both public health and public safety is a relatively recent phenomenon. While issues relating to people with mental illnesses at the intersection of the mental health and criminal justice systems are becoming better recognized, the issues remain poorly understood partly because of gaps in policy and legislation that prevent better integration of services (Goldman et al., 2008).

Another factor driving the crisis at the interface of the behavioral health and criminal justice systems relates to changes in criminal justice policy, particularly as it relates to criminal penalties for drug offenses and individuals identified as repeat or habitual offenders. Many of these shifts in criminal justice policy coincide with the period following the initiation of deinstitutionalization and the growth of the community mental health movement.

Beginning in the 1970s with the passage of new statutes, such as the Rockefeller drug laws in New York that substantially increased penalties for sale and possession of controlled substances, criminal justice populations began to grow (Mauer, 2001). During the 1980s, efforts to reduce disparities in sentencing practices led to further reduction in judicial discretion in determining penalties for criminal offenses by introducing presumptive and mandatory/minimum sentencing. This effort was led by the Sentencing Reform Act of 1984, which sought to create uniform sentences across federal district courts and was quickly adopted by legislatures seeking similar solutions for state courts. During the 1990s, federal and state laws aimed at popular political platforms such as "get tough on crime" and "truth in sentencing" further restricted sentencing options that did not involve incarceration. As these changes occurred, justice policy began to shift from principles of individualized and rehabilitative incarceration to more punitive principles that limited judicial discretion and disproportionately affected certain subgroups of individuals, including people with mental illnesses (Morrissey, Fagan, & Cocozza, 2009).

Criminalization of Mentally Disordered Behavior

The concept of the "criminalization of mentally disordered behavior" first appeared in the early 1970s (Abramson, 1972). Over the ensuing forty years, a tremendous amount of attention has been devoted to understanding and disentangling this deceptively complex concept—and to developing interventions to counter the unintended consequence of shifts in mental health policy and practice, and the incomplete implementation of the vision of the community mental health movement, that have occurred over the past half-century.

At face value, the logic behind the "criminalization hypothesis" appears straightforward: Lack of treatment for behavioral health disorders results in an exacerbation of symptoms, which in turn results in behaviors that are unlawful (or are misinterpreted as criminal acts rather than as manifestations of mental illness). This explanation offers intuitive appeal and suggests an elegant solution: Improving linkages to and involvement in community treatment services will decrease symptoms, which in turn will decrease behaviors that may become "criminalized" and will improve criminal justice outcomes. In other words, the hypothesis holds that the solution to the problem does not require the development of new knowledge or technologies, but rather simply working to improve access to and utilization of existing community-based behavioral health treatments.

Based on this reasoning, numerous programs have been developed that seek to establish collaborative relationships among stakeholders in the criminal justice and community behavioral health treatment systems, with the goal of improving linkages to community-based mental health and substance abuse treatment. Examples include crisis intervention team (CIT) programs, post-booking jail diversion programs and mental health courts, reentry programs that assist with linkages to treatment and support services, and community corrections programs that employ specially trained officers who apply problem-solving strategies to enhance compliance with terms of probation or parole (for an online database of collaborative criminal justice/mental health programs from across the United States, visit http://consensusproject.org/programs_start).

While these approaches have demonstrated effectiveness in improving behavioral health and criminal justice outcomes, the prevalence of SMIs among criminal justice populations has remained largely unchanged. This is not to suggest that these efforts are unnecessary: Many communities and states have demonstrated remarkable success in reducing costs and improving public health and safety through diversion and treatment linkage programs (see Cloud & Davis, 2013). Evidence of this, and the value placed on such strategies by governmental entities, is supported by continued funding made available through various state and federal legislation such as the Mentally Ill Offender Treatment and Crime Reduction Act authorized by Congress in 2004 and the Criminal Justice, Mental Health, and Substance Abuse Reinvestment Grant Program created in Florida in 2007.

Miami's Judicial Circuit Criminal Mental Health Project: A Case in Point

A combination of such funding sources was used to establish and expand the 11th Judicial Circuit Criminal Mental Health Project in Miami-Dade County, Florida more than a decade ago. To date, the project has provided CIT training to 4,000 law enforcement officers representing all thirty-eight local municipalities. Countywide, CIT officers respond to roughly 16,000 mental health crisis-related calls per year. In 2013 alone, CIT officers from the Miami-Dade Police Department and the City of Miami Police Department responded to more than 10,600 calls, resulting in over 1,200 diversions to crisis units and just nine arrests.

Post-booking jail diversion programs operated by the project serve approximately 500 individuals with SMI annually. Over the past decade, these programs have facilitated roughly 4,000 diversions of defendants with mental illnesses from the county jail into community-based treatment and support services. Recidivism rates among program participants charged with misdemeanors decreased from roughly 75% to 20% annually. Individuals charged with felony offenses have demonstrated reductions in jail bookings and jail days of more than 75%, with those who complete the program having a recidivism rate of just 6%.

Sustained Prevalence Rates

Despite these promising results, efforts to quantify the prevalence of SMIs among criminal justice populations over the past two decades suggest that little meaningful reduction has occurred—if anything, rates may have actually increased (Council of State Governments Justice Center, 2009; Epperson et al., 2011). Explanations for the inconsistency between these observations (more programs intended to divert people from the justice system to the community mental health system, and the relative stagnation of criminal justice SMI population estimates) are not entirely clear. In part, this may reflect the reality that involvement in one system is not mutually exclusive of involvement in the other, despite expanded diversion efforts.

Studies of mental health courts suggest that while people may continue to come into contact with the criminal justice system, they tend to be charged with less serious offenses or technical violations, experience longer times to first arrest, experience shorter lengths of stay in correctional settings, and are more likely to have charges reduced or dismissed (see Frank & McGuire, 2010; Heilbrun et al., 2012). Each of these outcomes potentially translates into significant public health and safety benefits, as well as reduced economic impacts.

Others attempt to explain the sustained prevalence rates by pointing to "tough on crime" and "zero tolerance" policies and laws that have emerged over the past several decades, coupled with steady reductions in funding for community-based treatment, as serving to increase the number of people who experience vulner-abilities leading to justice system involvement. While it is clear that the number of people with behavioral health disorders involved in the justice system is tied to a myriad of dynamic political, social, and economic influences, that people with behavioral health disorders continue to be overrepresented suggests that the policy goals of interventions designed around the criminalization hypothesis have yet to be achieved.

Further evidence that assumptions at the heart of the criminal justice/behav-ioral health debate may warrant reconsideration come from recent research suggesting that the presumed relationship between symptoms of mental ill-nesses and involvement in the criminal justice system may not be as robust or discernible as once thought (Junginger et al., 2006; Peterson et al., 2010; Skeem et al., 2011). Some even suggest that mental illness is not causally related to jus-tice involvement, and symptom improvement does not translate into improved criminal justice outcomes (see review by Skeem et al., 2011). If this were true, then it may be misguided social policy (rather than ineffective programs or "treatment-resistant" individuals) that is responsible for the absence of such progress.

The criminalization hypothesis does not identify mental illness as driving the demand for services in justice settings, but rather the limited availability of treatment services outside of the system. As such, rates of arrests and detentions should theoretically be reduced by increasing the supply of treatment services in the community. Research conducted to date, however, has failed to demonstrate a "dose–effect" relationship (Fisher, Packer, Simon, & Smith, 2000; Fisher, Silver, & Wolff, 2006). Furthermore, this argument, which implies that the mental health services delivery system is both the cause of and solution to the overrep-resentation of people with mental illnesses in the justice system, has been criti-cized as being parochial, resulting in recommendations for interventions that overemphasize "mental health" solutions while ignoring potential contributions of other disciplines such as criminology (Fisher et al., 2006).

Importance of Criminogenic Influences

Focusing too narrowly on symptoms of untreated mental illnesses and lack of traditional behavioral health services as primary antecedents of involvement in the justice system may distract attention from other possible causal fac-tors. It has been suggested that a potentially more fruitful approach may be to broaden the focus to describe offending patterns for people with mental illnesses involved in the justice system, rather than exclusively focusing on services for justice-involved people with mental illnesses (Fisher et al., 2006).

Recent research suggests that many people with behavioral health disorders who become involved in the justice system do so for the same reasons as people without such disorders (see Andrews & Bonta, 2006). Broadly applicable risk factors include social, environmental, interpersonal, and economic influences.

More specifically, they involve patterns of antisocial behaviors, personality traits, and thoughts; associating with individuals who engage in illegal activities; poor family or social supports; economic disadvantage; lack of adaptive or prosocial leisure activities; and substance use (Andrews & Bonta, 2006). The difference is that behavioral health disorders, particularly SMIs, may result in severe impairment in social and occupational functioning that, without adequate services and supports, may result in enhanced vulnerability to criminogenic risk factors.

NEED FOR IMPROVED SERVICES AND SERVICE COORDINATION

One of the ineffective aspects of the community mental health movement is the diffusion of responsibility for various services for people living in the community. Individuals often rely on a wide range of public programs to secure essential services such as treatment, housing, food, transportation, and income (Frank & Glied, 2006). Such services must be organized, coordinated, and financed to provide appropriate levels of needed care (Manderscheid & Hutchins, 2004).

The current system provides disincentives for the appropriate utilization of cost-effective, less intensive community-based services, which contributes to increased demand for expensive acute care and hospitalization services. Because the community-based system to which the person returns following crisis stabilization or hospitalization is unwelcoming and overburdened, the entire process—acute care episodes and subsequent psychiatric decompensation, all too often interspersed with justice involvement—begins again. Despite the development of effective treatment of serious mental illnesses, routine and efficient access to such evidence-based interventions in the public mental health system remains beyond the reach of many seeking care.

The National Leadership Forum

In 2008, the National Leadership Forum on Behavioral Health/Criminal Justice Services was established by the Substance Abuse and Mental Health Services Administration (SAMHSA) to address barriers to diversion from the criminal justice system and community reentry among individuals with SMIs. Forum members consist of national experts in the fields of public health, public safety, criminal justice, consumer advocacy, and behavioral healthcare service delivery. In September 2009, the group issued a report that details the current crisis, identifies barriers to more effective service delivery, and recommends immediate steps to decrease the criminalization of people with mental illnesses.

A key finding from the report is that communities lack accessible, high-quality services targeting the needs of individuals with SMI who are involved in the criminal justice system (or at risk of becoming so involved). Services that do exist tend to be "inadequately funded, antiquated, and fragmented" (p. 2).

Inefficiencies in service delivery are compounded by poor coordination and redundancies across the criminal justice and mental health systems.

Recommendations were made for an array of core services making up an essential system of care. These evidence-based practices, designed around the needs and experiences of justice-involved individuals, include forensic intensive case management, supportive housing, peer support, accessible and appropriate medication, integrated dual diagnosis treatment, supported employment, assertive community treatment/forensic assertive community treatment, and cognitive-behavioral interventions targeted to risk factors. Given the high rates of significant trauma histories in justice-involved individuals (Lynch, DeHart, Belknap, & Green, 2012; Policy Research Associates, 2011), the report also emphasizes the importance of ensuring that services are both trauma-informed and trauma-specific.

Needed Next Steps

Epperson and colleagues (2011) suggest that better behavioral health and criminal justice outcomes may be achieved by developing interventions tailored to the complex intrapersonal, interpersonal, and environmental factors that influence the likelihood of becoming involved in the criminal justice system. They point out that efforts to date that focus primarily on increasing involvement in mental health treatment, described as "first generation *mental health* and criminal justice interventions," (p. 3) have demonstrated positive outcomes, suggesting they are at least part of the solution. In addition, these efforts have been instrumental in substantially increasing awareness, particularly among legislators and policymakers, of the disproportionate number of people with behavioral health disorders involved in the justice system.

The next step is to improve outcomes by enhancing traditional mental health treatment to include services that address the complex needs and risk factors that drive justice system involvement among individuals with behavioral health disorders. While many of these needs and risk factors may be attendant to the experiences of people living with SMIs, they are not unique characteristics and, therefore, are often not a focus of traditional mental health treatment.

Described as the "next generation of *behavioral health* and criminal justice interventions" (p. 9) by Epperson and colleagues (2011), these services are recommended to address a more comprehensive "person and place" framework of risk factors and needs to include not only behavioral health treatments and interventions but also environmental/contextual characteristics of the community such as violence, homelessness, law enforcement presence, unemployment, poverty, and other indicators of social disadvantage that influence coping and resilience versus crisis and criminal offending among individuals with and without behavioral health disorders. The importance of attending to trauma and stress as critical mediators between person- and place-related factors is also emphasized.

To complicate matters, the current community-based treatment system was developed around the same time the criminalization hypothesis emerged, so it was designed for individuals with more moderate treatment needs. For most individuals who experience less severe and chronic functional impairments, are motivated for treatment, and possess adequate social and economic support, this typically does not present a barrier to service engagement and recovery. However, for a small but significant group of people with SMIs who experience severe and persistent psychiatric symptoms, have poor treatment compliance, and often experience co-occurring substance use disorders, the current system of care is inadequate (Lamb & Weinberger, 2011). Lack of intensive assessment and treatment planning, coupled with gaps in the availability of high-quality, evidence-based services targeting the needs, risk factors, and experiences of justice-involved individuals, has resulted in the delivery of interventions to certain individuals that are of limited effectiveness. This has contributed to patterns of service utilization characterized by episodic admissions to acute care and crisis stabilization settings, followed by referrals and linkages to services that are often insufficient in scope and intensity to address critical risk factors and vulnerabilities associated with outcomes such as criminal offending and homelessness.

Similar to the faulty policy implementation that led to large numbers of people with SMIs being released from state hospitals to communities without adequate treatment and supports, current policy governing the funding and organization of community mental health care has resulted in people with more intensive and chronic treatment needs being underserved or unserved in typical community-based settings. This is due in large part to rules and regulations that limit flexibility in designing service and reimbursement strategies targeting the specific needs of people with serious and persistent mental illnesses (National Leadership Forum, 2009).

For example, SAMHSA and the Centers for Medicare and Medicaid Services are two agencies housed within the U.S. Department of Health and Human Services. It would be fair to assume that both agencies work toward the common goals of the department, yet treatment providers often cannot be reimbursed for implementing evidence-based and promising practices promoted by SAMHSA because these services do not meet the Centers for Medicare and Medicaid Services criteria for "medical necessity." While it is true that interventions such as clubhouses, intensive case management, psychosocial rehabilitation, supported employment, and supported housing may not meet a medical necessity criterion, these strategies have proven to be among the most successful in supporting recovery outcomes for people with serious and persistent mental illnesses.

RELEVANT MENTAL HEALTH LAW: AN OVERVIEW

The Fifth Amendment of the U.S. Constitution guarantees that no person shall "be deprived of life, liberty, or property, without due process of law." The question of when a person with a mental illness may be deprived of liberty and forced to receive treatment is a controversial aspect of mental health law. Historically, there have been two legal principles underlying commitment. The first principle is *parens patriae*, which refers to the government's responsibility to intervene on behalf of individuals who are unable to act in their own best interest. The second principle is *police power*, which refers to the government's responsibility to protect the general welfare of the broader community and its citizens (Testa & West, 2010). These principles may be regarded as the government's responsibility to intervene on behalf of individuals who need treatment but lack the capacity to consent to care in order to satisfy the government's responsibility to protect the community from a dangerous individual.

Prior to the development of institutions and facilities to house people with mental illnesses during the nineteenth century, there was no obvious need for commitment procedures based on *parens patriae*, as therapeutic interventions did not yet exist. As such, the origins of commitment laws were based almost exclusively on the exercise of police powers to detain people deemed to be dangerous. As evidence of this, Deutsch (1946) provides the following excerpt from the very first commitment law to be enacted in New York in 1788:

> *Whereas,* There are sometimes persons who by lunacy or otherwise are furiously mad, or are so far disordered in their senses that they may be dangerous to be permitted to go abroad; therefore,
> *Be it enacted,* That it shall and may be lawful for any two or more justices of the peace to cause such person to be apprehended and kept safely locked up in some secure place, and, if such justices shall find it necessary, to be there chained. . . . (p. 419)

This law was almost identical both to a 1744 English law and to a law enacted in Massachusetts in 1797 revealingly entitled, "An act for suppressing Rogues, Vagabonds, Common Beggars and other idle, disorderly and lewd Persons." Clearly, the objective of initial commitment statutes was strictly a custodial exercise of police power, with no consideration given to the provision of treatment (Deutsch, 1946).

Therapeutic Commitment

It was not until the asylum era of the 1800s that the idea of commitment for therapeutic purposes emerged (Lindman & McIntyre, 1961). Initially, commitments required little procedure or formality, but the public became concerned about lack of commitment procedures and laws as asylum populations began to grow during the mid-1800s. Ironically, it was not out of concern for the rights of people with mental illnesses, but rather an exaggerated concern by the public that people without mental illnesses might be inappropriately committed to asylums.

The case of Josiah Oakes in 1845 fueled these concerns and drew public attention to the lack of legal protections against loss of liberty due to the possibility of wrongful civil commitment. It also marked a significant turning point in the evolution of commitment statutes. Mr. Oakes petitioned the Massachusetts Supreme Judicial Court on a writ of *habeas corpus,* claiming he had been wrongfully committed by his sons to McLean Asylum. Mr. Oakes was not alleged to be violent. Rather, as an elderly gentleman known to be "prudent and successful," he was accused of demonstrating unsoundness of mind and impaired judgment because of behavior just before and following the death of his wife, when he had taken up with a much younger woman of "bad character," whom he announced his intention to marry (Lindman & McIntyre, 1961). In ruling on the case, Chief Justice Lemuel Shaw wrote:

> The right to restrain an insane person of his liberty is found in that great law of humanity which makes it necessary to confine those who, going at large, would be dangerous to themselves or to others . . .
>
> The question must then arise in each particular case, whether a patient's own safety, or that of others, requires that he should be restrained for a certain time, and whether restraint is necessary for his restoration, or will be conducive thereto. The restraint can continue as long as the necessity continues. This is the limitation, and the proper limitation.
>
> —OAKES, *1850, p. 13*

Mr. Oakes' petition for release was rejected by the court, but this ruling defined the justification for and limitations on civil commitment of people with mental illnesses for the first time. In doing so, Chief Justice Shaw departed from the implicit standard of "detention of the violent," ruling that restraint was legally justified based not only on dangerousness, but on the grounds that restraint may be "necessary" or "conducive" to "restoration." This apparently represents the first time a justification for civil commitment based on the therapeutic principles of *parens patriae,* as opposed to police power, was cited by an American court (Deutsch, 1946).

Balancing Liberty, Due Process, and Public Safety

Over the ensuing 125 years, states crafted and recrafted civil commitment laws that attempted to balance individual liberty, due process, and public safety interests against the evolving field of psychiatry and a changing social and political landscape. As is often the case with wicked problems, each shift in policy was met with unforeseen consequences and calls for additional reforms. But mental health laws, as constructs with substantial political components, consistently lag behind advances in scientific and social technologies and understandings, creating a temporal disconnect that is often antithetical to progress.

In the preface to the first edition of *A Treatise on the Medical Jurisprudence of Insanity* published in 1838, Dr. Isaac Ray, one of the "Original Thirteen" members of the [Association of Medical Superintendents of American Institutions for the Insane (which would later become the American Psychiatric Association), lamented:

> Few, probably, whose attention has not been particularly directed to the subject, are aware how far the condition of the law relative to insanity is behind the present state of our knowledge concerning that disease. While so much has been done, within a comparatively short period, to promote the comfort of the insane, and so much improvement has been effected in the methods of treating their disorder, as to have deprived it of half its terrors, it is both a curious and a melancholy fact, that so little has been accomplished towards regulating their personal and social rights, by more correct and enlightened principles of jurisprudence. While nations are vying with one another in the excellence of their public establishments for the accommodation of this unfortunate class of our fellow men, and physicians are every year publishing some instance of an unexampled proportion of cures, we remain perfectly satisfied with the wisdom of our predecessors in every thing relative to their legal relations. (p. iii)

During the first half of the twentieth century, there was general consensus that inpatient care in hospital settings was the lesser of evils for people with serious mental illnesses. While the public had been aware of abuses and neglect that occurred in such facilities since the 1800s, the fact that there were no effective medications and few options for therapeutic intervention meant that there were often no viable alternatives for placement. People were assumed to be incapable of making decisions or acting in their own best interests, and civil commitment was often based on professional recommendation of need for treatment (Testa & West, 2010).

During the 1950s, the first effective psychotropic medications were developed, suggesting that people with mental illnesses could be treated more effectively, safely, and humanely in the community. This led to increasing agitation for change among those dissatisfied with the state of mental health policy and practice. Against the backdrop of the antipsychiatry and civil rights movements during the 1960s, and in the context of continued advancements in treatment, the traditional grounds for civil commitment began to be questioned (Large, Ryan, Nielssen, & Hayes, 2008).

In 1971, Kenneth Donaldson, a patient at Florida State Hospital for almost fifteen years, filed suit against the hospital's administrator and staff members, alleging they had intentionally and maliciously deprived him of his constitutional right to liberty. Over the years of confinement, Donaldson's frequent requests for release had been rejected despite repeated offers from a halfway house in Minneapolis and a friend of Donaldson's in New York to provide a home and supervision for him. While hospitalized, Donaldson had apparently refused treatment, denied he had an illness, and was neither dangerous to himself nor others.

In 1975, in *O'Connor v. Donaldson*, the U.S. Supreme Court held that "A finding of 'mental illness' alone cannot justify a state's locking a person up against his will and keeping him indefinitely in simple custodial confinement." Although Washington, D.C. and California amended their laws in the 1960s, following the *O'Connor* decision virtually every other state amended its laws to limit the provision of involuntary treatment to individuals deemed a "risk of harm" to self or others. In doing so, civil commitment laws have come to rest firmly on a foundation of "dangerousness," whereas basic "need for treatment" alone— which is arguably the primary justification for administering care in virtually every other situation in which a person may be incapacitated in some way and in need for medical attention—is no longer a sufficient threshold to trigger intervention. Over time, some states have added criteria to address "grave disability" or neglect of self-care to their definitions of dangerousness; however, none allows for involuntary commitment in the absence of some degree of risk of harm.

Shifting Civil Commitment Criteria: 1960s and 1970s

The shift in civil commitment criteria that occurred in the 1960s and 1970s was based on good intentions and a long-overdue response to an abusive system of care. But it is important to review the adequacy of these laws in the context of the current mental health treatment system, to ensure that the law both provides constitutionally mandated protections to guard against civil rights abuses and does not function as an unintended barrier to treatment in times of need.

For many individuals, an initial inpatient admission for crisis stabilization or short-term residential treatment is the first step toward recovery (Testa & West, 2010). Civil commitment laws predicated on narrow criteria of dangerousness as the threshold to trigger involuntary intervention mean that a person's functioning must deteriorate to a perilous level before this first step can be taken. Not only is this detrimental to the individual, it often places family members in the positions of fearfully watching as their loved ones become progressively more disabled.

Another reason to reexamine laws governing civil commitment is their potential effect on extending the duration of untreated mental illnesses, particularly psychosis. Longer duration of untreated psychosis is associated with numerous adverse outcomes, including poorer treatment prognosis (Marshall et al., 2005; Perkins, Gu, Boteva, & Lieberman, 2005), increased risk of suicide (Melle et al., 2006), and violence (Milton et al., 2001). Longer duration of untreated psychosis and more frequent episodes of acute psychosis may result in physiological changes in the brain that dispose the individual to greater long-term psychiatric impairment (Lieberman, Dixon, & Goldman, 2013). To the extent that policies and statutes governing civil commitment contribute to delays in access to treatment or expose individuals to more chronic episodes of psychosis, these laws may be contributing to long-term disability that could have been avoided through more timely intervention.

To consider the possible impact of civil commitment laws on duration of untreated psychosis, Large, Nielssen, Ryan, and Hayes (2008) examined studies of schizophrenia and other psychotic disorders from jurisdictions that incorporate dangerousness as a required commitment criterion with jurisdictions that utilize other criteria for involuntary treatment. Studies included in this analysis came from thirteen developed Western countries, including the United States. As such, findings should be interpreted with caution, as duration of untreated psychosis rates may have been influenced by factors specific to particular countries and jurisdictions, as well as shared characteristics of civil commitment laws. Results indicated that the average duration of untreated psychosis was nearly six months longer (79.5 versus 55.6 weeks) among individuals in jurisdictions requiring dangerousness as a criterion for involuntary treatment. The authors also point out that requiring dangerousness as a criterion for involuntary treatment can have a particularly detrimental effect on individuals experiencing the first episode of psychosis because commitment statutes often rely on historical information about the individual and past episodes of harm to self or others in the context of symptoms of mental illnesses. Individuals experiencing the initial onset of psychosis are unlikely to have demonstrated behavioral histories that would warrant the authorization of involuntary treatment. Similarly, most state statutes authorizing involuntary outpatient treatment require the demonstration of historical receipt of mental health services in acute care or correctional settings as a prerequisite to filing petitions for involuntary treatment. Individuals experiencing a first psychotic episode are less likely to have had these experiences, meaning they need to get more crisis treatment and/or incarceration before they meet criteria for outpatient civil commitment.

Objections to the broadening of civil commitment criteria generally hinge on arguments regarding autonomy, choice, and free will in refusing treatment. If one accepts these arguments, one must accept the assumption that people who are in crisis, but not dangerous, are competent to make decisions. One must also accept the implicit assumption that people in the midst of acute psychiatric crises are making reasoned decisions about their need and desire for treatment that would be consistent with decisions they would make if presented with a similar hypothetical scenario when not in crisis. While this may be the case in some instances, anyone who has experienced regret after making a decision in the "heat of the moment" or while experiencing a highly stressful situation may see the flaw in this reasoning. Furthermore, the mere existence and utilization of legal documents such as psychiatric advance directives demonstrate acknowledgment by law, medicine, and consumers of mental health services that there are times when, because of exacerbation of illness, one's decision-making ability may be impaired.

While it may be possible that a person gravely in need of treatment, who adamantly refuses care, is making a reasoned decision, it is more likely that the decision being made is at least partially determined by the illness. Given that false beliefs, suspicion, distrust, and other impairments in cognitive functioning not only are associated with acute expression of certain SMIs but are in fact diagnostic of them, it would seem unreasonable to regard all statements of people in acute psychiatric distress as reflecting competent and informed decision making.

In this sense, it has been argued that, in certain situations, the manifestation of illness has undermined the individual's capacity to consent to treatment (Large, Ryan, Nielssen, & Hayes, 2008). If this is the case, the person is not so much expressing autonomy but expressing symptoms of illness by refusing treatment. As such, authorizing involuntary treatment in such situations would not diminish autonomy, as that has already been accomplished by the illness.

Another criticism of civil commitment laws that require some form of dangerousness is that they effectively discriminate against people with mental illnesses in access to care (Large, Ryan, Nielssen, & Hayes, 2008). There are numerous circumstances in healthcare where a person may benefit from treatment but is unable or refuses to consent. Children, people who are unconscious, and those with severe dementia fall into this category. In such situations, there are typically legal provisions to act in the person's best interest or to secure consent for treatment through a proxy decision maker. Should we also require them to be dangerous before they can receive care? If not, requiring this of people in psychiatric crisis who are not competent to consent to services represents a unique barrier to care for people with mental illnesses.

Similar to commitment statutes that contemplate past admission to acute care and correctional settings, information regarding episodes of violence and self-harm is often critical to predicting future behavior. However, overreliance on prediction of harm, particularly in the context of a person experiencing a first episode of psychosis who has not demonstrated a history of dangerousness, results in an arbitrary differentiation of individuals in which many false-positive and false-negative assumptions will be made. Legislation authorizes loss of liberty for all people who *may* become dangerous to intervene among the smaller subset of those who *will* become dangerous. While it is not suggested that the ability to detain, examine, and treat people who present with a risk of harm should be removed, it is suggested that reliance on judgments about dangerousness as the primary criterion for civil commitment is problematic. To identify people who will become violent, criteria for those who are detained must be overly broad, but people with mental illnesses can become violent without exhibiting overt precipitating signs of dangerousness. For these individuals who may be in genuine need of involuntary treatment, current commitment standards may not apply. Furthermore, there are many more who do not experience mental illness who present a risk of harm—are there grounds to involuntarily detain them? A system that deprives a person of liberty based on assumptions about what he or she *might* do simply because he or she has a mental illness represents another example of state-sanctioned discrimination against people with mental illnesses (Large, Ryan, Nielssen, & Hayes, 2008).

MOVING FORWARD

Research and practice have generated many creative and inspired problem-solving initiatives at the interface of the criminal justice and mental health arenas.

By working collaboratively across systems and disciplines, a greater understanding of the causes and consequences of involvement in the justice system among people with SMI has blossomed. We now know much more about what works and what does not work in the effort to address the wicked problems associated with untreated mental illnesses and criminal justice system involvement. That said, in many communities it is likely that current efforts have achieved the majority of their potential in the context of existing policy and practice.

Going forward, the ability to effectively design, implement, and fund high-quality services targeting the specialized treatment needs of people with mental illnesses involved in or at risk of becoming involved in the criminal justice system will require a collective commitment to reevaluating some basic assumptions about the problems we are trying to solve. As history has demonstrated, these issues are very complex, driven and sustained by influences beyond the expertise of any particular discipline or profession. As such, it is important that we not remain professionally parochial in our efforts to build upon our investigations of problems and solutions.

The current state of affairs in mental health policy and practice has led to a "perfect storm" of sorts. The gap between research and practice is substantial. There are many examples of high-quality programs demonstrating "what works" in different communities and at different points in the criminal justice system. Yet one look at "treatment as usual" in many communities would suggest that our typical practice of mental health interventions in criminal justice settings has remained stagnant for decades. As states and communities struggle with economic hardships, maintaining funding for existing services (let alone securing additional resources) is challenging. One reason for this is that many jurisdictions have become acquiescent to systems of care driven by disproportionate investment in costly, deep-end crisis service at the expense of more effective and sustainable prevention and community treatment. We need to reexamine the ways in which existing resources are allocated to ensure that states and communities consistently purchase appropriate services that are likely to produce a favorable return on investment.

Technology permits the sharing of information around the world, yet organizations within local communities remain separated in their own siloes. We need to implement information technology solutions to improve information sharing, and analyses that provide better community coordination and organization of the systems of care. We also need to reevaluate policies and laws surrounding mental health and provision of involuntary treatment services, particularly during times of crisis and early episodes of onset of illness. Responding more effectively and strategically in these situations is critical if we are to prevent chronic impairment, reduce demand for services in acute care and institutional settings, and promote recovery in the community.

The policies and laws that guide much of what we do today were an effort to correct the consequences of an abusive and coercive system of care. There is no argument that bad treatment, in bad hospitals, driven by bad policies, was bad for people, but the circumstances that exist today are much different, and our policies and laws should reflect the contemporary landscape of science and the community. Statutes based on dangerousness-related criteria should be retained, but adding criteria to address need for treatment that would conceivably permit intervention before tragedy becomes imminent should be considered. Large, Ryan, Nielssen, and Hayes (2008) offer the following as a suggestion for need for treatment criteria that could be added to state laws: (a) it can be reasonably established by an independent party that a person lacks capacity to consent to treatment; (b) it can be reasonably established by an independent party that involuntary treatment will be beneficial or that the person would otherwise consent to it, given sufficient capacity; and (c) treatment is provided in the least restrictive environment practicable.

In 2007, the Florida Supreme Court issued a report summarizing the work of the Mental Health Committee, which included representatives from all three branches of government and experts from the criminal justice, juvenile justice, and mental health communities. This group reviewed the criminal justice and mental health systems and made recommendations to improve the way these systems interact and respond to the needs of people with mental illnesses involved in the criminal justice system or at risk for justice involvement. Recommendations included a comprehensive proposal targeting planning, leadership, financing, and service delivery strategies.

In outlining these recommendations, the committee emphasized the need to create a redesigned system of care that provides community-based services and supports, ensuring that people with mental illnesses and/or co-occurring substance use disorders can access care that is effective, efficient, safe, and appropriate to individual needs and circumstances. In addition, it stressed that services and supports must be available in the community and likely to contribute to adaptive and productive life in the community, while minimizing unnecessary or inappropriate involvement in the criminal justice system or other institutional settings. It also acknowledged that while the needs of each community are different, the efforts of each community must be guided by a common vision and current knowledge regarding evidence-based and promising practices. Key components of the recommendations included:

1. Phased-in implementation of a redesigned system of care targeting the provision of enhanced services to individuals involved in or at risk of becoming involved in the criminal and juvenile justice systems, with the provision of reasonable start-up costs
2. Creation of a statewide, limited enrollment network of treatment providers who demonstrate the ability, commitment, and readiness to deliver effective, high-quality services across systems of care to individuals at highest risk of becoming involved in the criminal justice system or other institutional levels of care
3. Amendment of the Medicaid state plan to leverage additional federal funding and increase the availability of home- and community-based

services targeting the needs of people with mental illnesses involved in the justice system

4. Development of financing strategies that create incentives to prevent individuals from inappropriately entering the justice systems, and to quickly respond to individuals who do become involved in the justice system

5. Establishment of a classification system based on risk of institutional involvement in the criminal justice, juvenile justice, and state mental health systems to target enhanced services based on necessary level of care

6. Establishment of partnerships between the state mental health authority and the state Medicaid authority to maximize funding streams and opportunities to serve individuals covered under public entitlement benefits as well as those not covered

7. Implementation of strategies to maximize enrollment in federally supported entitlement benefits such as Medicaid and SSI/SSDI

8. Establishment of a statewide leadership group to provide administrative oversight and facilitate technical assistance with the development of state and local plans

9. Development of comprehensive and competent community-based mental health systems based on evidence-based and promising practices

10. Development of comprehensive and competent interventions targeting adults involved in or at risk of becoming involved in the criminal justice system based on evidence-based and promising practices

11. Development of comprehensive and competent interventions targeting youth involved in or at risk of becoming involved in the criminal or juvenile justice systems based on evidence-based and promising practices

12. Recommendations to promote and sustain a more effective, competent, and sustained mental health/substance abuse treatment workforce

13. Recommendations for oversight of psychotherapeutic medication prescribing practices in the dependency system and child protective services

14. Recommendations for best practices in screening and assessment in the juvenile justice system

15. Recommendations for educating judges and other professionals in the courts

16. Recommendations for judicial leadership and the development of community collaborations

Based on these recommendations, numerous legislative and policy proposals have been developed. Not all proposals have been successful, and the state is continuing to work to implement the recommendations. However, this has resulted in the initiation of an important and long-overdue dialogue among legislators, policymakers, and advocates concerned with the health, safety, and welfare of our communities and citizens.

The future of the criminal justice/behavioral health interface—and indeed community behavioral health in general, as the demand for acute care and institutional services has forced states to divert funding from the community to pay for these deep-end services—requires a focused, strategic, and sustained commitment. Such a commitment involves funding and delivering services sufficient in scope and intensity to address the complex needs of individuals who experience the most severe and persistent forms of mental illnesses, and who are at highest risk for involvement in the justice system and other institutional settings.

The ability to respond more effectively and strategically to the public health and safety concerns associated with individuals with behavioral health disorders involved in the justice system depends on the ability of policymakers at all levels of government to work cooperatively across political and organizational party lines. Investing in a more reasoned and outcomes-driven approach, and focusing on what does work rather than what should, will help to address the problems described in this chapter.

REFERENCES

Abram, K. M., Teplin, L. A., & McClelland, G. M. (2003). Comorbidity of severe psychiatric disorders and substance use disorders among women in jail. *American Journal of Psychiatry, 160*, 1007–1010.

Abramson, M. F. (1972). The criminalization of mentally disordered behavior: Possible side effect of a new commitment law. *Hospital and Community Psychiatry, 23*, 101–107.

Andrews, D. A., & Bonta, J. (2006). *The psychology of criminal conduct* (4th ed.). Newark, NJ: LexisNexis.

Braslow, J. (1997). *Mental ills and bodily cures: Mental health treatment in the first half of the twentieth century*. Los Angeles: University of California Press.

Campbell, R. J. (1984). Flashbacks: scenes from psychiatry's revolutions. *Bulletin of the New York Academy of Medicine, 60*, 479.

Cloud, D., & Davis, C. (2013, February). *Treatment alternatives to incarceration for people with mental health needs in the criminal justice system: The cost-savings implications*. [Research Summary]. Vera Institute of Justice.

Council of State Governments Justice Center (2009). *Frequently asked questions about June, 2009 Psychiatric Services study of serious mental illness in jails*. New York.

Deutsch, A. (1946). *The mentally ill in America*. New York: Columbia University Press.

Earley, P. (2007). *Crazy: A father's search through America's mental health madness*. New York: Penguin.

Epperson, M., Wolff, N., Morgan, R., Fisher, W., Frueh, B. C., & Huening, J. (2011). *The next generation of behavioral health and criminal justice interventions: Improving outcomes by improving interventions*. New Brunswick, NJ: Center for Behavioral Health Services and Criminal Justice Research.

Fisher, W. H., & Drake, R. E. (2007). Forensic mental illness and other policy misadventures. Commentary on "Extending assertive community treatment to criminal justice settings: Origins, current evidence, and future directions." *Community Mental Health Journal, 43*, 545–548.

Fisher, W. H., Packer, I. K., Simon, L. J., & Smith, D. (2000). Community mental health services and the prevalence of severe mental illness in local jails: Are they related? *Administration and Policy in Mental Health, 27,* 371–382.

Fisher, W. H., Silver, E., & Wolff, N. (2006). Beyond criminalization: Toward a criminogenically informed framework for mental health policy and services research. *Administration and Policy in Mental Health and Mental Health Services Research, 33,* 544–557.

Florida Department of Children and Families (2007). *Substance Abuse and Mental Health Services Plan: 2007–2010.* Tallahassee, FL: Author.

Florida Mental Health Institute (2010). [Miami-Dade County heavy user data analysis]. Unpublished raw data.

Florida Supreme Court (2007). *Transforming Florida's Mental Health System: Constructing a Comprehensive and Competent Criminal Justice/Mental Health/Substance Abuse Treatment System: Strategies for Planning, Leadership, Financing, and Service Development.* Tallahassee, FL: Author.

Frank, R. G., & Glied, S. A. (2006). *Better but not well: Mental health policy in the United States since 1950.* Baltimore: Johns Hopkins University Press.

Frank, R., & McGuire T. (2010). *Mental health treatment and criminal justice outcomes.* Working Paper 15858. Cambridge, MA: National Bureau of Economic Research.

Goff, D. C., & Gudeman, J.E. (1999). The person with chronic mental illness. In A. M. Nicholi (Ed.), *The Harvard guide to psychiatry* (3rd ed.) (pp. 684–698). Cambridge, MA: Harvard University Press.

Goldman, H., Glied, S. & Alegria, M. (2008). Mental health in the mainstream of public policy: Research issues and opportunities. *American Journal of Psychiatry, 165,* 1099–1101.

Gronfein, W. (1985). Incentives and intentions in mental health policy: A comparison of the Medicaid and community mental health programs. *Journal of Health and Social Behavior, 26,* 192–206.

Heilbrun, K., DeMatteo, D., Yasuhara, K., Brooks Holliday, S., Shah, S., King, C., Bingham DiCarlo, A., Hamilton, D., & LaDuke, C. (2012). Community-based alternatives for justice-involved individuals with severe mental illness: Review of the relevant research. *Criminal Justice and Behavior, 39,* 351–419.

Junginger, J., Claypoole, K., Laygo, R., & Crisanti, A. (2006). Effects of serious mental illness and substance abuse on criminal offenses. *Psychiatric Services, 57,* 879–882.

Klerman, G. L. (1977). Better but not well: Social and ethical issues in the deinstitutionalization of the mentally ill. *Schizophrenia Bulletin, 3,* 617–631.

Lamb, H. R., & Weinberger, L. E. (2011). Meeting the needs of those persons with serious mental illnesses who are most likely to become criminalized. *Journal of the American Academy of Psychiatry and the Law, 39,* 549–554.

Large, M. M., Nielssen, O., Ryan, C. J., & Hayes, R. (2008). Mental health laws that require dangerousness for involuntary admission may delay the initial treatment of schizophrenia. *Social Psychiatry and Psychiatric Epidemiology, 43,* 251–256.

Large, M. M., Ryan, C. J., Nielssen, O. B., & Hayes, R. A. (2008). The danger of dangerousness: why we must remove the dangerousness criterion from our mental health acts. *Journal of Medical Ethics, 34,* 877–881.

Lieberman, J. A., Dixon, L. B., & Goldman, H. H. (2013). Early detection and intervention in schizophrenia: A new therapeutic model early detection and intervention in schizophrenia. *Journal of the American Medical Association, 310*, 689–690.

Lindman, F. T., & McIntyre, D. M. (1961). *The mentally disabled and the law.* Chicago, IL: University of Chicago Press.

Lynch, S. M., DeHart, D. D., Belknap, J., & Green, B. L. (2012). *Women's pathways to jail: The roles and intersections of serious mental illness & trauma.* Report submitted to the Bureau of Justice Assistance.

Manderscheid, R. W., & Hutchins, G. P. (2004). Building comprehensive community care systems. *Journal of Mental Health, 13*, 37–41.

Marshall, M., Lewis, S., Lockwood, A., Drake, R., Jones, P., & Croudace, T. (2005). Association between duration of untreated psychosis and outcome in cohorts of first-episode patients: a systematic review. *Archives of General Psychiatry, 62*, 975–983.

Mauer, M. (2001). The causes and consequences of prison growth in the United States. *Punishment and Society, 3*, 9–20.

McSherry, B., & Weller P. (2010). *Rethinking rights-based mental health laws.* Oxford: Hart Publishing.

Melle, I., Johannesen, J. O., Friis, S., Haahr, U., Joa, I., Larsen, T. K., Opjordsmoen, S., & Rund, B. R. (2006). Early detection of the first episode of schizophrenia and suicidal behavior. *American Journal of Psychiatry, 163*, 800–804.

Milton, J., Amin, S., Singh, S. P., Harrison, G., Jones, P. Croudace, T., Medley, I., & Brewin, J. (2001). Aggressive incidents in first-episode psychosis. *British Journal of Psychiatry, 178*, 433–440.

Minton, T. D. (2011). *Jail inmates at midyear 20010: Statistical tables* (NCJ No. NCJ 233431). Retrieved from Bureau of Justice Statistics website: http://bjs.ojp.usdoj.gov/content/pub/pdf/jim10st.pdf

Morrissey, J. P., Fagan, J. A., & Cocozza, J. J. (2009). New models of collaboration between criminal justice and mental health systems. *American Journal of Psychiatry, 166*, 1211–1214.

Munetz, M. R., & Griffin, P. A. (2006). Use of the Sequential Intercept Model as an approach to decriminalization of people with serious mental illness. *Psychiatric Services, 57*, 544–549.

National GAINS Center for People with Co-Occurring Disorders in the Justice System (2005). *The prevalence of co-occurring mental illness and substance use disorders in jails.* Fact Sheet Series. Delmar, NY: Author.

National Leadership Forum on Behavioral Health/Criminal Justice Services (2009). *Ending an American tragedy: Addressing the needs of justice-involved people with mental illnesses and co-occurring disorders.* Washington, D.C.: Author.

Oakes, J. (1850). *Matters of Josiah Oakes, Sen'r, Four Years Wrongfully Imprisoned in the Mclean Asylum, Through an Illegal Guardianship by Means of Bribery and False Swearing: Containing a Full Account of the Hearing Before the Supreme Court at Lowell with Judge Metcalfe's Interested Charge to the Jury, Contrary to Law and Evidence, and Chief Justice Shaw's Opinion on the Law Respecting Insane Persons, Confuted by Extracts from the Revised Statutes Showing it to be in Direct Opposition to the Law: Together with Opinions of the Press and Much Other Interesting Matter.* Boston: Published by special request.

O'Connor v. Donaldson, 422 U.S. 563 (1975)

Perkins, D. O., Gu, H., Boteva, K., & Lieberman, J. A. (2005). Relationship between duration of untreated psychosis and outcome in first episode schizophrenia: a critical review and meta-analysis. *American Journal of Psychiatry, 162*, 1785–1804.

Peterson, J., Skeem, J. L., Hart, E., Vidal, S., & Keith, F. (2010). Analyzing offense patterns as a function of mental illness to test the criminalization hypothesis. *Psychiatric Services, 61*, 1217–1222.

Policy Research Associates (2011). *Final report of the evaluation of CMHS Targeted Capacity Expansion for Jail Diversion Programs initiative*. Delmar, NY: Author.

Ray, I. (1838). *Treatise on the medical jurisprudence of insanity*. Boston: Little Brown & Co.

Rittel, H. W. J., & Webber, M. M. (1973). Dilemmas in a general theory of planning. *Policy Sciences, 4*, 155–169.

Scull, A. (2005). *Madhouse: A tragic tale of megalomania and modern medicine*. New Haven, CT: Yale University Press.

Sharfstein, S. S. (2000). Whatever happened to community mental health? *Psychiatric Services, 51*, 616–620.

Skeem, J., Manchak, S., & Peterson, J. (2011). Correctional policy for offenders with mental disorder: Creating a new paradigm for recidivism reduction. *Law and Human Behavior, 35*, 110–126.

Steadman, H. J., Osher, F. C., Robbins, P. C., Case, B., & Samuels, S. (2009). Prevalence of serious mental illness among jail inmates. *Psychiatric Services, 60*, 761–765.

Testa, M., & West, S. (2010). Civil commitment in the United States. *Psychiatry, 7*, 30–40.

Whitaker, R. (2002). *Mad in America: Bad science, bad medicine and the enduring mistreatment of the mentally ill*. Cambridge, MA: Perseus Publishing.

12

The Sequential Intercept Model as a Platform for Data-Driven Practice and Policy

EDWARD P. MULVEY AND CAROL A. SCHUBERT ∎

This chapter describes a particular application of the Sequential Intercept Model (SIM): its potential to shape research and other forms of data gathering, with direct implications for practice and policy in this area. Practitioners and policymakers often need immediate and specific information about program operations and impacts. In this chapter, we describe data-gathering processes that can provide such information. This process differs from the much lengthier undertaking of designing, implementing, interpreting, and publishing scientific research. We highlight the different ways that data can be collected and analyzed with validity, whether for immediate application to a specific set of questions or for the goal of conducting publishable research. We describe the role of SIM-guided data, some strategies for strengthening data collection and analysis (including identifying barriers to be overcome), and the overall organization of a data-collection project.

THE LOGIC OF THE SIM

The logic and utility of the SIM rests on three basic facts. The first is a simple observation: The people processed in the criminal justice and mental health systems are often the same individuals. Estimates are that as many as 64% of individuals in the criminal justice system have a mental health problem (James & Glaze, 2006) and anywhere from 42% to 66% of individuals in community mental health treatment have had criminal justice involvement (Draine & Solomon, 1992; Lafayette, Frankle, Pollock, et al., 2003; McGuire & Rosenheck, 2004).

Clearly, the populations of these two systems overlap; consequently, the types of problems faced in both systems overlap as well. The idea that these two systems can continue to operate in their own "silos" makes little sense considering the experiences of the individuals involved with them.

The second basic fact is that what happens to an individual in one system often affects his or her involvement and outcomes in the other system. Over their lifetime, people have "careers" of interrelated experiences in the mental health and criminal justice systems (Fisher, Wolff, & Roy-Bujnowski, 2002). In some instances, untreated mental health problems can lead to criminal involvement; in others, criminal justice processing may exacerbate mental health problems. Moreover, criminal justice involvement can possibly impede connections with services or work synergistically with mental health services to promote improved mental health. These two systems are tied together operationally. The success of each system depends somewhat on how it works with the other to reduce the risk of future offending and to address an individual's needs related to successful community functioning.

The third basic fact is that costs of separate treatment and control systems can-not be supported. Prior to the deinstitutionalization of the severely mentally ill in the early 1960s, both the mental health and criminal justice systems focused a great deal of energy and resources on developing policies and procedures related to "client management" in institutional settings. In both systems, a concerted effort was made to ensure the safety of individuals while providing appropri-ate services within the confines of institutional walls. The movement of men-tal health clients into less restrictive community settings (fostered by a shift in zeitgeist regarding individual rights as well as fiscal concerns) forced a shift in emphasis in this system onto community adjustment and long-term outcomes (Koyanagi, 2007). In many ways, the criminal justice system is now experienc-ing a similar shift in emphasis, motivated primarily by financial and practical considerations. There is a recognition that "building our way out" as a method of addressing crime cannot be sustained; it is too expensive to confine increas-ing numbers of individuals in criminal justice institutions for longer and lon-ger periods of time (Cowell et al., 2004). The current shift to community-based alternatives for low-level offenders comes from the awareness that alternative approaches are desperately needed and that recidivism, although relevant, pro-vides only a limited and often biased view of successful community integration. Outcomes such as employment status or the quality of social relationships have emerged as important considerations in assessing reentry adjustment or success-ful diversion (Petersilia, 2004).

The recognition of these simple facts implies a new way of doing business for both criminal justice and mental health professionals. Collaboration and joint problem solving have become the new standard practice for professionals in both systems. To address the realities of their situations, these professionals need to reconcile different worldviews, determine common goals, collaborate effectively on joint projects, and share common measures of program performance and success. Using the SIM process promotes these activities in a locale.

Other chapters in this book address how the SIM process can promote effective problem formulation and collaborative problem solving. This chapter addresses the issue of determining and measuring program performance and success in the context of the SIM process. This is a more complex undertaking than it might seem, requiring a range of activities related to the planning, execution, and follow-up of the SIM process. In this chapter, we address the issues surrounding the establishment of common goals and agreed-upon data systems and outcomes.

It is our position that these activities are essential building blocks for effective and continued collaboration between mental health and criminal justice professionals. Addressing data collection, analysis, and interpretation issues diligently provides an opportunity to expand the impact of the SIM process. A shared vision of desired outcomes and a common set of metrics for assessing operations and outcomes are building blocks for providing integrated responses to mentally ill individuals with criminal justice involvement. This shared vision also sets the stage for future productive collaboration and innovation between the criminal justice and mental health systems.

WHY CAN'T WE ALL JUST GET ALONG?

The mental health and the criminal justice systems have somewhat overlapping yet distinct missions. The mental health system primarily functions in a "helping" role, focusing on treatment and education and offering a range of services to address particular mental health disorders. The criminal justice system, on the other hand, is entrusted with ensuring public safety, mainly by detaining, monitoring, and punishing those who break the law. This is not to say that the mental health system is purely treatment-oriented and that the criminal justice system is purely punishment-oriented. Coercive practices linked to acceptable community behavior operate widely in the mental health system (Monahan et al., 2001), and interventions to provide skills and alter criminal thinking patterns can be found throughout the criminal justice system (Dvoskin, Skeem, Novaco, & Douglas, 2011; Lipsey, Chapman, & Landenberger, 2001). Nonetheless, the core functions of each system only overlap at their margins.

These distinct missions lead to different perspectives on what is important to record and track regarding the individuals involved in their system and the actions taken by the system's professionals. Mental health records are typically organized by individual and include clinical notes, indicators of symptom reduction and community adjustment, and information about the extent and type of services provided (needed at least in categorical form for billing purposes). A typical data system in the criminal justice system is incident-based (an arrest initiates a new record, with records linked to individuals) with a focus on issues related to the management of that incident (e.g., charge information, hearing dates and outcomes). Person-based data systems certainly exist in criminal justice, but these are not the most useful for everyday operations. Handling a situation and processing a person are usually the most pressing tasks; figuring out the factors that make an individual unique are usually secondary to knowing where someone is and why he or she is there. In both systems, professionals have limited knowledge of the characteristics and experiences of individuals beyond the bounds of what is recorded in their own particular system.

Differences in the types of information considered and the myopic view of information in each system are more than just operational barriers to collaboration. These are also indicators of a larger issue, a fundamental disconnect between these systems. Data collection and summary reports are constructed to reflect the important concepts to consider as system professionals pursue their activities and as administrators gauge effectiveness. The types of data collected in a public system legitimize particular frameworks for conceptualizing and addressing problems and thus subtly affect how professionals in each system formulate problems or gauge success.

The choice and use of outcome measures provide an example of how particular measures reflect the different orientations of these two systems. Criminal justice interventions often cite low recidivism figures as indicators of success. Lower rates of rearrest and return to an institution on a violation are indirect, and very policy-relevant, indicators of changed behavior in program participants. An individual who completes a program is assumed to have changed his or her attitudes, life situation, or level of skills sufficiently to reduce subsequent offense risk. Mental health system interventions, on the other hand, infrequently report the number of individuals who return for treatment as the primary indicator of success. The prevalence or timing of future hospitalizations may be linked to program impact, but such data are often interpreted as an indicator of the severity of the problem seen in a population or evidence that additional ancillary services are needed. In criminal justice, the mission of reducing continued involvement with the system is explicit; in mental health, this outcome is usually central only when costs are the major concern.

In addition to the choice of outcome measures, there are other examples of system differences, even in the interpretation of the same indicator. For example, mental health counselors may see engagement in treatment services as an indicator of positive adjustment, and such activity may be cited favorably in a case summary. Criminal justice professionals, on the other hand, may view continued reliance on mental health professionals as a marker of an individual's continued instability and difficulty with independent functioning, thus requiring continued strict monitoring.

In light of these realities, collecting and analyzing data regarding initiatives undertaken as part of the SIM process represent a formidable challenge. Not everyone is "on the same page" about what is valuable or meaningful information. Discussions of data often illustrate differences in perspectives about what interventions might be expected to achieve or the priority of certain life outcomes.

At the same time, having these thoughtful discussions can help these systems work together more effectively. Integrating discussions and activities regarding data collection, analysis, and application into the ongoing process of systems mapping is necessary, even though these activities are often considered an afterthought rather than a critical component of the process. Resolving issues of data availability, management, and interpretation present opportunities for collaboration and exchange that might be overlooked or underutilized. Taking on these challenges throughout the SIM process also creates opportunities for longer-term joint activities.

THE ROLE OF DATA IN THE SIM PROCESS

Ultimately, the potential of data lies in its ability to inform either practice or decision making regarding policy. Unfortunately, this potential is rarely met, particularly in the criminal justice and mental health systems. One estimate indicates that less than 10% of the information collected by jails is used to assist management in making decisions or in helping with planning the future activities of the jail (Ford, 1983, cited in Brennan & Wells, 2009). This state of affairs stands in stark contrast to some other areas with a longstanding tradition of using data to inform operations and decision making (e.g., business) or where data are increasingly used to improve service quality or reduce cost (e.g., healthcare, public schools). The criminal justice and mental health systems are moving toward an integration of data into service quality improvement and better-informed policy discussions, but these efforts are still relatively unsophisticated and lag behind other public and private sector initiatives (Counte & Meurer, 2001; http://www.pathwaystocollege.net/pdf/data.pdf).

Across a variety of settings, data collection and analyses serve several general organizational purposes (Nutley, Walter, & Davies, 2007). They can be useful in the following ways:

- *Instrumental*: In some situations, data can play a valuable role by informing a specific decision (e.g., the outcomes of two program approaches are identical, but program B is twice the cost of program A).
- *Conceptual*: Used more broadly, data can influence or inform how to think about issues, problems, or potential solutions (e.g., an analysis indicates that amount of family contact is the most important variable related to positive outcomes for released offenders in an aftercare program, although this was not a major emphasis of the intervention).
- *Tactical*: Data can often be used to justify existing positions in policy or program discussions (e.g., a single finding of an outcome study can be put together with other related findings to argue for a particular funding stream).
- *Imposed*: Initiatives that are seen as overall system improvements often use data to ensure that guidelines or prescriptions are being followed (e.g., state reporting requirements include indicators that a mandate to use evidence-based practices is being followed).

In each of these instances, empirical information about the processes or outcomes of interventions is used to either (a) frame the immediate problem or (b) identify the most effective approach within existing resources for having a favorable impact. Each of these roles may emerge at different points in the SIM process, and consideration of *how data might be used* is a key first step to using it efficiently and effectively in this process.

It is our experience that data may be used in any of the above ways during discussions of possible reforms in the mental health and criminal justice system—but the use of data does not always promote positive problem identification or the generation of innovative solutions. Often, individuals engaging in initial collaborative discussions cite data to defend their formulation of a problem (conceptual role) or to insist on the need for a particular approach (tactical role). This use of data can stifle problem-solving discussions and limit the potential for positive exchange among participants. For instance, recognition of the disproportionate number of mentally ill individuals in a jail may easily be diverted into a discussion of the arrest process. Data indicating that a large number of mentally ill individuals are admitted to the jail are often interpreted (accurately or inaccurately) as an indication that there is a problem with the police not making appropriate diversionary referrals. In another common example, individuals may cite data (often of questionable validity) about the demonstrated effectiveness of a particular program, excluding it from consideration as a point of intervention or highlighting it as a candidate for broader application. Individuals may base their high regard for a particular program on one widely accepted local study of program effectiveness or the fact that the program is implementing an evidence-based practice. The presentation of empirical data in this way often shields particular aspects of the system from more careful scrutiny, since few people want to "argue with success." In the process, however, groups often do not learn as much as they could about the lessons or limits of this perceived success.

The initial discussions surrounding the implementation of the SIM offer numerous opportunities to demonstrate the difficulties and potential pitfalls of interpreting data at a cursory level or through a biased lens. In the previous example about disproportionally high numbers of mental health clients in the jail population, discussions can center on the processes that might produce a heavy reliance on jail as an alternative (rather than diversion options) or the factors that could make the estimate of the prevalence of mental health clients suspect (e.g., the number of individuals who do not complete a screen). These discussions thus present opportunities for critical thinking about both data interpretation and problem formulation. In the example about the widely accepted figures regarding program success, a discussion of some outcomes that might not have been measured, or of the system or operational factors that might have changed since these outcomes were assessed, can again demonstrate how to think critically and talk openly about data. Emphasizing the role of data as a snapshot of the process at a particular time starts by addressing the seemingly "empirical" facts brought into the room initially by participants in SIM discussions.

The ideal situation is one in which data sources are identified prior to discussions about implementing the SIM (e.g., prior to cross-system mapping workshops) and preliminary data regarding system regularities can be presented to the group and discussed. This strategy avoids the possible difficulty of refuting widely accepted data in the initial discussions. Also, the integration of new data into the discussion process models the desired strategy of considering and critiquing empirical information to assess efficiency and effectiveness across systems. In reality, however, it can be difficult to persuade people to do more than simple, cursory examinations of the data in their local system prior to the cross-system mapping workshops and more general discussion about implementing the SIM. The relationships needed for in-depth sharing of information across (and often even within) systems are often not well established, and the time and effort required to do analyses come at the expense of more pressing tasks. Requesting the preparation of useful, detailed datasets prior to the initiation of the SIM process usually costs more in good will from participating agencies than seems reasonable.

An alternative strategy is to gather information during discussions regarding the implementation of the SIM (e.g., during the cross-systems mapping workshops). This could involve discussions about the availability of particular types of data relevant to activities identified by the group, and the use of this information for targeted follow-up projects. Group members can be asked to describe the data sources that might be useful to address particular issues (e.g., the need to conduct risk/need assessments prior to reentry from the prison system). Volunteering this information sets the stage for future collaboration on data-related activities and identifies the individuals in each organization who would be valuable to include in subsequent discussions.

Data analysis and interpretation become more central to using the SIM in the cross-systems mapping process as group members consider the impact of attempted system improvements. As noted earlier, the basic principles of the SIM imply system-level changes in policy and practice to prevent individuals with behavioral health concerns from entering or penetrating deeper into the criminal justice system. Determining whether changes have promoted the achievement of these broad goals is certainly not simple, however. Instead, it is the result of answering a sequence of questions about the processing and outcomes for individuals with mental disorders in the criminal justice system. Data can be used effectively to promote ongoing collaboration and system improvement—if such data are targeted toward providing information about the topics of most interest to the group participants. This can also facilitate continuing discussions following the completion of the cross-systems mapping.

Data can be a critical component at several points in this larger process of assessing system reform. Discussions of identified new policies or practices can be focused by providing information to stakeholders and/or administrators about the readiness of a locale for a particular change (e.g., the availability of requisite resources, the receptivity of stakeholders to this change) and the relative attractiveness of options (e.g., the comparative costs and payoffs of possible solutions). At the initial stages of problem assessment and formulation, data can assist in framing the issue and providing objective indicators for the assessment and comparison of available options. Once an option is selected, data can be used to monitor its implementation and identify aspects of operations that might undermine the success of a new policy or program. Finally, and arguably most importantly, after a program or policy has been in place for a sufficient period of time, data can be used to evaluate whether its goals were achieved, identify unintended effects, and inform future decisions regarding resource allocation (e.g., Do we have the funds to begin or sustain this new practice? What are the staffing requirements for this change?).

Assessments of the impact of the activities related to the SIM process might include the following types of broad inquiries:

- Has the momentum for systems change focused on the right places or practices? What aspects of the system in a jurisdiction have been identified as needing change? How were they identified? Were the most reasonable aspects of the system identified for intervention? In essence, this is a question about whether initiatives have focused on aspects of the system where a change will have a noticeable impact on how mentally ill individuals are treated.
- Has the adoption of a particular model for intervention or alteration in processing procedures produced any actual changes in the usual practice? How are professionals in the system acting differently? These questions ask whether people in the mental health and criminal justice system are doing their jobs differently than before.
- Have these changes made a difference in how justice-involved individuals with mental illness are handled compared to other individuals? These questions address how system involvement looks from the perspective of mentally ill individuals, and whether their experiences differ from those of individuals without an identifiable mental disorder.
- Has any differential treatment of justice-involved individuals with mental illness promoted or detracted from positive outcomes for these individuals? The issue here is whether there are demonstrable outcomes in the functioning of mentally ill individuals, either positive or negative, that have accompanied changes initiated by the SIM process.

Accurate answers to such questions are facilitated by systematic and focused data collection at a number of points in the process of providing mental health services and processing individuals through the criminal justice system. Without such systematic collection and integration of data, though, answers to these central questions inevitably rest on subjective impressions, isolated anecdotes, or conjecture.

The integration of data collection and analysis into implementation activities after initial discussion about implementing the SIM serves a purpose beyond simply determining whether the activities identified in these discussions were achieved adequately. These data-related activities also promote a common language and perspective for participants from different systems or for individuals with different roles within the same system. Agreeing upon data elements and methods for portraying outcomes requires that people talk to each other in specific terms about what is really known and what is worth knowing. This sort of exchange, if done positively, can pave the way for focused discussions of program activities and reasonable expectations that might not otherwise occur.

STRATEGIES FOR STRENGTHENING DATA COLLECTION AND ANALYSIS

These examples of when and how data can be useful seem persuasive. So why are data not used more frequently? Why are requests for such data often met with resistance? There are several barriers to the systematic examination of data in the mental health and criminal justice systems. It is often necessary to address these barriers in efforts to create data-informed reforms in which these two systems work together effectively.

Barrier #1: Sometimes Administrators Just Don't Want to Know

The successful use of data to drive decision making is not random happenstance; it usually arises in an organizational culture where empirical information is considered critical to successful management. Decisions about what data to collect, how to collect them, and how to apply them usually come from managers with the ability (and resources) to think ahead—about the eventual goal and the relevance of certain information for promoting desirable changes. For many managers without this orientation, data collection/use is usually an afterthought, not an ongoing part of the organizational conversation and planning processes. The priority of obtaining and considering solid data comes from the top of an organization and is reflected in how problems are framed and how actions are assessed.

Use of data in this way may be more of a requirement than an option in the future. The demand for using data and for thinking in empirically verifiable terms is increasing in response to comprehensive reporting requirements instituted by law (Brennan & Wells, 2009). Moreover, reliance on empirical information in program planning is becoming more common, as funding becomes linked to demonstrated change (Platz, Greenway, & Hendricks, 2006) (http://www.nationalserviceresources.org/filemanager/download/ProgramMgmt/Outcome_Measurement_Showing_Results_Nonprofit_Sector.pdf). Managers who recognize the promise of data are well positioned to meet these new requirements.

Our call for data to play a more central role in organizational planning and operations implies that decision makers in both the mental health and criminal justice system can build their capacity to use such data. At the very least, it is advantageous for decision makers to appreciate the positive potential of data, to know how to formulate data-related questions, and to understand the conceptual messages derived from analyses. These skills are increasingly important to be a knowledgeable participant in discussions that rely on research literature and statistics as frameworks for improvement strategies. They are also essential for promoting an agency-wide climate that supports taking the time and effort to focus on data and uses data to improve policy and practice. Even if a decision maker is fortunate enough to have personnel to design a data system and/or conduct analyses, his or her ability to guide the analytic agenda by formulating questions and to understand the conceptual implications of the findings are key to informed decision making. However, not all agencies or settings have yet reached this conclusion. For administrators who have not adopted an empirical orientation to problem formulation and solution, data can be a troublesome (or even threatening) intrusion. A good number of organizations still rely on the personal charisma or authoritative control of their leader to maintain stability, order, and direction. In these types of settings (in either mental health or criminal justice), data challenging current practices are often seen as naïve or politically motivated. The tone of an organization flows from the top, and skepticism about the accuracy or utility of data can permeate some organizational cultures.

These types of settings can become more receptive to the use of data that demonstrably improve or simplify operations. In the face of considerable resistance to data collection or analysis, it is important to begin these activities when there is high potential for immediate payoff to the completion of valued staff activities. In criminal justice settings, data collection might be useful for determining unit assignment more quickly and effectively, or reducing the likelihood of incidents that might result in staff injury. In mental health settings, systems for screening individuals for suicide risk or potential drug interactions might limit staff liability. Small successes in resistant settings can pave the way for more elaborate data collection and application.

Barrier #2: Often There Just Aren't Enough Resources

In most criminal justice and mental health settings, material and staff resources are stretched thin. There is little time, there are few computers, and there are even fewer skilled personnel who are not already overcommitted. The issue is often not a lack of will to collect and consider data; it is simply insufficient resources to do so with any focus or consistency.

This situation is particularly acute in the criminal justice system. Mental health programs have had data systems and personnel in place to track service delivery and to maintain billing records for some time and often have access to data analysts through affiliations with medical facilities or county human service departments. Criminal justice agencies, particularly local jails and county agencies, are "late to the dance" in some respects. Local jails are often run as standalone units (in contrast to state-level Department of Correction systems) and are particularly hard pressed for resources. However, in response to comprehensive reporting requirements instituted by law, criminal justice agencies at all levels are now confronting challenges associated with designing and monitoring databases, running analyses, and evaluating aspects of their operational processes (e.g., operational costs, utilization levels, population trends and statistics; Brennan & Wells, 2009).

The financial and personnel resources are often just not there to meet the increasing demand for data reporting, and there is no easy fix to this situation. There are, however, several strategies that locales and agencies have tried with some success. First, it is often useful to evaluate the skills of existing personnel and new hires with an eye toward data-management skills (ranging from data entry to data manipulation and analysis). Current employees such as clerical support staff members probably have the requisite skills for data entry, and most recent college graduates have exposure to at least basic data manipulation during their undergraduate training. These individuals may be brought together to form a data-management team under the direction of an individual with more sophisticated skills. Second, many agencies or settings reach out to local education programs. Universities, colleges, or technical/trade programs are often seeking internship/practicum opportunities for their students. These can often provide a steady source of skilled individuals with little associated cost. Third, some locales borrow what they can through cooperative arrangements. Working together with other agencies within or across counties can often provide a mutual opportunity for capacity building and can save time, effort, and money for each agency. Finally, there is the possibility of collaborating with resource centers. Many states have funded technical assistance centers at universities that can provide support services for specific data-related projects for free or at a reduced price (e.g., in Pennsylvania, the Pennsylvania Mental Health and Justice Center of Excellence, http://www.pacenterofexcellence.pitt.edu, or the Penn State Justice and Safety Institute, http://jasi.outreach.psu.edu).

Another reasonable alternative is to share information between the criminal justice and mental health systems to answer questions of common interest. Information sharing has implications for the maintenance of confidentiality (if individual-level data are being shared) and may require the formulation of memoranda of understanding between agencies. These issues are discussed in Chapter 13. In addition, there are a variety of mundane issues that must be addressed, such as the lack of common identifiers across the data systems and the sufficiency of any "matching" processes using multiple identifiers across datasets. If these issues can be addressed, however, the potential for sharing information across datasets can be considerable, and it can be done at a fraction of the cost for creating new data systems.

Barrier #3: The Questions and Issues Are Just Too Complicated

Designing and carrying out a conceptually sound and empirically rigorous evaluation in a criminal justice or mental health setting is a difficult assignment in itself; trying to conduct an evaluation of an initiative that spans both systems compounds the complexity. As mentioned earlier, common language, goals, and operations must be established that make sense to professionals in both systems. Sometimes coordinating data collection across both systems and interpreting it in light of the concerns of policymakers and professionals in both systems simply seems overwhelming.

The temptation in these situations is to create a new system of data collection—one that integrates the concerns of professionals in both systems as well as all possible services received or outcomes of individuals who move between the mental health and criminal justice system. This is a complicated task that can run amok in many ways. It is true that some locales have established "data warehouses" that compile and merge data from multiple human service and criminal justice systems, but truly functional systems like this are rare. Integrating data systems from mental health and criminal justice on a large scale is more often fraught with frustration and, unless there is a long-term strategic commitment, is difficult to maintain. Constructing large, integrated data systems across mental health and criminal justice may be an instance where, as Voltaire noted, "the best is the enemy of the good."

A preferred strategy is to take on targeted elaborations of the existing data systems. The substantial overlap between the criminal justice and mental health system populations suggests that these systems should be mutually informed about the sorts of information routinely tracked and to identify the information gaps relevant to their shared clients. Depending on the extent and nature of these gaps, it might suggest a need to add supplemental information to the current domain of data collected and/or to share information between systems. A range of broad and specific issues arise, however, when changing or expanding an existing data system.

Broad questions arise about the purpose of the data system overall. Who will be viewing the final data analytic products? For what purposes? How do we ultimately want to use these data? In many cases, existing data systems serve as administrative databases primarily, providing information about specific case actions rather than aggregate trends. In other words, these databases are designed to provide information such as whether an individual was in a facility during a particular time or received a particular type of service, rather than offering population-level profiles over time. Manipulating case files into usable summary datasets regarding samples of interest is thus a task that often takes specialized programming skills.

In addition, specific issues arise about the details of the data-processing tasks. Who makes the determinations about coding, what is this person's skill level, and how do we balance functionality with validity in any new data collected? In the course of these considerations, it becomes apparent that all of these seemingly mundane concerns matter greatly. The devil *is* in the details when designing systems for data collection, organization, and storage. If information is unavailable, unreliable, or invalid, it may not be possible to answer important questions; even worse, erroneous conclusions can be taken as fact.

Because of the complexities of starting new data-collection initiatives, it is usually advantageous to build more elaborate systems incrementally. Any new data collection or reorganization will create additional work for people who already feel overburdened, and the potential utility of this new activity to the organization as a whole or to the individuals themselves has to be communicated clearly and directly. People collecting data just because they "have to" generate little enthusiasm for attention to all the details that matter in the end. In addition, data changes focused on addressing a particular issue are easier to understand and endorse. Getting at a focused question (e.g., the proportion of people identified with a mental disorder in the jail who actually receive follow-up services when they return to the community) by gathering additional processing or outcome measures is usually more reasonable to people than simply overhauling the existing system. Incremental change in the ways that data are collected, organized, and analyzed can be achieved by addressing successive, focused questions. Changes implemented to answer one question can serve as the platform for changes to address the next question. Gathering immediately useful information in small steps can fuel incremental change.

ORGANIZING A DATA-BASED PROJECT

Taking these incremental steps usually requires a considerable investment in working with personnel to identify the specific problem to be addressed and the steps needed to generate useful information. We outline the key steps in this process below, in a linear and simplified form. We caution, however, that the world is rarely linear and almost always more complex than can be described here. We recommend that you consult additional resources for a more thorough understanding of how to do collaborative, action-based research and integrate these principles into using the SIM (some relevant websites and books on these topics are given in Appendix A).

A general framework for organizing a data-based inquiry includes several steps that can guide ongoing data-related and consultation activities. These include:

- *Question identification.* The process of planning a joint data-based inquiry begins with the clarification of the *general topic* and the specific question of interest. This can be facilitated greatly if efforts to collect and analyze data are coordinated with the mapping process in a locale. In the SIM exercises, priority issues are identified by the group, and these serve as accepted starting points for relevant inquiries. Pursuing data-collection and staff-consultation efforts aligned with the locale's goals allows discussion and data-related activities to occur while the consensus is still fresh in the minds of professionals in the system.

    The discussions regarding the question of interest provide an excellent opportunity to model the logical steps of narrowing a broad concern into

a manageable research question. Initially, the discussion can focus on
certain kinds of questions:

1. What is the purpose for conducting this inquiry? What do you want
   to be able to do/decide as a result of looking at this information?
2. Who is the audience for the information that is produced? Is it a
   funding agency, state or local legislators, clients?
3. What kind of information is needed to inform your decisions
   and/or enlighten your intended audiences? What comparisons or
   descriptions would be most compelling to your intended audience?
4. When is the information needed? What can be gathered and
   analyzed in the projected time period? Will the data be seen as
   still reflecting current needs or operations?
5. What resources are available to collect the information and at what
   cost?

These types of questions can help group members focus their question
and apply their efforts efficiently.

Group discussion can also highlight whether the question of interest
is related to observations at the system level or the individual level. This
distinction is often not immediately apparent to individuals trying to
examine the state of services across the criminal justice and mental health
systems. Some system-level questions can be addressed by examining
official, aggregate-level data sources (e.g., how much time do police
officers spend during booking with mentally ill individuals compared
to individuals without mentally illness?). Other questions require the
construction of datasets about individual patterns or outcomes (e.g., what
types of clients benefit most from a particular service?). The strategies,
resource needs, and design implications of addressing one type of
question over the other are considerably different.

• *Research design.* When a clear question has been identified, the
  discussions can move into more concrete terms about how it could be
  answered convincingly. In essence, this amounts to stating a hypothesis.
  A hypothesis is simply a suggestion about the specifics of the relationship
  of interest (e.g., minorities are more likely to end up in the deep end of
  the system, and this disproportionality is even stronger if the person is
  mentally ill). The purpose is to focus the research question so that data
  can determine whether the position is supported.

  Focusing the research question to a hypothesis also forces
  consideration of what would constitute appropriate variables. As
  Dometrius (1992) notes, "A variable is a characteristic of the object being
  studied (person, book, rock, or whatever) that varies; it implies differences
  of kind or degree" (p. 10). For example, the idea of "fruit" can be a variable
  of different kinds or categories (e.g., apples, oranges), while something
  like intelligence can be a variable with differing degrees (e.g., IQ scores).
  In focusing the research question, the group confronts the issues of what

variables to consider and in what form. In addition, the hypotheses force a statement of which variables are dependent (the outcome you are trying to explain) and independent (related to the variance of interest).

- *Determining the data needed.* The defined question and chosen method for investigation both have implications for the types of information (the data) that will be needed. If the area of inquiry has been defined independent of and prior to the development of a data system, then this stage would involve defining the specific information (variables) to collect. If the question is coming up later in the process (as is more likely the case in the context of the SIM), this would involve an examination of the existing data to determine whether the necessary information exists and/ or whether finding bits of missing information has to be done. Obviously, if the needed data are not readily available, the examination of the topic of interest may be slower and more complicated.

  The collection or compilation of data involves numerous decisions about the specifics of variable definition. How a variable is defined and measured has far-reaching implications for the rest of the research or evaluation enterprise. The decisions might range from whether to interview clients or rely on official records to being sure that the label given to a variable reflects its actual qualities. There are a variety of nuances about such seemingly mundane issues that go well beyond the scope of this chapter. There are several sources listed in Appendix A for exploring these issues. In addition, we have listed some variables and types of data that might be useful to consider in efforts to address questions arising from the use of the SIM (see Appendix B).

This outline of the steps for formulating questions about the impact of the SIM is rather rudimentary. The outline, however, does follow a very important sequence from problem definition to data specification. While in many ways it seems obvious, it is striking how often this logical pattern is reversed in practice. In many situations, groups of practitioners and researchers start with a survey of available data and then search for a question that can be answered in light of the potential or limitations of existing datasets. This strategy of "seeing what we can get out of what we have" usually produces a compromised product—a weak design addressing a relevant question or solid results about an irrelevant question.

CONCLUSION

Practitioners and policymakers in the mental health and criminal justice systems (and beyond) are constantly required to make decisions with limited information about a wide range of operational issues. They do not have the luxury of indecision—they must and will make decisions based on whatever information is available to them (Snyder, 2011), sometimes with far-reaching consequences. These decisions are influenced by many factors, including the agency's agenda, the political climate, and current views of "the field."

Empirical analyses are an important part of the stream of information confronting practitioners and policymakers, but they are only part of it. The availability of data doesn't always guarantee its use. Moreover, while solid empirical information may be the ingredient that tips the balance toward *informed* decisions, its use does not guarantee *good* decisions. Data analysis may be a valuable tool promoting sound decisions, or it can be a manipulated piece of a message driven by other considerations. The quality of public policy and practice decisions ultimately relies on the imposition of good judgment, using sound information generated with accepted analytic practices.

The SIM is a valuable platform for sparking collaborative efforts between criminal justice and mental health professionals and promoting the generation and use of solid empirical information. It brings a level of organization, consensus, and priority setting that can promote energetic innovation. We maintain that it can do more than this: It can also promote an appreciation for data-based answers to pressing problems and a commitment to measureable improvements in service provision. The key to achieving this largely unrealized potential is to meld data-collection and data-analysis tasks tightly to the SIM and to produce sound information that moves collaboration forward.

If this were an easy task, it would probably be a common occurrence by now. However, the barriers that confront efforts to find, improve, collect, and analyze data in the criminal justice and mental health systems are formidable. As we point out, administrators, policymakers, and front-line staff all have their own reasons for either avoiding or abhorring empirical information. Done well, empirical analyses can threaten long-held, secure positions; done badly, they can also create unwarranted havoc. Unfortunately, the ability of evaluators and researchers to adapt their methods to the realities of these systems is usually poor. The burden on researchers to improve their methods to capitalize on the potential of the increasing collaboration between these systems is great.

There can be little doubt, though, that the time has come for researchers to start getting it right. The integration of data into the operations of the criminal justice and mental health systems seems inevitable. The broader view of system integration and data-driven inquiry is currently seen as both possible (given advances in computer technology) and desirable (given a political climate of increased fiscal accountability). Data can be obtained, stored, and processed with increasing efficiency. In addition, both the mental health service sector and the criminal justice system have mounting pressure to justify budgets, meet certain standards of practice, and assess program effectiveness. The role of data has become increasingly important in efforts to meet these challenges. This presents an important opportunity for empirically based researchers to make valuable contributions to the development of innovative practices that are useful in both the criminal justice and mental health systems.

APPENDIX A: RESOURCES

Below is a list of resources that we have encountered in our work. This list is not exhaustive nor does it constitute an endorsement of the listed resources.

BASIC RESEARCH/OVERVIEWS

Brennan, T., and Wells, D. (2009). *Data driving policy and planning decisions: Policy making in criminal justice: The use of hard data at each stage of the policy/planning process.* Northpointe Institute of Public Management, Inc. Retrieved from http://www.northpointeinc.com/files/whitepapers/Data_Driving_Policy.pdf

Stiffman, A. R. (Ed.) (2009). *The field research survival guide.* New York: Oxford University Press.

Thigpen, M. L., Beauclair, T. J., Hutchinson, V., & Persons, V. (2007). *How to collect and analyze data: A manual for sheriff and jail administrators* (3rd edition). U.S. Department of Justice, National Institute of Corrections. Retrieved from http://static.nicic.gov/Library/021826.pdf

EVALUATION

An introduction to evaluation (Trochim, 2006):
www.socialresearchmethods.net/kb/intreval.php

A basic guide to program research:
http://managementhelp.org/evaluation/program-evaluation-guide.htm

An excellent overview of outcomes-based evaluation:
http://www.unitedway.org/outcomes/

Basic Guide to Program Evaluation
http://managementhelp.org/evaluatn/fnl_eval.htm.

BJS evaluation website:
http://www.ojp.usdoj.gov/BJA/evaluation/

What is an evaluation: A set of beginners' guides:
http://gsociology.icaap.org/methods/BasicguidesHandouts.html

Program managers' guide to evaluation:
http://www.acf.hhs.gov/programs/opre/other_resrch/pm_guide_eval/index.html

Key concepts in evaluation:
http://brunerfoundation.org/ei/docs/EvaluativeThinking.bulletin.1.pdf

STATISTICS

Healey, J. F. (2007). *The essentials of statistics: A tool for social research.*
Belmont, CA: Thomson Wadsworth.

APPENDIX B: POTENTIALLY RELEVANT VARIABLES AT EACH POINT IN THE SIM PROCESS

This list contains variables that might be useful in evaluating the impact of initiatives taken across the mental health and criminal justice systems in a locale. This list may be expanded to include data related to the specific priorities of the locale (identified during the Sequential Intercept Mapping workshop). This provides a starting point for the types of information that could be gathered in attempts to address hypotheses about the impact of innovations arising from the SIM process.

INTERCEPT 1: LAW ENFORCEMENT

1. Dispatch
   a. # of calls identified by dispatch as involving mental illness
   b. # of calls referred to: trained crisis workers, police, MH worker, other
2. Background/training of respondent
   a. Profession
   b. Age
   c. Training
3. Disposition from visit
   a. Arrest
   b. Arrest and transport to hospital for medical tx
   c. Arrest and transport to psychiatric evaluation
   d. Involuntary transport to psychiatric evaluation
   e. Transport for medical tx
   f. Transport to mental health facility other than hospital
   g. Referred to mental health/social services
   h. Contact only
4. Characteristics of the actor
   a. Age/DOB
   b. Gender
   c. Ethnicity
   d. SSN (or any other information that may serve as a unique identifier across systems)

    e. History of prior incidents and dispositions
5. Description of the incident
    a. Date of incident
    b. Time of day
    c. Location (specific address or categories [e.g., private residence, public place])
    d. Weapon involved?
    e. Violence against a person?
6. Subsequent history of the actor (attempts to track individual through the system)
    a. Unique identifier that crosses data systems
    b. Date
    c. Type of incident

INTERCEPT 2: INITIAL DETENTION/INITIAL COURT HEARINGS

1. Case identifiers (including charges)
2. Characteristics of the individual (as above)—check offender management system
3. Events/actions that preceded the arrest (e.g., crisis intervention prior to this appearance)
4. MH status from "booking interview"
    a. Suicide risk (y/n)
    b. MH status
    c. On medication (y/n)
    d. Substance use issues
5. Disposition outcome from initial detention & court hearing
    a. Specialty court
    b. Jail
    c. Treatment not associated with court
    d. Home

INTERCEPT 3: JAILS/COURTS

System-level information

1. What jail-based MH services are available?
    a. Is there a MH unit?
2. Does the system employ case managers to follow up with MH clients upon release?
3. Is there a forensic peer support program?
4. How does the system integrate MH information?

Case-level information

5. Was the case referred to MH court (y/n)?
   a. Was case accepted to MH court?
   b. If yes, what services were provided by the MH court?
6. Length of jail stay (date of admit, date of release)
7. Sequence/timing of various hearings
8. Receipt of medication while in jail (y/n)?
   a. Types
   b. Dosage
9. Any jail incident reports involving the client
10. Housing unit (general or MH unit)

INTERCEPT 4: REENTRY

System-level information

1. Is there a procedure for prerelease planning?
2. Is there a structured risk-need assessment at release?

Case-level information

1. Was there a prerelease planning meeting?
   a. Is there a plan in place?
   b. What are the conditions in that plan?
2. Where was the client released to (a specific address or to the streets)?
3. Living arrangement/type of place going to
4. Does the client have an identified MH service provider/agency?
   a. Appointment made?
5. Are there any community restrictions on the person (e.g., mandated treatment)?
6. Is the client on probation or parole?
   a. Is the client on a specialized probation caseload?
   b. Frequency of contact with probation
7. Employed at time of release?
   a. Date began working
8. Start and end dates for specialty court and/or probation involvement
9. Consult reentry checklist from GAINS Center (http://gainscenter.samhsa. gov/topical_resources/reentry.asp)

INTERCEPT 5: COMMUNITY CORRECTIONS

System-level information

1. Is there a screening?
    a. What screening is used?
2. Is there information sharing between agencies?

Case-level information

1. Detailed information about services received
2. Does the individual have a case manager?
3. Dates of contact with probation and other court services
4. Dates and reasons for violations of conditions of release and/or probation
    a. Outcomes from violations
5. Rearrest
    a. Dates and charges

REFERENCES

Brennan, T., & Wells, D. (2009). *Data driving policy and planning decisions: Policy making in criminal justice: The use of hard data at each stage of the policy/planning process.* Northpointe Institute of Public Management, Inc.

Counte, M. A., & Meurer, S. (2001). Issues in the assessment of continuous quality improvement implementation in health care organizations. *International Journal for Quality in Health Care, 13,* 197–207.

Cowell, A. J., Broner, N., & Dupont, R. (2004). The cost effectiveness of criminal justice programs for people with serious mental illness co-occurring with substance use: Four case studies. *Journal of Contemporary Criminal Justice, 20,* 292–315.

Dometrius, N. C. (1992). *Social statistics using SPSS.* New York: Harper Collins.

Draine, J., & Solomon, P. (1992). Comparison of serious mentally ill case management clients with and without arrest histories. *Journal of Psychiatry and the Law, 20,* 335–342.

Dvoskin, J. A., Skeem, J. L., Novaco, R., & Douglas, K. S. (Eds.) (2011). *Using social science to reduce violent offending.* New York: Oxford.

Fisher, W. H., Wolff, N., & Roy-Bujnowski, K. (2002), Community mental health services and criminal justice involvement among persons with mental illness. In W. H. Fisher (Ed.), *Community-based interventions for criminal offenders with severe mental illness (Research in community and mental health,* Volume 12) (pp. 25–51). London: Emerald Group Publishing Limited.

James, D. J., & Glaze, L. E. (2006). *Bureau of Justice Statistics special report: Mental health problems of prison and jail inmates*. Washington, D.C.: U.S. Department of Justice (NCJ 213600).

Koyanagi, D. (2007). *Learning from history: Deinstitutionalization of people with mental illness as precursor to long-term care reform*. Kaiser Commission on Medicaid and the Uninsured. Washington, D.C.: Kaiser Family Foundation.

Lafayette, J. M., Frankle, W. G., Pollock, A., et al. (2003). Clinical characteristics, cognitive functioning and criminal histories of outpatients with schizophrenia. *Psychiatric Services, 54*, 1635–1640.

Lipsey, M. W., Chapman, G. L., & Landenberger, N. A. (2001). Cognitive behavioral programs for offenders. *Annals of the American Academy of Political and Social Science, 578*, 144–157.

McGuire, J. F., & Rosenheck, R. A. (2004). Criminal histories as a prognostic indicator in the treatment of homeless people with severe mental illness. *Psychiatric Services, 55*, 42–48.

Monahan, J., Bonnie, R. J., Appelbaum, P. S., Hyde, P. S., Steadman, H. J., & Swartz, M. S. (2001). Mandated community treatment: Beyond outpatient commitment. *Psychiatric Services, 52*, 1198–2005.

Nutley, S. M., Walter, I., & Davies, H. T. O. (2007). *Using evidence: How research can inform public services*. Bristol: The Policy Press.

Petersilia, J. (2004). What works in prisoner reentry? Reviewing and questioning the evidence. *Federal Probation, 68*. [Online]. Available: http://www.uscourts.gov/fed-prob/September_2004/whatworks.html.

Platz, M. S., Greenway, M. T., & Hendricks, M. (2006). Outcome measures: Showing results in the non-profit sector. Retrieved April 9, 2012, from http://www.nationalserviceresources.org/filemanager/download/ProgramMgmt/Outcome_Measurement_Showing_Results_Nonprofit_Sector.pdf

Snyder, H. (2011). Socially responsible criminology: Quality relevant research with targeted, effective dissemination. *Criminology and Public Policy, 10*, 207–2151.

Trochim, W. M. K (2006). Introduction to evaluation. Retrieved November 16, 2011, from www.socialresearchmethods.net/kb/intreval.php.

13

Using the Sequential Intercept Model in Cross-Systems Mapping

PATRICIA A. GRIFFIN, CASEY LADUKE, DAN ABREU,
KATY WINCKWORTH-PREJSNAR, SARAH FILONE,
SARAH DORRELL, AND CHRISTINA FINELLO ■

As behavioral health and justice systems expand community alternatives to incarceration for people with serious mental illness, cross-system understanding and collaboration has never been more important. At a time when these systems are being asked to provide more services with fewer resources, behavioral health and justice representatives are recognizing the need to develop services that are efficient, cost-effective, and based on promising and best practices.

Toward this end, the Sequential Intercept Model (SIM; Munetz & Griffin, 2006) stands out as a tool to help generate cross-systems understanding and collaboration. Previous chapters have described the SIM, how it is being used, the interventions at each intercept, and the tasks to which it can be applied. In this chapter, we will discuss how the SIM can be used to increase cross-system collaboration, understanding, and planning around diversion strategies in local communities across the United States. This process, organized into the Cross-Systems Mapping (CSM) workshops, represents an application of the SIM that takes the collective understanding of promising practices across the behavioral health and justice systems and applies them directly to local communities in an intensive, collaborative manner.

DEVELOPMENT OF THE CSM WORKSHOPS

CSM workshops developed over the past fifteen years. In 1997, the Substance Abuse and Mental Health Services Administration (SAMHSA) funded a Knowledge and Development Application on jail diversion that included multiple sites throughout the United States. The goal of the SAMHSA jail diversion initiative was to develop ideas and data around different ways to improve the prevention and treatment of substance abuse and mental illness, and to work with state and local governments, providers, families, and consumers to apply that knowledge effectively in everyday practice (Steadman et al., 1999). In addition to the research component, this initiative included a technical assistance component coordinated through the National GAINS Center hosted by Policy Research Associates, Inc. in Delmar, NY, out of which the current workshops began to take shape.

In addition to assisting in data collection, the National GAINS Center sent staff to each of the nine sites selected as part of the initiative to complete a process and outcome evaluation of the community's jail diversion programs. The evaluations focused on producing a detailed description of the diversion programs at each site, a description of each individual's exposure to the diversion program, and a description of the community context of the diversion program. Staff worked with community representatives to inventory and describe the diversion services available to consumers in that community, as well as to show how those services fit into the larger behavioral health and justice systems. GAINS Center staff also worked with the local communities around strategies to promote further diversion programming.

Although initially focused on accessing information on the screening, assessment, and treatment of people with serious mental illness in the local community, GAINS Center staff discovered that the biggest obstacle they were encountering during the technical assistance process was how to get local stakeholders to work together in a more collaborative and productive fashion. In response, they began to modify the technical assistance sessions to make them more interactive with the local participants, particularly by having them share more information about their services with the other participants rather than having a general presentation of services through planned presenters. Over time, GAINS Center staff tried to make this information sharing more structured—for example, by dividing the local participants into groups based on their involvement within the justice, drug and alcohol, or mental health systems, and then having them each map out their system separately. Once this was completed, the larger group would move from system to system and hear presentations by the community representatives who had worked on each particular map. This provided much more information to all workshop participants. However, the mappings were done without an overarching model to help organize them. It soon became apparent that there were gaps in participants' understanding of how these three systems interacted in the local community.

To better address these cross-systems issues, the workshops were modified into larger group discussions in which GAINS Center staff worked to create one map composed of all three systems. These combined maps were based on what was becoming known as the SIM, which was then a modification by Patricia Griffin (a senior consultant from the National GAINS Center) of an earlier model being used by Mark Munetz (clinical director for the Summit County Alcohol, Drug Abuse, and Mental Health Board and Director of the Ohio Coordinating

Center of Excellence) (see Munetz & Griffin, 2006). The SIM was used to simplify the cross-systems discussion by structuring it around the justice system, where the organization and flow seemed more predicable that that of the behavioral health system. The goal of this more structured information-sharing process was to make the workshop discussions more understandable, collaborative, and productive.

The revised version of the workshops, based on the SIM, served as the primary method of technical assistance throughout the end of the SAMHSA jail diversion initiative. Recognizing the potential utility of this type of workshop, Policy Research Associates then secured a small business initiative grant (Vogel, Noether, & Steadman, 2007) to continue to develop the workshop to better address its own goals and national initiatives. Through this grant, Policy Research Associates drafted and tested a workshop curriculum, wrote a training manual, and began training facilitators to conduct CSM workshops (Policy Research Associates, Inc., 2007).[1]

Currently, the workshops are being implemented nationwide to help communities better understand their behavioral health and justice systems and to help them generate and promote diversion strategies. Implemented as a series of semistructured, manualized technical assistance workshops, the workshops are continually modified to better address the needs of local communities. Although overseen by a variety of individuals and organizations, the workshops have consistently held the same goal: to help generate cross-system collaboration to promote community alternatives for people with serious mental illness and often co-occurring substance use disorders involved in the justice system.

OVERVIEW OF WORKSHOPS

In their current form, the workshops have two components: the CSM workshop and the Taking Action for Change (TAC) workshop. These workshops may be done separately, although each has been developed to benefit from the inclusion of the other. The objectives of the CSM workshop are to introduce the SIM and provide examples of promising practices and services at each intercept, to create a detailed inventory of what the community is currently doing at each of the intercepts, to highlight opportunities and gaps in the current system, and to identify and prioritize what the community would like to change. Building on this work, the TAC workshop promotes cross-system collaboration by creating a series of workable action plans to accomplish the identified priorities of the community.

Much work goes into the planning and completion of each of these workshops, as well as developing useful outcome resources and continued support for community efforts. These workshops can be implemented at both local and statewide levels in a variety of ways and can have a significant impact on the services available in the communities being mapped. Each of these will be covered in turn. At their core, however, the workshops represent intensive technical assistance, structured around the SIM, with the goal of generating cross-system collaboration and promoting community alternatives for persons with mental illness in contact with the justice system.

The CSM workshop includes of a variety of activities that involve group discussion and collaboration. Facilitators and participants work together to create written and visual accounts of the services available in the community. Gaps in current services and opportunities across both systems are catalogued, which assists the participants to identify priorities for change in their community.

CSM WORKSHOP PLANNING

Workshop planning begins months before the workshop itself. This involves the distribution of a planning manual to the community contact person and gathering background information and data from the community.

Typically, workshop planning is done by the workshop facilitators, support staff from the technical assistance center organizing the workshop, and the local contact person. The local contact person is someone from within the behavioral health or justice system with the motivation, time, and resources to help coordinate the workshop. With support from the facilitators, he or she select potential dates for the workshop, coordinate the location, and generate awareness and interest in the workshop. He or she also invites local stakeholders to participate and maintains contact with them in the weeks and days leading up to the workshop. As broad participation is key to developing a useful and comprehensive cross-systems inventory and map of local services, a cross-section of local stakeholders should be invited to participate (Table 13.1). This includes individuals at all levels of the behavioral health and justice systems, as well as representatives of community organizations providing services for the target population. To assist in this process, the local workshop planning team typically includes various behavioral health and justice stakeholders to promote leadership buy-in from multiple groups. For example, it is very useful to have a judge from the local system be part of the team to add credibility and influence to the workshop.

Consumer and family participation is critical to ensure that the workshop outcomes are recovery-oriented and address consumer needs. Justice-involved consumers face many barriers to meaningful participation in community planning activities and to obtaining employment as peer specialists (Davidson & Rowe, 2008). Many communities have local chapters of the National Alliance for Mental Illness (NAMI), and those conducting the workshops can ask that NAMI and representatives from other relevant mental health groups be invited. In some communities, family and consumer advocates may be involved in community planning activities, employment as peer specialists, or working within consumer-run agencies providing recovery-oriented services. The range of consumer involvement in community planning activities varies greatly, however, and in most communities including justice-involved consumers has proved

Table 13.1 PARTICIPANTS TO INVITE

Whom to Invite—Sample Services and Roles

Mental Health	Substance Abuse	Criminal Justice	Consumers	Support Services	Others
Community mental health providers	Community-based treatment (public and private)	Emergency dispatchers (911)	People with serious mental illness	Case management	Elected officials
Mental health centers	Case management	Law enforcement (state and local)	People with co-occurring disorders	Housing	Social services (Medicaid/Medicare)
Mental health clinics	Detoxification programs	Correctional staff (administrators and service personnel)	Consumers with experience in the justice system	Peer programs	Social Security Administration (entitlements)
Behavioral health HMOs	Residential treatment programs	Probation and/or parole departments	Family members	Mutual support programs	Cultural organizations
Contracted service providers	Contracted service providers	Community corrections	Advocacy groups (local and national)		Faith-based organizations
		Specialized diversion program staff	Consumer-run programs		Vocational programs
		Court officials (criminal court and district court judges, pretrial services, prosecutor, defense attorney)			Veterans Justice Outreach Coordinator from local VA Medical Center

Modified from Policy Research Associates, Inc., 2007.

challenging—even when there is strong consumer participation in a community, justice-involved consumers are rarely included in these activities.

Facilitators work to address this disparity in the early stages of planning for the workshop. Working with the planning team, facilitators work to identify three to five justice-involved consumers who might be appropriate to participate in the workshop. While there are no specific requirements, we suggest that invited consumers be in recovery for a minimum of six months. The facilitators also offer to meet with the participating consumers on the afternoon or evening before the workshop so they become comfortable with the facilitators, know what to expect at the workshop, and provide enough information so that facilitators can elicit participation from them during the workshop should they be uncertain about when to speak up. If a meeting cannot be arranged, a conference call with the facilitators is arranged to prepare consumers for the workshop. It is important to involve multiple consumers to elicit varying perspectives, to provide a supportive atmosphere for consumer participation, to lay the groundwork for ongoing participation in planning, and to foster increased employment opportunities for justice-involved consumers.

In addition to planning for the workshop, the local contact person is also involved in locating and consolidating background information, current programming, and data from the community. Facilitators work with him or her to highlight what data might be available in the community and how it may be best accessed and transferred. Examples of important data may include the number of behavioral health crisis calls received by local law enforcement, the population of incarcerated individuals utilizing mental health and substance abuse services, and any statistics from existing diversion programs. This information is used to personalize the workshop as well as provide useful information for facilitators and participants throughout the workshop.

The CSM Workshop

The CSM workshop is a full-day, interactive workshop facilitated by field professionals with experience developing and implementing diversion strategies for persons with mental illness involved in the justice system. Generally, the workshop is structured to introduce local stakeholders to promising practices in the field of diversion, using the SIM as an organizational tool and point of reference, and then to construct a local inventory of the diversion programming, community alternatives, and resources that exist in the community.

At the beginning of the workshop, facilitators introduce the focus, goals, and tasks of the workshop, primarily to promote collaboration around improving services for individuals with serious mental illness, and often co-occurring substance use disorders, involved in the justice system. The SIM is introduced as a tool that can be used to attain this goal by providing a common language to be used across the different local systems, identifying what is being done and what the community sees as gaps in services, and prioritizing where the community would like to begin the process of addressing these gaps. Promising practices specific to each intercept are presented to give the participants an idea of what is being done locally and nationally around the issues; this also serves to reinforce the structure of the SIM and the benefits of cross-system collaboration.

This didactic part of the workshop focuses on the prevalence of co-occurring disorders in the justice system, characteristics of justice-involved consumers, and, more recently, the characteristics of justice-involved veterans. Due to the high prevalence of trauma in the justice-involved population, the importance of trauma-informed systems and trauma-specific interventions is discussed.

After the SIM is introduced, the facilitators then transfer the focus to the workshop participants. Using the SIM structure as a guide, the participants begin to construct an intercept-by-intercept inventory of the services that exist in the local community around the target population: justice-involved individuals with behavioral health problems. The facilitators start the conversation by asking participants to describe how individuals with serious mental illness first enter, then work their way through, and finally exit the justice system. Along the way, participants from the behavioral health system, justice system, and community resources are encouraged to describe the services they offer, how these services can be accessed, and any data they have related to these services.

If the participants raise issues beyond the scope of the workshop or have questions outside the expertise of the other participants, the facilitators refocus the conversation or provide relevant background information and examples. Based on their professional experience and impartial stance, the facilitators may also be helpful in providing objective feedback, asking previously unconsidered questions, and generating conversation around issues that local participants may be uncomfortable bringing up themselves. Since the goal of the exercise is to accurately describe the services being offered in the local community, facilitators work to maintain a respectful and honest conversation with input from various perspectives in the community.

In addition to encouraging and guiding the conversation around local services, the facilitators also work to capture both written and visual accounts of the inventory of services being discussed. The written account is a real-time transcription of the workshop discussions that consists of a detailed, intercept-by-intercept listing of the services offered by the community. This typically includes the name of the service, the organization that funds and manages it, the services that it provides, and how it can be accessed. For example, if the participants are discussing a mental health court they have established, the written report will typically include who initiated the project, how the funding was secured, when the court officially started, the criteria for eligibility, how participants can access it, what services are provided and by whom, and any data regarding the number and activities of the individuals being served. The facilitator responsible for these details will also be aware of what information is useful to include and can raise specific questions throughout the workshop that may be missed by the facilitator who is guiding the conversation more broadly.

The visual record of the discussion, called the cross-systems map, consists of a series of easel sheets located at the front of the room visible to all participants. On these sheets is a blank version of the SIM, including all five intercepts, onto which the facilitators add each of the services being discussed. Instead of an exhaustive description of these services, this map will be used to illustrate the location of each service along the SIM, and well as any connections between services in the local system. For example, a crisis response team that co-responds to crisis situations with law enforcement and is capable of transporting individuals to emergency rooms will be represented as a service in Intercept 1, with arrows used to show its relationship to both local law enforcement and local hospitals. Intensive case managers who provide in-reach into local jails and community reentry services will be represented in Intercept 4, with arrows used to designate both activities within the local correctional system (Intercept 3) and linkages to community support services (Intercept 5). The cross-systems map thus provides a visual representation of how individuals with serious mental illness flow through the local justice system, what institutional and community services are offered by the various systems at each intercept, and how these services and systems interact.

Gaps and Opportunities

During the mapping exercise, participants identify obstacles and challenges to providing services in the community, gaps in services, difficulties in cross-system communication and collaboration, and/or the lack of specific services offered in either justice or behavioral health system. These may be system-level issues (e.g., Social Security benefits for incarcerated individuals, or data sharing between the state prisons and local behavioral health authorities) or community-specific concerns (e.g., rural law enforcement being spread too thinly to implement specialized police responding, or the lack of an advocate within the court system to establish problem-solving courts).

These issues will be important as the community attempts to transform the services it offers as a result of the workshop. To consider them—but to avoid using most of the workshop to focus on what is not working—any obstacles raised by the community are documented as "gaps" by the facilitators on additional easel sheets. These gaps, also organized by intercept, are recorded throughout the day as they are brought into the conversation and used later in the workshop to identify priorities for change.

In addition to gaps, it is also likely that participants will identify services that are particularly well designed, funding prospects that are available, and/or collaborations that are already established or beginning. These positive aspects, labeled "opportunities," are also catalogued. As the participants plan to transform their services, they will choose to utilize and build from the opportunities that already exist across both systems, so it is vital to include these opportunities.

Priorities for Change

After the facilitators and participants have fully inventoried the services available in the community, the conversation turns to planning for the future. Participants are encouraged to review and add to the gaps that were raised and catalogued, after which the facilitators turn the discussion toward the community's primary priorities for change moving forward. Participants construct a list of their priorities for further work. These "priorities for change" may consist of issues the community has already identified but is struggling to implement, a combination of smaller gaps uncovered during earlier discussion, or a single but important gap that the majority of the group feels needs attention.

Once this list is constructed, participants prioritize these issues and select which ones to focus on first. Facilitators are careful to elicit the opinions of all participants to promote a sense of inclusion in identifying and advocating for priorities. For example, participants are given the opportunity to advocate for what they believe should be the community's top priority. After interested participants campaign for their top priority, all members of the group vote. Participants use a cumulative voting process to prioritize gaps, which allows a more proportional representation of the participants. Participants are each given three dots—one red for first priority and two of any other color for second and third priority—and instructed to place a dot on one of their top three priorities listed on the easel sheets. In this way, participants can influence the selection of multiple priorities, and there will be a higher number of participants who will have voted for the top priorities, increasing participant buy-in. Based on this voting, a final list of the top five priorities is established. These priorities are community-specific and serve focus the attention and action of local stakeholders as they plan and implement future changes in the services available in their community.

Closing

Once the top priorities have been tallied and reviewed, the facilitators bring the group back together to close the day. They summarize the day's accomplishments and offer congratulations for the work the participants have done. If the CSM workshop is to be followed by the TAC workshop, facilitators set the stage for the second workshop and give advice on how to prepare for the work ahead. For example, participants are encouraged to individually review the top priorities that have been set and consider what steps they would like to include in the action planning process. After receiving feedback from the participants about the day's activities, facilitators again thank the participants for their hard work and dismiss the workshop.

TAC WORKSHOP

The TAC workshop is designed to build on the momentum of the CSM workshop by developing a workable, community-driven action plan around each of the top priorities selected by the CSM workshop participants. It is typically completed during a half-day immediately following the CSM workshop and includes the same participants.

While the large majority of communities choose to complete both workshops, some choose only the mapping exercise. Rarely do communities request the TAC workshop without first completing the CSM workshop. Therefore, the discussion of the TAC workshop will assume that it follows the cross-systems mapping and the development of priorities for change.

Review of Cross-Systems Map and Priorities

Upon reconvening for the TAC workshop, participants are initially asked to review a printed version of the cross-systems map created the previous day. The map is reviewed for accuracy and clarity, with participants making any changes so that it can be modified prior to its inclusion in the final report. This not only ensures an accurate representation of the services available in the community but also reorients participants to the breadth of services discussed the previous day and the state of the systems they will be working to transform during the TAC workshop.

After the map is reviewed, the facilitators review the top priorities that were voted on by the participants the day before. Any remaining questions regarding what each priority includes should be resolved, and any modifications that the group agrees on should be made. Since participants may see the list of top priorities differently after having some time to think about them away from the larger group, short discussions are encouraged to tailor each priority to the participants' expectations before moving on to the action planning exercise.

Action Planning Exercise

After the top priorities have been finalized, the workshop participants are then tasked with collaboratively building a community-specific plan, called the "action plan," with clearly defined, attainable, prioritized steps aimed at addressing each priority. These should include both short- and long-term action items, and each should be accompanied by enough information and instruction to facilitate their completion.

Action planning can be completed in different ways. One option is for facilitators to guide the entire group through a priority-by-priority process that includes input from all participants. Another option is to break participants into smaller groups on a volunteer basis; each group works intensively on one priority's action plan and then presents that plan to the larger group. Regardless of how the action planning is organized, each top priority should be intensively and systematically considered to outline the steps the community plans to take to address the highlighted issues. Completed action plans include a series of substantive objectives and specific steps that address how the community will pursue the objective. Associated with each step should be a point person who will work on that step, as well as a timeframe within which it will be completed. Such action planning divides larger issues into more manageable tasks and then delegates responsibility to someone to lead the task to completion.

Just as the top priorities are tailored to the community, so is the action plan. Participants may choose to make their action plans highly detailed or more general outlines of steps to be taken in leveraging support from the larger behavioral health or justice communities. Some local communities may choose to tackle complex, system-wide obstacles during action planning, while others may select issues that are more easily, quickly, or inexpensively fixed in order to build momentum toward their community's larger changes. Regardless of how each community establishes its action plan, the top priorities typically require significant cross-system effort. Therefore, the individuals writing the action plans must also be those who will be involved in their advocacy, planning, implementation, and sustaining.

Closing

After the action planning has been completed and presented by the local community, facilitators turn to next steps. For example, they may ask when the next locally important behavioral health or justice meetings will be held—and foster cross-system interest in attending. Next, they discuss the final report—its contents and how it will be provided to the community. Volunteers are enlisted to review and edit the draft report. Participants are reminded of the additional services they can access through the organizing technical assistance center and are encouraged to remain in contact with each other and the facilitators as they work to carry out their action plans.

To evaluate the workshop, participants are asked to complete feedback forms that are summarized and reviewed by workshop facilitators and organizing centers. This gives participants the opportunity to anonymously offer feedback, including perceived benefits in completing the workshops, how they viewed the facilitators, and what they would have liked to see done differently.

Some communities like to include closing remarks by key stakeholders involved in the workshops. Whether by a local representative or the workshop facilitators, closing remarks are an opportunity to thank participants for their dedication and hard work, to make inspiring remarks about the journey ahead, and to encourage continued collaboration across the behavioral health and justice systems.

OUTCOMES AND CONTINUED SUPPORT

The Final Report

The most tangible product of the CSM and TAC workshops is a report that includes all of the work done throughout the workshops, as well as some additional information cultivated from outside sources. The final report starts by introducing the CSM and TAC workshops and how they came to be carried out in the local community. The community is briefly profiled, including basic information about its location and makeup, current diversion programming and cross-systems collaborations, and an overview of any significant data that was supplied by the community. Introductions by key stakeholders are included to personalize the report and to highlight the importance that it holds for the community.

The report then details the work done by the participants. First, the cross-systems map of the community is presented to offer a visual representation of how individuals with severe mental illness flow through the justice system, what services are provided for them, and how these services interact with one another. The report then provides an in-depth, intercept-by-intercept inventory and description of all of the services offered by the community for the target population. This includes all of the behavioral health, justice, and community programs discussed during the CSM workshop, as well as any additional programs identified through research of the community that may not have been represented at the workshop. In addition to the name, description, and contact information for each program, each intercept also includes all the gaps and opportunities raised by participants. These gaps are listed and are not edited or modified by the facilitators.

After the comprehensive review of the services offered by the community, the top priorities are introduced, with a brief description of how they were developed and selected. Any additional priorities that were discussed but not included in the action planning process are also listed to provide a complete picture. The top priorities are followed by a representation of the action planning process undertaken by participants, including the specific priority, the objectives and action steps, the point person for each action step, and the timeframe in which the action steps and larger objectives will be completed. If priority-specific groups completed the action planning process, the members of each group will also be listed. The action plan reflects what was decided by the participants and is not edited or modified by the facilitators. This ensures that the action plan is tailored exclusively to the community, incorporating the participants' opinions and decisions.

The report concludes with a summary of the goals, activities, and outcomes of the CSM and TAC workshops. The concluding section may also include a summary of recommendations, which allows the facilitators to include their own opinions on gaps, opportunities, and resources in the community; this may include items discussed by participants or other issues that facilitators noticed outside of the workshop discussions. This may also be accomplished through a series of appendices or a separate resource guide that describes national efforts around some of the larger issues typically encountered during diversion planning and implementation. These can range from examples of law enforcement training around deescalation and different types of specialized reentry programs to the basics of information sharing across systems and typical barriers to housing for people with serious mental illness. Finally, a brief conclusion refocuses the discussion on the larger issues covered by the workshop and encourages the community members to continue their efforts to improve services for justice-involved individuals with serious mental illness.

The final report serves a variety of purposes. It makes cross-system collaboration more attainable by providing background information on the behavioral health and justice systems, as well as a guide to all current services dealing with the diversion and treatment of individuals with serious mental illness. It provides a personalized, visual representation of where these services are placed within the local system, as well as how they interact. The report may also be used as a catalyst to highlight critical and imminent needs and gaps and to attract the attention of public officials and funding agencies. It documents the action planning process, including the steps being taken, who is responsible for each, and the timeframe within which top priorities are to be completed. It demonstrates that the community leaders have been proactive in maximizing system collaboration and efficiencies, yet there remain critical areas of need. Finally, it gives the local professionals guidance and perspective on attaining the selected priorities and how the community can best move forward. Since the report reflects the consensus of leadership in both behavioral health and justice areas, the report findings can be leveraged to influence both policy and funding priorities of local and state legislatures, or local and state agency leadership. It should be provided in both pdf and Word formats so it can be distributed broadly but also excerpted for use in annual reports, planning documents, and grant proposals.

Overall, the final report provides detailed documentation of the CSM and TAC workshops. It can be used by the local community to improve the understanding of its current system and to work on addressing the highlighted priorities for change. The report describes the cross-systems collaboration involved in completing the workshops and helps to sustain the momentum generated during the workshops as the community moves forward in transforming services for people with serious mental illness involved in the justice system.

Next Steps: Follow-Up and Continued Support

The work done in the CSM and TAC workshops constitutes a significant benefit to the community, but there is another potential benefit: Continued technical assistance and facilitator support can be made available to the community after the workshops. Often the action planning process will identify areas in which the community needs additional training or information (e.g., information sharing, housing options, benefit issues, or data collection). These are areas where local or national technical assistance centers can provide continued support.

Follow-up meetings can be scheduled to allow facilitators to return to the community and provide continued assistance and support. This is particularly useful for large, specialized action items such as securing and sustaining competitive grants, or designing and implementing diversion programming. Occasionally, communities may decide to track their system-wide transformations by reconvening to map their local systems again. More typically, however, communities track their own progress following these workshops, occasionally contacting the facilitating agency for specific technical assistance.

IMPLEMENTATION OF CSM WORKSHOPS

To date, the CSM and TAC workshops have been implemented in two different ways. The first involves community-specific implementation facilitated by a national technical assistance center, and the second is through county-by-county implementation organized by a statewide technical assistance center.

National Implementation

The CSM and TAC workshops were developed over time through their use by national organizations focused on policy, research, and training around diversion. Currently, the workshops are overseen by SAMHSA's GAINS Center for Behavioral Health and Justice Transformation hosted by Policy Research Associates, a national technical assistance and training center focused on transforming mental health services for vulnerable populations (see Chapter 8). Interested parties contact Policy Research Associates to make arrangements for the workshops to be implemented in their community. The workshops are delivered by two facilitators who are selected from a national network of consulting experts based on their availability and expertise. The community, facilitators, and support staff at Policy Research Associates then work together to plan and implement the workshop, edit and finalize the cross-systems map and report, and provide follow-up support or technical assistance as needed.

As of mid-2014, Policy Research Associates had mapped approximately one hundred communities throughout the nation. Their services have been requested by individuals from both the behavioral health and justice systems, and by some communities that are highly experienced in their planning and implementation of diversion programming and others that are just beginning the process of transforming their system.

Statewide Implementation

As awareness of the benefits of diversion programming has increased, some states have become more active in planning and implementing community services for justice-involved people with serious mental illness. While some states (e.g., Connecticut) have implemented diversion programming statewide, another option is to provide community-specific diversion planning and implementation, often organized through a state technical assistance and training organization such as a Center of Excellence (see Chapter 10 for a more intensive discussion of these centers). Policy Research Associates has trained seven states to deliver mapping workshops to their counties.

An example of this latter statewide implementation is seen in Pennsylvania. Since 2010, the Pennsylvania Mental Health and Justice Center of Excellence (CoE), a collaborative project between two local universities that is funded through the Pennsylvania Commission on Crime and Delinquency and the Pennsylvania Office of Mental Health and Substance Abuse Services, has assisted local counties with diversion planning and implementation through a systematic, county-by-county implementation of the CSM and TAC workshops. The workshops are supplemented by data collection and continued technical assistance; all are provided at no cost to the counties. Through these workshops, the CoE has been able to assist counties across Pennsylvania in better understanding their local behavioral health and justice systems, increase cross-system collaboration, and construct county-specific action plans to transform their services for people with serious mental illness. By implementing structured data collection and technical assistance, the CoE has been able to update and modify the CSM and TAC workshops to better serve the counties participating in this statewide initiative.

As of mid-2014, the CoE had mapped thirty-one of the state's sixty-seven counties (an additional four counties were mapped by the GAINS Center prior to the CoE), with ten more workshops scheduled in additional counties through 2014 and 2015.

Measuring Mapping Impact: Three Levels of Evaluation

To capture the impact of the mapping workshops, the CoE uses a three part evaluation process to assess the impact of the mappings on how counties collaborate, their progress in implementing local action plans, and their success in addressing gaps identified in the mappings. The three level process includes an evaluation completed by workshop participants during the mapping and a two part follow-up survey conducted at least six month after a mapping is completed.

Level 1: Workshop Evaluation and Feedback. At the conclusion of each mapping workshop, participants are asked to complete a feedback and evaluation form. On average, twenty-three participants from a variety of county services completed the surveys during each workshop. The highest rate of completed responses were from mapping participants working in the mental health (32%) and criminal justice (27%) systems. A total of ten questions are asked and ranked on a scale of 1 (strongly disagree) and 4 (strongly agree). Responses ranged from 3.41 to 3.83, demonstrating high levels of satisfaction with the workshop. More specifically, results from the evaluation indicate the mappings helped identify gaps and opportunities, and prepare the county for systems change as a result of the action plan developing during the mapping.

Level 2: Online Follow-Up Survey. The online survey is distributed via email to all workshop participants through the Qualtrics Survey System. On average, there was a 47% response rate. Responses from the online survey came from a variety of county systems, including mental health, criminal justice, 911, social services, housing, substance abuse, crisis services, and consumers/family. The highest rates of completed responses were from mapping participants working in the criminal justice and mental health systems, with 35% and 27% response rates, respectively.

Results indicate that the mappings have fostered increased collaboration and significant progress in each county's action plan. Roughly 81% of the survey respondents perceived the mapping as improving the county's ability/willingness to collaborate across systems. When asked to elaborate on specific areas of improvement, one participant stated: "[T]he Mapping exercise fostered open communication and joint planning among the various agencies and entities that are integral participants in the areas of [Mental Health/Drug and Alcohol] and the Criminal Justice system. It identified the joint responsibilities, the benefits and the barriers with and among each of the separate systems. It has offered the opportunity to better coordinate and establish MOU's." In addition, 83% of respondents reported that the action plan developed during the mapping was helpful to the initiation or continuation of programs in their counties. For example, one participant wrote: "The action plan helped us identify and execute trainings for first responders who deal with crisis situations involving individuals exhibiting symptoms of mental illness. It also helped us to define our top priority issues and how we are addressing them." Finally, 95% of the respondents indicated that they would recommend the mapping workshop to other counties in Pennsylvania.

Level 3: Telephone Follow-up Interviews. The telephone survey was divided into three sections: general questions, priority-specific questions, and questions designed to assess other aspects of the CoE's mission. Nearly all of the respondents indicated that the mapping fostered better communication. In addition, all respondents reported at least one actual system change that could be attributed to the cross-systems mapping. Some examples included using a screening tool to identify veterans, employing more mental health personnel in jail to provide psychotropic medication more quickly, implementing Mental Health First Aid training for public safety staff, beginning to use peer support specialists and forensic peer support professionals, improving collaboration with police and community providers, and implementing training for various groups (e.g., police, community providers).

Respondents described improvement in communication between the mental health and criminal justice systems, with one county representative stating: "A byproduct of the mapping meeting was to bring the MH and CJ people to the table. In the end, the CJ now understands the MH position better and the MH people now understand the job of law enforcement and their position better. It helped to dispel a lot of stereotypes." Another respondent noted, "There are several benefits of the mapping. It gives credence to what we (the MH system) have been trying to do. It brought people together who wouldn't normally get together, and it gave us a format/template to work from." Finally, respondents described gaps and challenges that counties continue to face. There was near-universal agreement that funding/sustainability was an ongoing area of concern, while some counties also described encountering specific groups or organizations that were not open to change.

CONCLUSION

The CSM workshops have been received well by communities. Participants have reported high levels of satisfaction with the expertise of the workshop facilitators, the workshops, and the related planning and information-dissemination processes. Participants from both the behavioral health and justice systems have reported continued benefits from the workshops, primarily involving increased within- and between-system communication and understanding. While gaps in services and communication may remain, many participants report having a better understanding of why such difficulties are being experienced and how they can be addressed more effectively. Many communities report benefits from the workshops in the initiation and continuation of diversion programming. These may include many of the tasks developed during action planning, with participants reporting the initiation and completion of a variety of short-term and long-term goals.

Despite these positive outcomes, the workshops have limitations. As system personnel and policies change, highlighted priorities and developed action plans may need to be reorganized and modified. As some obstacles are overcome, communities may encounter larger obstacles. Funding is a consistently limiting factor for achieving many of the goals and is one of the most frequently cited reasons for limited progress around a variety of priorities. Follow-up sessions and intensive technical assistance can be useful in overcoming some of these shortcomings, but systemic change is often slow and challenging. This highlights the importance of establishing the CSM workshops as a rallying point as stakeholders continue to work together to transform their system over time.

The impact of the workshops in local communities is tied to the larger field of diversion itself. Fortunately, the field of diversion continues to develop promising practices around the issues frequently raised by local communities. Thus, one of the most pressing issues relevant to competent and current technical assistance is how best to disseminate these promising practices to communities. More efficient and effective information dissemination would greatly facilitate much of the work in the area of diversion.

The CSM workshops represent a useful application of the SIM to promote cross-system collaboration and community-specific action planning. They directly apply promising practices from across the behavioral health and justice systems to action planning around community alternatives to incarceration, developed by representatives from the systems involved in transforming these services. As the obstacles are better understood and the field of diversion becomes more highly specialized, the workshops will continue to provide a tool to be used toward the larger goal of transforming these services.

NOTE

1. Effective 2011, the CSM workshops conducted by Policy Research Associates were renamed "Sequential Intercept Mapping Workshops."

REFERENCES

Davidson, L., & Rowe, M. (2008). *Peer support within criminal justice settings: The role of forensic peer specialists.* Delmar, NY: CMHS National GAINS Center.

Munetz, M., & Griffin, P. (2006). Use of the Sequential Intercept Model as an approach to decriminalization of people with serious mental illness. *Psychiatric Services, 57,* 544–549.

Policy Research Associates, Inc. (2007). *Cross-systems mappings and taking action for change.* Delmar, NY: Author.

Steadman, H. J., Deane, M. W., Morrissey, J. P., Westcott, M. L., Salasin, S., & Shapiro, S. (1999). A SAMHSA research initiative assessing the effectiveness of jail diversion programs for mentally ill persons. *Psychiatric Services, 50,* 1620–1623.

Vogel, V. M., Noether, C. D., & Steadman, H. J. (2007). Preparing communities for re-entry of offenders with mental illness: The ACTION approach. *Journal of Offender Rehabilitation, 45*(1/2), 167–188.

14

Sequential Intercept Mapping, Confidentiality, and the Cross-System Sharing of Health-Related Information

JOHN PETRILA, HALLIE FADER-TOWE,
AND ALLISON B. HILL ■

Maintaining the confidentiality of health-related information is a core legal and ethical principle. Yet confidentiality is not an absolute value, and few would argue that it should be. The disclosure of otherwise confidential health information is essential to continuity of care. It is required for the reimbursement of services. And in some cases, for example with infectious diseases, disclosure to public health authorities is mandatory because of potential threats to the public's health.

In the context of Sequential Intercept Mapping, confidentiality is also an important but sometimes controversial topic. On one hand, if a person is being diverted from the criminal justice system to treatment, disclosure of the person's treatment history is important for continuity of care, and a failure to disclose information can have negative and sometimes even fatal consequences (Shuchman, 2007). On the other hand, a person with both an arrest record and a history of being treated for mental illness can face significant social stigma that can create barriers to gaining access to housing, employment, and other benefits. This social stigma can create an incentive to keep private as much personal information, including health-related information, as possible. In many situations, the issue becomes even more complex because the disclosure would be across systems, not simply within the healthcare system.

The laws governing confidentiality are also sometimes confusing, leading to uncertainty over when health-related information must be kept confidential and when and under what circumstances it may be disclosed. The emergence of the

Health Insurance Portability and Accountability Act of 1996 (HIPAA) has contributed to the confusion. As a result, the typical default position of many health-care providers on the disclosure of health-related information is to simply assert that "legally we are prohibited from disclosure."

We suggest that just as the Sequential Intercept Model (SIM) uses an individual's passage through the criminal justice system as a map for identifying "intercept" points for connections with behavioral health systems, it also provides a map for potential collection and sharing of information that can facilitate these collaborations between criminal justice and behavioral health. As individuals with mental health and substance use needs move through the intercept map, community-based treatment providers, behavioral health administrators, family members, and, indeed, many traditionally "criminal justice" actors are collecting information about treatment needs, compliance, and outcomes, as well as information specific to the person's arrest and disposition in the criminal justice system.

This chapter discusses confidentiality and privacy issues in the cross-system sharing of information, focusing on health-related information and its potential disclosure at the different intercepts. The chapter begins with a description of the basic legal principles and sources of law for the confidentiality of health-related information. It then applies those principles to specific exchanges of information that might occur at each of the five SIM intercepts. Following that, it discusses strategies to facilitate cross-system information sharing. Finally, the chapter briefly discusses penalties for violating privacy rights. The chapter does not purport to provide legal advice to be relied upon by readers. Rather, the intent is to provide a framework that those involved in intercept mapping can use to consider confidentiality, at either the planning or implementation phase.

BASIC LEGAL RULES

The fact that no single source of law governs the confidentiality of health-related information can lead to misunderstanding. Three of the most important sources of law are considered here. HIPAA and its implementing regulations address health information, while 42 CFR Part 2 of the Code of Federal Regulations applies to alcohol and substance abuse treatment information. The confidentiality laws of each state are also an important source of law in this area.[1] HIPAA applies to "covered entities." 42 CFR Part 2 applies to "federally assisted programs." State laws, depending on the state, apply to mental health and substance abuse treatment records, information about such treatment, and providers. Understanding which law applies depends on understanding some basic definitions and concepts.

HIPAA

A stock answer to requests for health information is "I cannot give you the information because of HIPAA." Sometimes this answer is correct, but most often it is not (Houser, Houser, & Shewchuk, 2007). To understand when HIPAA affects information sharing, it is essential to understand three things about the legal framework HIPAA establishes: *what* sort of information it applies to, *who* it applies to, and *when* state laws take precedence.

To what sort of information does HIPAA apply? HIPAA was enacted by Congress (Health Insurance Portability and Accountability Act of 1996) and then implemented by regulation by the U.S. Department of Health and Human Services (HIPAA Privacy Rule, 2002). HIPAA applies to "protected health information," also commonly referred to as "PHI." Federal regulation (45 CFR 160.103) defines PHI as follows:

> Individually identifiable health information that is (i) transmitted by electronic media; (ii) maintained in electronic media; or (iii) transmitted or maintained in any other form or medium.

This "individually identifiable health information" embraces two concepts. The first is "health information" (45 CFR 160.103), which means "any information, whether or oral or recorded, that

(A)   is created or received by a health care provider, health plan, public health authority, employer, life insurer, school or university, or health care clearinghouse; and
(B)   relates to the past, present, or future physical or mental health or condition of any individual, the provision of health care to an individual, or the past, present, or future payment for the provision of health care to an individual."

The second is "individually identifiable" information (45 CFR 160.103). This is a subset of health information, including demographic data, that meets the definition of health information and also either identifies the individual or creates a reasonable basis to believe the information could identify the individual.

Note that health information contained in most educational records (Bergren, 2004) as well as health records held by an employer in its role as employer (Rothstein, & Talbott, 2007) are excluded from coverage by HIPAA. Sorting out the applicability of federal law on educational records and HIPAA is beyond the scope of this chapter, but the federal agencies charged with implementing these laws have provided very useful guidance on the relationship between the two (U.S. Department of Health and Human Services & U.S. Department of Education, 2008). The impact of HIPAA in employment contexts is discussed by Rothstein and Talbott (2007).

To whom does HIPAA apply? While the definition of PHI is broad, HIPAA applies only to "covered entities," which are specified as a "health plan," a "health clearinghouse," and a "health care provider." Health plans are payers of healthcare services, such as Medicare, Medicaid, and private insurers. Healthcare clearinghouses, which are not particularly relevant here, are entities that take electronic information such as healthcare information received from a provider and transform it into a format acceptable to a payer of services. Healthcare providers include doctors, nurses, psychologists, nursing homes, pharmacies, and other providers of care, but health providers are covered entities only if they transfer information in electronic form in connection with a transaction for which HIPAA has adopted a standard (such transactions include things such as requests to obtain payment [45 CFR 162.1101], determination of eligibility for a health plan transaction [45 CFR 162.1201], and enrollment in a health plan [45 CFR 162.1501]). Therefore, a healthcare provider who does not bill electronically or keep health records electronically or engage in any electronic transactions for which HIPAA has established a standard is *not* a covered entity. For example, in the context of mapping, a case manager who provides independent case management for individuals diverted to treatment but who does not engage in any electronic transactions is not covered by HIPAA.

In addition, many other parties involved in intercept mapping are not covered entities and so HIPAA does not apply *even when that entity comes into possession of PHI.* Judges, including judges administering therapeutic courts, are not covered entities, nor are probation or parole officers. This means that HIPAA does not apply to them, absent specific rules, such as those establishing criteria for obtaining PHI by judicial order. As a result, judges, probation officers, and others are not bound by the HIPAA provisions that create obligations for covered entities.

When does HIPAA apply? HIPAA applies only if it provides more stringent protections for privacy than state law. In other words, HIPAA creates a minimum standard for the privacy of PHI, and if a state law is more protective, then the state law applies (Cohen, 2006). State laws for the disclosure of mental health treatment information are often more restrictive regarding disclosures than HIPAA, so the state law would take precedence.

42 CFR Part 2. Federal statute (42 USC 290dd-2) and regulations enacted in the early 1970s protect the confidentiality of alcohol and substance abuse treatment records (Confidentiality of Alcohol and Drug Abuse Patient Records, 2012). These regulations are among the most restrictive privacy rules in U.S. law (Gentiello, 2005), and their relationship to HIPAA and state privacy laws can be confusing. Kamoie and Borzi (2001) have prepared a helpful guide discussing the relationship between HIPAA and 42 CFR Part 2.

To what sort of information does 42 CFR Part 2 apply? 42 CFR 2.12 applies to "any information, whether or not recorded," which

(i) Would identify a patient as an alcohol or drug abuser either directly, by reference to other publicly available information, or through verification of such an identification by another person; and

(ii) Is drug abuse information obtained by a federally assisted drug abuse program . . . diagnosis, or treatment of any patient which are maintained in connection with the performance of any drug abuse prevented function.

This is a very broad definition and focuses primarily on preventing the revelation of a person's status as someone who has been treated for alcohol or substance abuse. The type of information that might provide that identification is much less important than whether it identifies or can be used to identify a person who has received treatment.

To whom does 42 CFR Part 2 apply? 42 CFR Part 2 applies to a "program" that is "federally assisted" (42 CFR 2.12(a)(ii)). The definition of "federally assisted" is quite broad and includes programs receiving *any* federal funds, whether or not those funds pay for alcohol or drug abuse services (42 CFR 2.12(3)(i)). The regulation (42 CFR 2.11) defines a "program" as

1. an individual or entity (other than a general medical care facility) who holds itself out as providing, and provides, alcohol or drug abuse diagnosis, treatment, or referral for treatment; or
2. an identified unit within a general medical facility that holds itself out as providing, and provides, alcohol or drug abuse diagnosis, treatment, or referral for treatment; or
3. medical personnel or other staff in a general medical care facility whose primary function is the provision of alcohol or drug abuse diagnosis, treatment, or referral for treatment and who are identified as such providers.

Note that the first two parts of this definition require that the individual, entity, or unit "hold itself out" as providing alcohol or substance abuse services and the third part covers medical personnel in a general medical care facility who "are identified" as providers with the primary function of providing such services. This means that 42 CFR Part 2 does *not* apply to the incidental provision of such services by other care staff, or to services provided in a facility that does not "hold itself out" or identify itself as a provider of such services. If a mental health facility provides some substance abuse services but does not advertise itself as doing so, 42 CFR Part 2 would not apply. However, if the mental health facility "holds itself out" as providing such services (e.g., stating that it provides co-occurring mental health and substance abuse services), then 42 CFR Part 2 would apply. Note also that some have concluded that drug courts meet the definition of a program under 42 CFR Part 2, a topic considered in the discussion of Intercept 3 below.

A program governed by 42 CFR Part 2 also must comply with HIPAA if it is a covered entity (discussed below). A good overview of this and related issues has been prepared by the Substance Abuse and Mental Health Services Administration (SAMHSA) of the U.S. Department of Health and Human Services (SAMHSA, 2004).

When does 42 CFR Part 2 apply? All states have laws that apply to alcohol and substance abuse information. Because 42 CFR Part 2 is so strict concerning the release of information, many states simply track its provisions. However, if the state law is more protective of privacy (and some are), then as with HIPAA, state law applies. For a discussion of this issue specifically and the relationship between state and federal law governing consent for disclosure of health information, see RTI International (2009).

State Confidentiality Laws

Most states have separate laws for the confidentiality of mental health and substance abuse treatment records and information. Because state mental health laws, in particular, are often more restrictive than HIPAA, it usually makes sense to begin an analysis of confidentiality protections with the state law before moving to HIPAA. Some states have provided guides that compare HIPAA and state mental health law. A particularly good example is that prepared by the New York State Office of Mental Health (2009; see also RTI International, 2009; http://www.networkofcare.org/library/HIPPABooklet.pdf).

There are a handful of situations where HIPAA typically will provide greater rights to the individual than state law. The first is when an individual requests access to his or her record. HIPAA provides a broad right of individual access (45 CFR 164.524) with few restrictions and provides rights of appeal for denials of access. Access can be denied to information given by a third party under an assurance of confidentiality where access might lead to disclosure of the informant's identity; when the healthcare professional reasonably concludes that access may endanger the life or physical safety of a third party or the individual; and when an inmate requests access and a correctional facility determines that providing access could jeopardize the safety of correctional employees or inmates. Access can also be denied to information prepared in anticipation of a legal proceeding.

The second situation in which HIPAA is more restrictive than state law is in HIPAA's protection of "psychotherapy notes" from virtually all disclosure, including disclosure to the individual. "Psychotherapy notes" are

> notes recorded (in any medium) by a health care provider who is a mental health professional documenting or analyzing the contents of conversation during a private counseling session or a group, joint, or family counseling session and that are separated from the rest of the individual's medical record . . . notes exclude medication prescription and monitoring, . . . session start and stop times, the modalities and frequencies of treatment furnished, results of clinical tests, and any summary of . . . diagnosis, functional status, the treatment plan, symptoms, prognosis, and progress to date. (45 CFR 164.501)

Individual authorization is required before disclosure in nearly all circumstances, and generally state laws do not have a correlate for this protective shield for psychotherapy notes (Maio, 2003).

Consent/Authorization and Disclosure

While in practice most care providers will require the individual's consent as a predicate to disclosure, it is worth noting that there are significant differences in the way each of these laws addresses the issue. Note that even in this context, terminology may cause confusion. Generally, except in a handful of situations described below, HIPAA uses the term "authorization" for disclosure rather than consent, while 42 CFR Part 2 (and most state laws) use the term "consent." When the term "authorization" is used below, it refers specifically to HIPAA's use of that term.

First, HIPAA does *not* require individual consent for the disclosure of PHI for purposes of treatment, payment, and healthcare operations (45 CFR 164.506).[2] This means that absent a state law requirement for consent, one treatment provider can disclose information to another treatment provider for aftercare or submit a bill for payment of services without the individual's consent. HIPAA also does not require individual "authorization" in a variety of circumstances, such as reporting potential child abuse, for certain law enforcement purposes, and for various public health reporting purposes. A good discussion of incidental disclosures under HIPAA can be found in a paper by Lo and colleagues (2005). In addition, the U.S. Department of Health and Human Services has an excellent guide to the rules governing authorization at http://www.hhs.gov/hipaafaq/use/index.html.

In contrast, 42 CFR Part 2 requires individual consent prior to almost any disclosure of information by a federally assisted program, and the consent form has to contain those elements set forth in the regulation (42 CFR 2.31). Information can be shared by treatment staff within the same program, but disclosure to another treatment provider requires consent. In addition, state laws typically have their own consent requirements (RTI International, 2009). Based on the "most restrictive law governs" principle, if a state law requires consent for disclosure where HIPAA does not, then consent is required. Some states (e.g., Ohio) have reconciled their mental health confidentiality laws with the provisions of HIPAA to facilitate the exchange of information within and across systems (Ohio Coordinating Center for Integrating Care and Ohio Department of Mental Health, 2010).

Redisclosure

If PHI is disclosed under HIPAA, the party receiving the information is not bound by HIPAA unless it is a covered entity or business associate, a type of entity discussed below. Therefore, it is legally permissible under HIPAA for a noncovered entity to disclose PHI unless otherwise prohibited from doing so—for example, by terms of a court order that has caused the initial disclosure (Goldstein, 2012). On the other hand, any party receiving information from an entity covered by 42 CFR Part 2 is obligated to not redisclose the information except as permitted by 42 CFR Part 2 (42 CFR 2.32). This creates contrasting rules for redisclosure. For example, a judge or police officer who receives PHI is not bound by HIPAA provisions because he or she is not a covered entity, and HIPAA covers only covered entities. Exceptions would be if the individual's authorization expressly bars redisclosure or if a court order directing the production of PHI bars redisclosure. However, if the judge or officer receives information from a 42 CFR Part 2 provider, the information cannot be redisclosed except under rules established by 42 CFR Part 2, and those rules require consent before virtually all disclosures.

The Principle of Minimum Necessity

HIPAA incorporates the principle that the disclosure of PHI should be limited to the minimum necessary to accomplish the intended purpose for which the disclosure is made (45 CFR 164.502(b), 164.514(d)). However, this principle does not apply to disclosures for treatment purposes, disclosures made pursuant to the individual's authorization, disclosures to the individual who is the subject of the information, and disclosures to the federal government for enforcement of HIPAA or as otherwise required by law. Information released under 42 CFR Part 2 must be restricted to that necessary to the purpose of the disclosure. While the HIPAA requirement does not apply to some types of disclosures, the principle of minimum necessity is a useful construct in considering disclosure, particularly when one considers that most people would prefer to have information about their health kept private except where necessary.

INFORMATION SHARING AND THE INTERCEPT MAP

Application of laws on confidentiality will vary, depending on the source of law and the intercept. The following examples illustrate the application of confidentiality rules at different intercepts. Other examples can be found in guides available elsewhere (Petrila & Fader-Towe, 2010).

Intercept 1: Law Enforcement/Emergency Services

The Crisis Intervention Team (CIT) model has been adopted by many jurisdictions to provide law enforcement officers with training in recognizing and intervening safely with individuals who may present a mental illness (Compton, Bahora, Watson, & Oliva, 2008). Assume that a police officer trained in the CIT model is called to check on a middle-aged man walking through traffic in an apparently random manner, endangering himself and the motorists around him. The officer would like to know whether the person has received mental health or substance abuse treatment in the past.

She calls the two treatment centers in town to request the information. Can it be provided?

Generally, the answer is no. Even if state law permitted it, no provision in HIPAA permits an officer to receive such information from these sources, and 42 CFR Part 2 requires consent for virtually all disclosures relevant here. However, HIPAA *does* permit disclosure of PHI if the covered entity believes it necessary to prevent or lessen a serious and imminent threat to the health or safety of a person or the public, and if the disclosure is to a party reasonably able to prevent or lessen the threat (45 CFR 164.512(j)(1)(i)). This suggests that in an emergency that meets this definition PHI could be disclosed to the officer—for example, to prevent a suicide or assault. Note also that a covered entity may disclose PHI in response to a request from law enforcement for purposes of identifying or locating a suspect, fugitive, material witness, or missing person, although disclosure is limited to identified types of information (45 CFR 164.512(f)(2)).[3]

Assume that at Intercept 1 the officer brings the person to an emergency room and that the healthcare provider wants information from the officer regarding the officer's knowledge of the person's mental status or treatment history. In this situation, the officer is neither a covered entity under HIPAA or a federally assisted program under 42 CFR Part 2. Therefore, the officer may disclose the information in her possession, even if the information would otherwise meet the definition of PHI under HIPAA or be covered by 42 CFR Part 2. The only limitation on this type of disclosure would be if the officer received the information pursuant to a 42 CFR Part 2 disclosure, in which case the prohibition on redisclosure just noted would govern.

Finally, assume the police decide to create a roster of individuals whom law enforcement knows have received treatment or have been suspected of mental illness in the past, and that the roster would be available to officers on the street for use when they encounter an individual. If this information is not subject to rules governing redisclosure, there are no prohibitions on the creation of such a roster.

Intercept 2: Initial Detention/Initial Court Hearings

Some jurisdictions organize diversion at Intercept 2, either at initial detention or an initial court hearing (Clark, 2004). In this situation, either the jail or a judge/magistrate might desire information regarding the person's mental state or the person's past or current treatment. In addition, jails may provide daily booking information to providers so that the providers can screen their rolls to determine if an individual is or was in treatment. To dispose of the last issue first, booking information is not covered under HIPAA, 42 CFR Part 2, or state mental health confidentiality statutes. Therefore, these laws are not relevant to whether booking information is shared with treatment providers. A state may have a law addressing disclosure of booking information, but that is a separate issue from disclosure of health-related information.

Can a jail receive PHI without consent of the individual? HIPAA permits this, explicitly providing for unconsented disclosure of PHI to correctional or other custodial facilities for several purposes, including the provision of healthcare to the inmate, protecting the health and safety of inmates and officers and other correctional employees, to persons involved in transporting the inmate, or other activities necessary for the maintenance of "safety, security, and good order of the institution" (45 CFR 164.512(k)(5)). In other words, unless barred by state law, treatment providers can provide PHI to a correctional facility without the person's authorization, for these purposes. That means that a treatment provider, under HIPAA at least, could notify a jail after reviewing booking data which individuals had received or were receiving treatment. On the other hand, a provider regulated by 42 CFR Part 2 cannot do the same without the person's consent.

The situation is somewhat more complex if a court would like to receive PHI. For example, suppose a magistrate would like to know whether an individual appearing before her has received emergency medication in the jail. Under HIPAA, the in-jail mental health/health provider may be a covered entity, particularly if the jail has contracted the services out to a healthcare provider organization (Bizzell, 2005). However, the law enforcement or correctional official who administers the jail may or may not be a covered entity, or the jail may be a "hybrid" entity, meaning that part of the jail has been designated a covered entity but the rest has not (Dimitropoulos & Rizk, 2009). Therefore, if the sheriff is not a covered entity, he or she can receive PHI without the individual's authorization under the rules governing disclosure to correctional officials and in turn may redisclose that information to a magistrate in this situation. Whether that *will* occur, *should* occur, or will be *permitted* to occur by defense counsel, or whether state law permits it, is a different matter, but if HIPAA governs, it is not prohibited. Otherwise, a covered entity providing services in a jail (or in the community) can provide PHI to a court ordinarily only pursuant to court orders that meet either the conditions established by HIPAA (if applicable) or a more restrictive state law. Given that HIPAA does not bar redisclosure by a noncovered entity, a jail administrator in theory could provide PHI to a prosecuting attorney as well; however, this would undoubtedly raise ethical concerns as well as arguments that such disclosures could undermine the defendant's defense.

Intercept 3: Jails/Courts

Some issues that may arise in Intercept 3 (e.g., court access to PHI) are discussed in the section on Intercept 2. Other issues may arise in Intercept 3—for example, confidentiality issues that may be associated with therapeutic courts such as mental health courts and drug courts.

Mental health courts. As noted earlier, a court is not a covered entity under HIPAA. However, assume that a mental health center that *is* a covered entity provides a staff member to the court who performs mental health screenings to determine eligibility for admission to the mental health court program. In this context, a cautious reading of HIPAA would suggest that authorization should be obtained from the individual to share the results of the screening with the court; one can readily imagine that if a person withheld authorization, a mental health court team might decide that the person is not appropriate for participating in the program. On the other hand, if the court independently employs a mental health professional to perform eligibility screening, and that professional is not a covered entity, authorization to release the information to the court would not technically be required under HIPAA but presumably would be obtained anyway as a standard part of performing such an assessment.

In addition, mental health courts may discuss an individual's mental health status, treatment, and related issues in open court. HIPAA does not prohibit such discussions. However, for a variety of reasons, including stigma and potential impact on the person's court case, commentators have strongly suggested that clinical information regarding the person should not be discussed in open court (BJA, Council of State Governments, 2008).

Drug courts. It is extremely unlikely that a court would meet the definition of a covered entity under HIPAA, barring a situation where the court became a direct provider of services and engaged in the types of electronic transactions that would bring it under the definition. On the other hand, as early as 1999 the U.S. Department of Justice conducted an analysis that concluded that when an employee of a drug court did an assessment of a drug court participant, the drug court was a "program" under 42 CFR Part 2 (U.S. Department of Justice, 1999; for a more general discussion of confidentiality and drug courts, see Freeman-Wilson, Sullivan, & Weinstein, 2003). Many drug courts have received federal funding (making them "federally assisted" within the meaning of the regulation). In addition, given that some drug courts provide services directly, and "hold themselves out" as doing so, the conclusion that a drug court is covered by 42 CFR Part 2 is not unreasonable. Whether or not one accepts this premise, drug courts will be obtaining services from providers covered by Part 2, so the consent rules established in the regulation will apply.

Intercept 4: Reentry; and Intercept 5: Community Corrections/Community Support

Reentry has become a major issue in both prison and jail contexts and is not restricted to U.S. jurisdictions. It is linked with Intercept 5, since community supervision is an essential part of reentry efforts, whether through treatment providers or probation or parole officers. Two issues illustrate the types of questions that can arise with information sharing in these intercepts.

First, information sharing is indispensable in reentry planning (Osher, Steadman, & Barr, 2003). For example, a treatment provider may wish to do in-reach to the jail (or prison) to begin treatment planning so that the individual receives care on release (Buck, Brown, & Hickey, 2011). Alternatively, the jail (or prison) may wish to share PHI with community treatment staff or with a probation or parole officer. In either case, HIPAA permits the unconsented sharing of PHI between caregivers. So if the community provider doing in-reach wishes to discuss the individual's care with the covered entity providing in-jail mental health services, HIPAA permits this. Similarly, HIPAA would permit a covered entity doing prerelease treatment planning in the correctional facility to share PHI with community treatment providers for the purpose of aftercare. As always, however, state law may mandate that the person's consent be obtained prior to disclosure.

The situation with parole or probation officers is more complex, because HIPAA does not provide for disclosure of PHI to either, absent the person's authorization (Petrila & Fader-Towe, 2010). Yet probation officers often require at least limited health-related information, and with the emergence of specialty probation for people with mental illnesses, this need will only grow (Skeem, Emke-Francis, & Louden, 2006). However, while HIPAA permits virtually unlimited flow of PHI to a correctional facility, ordinary consent rules govern when the individual "is released on parole, probation, supervised release, or no longer in lawful custody" (45 CFR 164.512(k)(5)(F)(iii)). In addition, 42 CFR Part 2, here as in nearly all other circumstances, requires consent before a "program" can release information either to another provider or to a probation or parole officer. However, 42 CFR Part 2 does have a provision explicitly permitting disclosure of information to criminal justice officials who require the information for monitoring and supervising individuals who are to receive substance abuse or alcohol treatment as a condition of their case disposition (42 CFR 2.35). The individual's consent is still required, but the individual cannot revoke the consent at will as he or she can under the usual provisions of the regulation.

A probation officer who receives information from the individual on probation regarding his or her health status can redisclose the information (e.g., to a court). This is because the probation officer is not a covered entity or a federally assisted program. Similarly, if the probation officer receives PHI from a care provider, for example that the person has attended treatment appointments, the officer can redisclose this information under HIPAA, although state law may differ. However, the same is not true of information received from a caregiver under 42 CFR Part 2, unless the person consented to the redisclosure.

The best solution to address information sharing with probation and parole officers is for courts who place people in the community to either (a) insist that the defendant sign an authorization permitting the disclosure of treatment information as a condition of supervision and/or (b) enter a court order, compliant with governing state or federal law, that orders disclosure as appropriate to monitor adherence with the regular and treatment-oriented conditions of probation/parole. Further discussion, and examples of court orders, can be found elsewhere (Petrila & Fader-Towe, 2010).

STRATEGIES FOR ADDRESSING INFORMATION SHARING

A variety of strategies can be employed to facilitate information sharing, including the most obvious, which is obtaining the individual's authorization/consent. These strategies are discussed briefly below.

Uniform Authorization/Consent Form

There are sound ethical and treatment-related reasons for obtaining the person's consent to disclosure even if the law permits information sharing without it. For example, providing the person with control over the circumstances in which personal information is revealed to others is consistent with the commitment to recovery that is the foundation of treatment today.

At the same time, in many jurisdictions consent is obtained each time the person comes into contact with a new entity. This can create delays in sharing information and can lead to discontinuity in treatment. An alternative is to use a common form that is available at each point in an intercept the person might touch and that meets the requirements of HIPAA, 42 CFR Part 2, and state law. While agencies sometimes cling to their own forms, system mapping can force issues of information sharing to the forefront of stakeholder discussions and may create the opportunity to begin a discussion of developing consent/authorization forms with common elements. A consent to release information form can require the individual to "opt in" to each disclosure (e.g., through a list of agencies that the person must check to authorize) or "opt out," whereby the person consents to release to the agencies noted on the form absent explicit refusal to endorse particular agencies. As health networks increasingly turn to shared electronic health records, a uniform authorization/consent form can become an essential tool in facilitating information sharing (Goldstein, 2010). For those interested in obtaining samples of uniform authorization forms, a Google search with the term "sample HIPAA compliant authorization form" will yield a number of results. Of course, any authorization form produced by such a search should be checked against the requirements of HIPAA or the applicable state law. 42 CFR Part 2 contains a sample consent form (42 CFR 2.31).

Standard Judicial Language

Courts play an important role in diversion. Even if a jurisdiction focuses on prebooking diversion or jail-based diversion, many individuals with mental illnesses who encounter the criminal justice system do so repeatedly and inevitably find themselves before a judge. Judges can facilitate information sharing by employing three strategies. First, a judge can insist that an individual authorize release of his or her records as a condition of entering judicial programs such as a therapeutic court. To do this, courts should have consent/authorization forms available that comply with the various laws governing disclosure. Second, courts can direct a person to authorize release of information as a condition of case disposition—for example, when a court places an individual on probation. The authorization can effectively become part of the probation record and can be shared with treatment providers who may treat the individual during probation or parole. Finally, in the absence of the individual's authorization/consent to disclosure, the court can adopt standard language to incorporate in any court order issued in diverting a person into treatment, either before or after adjudication of the charges. As with an authorization/consent form, the language for a judicial order must comply with applicable federal and state law. The criteria for court orders to produce PHI under HIPAA are at 45 CFR 164.512(e), and the criteria to produce records covered by 42 CFR Part 2 are at 42 CFR 2.61-2.67. A court order that directs disclosure as a routine part of any order relevant to diversion can provide protection for providers asked to release information as part of the person's treatment and monitoring.

In short, courts should first attempt to gain the person's authorization or consent for disclosure. In its absence, the court can rely on its judicial authority to permit and structure disclosure through the use of standard language in court orders disposing of the individual's case.

Business Associate Agreements and Qualified Service Organization Agreements

Sequential Intercept Mapping is a planning exercise designed to result in programmatic change. Part of that change might involve bringing other parties into the community to assist with technical, nontreatment matters. For example, a large jurisdiction might decide to contract with an entity to create an integrated database or management information system.

Both HIPAA and 42 CFR Part 2 provide tools under which this can occur. HIPAA provides for establishment of a Business Associate Agreement, and 42 CFR Part 2 permits creation of a Qualified Service Organization Agreement. A "business associate" is a person or entity that performs certain types of activities for a covered entity in which PHI is revealed—for example, claims processing, providing legal advice, or quality assurance (45 CFR 164.502(e), 164.504(e), 164.532(d) and (e)). A "qualified service organization" provides similar services to 42 CFR Part 2 providers, such as bill collecting and data processing (42 CFR 2.11). The Office of Civil Rights of the U.S. Department of Health and Human Services, which has primary authority to enforce HIPAA, provides sample business associate agreements at its website, which at the time of writing could be

located here: http://www.hhs.gov/ocr/privacy/hipaa/understanding/covereden-
tities/contractprov.html

Health Information Exchanges

As a way to facilitate the flow of PHI among networked care providers, HIPAA
provides for the creation of a "health information exchange," which is the electronic movement of health-related information among organizations according
to nationally recognized standards. This type of exchange is designed to ensure
access to and retrieval of clinical data for care. This is part of a larger national
agenda to create electronic health records; the ultimate goal is to create a national
health information network (Bostick, Crayton, Fishman, et al., 2011), and health
information exchange is facilitated by developing smaller networks that are often
referred to as health information organizations.

A series of technological and substantive issues are involved with the creation
of health information organizations, including whether and how to incorporate
mental health information (often stringently protected by state law) and alcohol
and substance use information protected by 42 CFR Part 2 (Bostick, Crayton,
Fishman, et al., 2011). To date, there have been few efforts to bring jails and other
stakeholders essential to the success of the intercept model into an electronic
health information environment (New York City is an exception, with creation
of an electronic health record for Rikers Island; see Stazesky, Hughes, & Venters,
2012). However, as the nation moves increasingly toward reliance on electronic
health information and its availability to networked providers, it will become
increasingly an issue for care providers and law enforcement and correctional
officials at the intersection of the criminal justice and treatment systems.

PENALTIES

One barrier to the appropriate sharing of health-related information is a concern
that even minor violations of confidentiality laws will lead to significant penalties. This fear is exaggerated for several reasons.

First, there is no private cause of action for violations of HIPAA. The federal
courts have been very clear about this. This means that an individual cannot
bring a lawsuit for money damages against a covered entity that violates HIPAA
in some manner (Collins, 2007). Nor is there a private cause of action for violation of 42 CFR Part 2 (Jade, 2006).

Second, enforcement is primarily left to the federal government, with the
Office of Civil Rights of the Department of Health and Human Services having
primary enforcement power. The Health Information Technology for Economic
and Clinical Health Act (HITECH), which was part of the Recovery Act of 2009
(also known as the Stimulus Bill), did extend authority to state attorneys general
to bring enforcement actions and permitted assignment of at least a portion of

any damages won to a private individual causing the Attorney General to act (HITECH and its implications for health care providers is discussed by Murray, Calhoun, & Phillipsen, 2011). In addition, penalties were raised for civil violations, from a maximum of $100 per violation to $50,000, and the overall cap for multiple violations was raised from $25,000 to $1.5 million in a calendar year. It is also true that enforcement activities seem to be increasing. However, neither the federal government nor state attorneys general are pursuing inadvertent or minor violations of HIPAA. Rather, they have focused their attention on egregious conduct or patterns of violations by a covered entity. In the context of those activities involved in implementing programs as part of mapping, there is little cause to worry about penalties, absent intentional or systematic violations of the privacy rights of individuals. The Office for Civil Rights, which has primary enforcement authority over HIPAA, maintains an excellent website devoted to enforcement actions and penalties. It can be found here: http://www.hhs.gov/ocr/privacy/hipaa/enforcement/.

SUMMARY

It is impossible to intercept individuals from deeper involvement in the criminal justice system and divert them to treatment without sharing health-related information at critical points. Yet this often does not occur, because of misunderstanding of legal rules, because of exaggerated concern over potential liability, and because of a failure to take advantage of tools that can facilitate the responsible sharing of information.

It is usually the case that obtaining an individual's consent (or, in the case of HIPAA, his or her authorization) is preferred. It makes the exchange of information easier; it is consistent with the principles of recovery and empowerment that inform most care today; and it is favored by healthcare providers. However, as this chapter makes clear, there are circumstances in which health-related information can be shared without consent, and there are tools that can make information sharing easier to accomplish.

Confidentiality of health information is important, legally, ethically, and as part of an individual's decision to seek healthcare. When information is shared, only that minimally necessary for the transaction at hand should be disclosed. However, confidentiality is not an absolute value. Finding the right balance between protecting the privacy of health information and sharing it to provide better care is essential to the success of community efforts to use intercept mapping as a tool for a more rational system of care.

NOTES

1. Because of space limitations, this article does not address limitations on information sharing within criminal procedural law, the rules of evidence for court cases, or professional ethical canons.

2. "Health care operations" are certain administrative, financial, legal, and quality improvement activities of a covered entity that are necessary to run its business and to support the core functions of treatment and payment (45 CFR 164.501). They include quality assurance activities, reviewing the qualifications of health-care professionals, for purposes such as credentialing, and other business practices. Only those activities specified in the definition qualify as "health care operations."

3. Disclosure of PHI to law enforcement in this circumstance is limited to name and address, date and place of birth, social security number, ABO blood type and Rh factor, type of injury, date and time of treatment, date and time of death, and a description of distinguishing physical characteristics. Other information related to the individual's DNA, dental records, body fluid or tissue typing, samples, or analysis cannot be disclosed under this provision but may be disclosed in response to a court order, warrant, or written administrative request (45 CFR 164.512(f)(2)).

REFERENCES

Bergren, M. D. (2004). HIPAA-FERPA revisited. *Journal of School Nursing, 20,* 107–112.

Bizzell, W. D. (2005). Meeting the HIPAA privacy challenge: A road map for jails. *American Jails, 18,* 122–24.

Bostick, M. R., Crayton, G., Fishman, E., Peters, E., & Smith, V. (2011). *Sustaining state health information exchange: A state toolkit.* Washington, D.C.: National Governors Association Center for Best Practices.

Buck, D. S., Brown, C. A., & Hickey, J. S. (2011). The jail inreach project: Linking homeless inmates who have mental illness with community services. *Psychiatric Services, 62,* 120–122.

Bureau of Justice Assistance (BJA) & Council of State Governments Justice Center (2008). *Improving responses to people with mental illnesses: The essential elements of a mental health court.* New York: Council of State Governments Justice Center.

Clark, J. (2004). *Non-specialty first appearance court models for diverting people with mental illness: Alternatives to mental health courts.* Delmar, NY: Technical Assistance and Policy Analysis Center for Jail Diversion.

Cohen, B. (2006). Reconciling the HIPAA privacy rule with state laws regarding ex parte interviews of plaintiffs' treating physicians: A guide to performing HIPA preemption analysis. *Houston Law Review, 43,* 1091–1142.

Collins, J. D. (2007). Toothless HIPAA: Searching for a private right of action to remedy privacy rule violations. *Vanderbilt Law Review, 60,* 199–233.

Compton, M. T., Bahora, M., Watson, A. C., & Oliva, J. R. (2008). A comprehensive review of extant research on crisis intervention team (CIT) programs. *Journal of the American Academy of Psychiatry and the Law, 36,* 47–55.

Confidentiality of Alcohol and Drug Abuse Patient Records (2012). 42 C.F.R. Part 2.

Dimitropoulos, L., & Rizk, S. (2009). A state-based approach to privacy and security for interoperable health information exchange. *Health Affairs, 28,* 428–434.

Freeman-Wilson, K., Sullivan, R., & Weinstein, S. P. (2003). *Critical issues for defense attorneys in drug court.* Alexandria, VA: National Drug Court Institute.

Gentiello, L. M. (2005). Confronting the obstacles to screening and interventions for alcohol problems in trauma centers. *Journal of Trauma-Injury and Critical Care, 59,* 137–143.

Goldstein, M. (2010). Health information technology and the idea of informed consent. *Journal of Law, Medicine & Ethics, 38,* 27–35.

Goldstein, M. (2012). Issue paper: Health information privacy in the correctional environment. *Community Oriented Correctional Services, April,* 1–18. Accessed November 6, 2012, at http://www.cochs.org/files/hieconf/PRIVACY.pdf.

Health Insurance Portability and Accountability Act of 1996. Pub. L. 104-191, 110 Stat. 1936.

HIPAA Privacy Rule (2002). 45 C.F.R. Part 160; Part 164 Subparts A and E.

Houser, S. H., Houser, H. W., & Shewchuk, R. M. (2007). Assessing the effects of the HIPAA privacy rule on release of information by healthcare facilities. *Perspectives in Health Information Management, 4,* 1–11.

Jade, R. (2006). The secret life of 42 CFR Part 2—What every defender and investigator needs to know about patient records from federally funded drug or alcohol treatment centers. *The Champion, 30,* 1–19.

Kamoie, B., & Borzi, P. (2001). A crosswalk between the final HIPAA privacy and existing federal substance abuse confidentiality requirements. *Behavioral Health Issue Brief Series, Double Issue Brief # 18-19.* Center for Health Services Research and Policy. The George Washington University Medical Center. Accessed November 5, 2012, at http://www.duncan-associates.com/crosswalk.pdf.

Lo, B., Dombrand, L., & Dubler, N. N. (2005). HIPAA and patient care: The role for professional judgment. *JAMA, 293,* 1766–1771.

Maio, J. E. (2003). HIPAA and the special status of psychotherapy notes. *Lippincotts Case Management, 8,* 24–29.

Murray, T. L., Calhoun, M., & Phillipsen, N. C. (2011). Privacy, confidentiality, HIPAA, and HITECH: Implications for the health care practitioner. *Journal for Nurse Practitioners, 7,* 747–752.

New York State Office of Mental Health (2009). *Understanding HIPAA, NYS mental hygiene law, and the confidentiality of mental health treatment and information in New York State: A how-to guide for communication between families, patient/clients, providers and others.* Albany, NY: New York Office of Mental Health. Accessed November 3, 2012, at http://www.networkofcare.org/library/HIPPABooklet.pdf.

Ohio Coordinating Center for Integrating Care and Ohio Department of Mental Health (2010). *Integrated care: Confidentiality and release of information fact sheet.* Accessed November 6, 2012, at http://www.occic.org/documents/Integrated%20Care%20Confidentiality%20and%20Release%20of%20Information%20Fact%20Sheet%202-10.pdf.

Osher, F., Steadman, H. J., & Barr, H. (2003). A best practice approach to community reentry from jails for inmates with co-occurring disorders: The APIC model. *Crime & Delinquency, 49,* 79–96.

Petrila, J., & Fader-Towe, H. (2010). Information sharing in criminal justice-mental health collaborations: Working with HIPAA and other privacy laws. New York: Council of State Governments Justice Center.

Rothstein, M. A., & Talbott, M. K. (2007). Compelled authorizations for disclosure of health records: magnitude and implications. *American Journal of Bioethics, 7*, 38–45.

RTI International (2009). *Privacy and security solutions for interoperable health information exchange: report on state law requirements for patient permission to disclose health information*. Chicago, IL: RTI International.

Shuchman, M. (2007). Falling through the cracks—Virginia Tech and the restructuring of college mental health services. *New England Journal of Medicine, 357*, 105–110.

Skeem, J. L., Emke-Francis, P., & Louden, J. E. (2006). Probation, mental health, and mandated treatment. *Criminal Justice and Behavior, 33*, 158–184.

Stazesky, R., Hughes, J., & Venters, H. (2012). Implementation of an electronic health record in the New York City jail system. *Community Oriented Correctional Services, April*, 1–6. Accessed November 6, 2012, at http://www.cochs.org/files/hieconf/IMPLEMENTATION.pdf

Substance Abuse and Mental Health Service Administration (SAMHSA) (2004). *The confidentiality of alcohol and drug abuse patient records regulation and the HIPAA privacy rule: Implications for alcohol and substance abuse programs*. Rockville, MD: U.S. Department of Health and Human Services, Substance Abuse and Mental Health Service Administration.

U.S. Department of Health and Human Services & U.S. Department of Education (2008). *Joint guidance on the application of the Family Educational Rights and Privacy Act (FERPA) and the Health Insurance Portability and Accountability Act of 1996 (HIPAA) to student health records*. Accessed November 4, 2012, at http://www.hhs.gov/ocr/privacy/hipaa/understanding/coveredentities/hipaaferpajointguide.pdf.

U.S. Department of Justice (1999). *Practical guide for applying federal confidentiality laws to drug court operations*. Washington, D.C.: U.S. Department of Justice, Office of Justice Programs, Drug Courts Program Office.

15

The Sequential Intercept Model

Current Status, Future Directions

KIRK HEILBRUN, EDWARD P. MULVEY, DAVID DEMATTEO, CAROL A. SCHUBERT, AND PATRICIA A. GRIFFIN ■

This book represents the first attempt to describe the Sequential Intercept Model (SIM; Munetz & Griffin, 2006) in sufficient detail to promote nuanced discussion of its development, its application for various purposes (training, technical assistance, research, and consultation), and particularly its use as a tool to promote systems change. In some respects, the literature in these areas is already well developed. In other ways, there are clearly gaps and needs that must be addressed to maximize the effectiveness of the SIM for accomplishing certain tasks.

In this final chapter, we begin by highlighting important points made in the first 14 chapters. We discuss each briefly and illustrate how researchers, practitioners, policymakers, and consumer advocates might apply these lessons now and develop new methods for future use. We next offer suggestions about one concrete way that the use of the SIM might be expanded: by applying this approach to populations of individuals for whom it has not yet been used. Finally, we summarize important implications for research, policy, and practice. A reasonable place to begin is with some essential maxims drawn from experiences using this approach.

CURRENT STATUS OF THE SIM: LESSONS LEARNED

1. The SIM may be considered a theoretical/descriptive model or an organizing tool. Its applications help to identify empirical questions that can be addressed through research.

The SIM's value lies in its identification of the successive stages of criminal justice processing, from initial contact with police or first responders through booking, arraignment, pretrial incarceration, conviction, postsentence incarceration or community supervision, and specialized treatment in the community while still under justice supervision. In identifying stages in this fashion, the SIM both offers hypotheses about how existing justice processing works and provides a tool for understanding how interventions might be designed or such processing modified. Using the 5 intercepts to consider the existing research evidence at each one allows illustration of areas in which the research is adequate to strong and other areas in which it is quite limited. In addition, the SIM facilitates planning for how research might be designed to address existing gaps and limits (see Chapter 1).

2. As an organizing tool, the SIM serves multiple purposes.

The SIM is often useful to users by simply identifying the discrete steps involved in criminal justice processing. But its greater strength involves illuminating the process through which a justice-involved individual must go if he or she is to be eventually convicted and incarcerated (or otherwise under justice supervision). The SIM was originally conceptualized as a series of filters, each of which could divert the individual from standard prosecution into an alternative intervention (Munetz & Griffin, 2006). When the SIM is applied for this purpose, it can be useful for those concerned with possible innovations in any single intercept or intervention (e.g., Crisis Intervention Team, mental health court). In addition, it can be enormously helpful to those thinking about the intercepts as interactive parts of a larger system and planning to intervene (or to develop new interventions) with consideration of all intercepts, processes, gaps, and opportunities. By having a complete map of the system, the planning process can accommodate input from representatives of the various systems (courts, corrections, law enforcement, parole and probation, mental health, drug and alcohol, veterans affairs, consumers) involved in the system's functioning.

3. HIPAA and other laws applicable to information sharing are often misunderstood. Information sharing is limited by law significantly less than it is widely perceived to be.

There is perhaps no more widely misunderstood influence on the functioning of the criminal justice system than federal law (particularly HIPAA) regulating health-related information sharing. The exchange and use of health and mental health information is essential for the effective functioning of many of the rehabilitative alternatives to standard prosecution described in this book. It is thus necessary to begin discussions of possible innovations or approaches with a clear understanding of applicable regulations in this area. This is provided in Chapter 14. Negotiation across agencies and systems about respective policies on information sharing that might differ must occur, with an eye toward what is needed, what is feasible, and what strikes a balance between the public good and the individual's privacy rights. This negotiation can only occur, however, when all participants have a shared, clear, and correct understanding of HIPAA regulations and restrictions.

4. Planning for diversion and other important system change is best accomplished using wide representation from multiple systems.

Just as the role of "boundary spanner" (Steadman, 1992) facilitates the effective functioning of a system that has contributors from different disciplines and systems of their own, input from various contributors is necessary when planning for change or increasing the effectiveness of present system functioning. Throughout most of the chapters in this book, there are references to the multisystemic and multidisciplinary nature of criminal justice processing, interventions, and alternatives. Reasonably, then, the planning process requires widespread contributions so there is sufficient commitment on the part of all planners toward making the changes work.

5. The SIM can guide research, identifying gaps at different intercepts, and can also organize and clarify thinking and planning. Both applications have research implications.

Comparison of the available research on SIM intercepts (Chapters 1 and 3-7) and the research that could be conducted using the SIM (Chapter 12) with other applications (e.g., cross-systems mapping; Chapter 14), leads to a two-part conclusion. First, the SIM is sometimes used as an organizational tool, facilitating system change with widespread participation. In these circumstances, the SIM plays a role as an educational tool rather than as a theory, and efforts to investigate its impact would focus on its role in institutional change. Second, the SIM is used to identify the intercepts discussed in Chapters 3 through 7, along with their accompanying interventions. In this role, the SIM often highlights the importance of conducting research on the interventions seen at each intercept. In this way, the SIM acts as a broad guide for researchers concerned with the effectiveness of interventions at each intercept. These two applications can work together as well. A jurisdiction seeking to make changes yielding maximum impact of time and money investments on treatment and public safety outcomes would do well to consider the empirical evidence on interventions at each of the SIM intercepts.

6. There are different models for interventions described by SIM intercepts. Flexibility is important to select the model most applicable in a given jurisdiction, even though this creates challenges to cross-jurisdictional research.

It should be clear from Chapters 1 and 3-7 that there are different models for the interventions made at the various SIM intercepts. Even when empirical evidence appears more supportive of a given model, there are additional considerations (e.g., cost, other resources, political climate, the negotiated preferences between representatives of different systems) that inevitably affect which model is adopted. In most respects this is a good practice: It means that jurisdictions that plan carefully and consider various alternatives can ultimately adopt a model at a particular intercept that is best suited to their priorities and resources. The challenge that this presents for effectiveness research across jurisdictions is a small price to pay. The limitations on the precision and generalizability of research outcomes are typically outweighed by the capacity of a jurisdiction to design a change that fits well with its particular locale and has an increased chance of sustainability.

7. The SIM has broad applicability across a range of locales. It has been used by national organizations (GAINS, Council for State Governments) and state-level organizations (in Florida, Illinois, Massachusetts, Ohio, Pennsylvania) for multiple purposes (cross-systems mapping, other training, technical assistance, program evaluation, research).

One good illustration of the usefulness of the SIM, particularly for organizational, technical assistance, and cross-systems mapping purposes, has been its adoption as a core tool by the GAINS Center and the Council for State Governments (Chapter 8) and the respective centers of excellence established in 5 states (Chapter 10). Certainly the priorities of each of these differ somewhat, but a common theme is the provision of services and the development of alternatives to standard prosecution for people with serious mental illness. The SIM's use by organizations devoted to describing empirically supported and best practices underscores both its versatility and its potential impact in promoting diversion and the planning and delivery of alternative interventions.

8. The SIM may be useful in promoting a legislative agenda, but it has not yet been applied much in this way.

To our knowledge, the SIM has rarely been used by legislators. Some of its potential applications in this area are illustrated in Chapter 11. The SIM does offer a way to provide legislators with a succinct and easily understood description of the criminal justice process, so focused legislation could well be promoted by using the SIM as a heuristic in these efforts.

9. Research guided by the SIM is important but faces multiple challenges.

There are several major challenges to conducting research on diversion and treatment alternatives guided by the SIM. These are described in some detail in Chapter 12. One of the most important challenges involves the lack of standardization in the implementation of interventions at the various intercepts. A second challenge concerns the inconsistency of outcome measures used by researchers in this area; while most employ some kind of criminal justice outcome and some measure of treatment involvement, there is considerable variability even within these variables. Both of these issues make it difficult to generate generalizable knowledge that would apply across studies and jurisdictions. A third challenge is funding; it is difficult to conduct good research in this area without adequate support, but such support (unless from a grant or contract) may be seen as coming only at the expense of intervention dollars. Finally, as noted in Chapter 12, there are occasions when those who run programs do not wish to obtain and be guided by empirical evidence about outcomes.

> 10. Sustainable funding for SIM-facilitated systems change is a major barrier to such change. To address this challenge, jurisdictions need multisystemic planning, institutionalized commitment, and creativity to incorporate cost-effective approaches for promoting both public safety and rehabilitation/recovery goals.

Developing sustainable funding for the kind of systems change that can be facilitated by the SIM is a major barrier to implementing such change. This is discussed in some detail in Chapter 9. The experiences in San Antonio and Miami (see Chapters 9 and 11) in particular demonstrate, however, that a combination of strategies can produce such sustainable funding. However, in most locales, lack of funding is seen as one of the major barriers to achieving the goals identified during mapping (see results from Pennsylvania counties who have done cross-systems mapping in Chapter 13). Funding is an inevitable, and important, consideration that has to be addressed as part of the planning process.

EXTENDING THE USE OF THE SIM

The primary focus of this book has been on individuals with severe mental illness, who may also have co-occurring substance use problems. There is no reason why the use of the SIM could not be extended to other populations as well; whenever rehabilitative alternatives to standard arrest/prosecution/incarceration are feasible, the SIM might be a useful tool for both organization and planning. Several of these additional populations include individuals with substance use problems (but without co-occurring mental illness), veterans, juveniles, and those with intellectual disabilities. But we caution against the application of the SIM with these populations, particularly in cross-systems mapping, without taking possible system differences into consideration. Using the SIM to organize (by intercept) the current status of diversion alternatives and the empirical support for their effectiveness can provide a comprehensive perspective on existing practices, their research support, and the gaps in support for such practices. To do so effectively, however, it is important to have a mapping facilitator who is experienced both with the population being discussed and the current system-level practices with such individuals. If this step is taken, however, it appears that the SIM has the potential to provide organizational and planning assistance comparable to what it offers for the individuals who are discussed in the present book.

IMPLICATIONS FOR RESEARCH

Research relevant to the SIM has been discussed in a number of chapters throughout this book. We have noted that the SIM is most effectively used as an organizing guide and as a planning tool; each use has different research implications. When the SIM is used to organize the description of the traditional criminal justice process, accompanied by alternative possibilities identified at each of 5 intercepts, it yields a description of research regarding these areas. From this work, it is possible to identify strengths and limitations, consistency with national benchmarks, and costs and benefits of existing treatment alternatives. It is also possible to observe that some areas have had relatively little associated research.

There are a number of ways in which further research could benefit the interventions associated with each of the SIM intercepts. We identify three important areas:

- *Research associated with Intercepts 1 and 2.* A Crisis Intervention Team (CIT) program is a relatively well-established and widely recognized form of specialized police responding (Intercept 1) that needs additional empirical study. Because it is a pioneering effort that has made substantial inroads in a number of police departments nationally, such research would not be conducted for the purpose of deciding whether CIT is advantageous compared to existing practice. Rather, research would be valuable regarding several focused questions about the implementation of this intervention: how widespread CIT might become while maintaining effectiveness, how it might be most effectively implemented through training, how its impact might be documented using information-management systems, and how it might be adjusted to be maximally effective in terms of costs, perceptions, harm reduction, and treatment delivery. Research on Intercept 2 interventions, by contrast, does not illustrate a single model (court-based, jail-based, or unspecified) or point (pre-booking versus post-booking) for diversion. Better-controlled studies at this intercept would help to identify the strengths and limitations of each model and point of intervention. Although we have noted that jurisdictions need the flexibility to select a model best suited to their needs, it is also clear that good research on Intercept 2 would help inform jurisdictions about the relative advantages of each approach.
- *Research on information sharing in the context of criminal justice and treatment alternatives.* The sharing of relevant information about justice-involved treatment participants who have been diverted at one of the intercepts is clearly a central issue for making diversion work effectively. It is our impression, however, that policies and practices

associated with such information sharing are often based on inaccurate perceptions of the limitations imposed by HIPAA and other relevant federal law. Our impression, however, is just that—an impression. There is very limited solid empirical research on the role of information sharing in mounting reforms regarding mentally ill individuals in the criminal justice system. What are the limitations on information sharing associated with the various kinds of interventions and programs discussed in this book? How often do jurisdictions refrain from developing a rehabilitation-oriented alternative to standard prosecution because appropriate information sharing cannot be developed? Research on these topics would be quite useful; among other things, it would identify a number of programs that have developed policies that appropriately balance privacy rights and public safety.

- *Research on the costs and benefits of such treatment alternatives.* We observed earlier that sustainable funding is often a barrier to the development of programs and interventions along the 5 SIM intercepts. Part of the difficulty in obtaining such funding is the lack of information demonstrating the cost-effectiveness of diversion and treatment. Much of the research on such reforms (see Chapters 1 and 3-7) does not provide any information about costs and provides only limited information about benefits, such as symptom reduction, housing, and work or disability income. Most do include some measures related to public safety, such as rearrest or reincarceration. But information about costs and benefits— considered from a funding perspective as well as from public safety and behavioral effectiveness perspectives—is sufficiently important to receive routine attention from researchers studying diversion and interventions.

IMPLICATIONS FOR POLICY

The SIM can be an integral part of efforts to change policy in this area. For example, a cross-systems mapping workshop (Chapter 13) can bring together representatives of the judiciary, prosecution, defense, law enforcement, corrections, parole/probation, mental health, and consumers/participants in a problem-solving, rather than confrontational, environment. In such a mapping, participants describe their interactions on relevant points and then prioritize their preference for how the entire system (mapped using the SIM) might function differently. This allows a jurisdiction to first decide on the priority for changing policy, and then (using the same representation from multiple systems) develop the plan for implementing this change.

This approach has the potential to be very effective, but it requires two important features. First, there must be sufficient advance coordination and representation from relevant parties in the various systems to make the mapping exercise meaningful. With limited participation, neither the priority selected nor the subsequent implementation of the plan developed is likely to be seen as a consensus by participants representing the different aspects of the system. Without representative participation, the exercise lacks the participation of those who can make changes directly, or persistently advocate for such changes. Second, the mapping exercise leader must be experienced with the population and associated criminal justice system and able to work with diverse groups to move them toward consensus. This allows the leader to move the group away from suggestions that have been unsuccessful elsewhere or are otherwise inconsistent with relevant law, ethics, or available empirical evidence. It also means that obstacles to consensus presented by particular participants can be managed without impairing the larger mapping exercise.

Another application of the SIM can occur around lawmaking and interpretation at the legislative and appellate court levels, respectively. This has not been used much, to our knowledge, but there is certainly considerable potential in its application (see Chapter 11). The SIM offers a clear and straightforward way to describe the functioning of the system and the points at which alternatives might be developed. As such, it provides a framework for developing focused law that is oriented toward rehabilitation and diverts justice-involved individuals from standard prosecution. More work could be done applying the SIM to discussions of statutory construction and application as a method to foster reform in this area.

IMPLICATIONS FOR PRACTICE

The SIM has the potential to identify practice needs and to highlight methods to meet these needs, including research on innovations and bolstering of professional competencies. Simply noting the nature of the services (the rehabilitation-oriented interventions at the 5 SIM intercepts) provided to justice-involved individuals who go through diversion often clarifies what is needed to improve practice in these areas. There are a variety of ways, for example, that specialized services might be delivered more effectively to individuals with severe mental illness returning to the community on parole. One involves the use of smaller caseloads to promote greater intensity of supervision; another is the incorporation of the "firm but fair" approach into parole officer practice (see Chapter 7). Another potentially useful practice in this area (highlighted by Eno-Louden and colleagues) is to focus services to justice-involved individuals on risk factors for offending (e.g., criminal thinking) as well as areas that are both criminogenic risk factors and relevant to effective behavioral functioning (e.g., family, peers, substance abuse). Although it is important to help individuals under these circumstances maintain clinical stability, avoiding reoffending is still a major goal, and one addressed most effectively through a direct focus on risk factors relevant to crime.

Another set of implications for practice involves the program- and system-level interventions that are identified by using the SIM as an organizing tool (for research and benchmarking at each intercept) and a planning guide (for mapping and technical assistance). For example, how much should police officers know about interacting with individuals with severe mental illness? The more established and intensive approach to officer training is CIT; a less demanding but still useful approach might also be employed (e.g., Mental Health First Aid; NREPP SAMHSA, 2014). Communication and information sharing are key components to effective practice in a system, so the work that is done as part of systems mapping can be most effective when individual connections made during the mapping are continued into the practice of future integration of services.

CONCLUSION

The SIM is a relatively recent innovation that has been used primarily for organizational and planning purposes in diverting individuals in need of mental health treatment from the standard process of arrest, prosecution, conviction, incarceration, and community supervision. This book provides a description of the model itself as well as explanations of its role in promoting intervention development, planning, and technical assistance. The areas of particular strength, the gaps in need of further work, and the opportunities for developing these methods more fully are clarified in these chapters. We hope it is useful for those working to increase the effective diversion of justice-involved individuals with behavioral health needs from standard prosecution.

REFERENCES

Munetz, M., & Griffin, P. (2006). Use of the Sequential Intercept Model as an approach to decriminalization of people with serious mental illness. *Psychiatric Services, 57,* 544–549. doi:10.1176/appi.ps.57.4.544

National Registry of Evidence-based Programs and Practices, SAMHSA (2014). *Mental health first aid*. Retrieved Jan. 26, 2014, from http://www.nrepp.samhsa.gov/ViewIntervention.aspx?id=321.

Steadman, H. (1992). Boundary spanners: A key component for the effective interactions of the justice and mental health systems. *Law and Human Behavior, 16,* 75–87.

Note: Page numbers followed by an n *indicates notes*

Autonomy, civil commitment criteria
and, 207–209
AXT. *See* Adult Cross-Training
Curriculum (AXT)

Barnes, F., 68
Behavioral health services
criminogenic influences and, 200–201
legal policies and practices and, 188–192
National GAINS Center initiatives in,
141, 150
Re-entry After Prison/Jail (RAP)
treatment program, 105–106
Risk-Need-Responsivity (RNR)
assessment model and, 98–100
Best practices
drug courts, 88–89
future proposals for, 212
Sequential Intercept Model (SIM), 74
specialty corrections and, 131–132
wicked problems concept and, 194–197
Bexar County Jail Diversion Program,
157–162
Boccaccini, M., 66–67
Bonta, J., 125–128, 129
Borzi, P., 260–261
Boston Diversion Consortium, 170–172
Boston Foundation, 169–172
Boston Police Study, 171–172
Bottom-up research methods, outcomes
assessment and, 125–128
"Boundary spanners" in diversion
programs, 27–28, 73–74, 158, 278
Brief Jail Mental Health Screen, 149–150
"Broken windows" theory, 84–86
Broner, N., 58, 62–63
Burke, C., 122
Business associate agreements,
confidentiality of health-related
information and, 270–271

Calgary Diversion Program, 68
Canada
diversion programs in, 68
specialized police response in, 52
Case, B., 67–68
Case management protocols

barriers to data analysis and, 225–229
case load size and, 128, 131–132
diversion programs, 72–73
reentry models for mentally ill
offenders, 101–104
relevant variables in SIM concerning,
235–236
specialized community correction
caseloads, 106, 128–130
specialty probation caseloads, 121–123
CCoE. *See* Coordinating centers of
excellence (CCoEs)
Center for Mental Health Services
(CMHS), 138, 140–141
Center for Substance Abuse
Treatment, 24–26
Centers for Medicare and Medicaid
Services and, Substance Abuse
and Mental Health Services
Administration and, 203
"Central eight" risk factors, clinical *vs.*
criminal justice outcomes and,
125–128
Chesterfield County (Virginia) Dual
Treatment Track Program, 65
China, specialized police response in, 53
Clark, J., 59–60
Client engagement, diversion
programs, 71–73
Client management policies, mental
health and criminal justice systems
focus on, 218
Clinical evaluations
diversion programs, 70–73
lack of association between clinical
and criminal justice outcomes and,
125–128
post-arrest diversion of mentally ill
offenders, 58–59
recidivism rates and, 124–125
Risk-Need-Responsivity (RNR)
assessment model and, 98–100
Code of Federal Regulations
business associate and qualified service
organization agreements, 270–271
confidentiality rules for health-related
information and, 258–264

Printed in the USA/Agawam, MA
February 12, 2024

861004.029